a special gift

presented to:

_____

from:

_____

date:

_____

_"And these are but the outer fringe of His works;
how faint the whisper we hear of Him!
Who then can understand the thunder of His power!"_
—Job 26:14 NIV

heaven's whisper

The Women's Devotional Series

To order, call **1-800-765-6955.**
Visit us at **www.reviewandherald.com**
for more information on other Review and Herald® products.

heaven's whisper

edited by Ardis Dick Stenbakken

REVIEW AND HERALD® PUBLISHING ASSOCIATION
Since 1861 | www.reviewandherald.com

Published by Review and Herald® Publishing Association, Hagerstown, MD 21741-1119

Review and Herald® titles may be purchased in bulk for educational, business, fund-raising, or sales promotional use. For information, e-mail SpecialMarkets@reviewandherald.com

The Review and Herald® Publishing Association publishes biblically based materials for spiritual, physical, and mental growth and Christian discipleship.

The author assumes full responsibility for the accuracy of all facts and quotations as cited in this book.

This book was
Edited by Jeannette R. Johnson
Copyedited by James Cavil
Designed by Patricia Wegh
Cover photo by JupiterImages
Typeset: Minion 11/13

PRINTED IN U.S.A.

11 10 09 08 07   5 4 3 2 1

Library of Congress Cataloging-in-Publication Data

Heaven's whisper / edited by Ardis Dick Stenbakken.
    p. cm.
  ISBN 978-0-8280-2016-9
  1. Seventh-Day Adventist women--Prayers and devotions. 2. Devotional calendars--Seventh-Day Adventists. I. Stenbakken, Ardis Dick.
  BV4844.H37 2007
  242'.643--dc22

                              2007022520

ISBN 978-0-8280-2016-9

There is an aspect of this book that is unique.

None of these contributors has been paid—they have shared freely so that all profits go to scholarships for women. As this book goes to press, 1,223 scholarships have been given to women in 105 countiries. For more current information, or to contribute to these scholarships, please go to http://wmgc.adventist.org/Pages/Wmscholarshiip—html#sos. In this way, you too can help to spread Heaven's whispers.

∞

Jonah and Me

I can do all things through Christ which strengtheneth me. Phil. 4:13.

 JONAH IS ONE of my favorite biblical characters because I can identify with him. He was a steward to whom God gave talent, money, and time to manage. (At least, that's what stewards are *supposed* to do.)

Then God asked Jonah to go tell the people of Nineveh to repent of their wicked ways. Instead, Jonah took the money God had provided for the trip and went to Joppa, where he bought a ticket to Tarshish. He boarded the ship, made himself comfortable, and fell asleep. As a result of his disobedience a storm arose, and Jonah was tossed overboard and spent three days and three nights in the belly of a fish (Jonah 1). Jonah prayed, probably as he had never prayed before.

I wonder how many times I've been like Jonah. Perhaps the Holy Spirit impressed me to witness to my neighbor across the fence and, instead, I waved at her and rushed into my house as though someone were chasing me with a weapon. How many times have I been prompted to witness to the person sitting next to me in the doctor's office, or standing in line in the supermarket or in the bank? Instead, I've chosen to read magazines. How many times has God given me a specific time to do something for Him, and I've made myself comfortable doing what I wanted to do? How many times have I taken money that God has provided for me to return to Him that which is rightfully His, and spent it to my own satisfaction? How many times has God sent me in one direction, and I've fled in the opposite? I've not spent any time in the belly of a fish, but I have occasionally run into a brick wall while running away from God.

Just as God gave Jonah an opportunity to start over, so He has given me that same privilege. I now witness to my neighbors and to those I come in contact with in the supermarket and at the bank. I return a faithful tithe and offerings—but I sometimes struggle with the way I spend my time. I am convinced that I can't do right things on my own; however, "I can do all things through Christ which strengtheneth me" because God said so Himself.

Father, thank You for giving me more chances. Please help me to be obedient to Your Word, a faithful steward today—and every day—of this new year. Amen.

CORA A. WALKER

9

A Lesson From the Christmas Lights

Let your light so shine before men, that they may see your good works, and glorify your Father which is in heaven. Matt. 5:16.

 IT WAS JANUARY OF 2004, and southwest Washington and northwest Oregon were in the midst of one of the worst winters ever. It had snowed for several days, and then the freezing rain began to fall on top of the snow. We hadn't taken down our outdoor Christmas lights yet, and we hoped they wouldn't be ruined by the ice.

One evening as we sat looking out our patio door, the sight nearly took our breath away. There, magnified by the ice and snow, were the colored lights shining up through the frozen snow and ice. It was awesome! We were among the fortunate ones who still had electricity, and the current was still flowing through those lights. We tried to take pictures, but the flash on our camera just washed out the beautiful colors. Then our son, who was visiting, brought out his digital camera and was able to take one of the most beautiful pictures by stopping the flash.

As I reflected upon those beautiful lights, which we were able to enjoy for several evenings until the ice and snow melted, it seemed to me that there surely was a lesson in this for me. It is so easy to let our light shine when our families are doing well, and we have no financial burdens, and our relationships are all on firm ground. But what happens when you have just laid your own son or daughter to rest in death, or your husband has walked out on you, or you have lost all your earthly belongings? It may not be so easy then; but that is the time folks look at you to see what kind of connection you have with the Lord. Will your light go out, or will you shine even more beautifully because nothing can break your connection with the Lord?

Satan will try to lure us with the bright lights of this world, which can cause our own lights to fade, but I will not allow that. God loved me enough to send His only Son to die for me, and I want to always keep that connection with Him, so that when the cold darkness creeps into my life I may shine even more beautifully for Him than ever.

Lord, help me today to let my light so shine before others, even in the cold darkness of life, that they will also glorify You always.

ANNA MAY RADKE WATERS

Praising God in the Midst of Trouble

I will bless the Lord at all times: his praise shall continually be in my mouth. Ps. 34.1.

DAVID RAN AWAY from King Saul, who was after his life, and sought refuge from the Philistine king Achish. This king soon sent him away too when he discovered that David had slaughtered Goliath, the Philistine giant. From there David hid in a cave near Adullam. While in this miserable cave David wrote a song to God, praising Him in the midst of his troubles.

I was in the depths of financial problems when I read and studied Psalm 34. For two years the devil attacked my finances. My business projects showed losses. Funds dried up. The children needed to go to school, but there was no money. Debts needed to be paid, but there was no money. Every business project I put my hand to failed. It seemed as if a curse had been cast on me, on my business, and on my household. My faith in God was low; a grumpy attitude set in, and doubt built up.

As I studied Psalm 34 I realized that David had made a decision to praise God at all times and in all circumstances—when things were going well, and when they were not going well. David praised God when he was in the cave of isolation and dismay, not when he was in the palace. It is easy to praise God when things are going well, but to do so when things are bad is a challenge.

So I also made a decision to praise God in the midst of my financial trouble. It was very difficult to praise God from an empty stomach and with an empty bank account, but something began to happen as I continued to praise the Lord in the midst of my trouble. The burden began to lift slowly from my grieved heart, as if Someone were helping me carry the financial burden. The dark cloud over my heart began to lift. I continued to praise the Lord, and my faith in Him rekindled as my focus shifted from my problem to my God. I realized that God is my provider—He owns everything in heaven and on earth—and my problem was small compared to my God.

Within a month of praising God continually for my fiscal problems, the financial doors began to open, one by one. The business started picking up slowly but steadily. New profitable projects came in, and my situation began to improve. Today I am back on my feet again, and I praise the Lord even more!

CONISIA ANTHONY

Influential Women in my Life

O God, thou hast taught me from my youth: and hitherto have I declared thy wondrous works. Ps. 71:17.

WHEN I WAS ABOUT 7 YEARS OLD, my aunt Fern lived with us. She taught me to say my prayers before I went to bed, a habit I continue to this day. Aunt Fern was an early influence in my life, especially since neither of my parents seemed interested in spiritual things. Thinking of her made me think about other women who contributed to my growing-up years.

My mother is number one on my list. Even though she didn't attend a church and I never heard her pray, she still had her own set of ethics that included patience and fairness in raising her 16 children. I can't recall hearing her ever raise her voice to me or my siblings.

Miss Mann was my teacher and mentor when I attended the little neighborhood Mennonite Sunday school from age 6 to 13. I loved her—and her class parties.

Miss Crabb was my fifth-grade teacher who saw my need to be included in the Christmas program that year—a first for me. I wore a white dress with a red sash and did a little routine on the stage.

My aunt Nora and her preacher husband lived on a farm with their six children. I loved to visit my cousins in the summertime, and I always enjoyed my aunt's country breakfasts and family worship around the kitchen table each morning.

The wife of the manager of the Mennonite Board of Missions in our town took me under her wing. I remember the Sunday night suppers by the fireplace that Mrs. Reiff invited me to.

Mrs. Leininger, another woman in the church, introduced me to white linen tablecloths and napkins, fine china, and delicious riced potatoes at special Sunday dinners when they had guests in their lovely home and included me.

Miss Fishley was my seventh-grade English teacher. She saw something in me I didn't see in myself. She encouraged me to always choose friends wisely. Referring to one close classmate, she said, "You can do better." I never forgot her kind words of wisdom.

Train up a child in the way she should go, and when she is old she will not depart from it (see Prov. 22:6). To whom do you owe a thank-you for a good influence? How can you pass on such an influence?

CLAREEN COLCLESSER

A Frantic Trip to the Hospital

And the prayer of faith shall save the sick. James 5:15.

LATE ONE FRIDAY NIGHT our daughter called to say that our 2-year-old grandson was having seizures, one after the other, with projectile vomiting. They had admitted him to the hospital in Lincoln, Nebraska. Would we come?

We left immediately from Minnesota and drove all night. It was so hard to see our poor little boy so sick. Because it was the weekend, the doctor didn't come to see him. The nurses were instructed to give medications to stop seizures, but the medicines didn't help. On Sunday afternoon David and Sandi took Clint out of the hospital and made a flying trip in their beat-up old car, driving into the wee hours of the morning to the Mayo Clinic, where he was admitted to St. Mary's Hospital, Rochester, Minnesota. Sandi and David, who were both still college students, had no insurance and not much money,

By the time we arrived, there were seven pediatric neurologists in Clint's room. They immediately began planning extensive testing. It was a mystery as to what was going on. They decided that if the testing didn't show the problem, they would do investigative brain surgery. All this was very frightening to us.

The next morning, while Clint was having a spinal, our daughter and I sat in a small café across the street from the hospital and, hand-in-hand across the table, we prayed. We pleaded with God to save Clint's life. Arriving back at the hospital, we learned that they had gotten the seizures under control and had put off the idea of the investigative surgery until more was learned. We thanked God for this blessing.

Today our grandson is 28 years old, has never had another seizure, and takes no medications. Later we learned they suspected Reye's syndrome, and as sick as he was, it was a miracle of God that he survived. An added blessing: the district managers I worked with took up a collection so that Sandi and David would have money to get back to Nebraska.

Whenever I'm tempted to doubt the Lord, I always remember the day I prayed with our daughter over the breakfast table for our little boy. God is good.

DARLENE YTREDAL BURGESON

Just Look

O God, thou art my God; early will I seek thee. Ps. 63:1.

A FEW YEARS AGO my sister moved into an apartment. She had unpacked some of her things, but there were still a couple boxes yet to unpack. She placed one of these boxes by the door. When I visited her one weekend, she mentioned that she needed some money. I gave her what I had, not knowing if she had all the money she really needed.

Soon she had her apartment the way she wanted it, and most of her things were unpacked. However, she never got around to unpacking that box by the door. It just stayed there, becoming a part of the furniture. Daily she passed the box, leaving it ignored, its contents unmoved.

Weeks later she finally got around to opening that box, and she found a check for $80 that she had forgotten about and so had not cashed! Every day she had passed by that box, not knowing that the money she needed was right there.

How often do we "pass by" God? We don't pray to Him, or talk to Him about our needs. That box had only some money that my sister needed, but God has everything we need. Not only does He have the money—He has the love, that second chance, the shelter, that job, that healing, that friend we need. He has all the answers and can help us with all that we may deal with—marriage, school, spiritual growth, unhappiness. Whatever you face, in faith go to God. Talk to Him constantly. Ask Him for what you need, ask Him not only to answer your prayers but also to bless you according to His will. He might have something better waiting for you to bless you more than you could ever ask or think.

Not only do we pass by and ignore God; we often ignore His Word. Just as my sister didn't open the box and find the needed treasure, we don't open the Bible and therefore miss the blessing we need. The Bible has promises, instructions, guidance, invitations to praise and prayer, and lessons for daily life.

In faith, wait on Him. He loves you, He loves me, and He will help us. In Him we will find our answers. He has sent His love and His Word—all we have to do is open the box. If we just ask—if we just look—we will be blessed.

KRISTINA BROWN

Trusting

Trust in the Lord with all your heart, and lean not on your own understanding; in all your ways acknowledge Him, and He shall direct your paths. Prov. 3:5, 6, NKJV.

LITTLE CHERUBS DAY CARE is my mission field. Even though I am the director/owner, in truth the day care belongs to God, not me. I spend a good part of my days observing children at play, and I love it! Children are so carefree. They have no worries—except for bugs and bees. Most "cherubs" run with fear at the sight of a bug or bee—but not Tristan. He's a unique child, full of smiles. As I sit here on this sunny, windy day I watch Tristan interact with a big black-and-yellow bumblebee. He runs and laughs, unafraid, in a playful game of "chase the bee." The funny thing is, the bumblebee stops and seems to say, "Here I am! Catch me if you can!" Tristan laughs and runs this way and that. When Tristan stops, Mr. Bee buzzes, "You missed me! Here I am."

Some children are easy to entertain; others are not. Take Martez, for example. Mr. Bee came to play on a different day, but Martez was not happy. The only expression on his face was fear. Terrified, he ran from the bee, screaming, "The bug is trying to get me!" He wanted no part of the bumblebee's game.

What causes one person to be afraid, and another not? I think of it this way: the closer you are to God, the less you have to fear. What about the children who don't know God? Where do they turn when they are in trouble, or if fear overtakes them? Where do they go when it seems as if their world is caving in?

I try to teach all my little cherubs that they can run to their Father in heaven. I want them to know that there is nothing in their life that is too big for Him to handle. If my spiritual life is not what it should be, they won't learn these truths from me. I can't teach what I don't know. How is it with you? Do you share Jesus with your children? Do they see Jesus in you?

Lord, may we all know that we are an example. May we show our love for You so that everyone we meet sees something in us that will give them the desire to know You as their Savior. Please handle all the big and little things in our lives.

TAMMY BARNES TAYLOR

Daughter,
Not a Granddaughter

Commit your way to the Lord; trust in him and he will do this. Ps. 37:5, NIV.

I HAD GOTTEN UP VERY EARLY to attend to one of my children, and since daylight was breaking, I wasn't able to get back to sleep. My thoughts turned to the future and to problems that I knew needed to be resolved soon. What would I do this year? What doors would open for me?

I didn't have to ask my questions very long, because my Lord answered me by reminding me of today's text. This verse was a comfort to my anxious mind because I could feel the depth of these words. This had been my favorite verse during my childhood and part of my youth, but for a long time I had forgotten it. Where along the way, or in what curve in the road, had I lost the sense of divine leading? Why the anguishing and depressive suffering during the past years?

In an attempt to decipher the questions in my life, I remembered that this verse was also a favorite of someone I admire a great deal because of his faith and trust in God—my father.

As the day grew brighter, my thoughts also became more enlightened. God allows rocks and holes along my paths so that my trust in Him can be whole. My trust should be based on a personal experience and not on what my father had with Him. I realized that my trust and assurance were more in my earthly father than in my heavenly Father. God wanted me to be His daughter—not His granddaughter—and I needed to continue learning to trust and depend on my heavenly Father more and more.

With the apostle Paul I can say, "I do not consider myself yet to have taken hold of it. But one thing I do: Forgetting what is behind and straining toward what is ahead, I press on toward the goal" (Phil. 3:13, 14, NIV).

Is it possible that you too might be living (or perhaps surviving) through a faith that is not yours but that of another? That you are a granddaughter, rather than a daughter, of faith?

Allow yourself to have a personal experience with God so that your faith may be a direct, legitimate relationship, and not an adoptive faith. Give yourself to Him. Trust in Him. He has done great things, and He wants to do more for you. Actually, He wants to do everything—and even more.

DENISE MÜCKENBERGE LOPES

Pink Hope

The Lord bless you and keep you; the Lord make his face shine upon you and be gracious to you; the Lord turn his face toward you and give you peace. Num. 6:24, NIV.

I RUMMAGED THROUGH MY CARD BOX, selected some delightful greetings, and gathered my pen and stamps at the kitchen table. I tucked a few birthday wishes into envelopes. A widowed friend had given me a calendar featuring my favorite artist. My brother-in-law had slipped $25 in my son's pocket during his recent visit. A thoughtful calendar, a surprise monetary gift for my son—two nice treasures for which I was thankful.

I chose a card designed with glorious hats for my next greeting. Varied in color, some had flowers, others had feathers—they all looked fun and pretty to me. Inside it read: "Under every great hat there is a great woman." I drew a smiley face telling my friend we needed great hats. Some misunderstandings had burdened our friendship, but during the year healing forgiveness had restored our joy of being friends.

My teenage son had spent the past few nights with friends. The house was quiet and lonesome without his presence. A note to my sister-in-law, who lives next door, shared thoughts of the empty nest syndrome. Her children are long grown and live in distant cities.

The previous day my sister, who lives in a nearby town, had come to visit Mom and Dad, who also live nearby. She brought us gifts of color and hope: a purple crocus for Mom; and for me, hyacinths with a hinting promise of pink barely visible. They stood tall in a tiny pot on the table in front of me. My note assured her that dawn had proved the promise of a soft shade of pink as she had wished. It offered pink hope.

A premature thought of spring on this January morning warmed me with peace and reassurance. I snuggled into thoughts of God's gifts of hope, faith, and love. Deep in the cold of January we exercise the energy of hope. We trust the frozen beds of tiny seedlings will be nudged by God's warmth and gentle rains, and spring will return.

Dear God, my friend, thank You for my "pink hope," spring, family, friends, and Your touches of love in boundless ways and boundless friends. Thank You for turning Your face toward us with Your graciousness and the gift of life, blessed with Your abiding peace, hope, and love.

JUDY GOOD SILVER

Grandma's Quilt

"For I know the plans I have for you," declares the Lord, "plans to prosper you and not to harm you, plans to give you hope and a future. Then you will call upon me and come and pray to me, and I will listen to you. You will seek me and find me when you seek me with all your heart." Jer. 29:11-13.

"GRANDMA, WHEN YOU DIE, can I have that nice statue in the corner?" I can't believe now I said that to my grandma, but I did back when I was little. And, of course, your next question is probably "Did you get the statue?" No, I'm sad to say, I didn't; but I did get something very special from my grandmother. She loved to sew, and often on birthdays she would give me one of her hand-made flowery-print aprons. Years later, after Grandma died, all of her granddaughters were given one of her beautiful quilts. There were several of us girls, so making a quilt for each of us was no small task—especially considering Grandma died in her early 60s, just when life was slowing down. What was so precious about my quilt was that the material was the same flowery material in all the aprons she gave me over the years. I treasure Grandma's quilt and still have it to this day, even though it is now a bit fragile. I didn't pack it away like fine china, but I used it, spreading it on my bed or just cuddling up in its surprising warmth.

Jesus said that He wouldn't abandon us if we call on Him. He knows what He's doing; He has it all planned out! Right now I'm smiling inside as I think about Jesus. Over the years the precious Son of God has been giving us beautiful gifts. He has given me the gift of a wonderful family, both in my childhood and present life. He has given me friends who are near and dear to my heart. He has given me talents and memories and so much more that I probably am not even aware of. I know that when I get to heaven Jesus is going to wipe away the tears from my eyes so that I can see His master plan, so that I can see the whole picture of why things happened the way they did. I think it will be as beautiful and full of memories as my Grandma's quilt!

NANCY ANN NEUHARTH TROYER

Thought: If God made you a quilt, what do you think it would look like? What colors, what pattern, might He use? Would you snuggle up in it, hang it on the wall, or hide it in a trunk?

I Am a Person Too

Then Peter began to speak: "I now realize how true it is that God does not show favoritism." Acts 10:34, NIV.

IF AN INANIMATE PICTURE is worth a thousand unspoken words, then the impact of a silent lesson taught in living, breathing color surely tells even more.

I didn't recognize the dirty, sore-infected, urine-stained homeless man as he sat on the curb outside the Seven-Eleven. I hurried past him as he looked at me with a cheery, toothless grin, yelling, "Hello, hello!" trying to get my attention to give a contribution to him. I totally ignored his loud greeting.

When I came out after making my purchase, he peered at me, bleary-eyed, and said, "Say, don't I know you from somewhere?" I stopped and really looked at him, and then I remembered him from his frequent appearances at church on Sabbaths.

I am sure my face was red as I responded, "Yes, yes, of course, you do know me," I said. "From the church."

He couldn't possibly have known the pangs of guilt that stabbed my heart for having ignored him. In spite of his outward appearance, he was a person created in God's image, just like me. Here I was shown, in living color, a picture of how I stood before God, without Christ my intercessor.

With my dirty, infected, and sin-stained life, Christ not only washed me and made me clean through His blood, but even now intercedes for me before God. He has made a provision for me to become a joint heir with Him. How dare I then be a respecter of persons? I certainly was not being like Christ as I wanted to be. I thought of the text "For God does not show favoritism" (Rom. 2:11, NIV).

The dollar I gave the homeless man represented a handout to him, but my smile assured him of my acknowledgment of his intrinsic value as a fellow creature of our God who had just taught me a significant lesson. My prayer is that God will always help me to be conscious of the fact that every person is precious in His sight, notwithstanding any outward appearance.

DOROTHY D. SAUNDERS

Never Give Up!

I have learned, in whatsoever state I am, therewith to be content.... I can do all things through Christ which strengtheneth me. Phil. 4:11-13.

AS A PAINTER AND PAPERHANGER, I worked several months for a family who had a chocolate seal point Siamese cat named Sam. One day Sam came limping into the yard. We took him to a veterinarian, who discovered that Sam had somehow broken his left rear leg. We thought it must have been an accident. The veterinarian encased Sam's leg in a plaster cast and instructed, "This cast needs to stay on for six to eight weeks, and he shouldn't be running, jumping, or climbing."

But after three days of being quiet and still, Sam began to feel better and became quite active. He pushed through the screen door and sunned himself out on the side porch. He thumped up and down the stairs to join Pat and Jerry in the playroom or to take a nap on one of their beds.

He went into the kitchen, jumped up on an empty chair, and made a flying leap that landed him on the kitchen sink countertop. Once there, he ate a bowlful of breakfast leftovers before they could be put into the garbage

One morning he stood in the hall—minus his cast. Because of his lively antics, his cast had spit in two! When Dr. Payne put a fiberglass cast on his leg for several more weeks, Sam didn't seem to mind. How happy everyone was when the cast came off for good!

I thought about all of Sam's adventures and wondered how most people would handle this type injury or misfortune. Do we moan and groan and complain a lot? Or do we, like Sam, make the best of our less-than-ideal situation?

When times are hard and we are hurting physically, mentally, or spiritually, and feel like giving into depression, God can help us make it through. All we have to do is ask for grace to cope. Things will get better someday—if not on this earth here and now, then when Jesus comes. We have this hope! So let's adopt what seems to have been Sam's motto and never give up.

Bonnie Moyers

Thought: Many Bible women faced challenges. Leah was one such woman—she knew her husband did not love her. Read Genesis 29:31-35 and note what she named her boys. When Judah was born, she seemed to change. Why? And what difference do you think this made?

Heaven-sent Nylons

How gracious he will be when you cry for help! As soon as he hears, he will answer you. Isa. 30:19, NIV.

THE YEAR WAS 1960, and I was attending a Christian boarding school in California. I was 17 and a junior. Life was fun but not always easy, because my parents had adopted two Korean girls, and they didn't have money to send to me for any extras. In fact, they had a difficult time just keeping up with the tuition, even though I worked part-time.

Back then it was required that all the girls wear nylon stockings to church functions on the weekends. Period. Even though I had been very careful with mine and they had lasted a long time, I got a run in one and had no money to replace them. I discovered this on a Wednesday. That night, on my knees, I said, "Lord, I don't have any money, and my nylons are ruined, and if I don't have any to wear this weekend I will get in trouble. Could You somehow solve this for me?" Then I went to sleep. Truthfully, I didn't expect any solution in the near future.

The next day, Thursday, the mail came about noon, and behold—I had a letter! I rarely got mail because I was too busy to write. I didn't recognize the Canoga Park, California, return address. When I opened up the letter, there was a single sheet of paper and two $10 bills! This was a lot of money to me! On the paper was typed, "To be used as needed." Not only had I gotten the needed funds to replace my nylons; I had enough so that I could buy other necessities and my parents wouldn't have to send me any money for that month. What a blessing! I was ecstatic! I ran up and down the hall, showing everyone that I had gotten money in the mail and telling them that I didn't know where it had come from!

I still don't know where the money came from! I never found out who my benefactor was. That person will never knew how very important that incident was in developing my spiritual relationship with God. I knew it was an answer to prayer because that letter had been mailed the day *before* I had even prayed my request! I was so awed to think that such a minor thing was so important to God that He had rewarded my faith even before I petitioned Him! The next day was "town day," and I immediately bought the necessary nylons.

I was—and am—so very thankful to be a child of God, aren't you?

LaVella Pinkney

Let's Look
to the Eternal Things

For our light affliction, which is but for a moment, worketh for us a far more exceeding and eternal weight of glory; while we look not at the things which are seen, but at the things which are not seen: for the things which are seen are temporal; but the things which are not seen are eternal. 2 Cor. 4:17, 18.

WHEN HARDSHIPS come your way, remember that Jesus is beside you, an ever-present source of help. Facing the difficulties with courage is part of the daily Christian walk. Christ knows that when somebody accepts Him as Savior she also has to carry a cross. But He is ready to give her assistance and consolation.

I say all this from my own experience. Several years ago our family suffered some terrible blows. One of them was the death of our 38-year-old daughter. After a long but quiet suffering, she slept in the Lord, leaving behind three children. Oh, it was a hard blow, but I held firmly to the arm of Jesus, and He gave me strength to endure. Meanwhile a group of women from the church supported me in prayer.

Before she died, my daughter entrusted me with her children to raise and educate. Her unwavering faith was proven by telling me that when she opens her eyes in the resurrection, she will look for the children. I trembled at the enormous responsibility.

But then the evil one hit once more shortly after, and I lost one of my sons. I told the Savior that the responsibility of raising these three grandchildren was too heavy—I asked Him to give them a mommy who would continue the work started by my daughter.

And the miracle happened, although humanly speaking it seemed impossible. Now the children have another mommy, faithful and loving, and I have a second daughter. But her work is more difficult than it would have been for my daughter. That is why we need to pray for her and for all those who are in her situation.

As for me, I am longing for Jesus to come—to see my children again and to embrace those children I have lost. And I am sure that the two daughters of mine, although they never knew each other, will embrace while surrounded by their children. Oh, what a wonderful day that will be! *Come, Lord Jesus! Come as soon as possible!*

ELISABETA MORARU

Answered Prayers

Yea, though I walk through the valley of the shadow of death, I will fear no evil: for thou art with me. Ps. 23:4.

FEAR FILLED MY BONES, and I shook, though it was not cold. My mother-in-law lay in the hospital bed groaning in pain that had become so intense that she was almost oblivious to her surroundings. She suddenly gave a frightened cry, a cry of death.

Within minutes she was surrounded by nurses and doctors, struggling to save her life. She was to undergo an operation, but unfortunately the doctor went on a journey that day and wouldn't return until evening. I silently committed Mom's life into God's hands, asking Him to perform a miracle and save her life. Then came the frightening message that the doctor had had an accident but was safe. I became tongue-tied, shivering from my head to my toes. My legs refused to support my body. My tears flowed unchecked; I wondered how this would all end.

Many people got on their knees, praying for the doctor and for the patients who needed him urgently. Soon he arrived and was X-rayed to confirm that he was out of danger. Fortunately he was fine.

Before long my mother-in-law was taken to surgery; the operation was successful, but this was just the beginning of her problems. She had high blood pressure, breathing difficulties, high sugar content in her body, and heart problems. The bad news about her serious sickness spread far and wide.

Sons and daughters, aunts, uncles, and friends flooded to the hospital to see her. Rumors spread that she could not survive; all eagerly waited for reports from the hospital. Day and night, family members prayed. She was on oxygen for three days. She remained in a coma until we lost hope. We saw darkness before us—our minds were in turmoil. Any scream from the direction of the hospital filled our hearts with fear.

Our merciful God did not leave her in this condition long. She started regaining strength, bit by bit, until she could sing, pray, and praise God. We continued to claim promises and pray.

In the valley of death God was still there. He delivered her from the shadows of death. Our God is able to deliver us from all sorts of problems. He requires only faith and trust.

MARGRET NYARANGI BUNDI

Cleanse My Heart, O God

Wash me clean from my guilt. Purify me from my sin. Ps. 51:2, NLT.

WE CAUTIOUSLY TURNED INTO THE LITTLE STREET whose sign was hidden behind six-foot sprigs of pampas grass. The roadbed declined before us, showing off giant old trees standing guard over quaint little wood-framed houses.

Immediately we felt at home as we inspected the small but comfortable house. All it seemed to need was a little scrubbing and paint.

Not until later did I discover a liver-shaped, dark-red candle stain on the carpet. Someone had unsuccessfully attempted to remove the wax, and now the hardened, matted mess marred the beige carpet. Wax is tough, and old wax is particularly troublesome. But there is a solution. One evening I sat down on the floor next to the spot with my iron and lots of paper towels. I made sure that the iron's heat was set very low, because too much heat could melt the carpet. As I gently moved the iron over the towel and wax, the wax began to absorb into the towel. The process had to be repeated many times before the top layer began to move more freely, leaving the towels covered with red blotches.

Even though the carpet looked much better, the job wasn't finished. Just beneath the surface, lumps of wax were still caught in the fibers. Carefully I pushed my fingers into the pile, separating the strands and opening up a tiny valley. The towels bloomed red with each push of the edge of the iron into the base of the carpet. Fiber by fiber, section by section, the heat of the iron released more and more of the wax and stain. It is easy to feel when the heat has completed its work. As the wax melts, the fibers relax and become more soft and pliable. After long, tedious work, the carpet was finally free of wax. A special solution helped to remove much of the remaining dye, and now the deep-red stain was replaced by a soft pink splotch—a hint of what it once was.

The cleansing process that God is working out in me is much like that stain-removing effort. My old habits, hurts, and hang-ups have produced a hard heart, but God uses just the right amount of heat, discomfort, and pressure to make me soft and pliable. Healing doesn't take place all at once—it's a long-term process. Now with each pass of heat over my life I say Thank You for the good work.

SHIRLEY KIMBROUGH GREAR

Even the Train Stopped

So that all the peoples of the earth might know that the hand of the Lord is powerful and so that you might always fear the Lord your God. Joshua 4:24, NIV.

EVERYONE WAS IN PLACE for the march that would take place that Saturday afternoon. The enthusiastic group of young people waited for the moment to move into action; the joy of participation showed on each face. When the leaders gave the order, everyone began to march.

As we passed through the streets and avenues, we saw many residents coming out of their homes and business establishments to see what was happening. We carried informative posters about the bad effects of alcohol and smoking, and we sang during our entire march. From afar, we could be heard. We distributed all of the literature we had with us.

Finally we reached the train tracks. The first groups crossed the tracks, and everything proceeded as normal. What we didn't know was that the train was already near, right before the curve, but because we were singing at the top of our lungs we hadn't heard the whistle.

When we realized where the train was, it was very near, and the last groups were still crossing the train tracks. What could we do? There wasn't enough time for everyone to cross the tracks. We felt paralyzed, not knowing what to do.

To our surprise, the train stopped! The train had never stopped in our town, but on that day it did—and everyone crossed the tracks calmly. When the last group had crossed, the engineer blew the train's whistle and continued along the track.

That afternoon I was certain that the angel of the Lord was at our side, between us and the train. The Lord had worked with the engineer so that he had stopped the train in time.

The march that afternoon was unforgettable. The entire town commented about it during the days that followed. The work carried out by the young people, as well as the providential way the train stopped for the youth to cross the track, was a true witness to our God who sees everything and acts at the right time. This episode touched my life and the lives of those young people who participated. How wonderful it is to have a holy God who cares for His children, intervening with His protecting hand at just the right time.

TÂNIA CELEIDE TEIXEIRA DAMASCENO

Friendly Neighbors

For I have given you an example, that ye should do as I have done to you.
John 13:15.

OUR NEIGHBORS, Virginia and Elmer, stopped to chat while on their evening walk on the dirt road that runs in front of our house. They knocked on the door of our family room in this remote area of Virginia. I hastened to let them in. How we all yearn for unexpected visitors to stop and chat awhile!

We have wonderful neighbors! Everyone knows everyone else up and down the roads of this country area. And families, as a rule, do not go running off somewhere else, but settle down in the same area, often on the same property that had belonged to their parents. It is a wholesome, loving relationship that families have and share. I left home many years ago to attend college in a big city, and there was no reason to turn and look back other than to remember pleasant memories. People in the North are not as closely entwined as those in the South, I think. Even the graves and minicemeteries nestled right next to the houses attest to the family closeness. They were never to leave where their roots flourished.

Our neighbors knew all about us before we ever moved in—word of mouth informed those sitting on the worn benches around the potbellied stoves in the corner markets. But as we settled into this rural place we found that there was room for outsiders and nonrelatives. Neighbors made us feel welcome as we unpacked. They stopped to introduce themselves and to get acquainted.

As Virginia and Elmer were leaving, I mentioned that I would be very happy to help them, or any of the neighbors, if they ever needed help of any kind. "You already have," Virginia said, "just by living here!"

To be accepted and loved is the greatest gift one can know. That is how Jesus feels about us. While He was on this earth, walking among men, He wasn't always accepted and loved by the creatures He created. Even so, He loves and accepts us. He gave us a wonderful example of Christian living in all He said and did.

LAURIE DIXON-MCCLANAHAN

Thought: Read John 14:1-3. Jesus says He wants us to be where He is—neighbors!

Giving Thanks
to the Lord Always

Give thanks in all circumstances, for this is God's will for you in Christ.
1 Thess. 5:18, NIV.

THAT SABBATH MORNING I arrived at church with great anticipation. I wanted to find my friend to learn what the examination
results were for a woman who was going blind. My friend sold
health plans and had contact with several physicians, so she had set
up an appointment. It was becoming more and more difficult for
the woman to get around without help, because she could no longer see. She
really wanted to read the Bible again, something that she had dearly loved.

So I looked for my friend, and when we met I asked about the test results. I did so hope that the report would be that the woman had cataracts,
or something that surgery or some treatment could fix, or that the use of
glasses would resolve. Unfortunately, the doctor reported that her optic
nerve had been damaged because of the lack of vitamin A, and that nothing
more could be done. No cure existed. This news made me very sad. Losing
something so precious as one's vision and having to live in darkness would
really be something to cause despair.

Then my friend said something that surprised me: "When I attempted
to console this woman, she was the one who consoled me, saying, 'I am
blind, yes, but I can still do something for my Master. I still have a voice to
speak of the love of God to others. I can hand out tracts, and witness for
God to those I love. Praise the Lord, I can still do that!'"

And she did! She handed out tracts, spoke of Jesus, and invited people
to receive Bible studies. She never complained and always had a smile on
her face. A true example!

Today her witness remains alive in my memory. How many of us, who
can see, do not do even half of what she has done throughout her life. Her
spiritual vision has inspired me, and I believe she has been an inspiration to
many others also.

May we today witness for Jesus to people with whom we come in contact, using whatever faculties we have, rather than complaining about those
we don't have.

Have a wonderful day—and never forget to be grateful for what the
Lord has accomplished in your life!

CRISTINA FLORÊNCIO

27

Tested but Alive

I didn't die. I lived! And now I'm telling the world what God did. God tested me, he pushed me hard, but he didn't hand me over to Death. Ps. 118:17, 18, Message.

A TREMENDOUS CRUNCH OF METAL—then unconsciousness. Faint voices, seemingly far away, carried me to a waiting ambulance. I heard scissors ripping through my clothing, but was unaware of the battery of tests given in a nearby hospital or the helicopter flight that carried me to a big-city trauma center.

The precious voices of those I loved reached out to me through the "fog" during the hours and days in intensive care. "What happened?" was my constant query. Patiently my husband explained that on our way to a scheduled musical program on that beautiful spring Sabbath morning, a man had sped through a stop sign at nearly 60 miles (97 kilometers) per hour and broadsided our car. A witness watched him run from the scene, never to be apprehended.

For three weeks I was under the care of four extremely competent teams of doctors. They dealt with multiple broken bones and numerous internal injuries. When the orthopedic doctor told me they had debated about whether to put me in a halo for the broken bones in my neck, I almost hugged him for his decision to use the brace instead.

The protection of angels at the scene will never cease to amaze me. If the main impact had been one split second sooner, my driver's-side door would have been smashed into the middle of the car. That was where the armrest on the back door landed. As my husband describes it, if angel hands hadn't taken over the steering wheel after the impact, we would have also hit a power pole. Instead we sailed through an opening between the pole and a fence, and into a plowed field.

My praise is unbounded for a loving, praying church that showered me with cards, visits, phone calls, food, encouragement, and much more during the many weeks of recovery.

As I wake up each morning I am so grateful for the life God has extended to me. When the heat of summer makes my neck brace uncomfortable, I thank God for the many opportunities it has given me to offer Him praise for His blessings of protection and healing. Whatever life He grants me I want to spend in witnessing to His mighty, saving power. Will you join me in this?

DONNA LEE SHARP

The Power of One

Only Jesus has the power to save! His name is the only one in all the world that can save anyone. Acts 4:12, CEV.

KING DAVID FACED TROUBLE ONCE AGAIN. Absalom had tried to take the throne and had been defeated. But now a troublemaker, Sheba, had persuaded Israel to follow him instead of David. Joab, David's army commander-in-chief, had chased Sheba into Abel-beth-maacah and laid siege to the town. The army built a siege ramp and began to batter the walls. Suddenly a wise woman called down to the army from the wall: "Listen! Tell Joab I want to talk to him." Joab responded. This woman told Joab that their town had been a peaceful town—a good town. So why was Joab trying to destroy it? Joab replied that he didn't want to destroy the town; he only wanted Sheba. If the town would deliver Sheba to Joab, the town would be saved. The unnamed woman replied, "His head will be thrown to you from the wall" (2 Sam. 20:21). The woman talked to the townspeople and delivered on her promise. Joab withdrew (verse 22). The power of one.

Cutting off someone's head is revolting to us, but because of this one woman's wisdom and bravery many, many lives were saved.

The power of one. Other Old Testament women also made a difference alone: Tamar, Rahab, Deborah, Jael, Abigail, and Rizpah are a few of those who acted significantly in a time in which we generally think women didn't take much of a role. And many women in our day have also exhibited the power of one. I hesitate to mention names because there are so many, but I will name two: Rosa Parks, who alone did much to start the civil rights movement in the United States; and Betty Ford, the United States president's wife who revealed publicly that she had breast cancer. Both have made a tremendous difference to both men and women.

The ultimate power of one, of course, belongs to Jesus Christ. Each of the women had to have support from others, but Jesus alone died for us. In fact, I believe He would have died for just one of us if that person had been the only one lost without His sacrifice. That is the power of one! All we have to do is to accept or reject this sacrifice. As today's text says, His name alone saves. That is the power of one that every one of us can exercise. I want to accept that offer today, don't you?

ARDIS DICK STENBAKKEN

An Evening Disrupted

Not one sparrow (What do they cost? Two for a penny?) can fall to the ground without your Father knowing it. Matt. 10:29, TLB.

ANNOYING! There was no other word for it. A damaged pair of glasses on a Friday evening. My husband and I had settled in for a relaxing time when he sat down and heard a pop. His glasses were not broken, just bent. It was 8:00, and the optician's office was still open. He got the glasses straightened, and we began driving home.

I saw something lying in the road just as my husband swerved around it. It was a brown-and-white beagle. "He's alive!" I exclaimed. We pulled over and turned on the car's emergency lights. We lifted the shivering dog gently to its feet, and it was able to limp into the yard of a nearby house and collapse under a bush. I used my cell phone to dial the police department to report an injured animal. They said they would send out the humane society truck, and I said we would wait until help arrived.

About an hour and a half later the truck turned the corner, followed closely by a small car that stopped behind it. Two young women jumped out of their car and ran to me.

"Do you have our dog?" they excitedly asked. "He's a brown-and-white beagle."

It was my turn to be amazed. "Yes," I said. "He's lying under that bush."

"We have been driving all over looking for him. He got out of the yard a little while ago. He's such a sweet dog, and he's rather old. We've had him a long time," one woman explained.

They gently picked up the injured dog, comforting him with soothing words. I told them about a nearby emergency veterinarian. "I don't think he's badly injured," I said. "He has a hurt leg." They thanked us for staying by, but their smile of gratitude was thanks enough. "Our prayers were answered," they said to each other as they carried their precious bundle.

Sometimes it's nice to know that an evening is interrupted for a purpose, and that God's care extends to all His creatures, even to the sparrows—and beagles.

EDNA MAYE GALLINGTON

Thought: Have you noticed how often a blessing flows out of an annoyance (an evening disrupted, or some other event you thought was bad), only to find a blessing?

And the Trumpet Shall Sound

In a moment, in the twinkling of an eye, at the last trump: for the trumpet shall sound, and the dead shall be raised incorruptible, and we shall be changed. 1 Cor.15:52.

AFTER A PRAYER MEETING one Wednesday night the first elder called for a short board meeting. The item on the agenda was heart-wrenching. He told us that a young man in our community had suffered a fatal motorcycle accident. The parents were requesting that the funeral service be held at our church since the facilities at the funeral home were inadequate. Without a moment's hesitation the members of the board voted unanimously to grant their request.

My husband and I gladly agreed to visit the home and offer comfort and help to the grieving family. As we talked with Eddy's mother, I discovered they were friends of one of my sisters. We learned too that Eddy, the second of four children, was such a kind, caring person that he had left college to come home to help in the family business. But on his way home one evening his motorcycle crashed into the back of a parked bus. He was thrown to the ground, and subsequently died of the massive injuries he sustained.

We told Eddy's mother of God's love for each of His children and prayed with her, entreating her to be faithful so that she could look forward to the resurrection.

On the day of the funeral the church was so crowded that there was hardly any parking space at the church or on either side of the street for the entire block. Thirty-two dump trucks, each decorated with yellow ribbons, lined up bumper to bumper on the street. It was a sight to behold!

The service was a wonderful but sad celebration of Eddy's life. The church was filled with teenagers and young adults testifying of Eddy's wonderful 22 years.

After the service many cars, a motorcycle squad, and the dump trucks drove in a long, slow procession toward the Memorial Gardens. Once there, the trucks all lined up on the opposite side of the road, facing the cemetery. As the pastor offered the committal, every one of those 32 trucks began blowing their horns for a minute, or more. As I looked on, I recalled today's text. I pray that we will all be able to hear that blast of the trumpet and awaken to newness of life.

LEILA FAY GREENE

The City or the Field

How much more shall your Father which is in heaven give good things to them that ask him? Matt. 7:11.

 IT HAD BEEN A GREAT TRIP to the Ukraine to visit friends I had made on previous trips. All had gone well, and we were happy to be together again. Now I was on my way back to Bucharest, then Zurich, and on home.

It was 6:30 in the evening when we arrived in Kishenev, Moldova. Here it was necessary for me to buy one more ticket for the last train into Bucharest. A courteous young man carried my bags up the steps and over to the ticket counter before disappearing into the crowd. I patiently stood in line behind a pretty blond young woman; not often did I see blonds here. I spent my few rubles on my ticket and struggled with my baggage back to the edge of the platform to wait an hour for train 619 from Moscow. I enjoyed watching the bright fading sun in this old city where years ago my grandfather had been born of German parentage.

As it neared time for the train to arrive, I checked my belongings. I looked into my bag around my neck, but there was no passport. Frantically I checked my entire luggage—but no passport. I was in trouble—my most precious item for traveling in these lands was gone! I quickly bowed my head and asked my God for help. As I saw it, I had two choices: I could remain here in this big city, where I knew no one or the language; or I could ride the train until we crossed the border into Romania, where they would discover I had no passport and put me in an empty field in the dark. I made the decision to go with the train.

Just then the blond young woman I had seen earlier came running up to me and tried to grab my luggage as she pantomimed "Do you have your passport?" Quickly we ran up the stairs to the ticket office. There, as the woman who had sold me the ticket earlier was putting on her coat preparing to leave her job, she handed me my passport. I had neglected to pick it up earlier. I thanked them both gratefully for their help in remembering me and finding me.

I was saved from the dire circumstances of this city or the dark field at the border. Our God is always near by and hears us. He has ways beyond our imaginings to answer and solve our problems. I am so thankful.

DESSA WEISZ HARDIN

The Miracle of the Potatoes

The kingdom of Heaven belongs to little children like these! Matt. 19:14, Phillips.

"WE SHOULD HARVEST THE GARDEN TODAY," my husband, Larry, announced as he flipped pancakes and poured orange juice. "It's supposed to start snowing, and the temperature will drop all day."

"I'll help, Daddy," stated Garrick, our 4-year-old son, as he reached for the syrup.

Garrick, who had lived in the Philippines until he was 3, liked gardens. He'd sat in the shade of a passion fruit arbor. He'd helped Larry plant the spiky tops of pineapples. If someone lifted him up, he would pick papaya. And after eating tiny, sweet bananas, he had helped chop down banana plants so that new ones would spring up. He enthusiastically helped to spread manure, watered the bougainvillea—and his dad—and checked to see if the guavas were ripe. But he knew little about gardening in Alberta, Canada.

Soon the table was wiped, the dishes were stacked in the sink, and Larry and Garrick were pulling on coats, mitts, and caps. "I'll join you when I get the laundry started," I called as they searched for the garden fork. While the washing machine was filling, I donned my jacket, opened the door, and watched Larry and Garrick. The day was chilly and overcast, damp and threatening, but they laughed together as they worked. Larry thrust the tines of the garden fork into the wet, heavy soil. Garrick, his knitted cap almost covering his eyes, his cheeks already streaked with dirt, dropped to his knees when Larry said, "OK." He reached into the hole, and then stood up, grasping a large red potato in each hand, his eyes full of amazement.

"Look, Mom!" he shouted as he saw me standing on the porch. He waved the potatoes excitedly. "Look what we found!" And then his voice dropped in awe. "We don't know where they've come from."

The day was no longer bone-chilling and gray. Instead, it was filled with joy and excitement. A miracle had happened in our garden. A miracle of potatoes. Garrick plunked them into a pail and knelt again to see if he could discover more. "Come on, Mom," he encouraged, wanting to share this wonder that was occurring in his garden. "You can find some too!"

When we look at God's world with the eyes of a child, heaven comes close to earth as we savor the blessings that surround us.

DENISE DICK HERR

Apparently Common

My grace is sufficient for thee: for my strength is made perfect in weakness.
2 Cor. 12:9.

 TUESDAYS HAD BECOME a true torment for me. In my pathology class I had an examination every week on Tuesdays, no exceptions. I was already tired and tense; now my grades had been dropping. It didn't matter how much I studied; my grades did not improve.

Alone and far from home, a feeling of impotence consumed me. It is at times like this that we remember God, and I knew that I needed Him, only I didn't know what to do.

At my morning worship I read 2 Corinthians 12:9. Soon after, I saw this thought by Rick Warren: "You will never know that God is everything that you need until He is everything that you have." I felt that this had been written especially for me.

I understood that if I wanted a miracle, I would have to ask for it. One miracle was not all I needed—improving my grades immediately was necessary, and long-term results were also my goal. So that is what I asked for.

Then I received an e-mail from my father. I became more encouraged. He told me, "Weakness is any limitation that you inherited and cannot alter. It is not an accident. God has allowed this in your life deliberately with the purpose of showing His power through you."

From this moment forward I stopped worrying, and dedicated myself to doing my part. I continued studying and asking for God's guidance.

The days were difficult, and I felt afraid. This is when I learned a lesson: It is not during every single moment of our friendship with God that we will feel He is close to us. God wants us to have faith even when we cannot feel that He is near.

The day of the test arrived. After doing my part, I prayed again for that miracle, and a deep peace took hold of me. To my surprise, the professor asked only about things that I knew.

I received much more than I had asked for. Between the oral exam and the written exam I received a 98 average, one of the highest grades in the class, something unimaginable for me.

If at times you consider yourself as just another person in this world, do not be discouraged. Trust in God and let Him show you that appearances may deceive; you are someone who is important to Him.

MARESSA STEINER MARRONI

Gone Forever

For ye have the poor always with you; but me ye have not always. Matt. 26:11.

I AM THE CAREGIVER to two 83-year-old women. One has emphysema and has had some mini strokes and cannot get around very well; parts of her face droop. The other woman has Alzheimer's disease, and has lost the ability to reason and understand anything—her mind is gone.

We see visions of families on the TV screen who have sparse rations of food, no medical help, no jobs, and certainly no luxuries such as we have here in North America. How long has it been since you considered the value of the things you take for granted? Someone once said that "salt is what ruins the potatoes when you don't have any, water is what makes you thirsty when the well goes dry, and smoking is what makes you healthy when you don't do it." Often the things for which we are the most thankful are the things we have been without. And we often take for granted the things we have, forgetting that someday we may have them no longer.

The one who most appreciates being able to walk is the one who has not been able to—and will jump the highest and shout the loudest in heaven. A few years ago I had cataracts removed on both eyes. Until my eyes were clear again I didn't know I had freckles on my arm or that the ceiling in my bedroom had speckles on it.

We tend to take our blessings for granted while we have them. We take our health, eyes, ears, and speech for granted. When, one by one, we begin to realize that these things will not last forever, we then appreciate them more.

Lucifer did not appreciate his blessings. He valued them lightly, and as a result eventually rebelled. The disciples did not appreciate Christ as they should have. Only after His death did they feel like sheep without a shepherd. How many boys and girls have a toy chest full of things that were longed for and now lie forgotten? How often do the "I do's" little by little become the humdrum of daily life and are no longer valued? Many of us do not value health until it is gone. We do not appreciate loved ones or friends until they are not with us anymore.

When Jesus comes again, we will realize that death is what makes you glad when it is gone forever; sorrow is what makes you happy when it is no more; and tears are what bring joy when they are wiped away.

VIDELLA McCLELLAN

Child Life: Adult Life

You shall not bow down to them or worship them; for I, the Lord your God, am a jealous God, punishing the children for the sin of the fathers to the third and fourth generation of those who hate me, but showing love to a thousand (generations) of those who love me and keep my commandments. Ex. 20:5, 6, NIV.

HAVE YOU EVER AT TIMES just wanted to be rid of the emotional and environmental impacts on your life as a child that now impact your life as an adult? I have. Several times. I would like to share with you the prayer I cried out to God at one of those times, and it is my prayer that this might be your prayer too.

"Father God, it is my desire, my earnest desire, that You dig deeper and totally renovate my core being to be what You, heavenly Father, have in store for me. Take the filthy rags of my inner core and replace them with the desired spiritual, physical, emotional, social, and intellectual content that You have ready for me.

"You created me of my parents, knowing Your plans for me, and the choices I would actually make in my life. Save me from myself; cleanse me, make me whole in You and in Your expectations—but Father, be gentle. Please let the changes be permanent; please forgive me. Thank You for forgiving me."

Since this prayer God has continued to retrain me, to remove the childhood negative experiences that have colored and clouded my life as an adult. He has become my mother and my father, my brother and my sister. I'm reminded of Isaiah 54:5: "For your Maker is your husband [or father or mother]—the Lord Almighty is his name— the Holy One of Israel is your Redeemer; he is called the God of all the earth."

If you have anything in your life as an adult—or as a child—preventing you from being the best you can be for and with God, surrender it to Him today! He is waiting just for you and the issue that comes to your mind right now.

Father God, I yield to You this event in my life that continues to distract me from full and continuous surrender and service to You. I claim the power in the blood and name of Jesus Christ to release me from the evil one, who distracts me from being wholly Yours.

JULIE NAGLE

My Heart Will Go On Singing

I will sing unto the Lord as long as I live: I will sing praise to my God while I have my being. Ps. 104:33.

I HAD BEEN ASKED TO ORGANIZE the musical program for a women's retreat in Germany. We wanted these meetings to be inspiring, so music was important. I looked at the list of participants to identify possible musicians. I contacted the people and made a detailed plan. Of course, there were some last-minute changes, so I had to fill in the gaps at the last moment.

I had considered organizing a choir at the retreat, but dismissed the idea. The meeting schedule was very tight, and I couldn't imagine anyone giving up their spare time for choir practice. When I packed for the retreat, I put in the sheet music I had prepared—just in case.

The first days passed, and I refused to even think of the song, but deep in my heart I knew that we needed this song. So I asked Kirsten, a good singer, if she would sing it as a solo at the end of the retreat. We arranged to meet at the grand piano the next morning. She looked at the song and sang it a couple of times, and we agreed to put it in the final morning.

After a while she said, "I would like to ask Martina to sing the alto voice. Would that be OK?" I agreed. In the evening, at the end of the day's meetings, we got together around the piano again as Martina had a look at the song. They sang it beautifully. As they were singing, another woman was attracted to the singing and came closer to hear better. We asked her if she wanted to join in. She did. And, one by one, other women came. One took over the piano part. This was a case of infectious enthusiasm. Finally the only singing male in our midst joined us, and the song became richer in harmony as all four parts blended together beautifully.

It was such a happy moment of singing, as if all of these people had wanted to join their voices in praise and had finally found the opportunity to do so. This spontaneous choir was radiant, full of the joy only such an experience can bring. Furthermore, our song touched hearts.

I had not wanted to ask people to sing in a choir. I had thought it too much trouble. But obviously God had wanted us to sing this song and had invited the singers through the prompting of the Holy Spirit. God can do so much more than we ever expect of Him. I learned that God blesses our efforts and that singing is such a boost to our spirits. It should be no trouble at all!

HANNELE OTTSCHOFSKI

Birds of a Feather

Two people are always better off than one because they can work together and enjoy each other's company. If one of them falls, the other can help him up. But I pity the man who walks alone, because when he falls, he has no one to help him. When two people sleep together, they can keep each other warm, which is better than if each one sleeps alone and is cold. Two can resist an attack better than one trying to do it alone. A rope made from three strands is much stronger than a rope made from one. Eccl. 4:9-12, Clear Word.

"LOOK OUT THE WINDOW!" my husband said excitedly. "There's a bluebird on the deck!" It wouldn't have been unusual to see an eastern bluebird in our yard except that it was the end of January in Michigan. I felt sorry for the bird—left behind while the rest of its kind had flown south.

A couple days later I was looking outdoors. Along one side of our yard is a tree line where we hang a bird feeder, suet, and ears of dried corn. There is also a bluebird house attached to a tree trunk. And what to my wondering eyes should I behold but two bluebirds sitting on the long perch outside the birdhouse!

What I saw next truly amazed me. One of them went into the birdhouse, and another flew from the trees to take its place. Then that bird went inside too. This was repeated several times as more birds flew to the perch and went inside. Finally the last bird went in too.

I stood, mesmerized, with my eyes riveted on the birdhouse, letting what had just happened sink in. I failed to count how many birds there were, and I could only imagine what was going on inside. I laughed as I thought of feet on heads and wings not folded amid grumbling about who poked whom.

It wasn't long before one bird came back out on the perch and stood as a sentinel while one by one they came out and flew into the trees again. This time I counted—nine birds had crowded together! Once they were all out, they flew away. Over the next few days this process was repeated.

Now I was happy for the little flock that stuck together, making life easier for all. As Christians we need each other too, and with the Lord we can face any hardships that come our way.

DONNA MEYER VOTH

O Love That Will Not Let Me Go

I have loved thee with an everlasting love: therefore with lovingkindness have I drawn thee. Jer. 31:3.

SHE WAS YOUNG AND FULL OF LIFE, and at 16 she joyfully gave that life to the Lord and was baptized. However, a few years later there were some problems. Discouraged, she left for a far country, putting as many miles as possible between her and her family, her and her God—or so she thought.

After working as a nurse for several years, she married a young man from a prestigious family, not realizing that he had a serious problem with both alcohol and tobacco, to which she, too, soon became enslaved. One day, in desperation, she took her two children, left her beautiful country home, and settled in a distant city, where she worked hard to bring up her family. Though she gave no thought to God, He was always there for her when she needed Him most, even though she attributed His providential working to luck, coincidence, or her own hard work.

But everything changed in the summer of 2003. Though she had stopped smoking seven years earlier, terminal lung cancer was diagnosed. She was terrified, and for the first time in 45 years she started to think seriously about her life, turning slowly toward God.

One day her eldest sister, who was a Christian, phoned and asked if she could come and spend the month of December with her. She accepted joyfully, even though her doctors warned her that she probably would not still be around by Christmas. In 45 years she had seen this sister only once, 15 years before.

It was an unforgettable month. A time of reminiscing, of much laughter and some tears, of joking and serious talk. Though still physically in that far country, she had started spiritually on the long road home.

The sisters bought a Bible and read together the beautiful promises of God's love and forgiveness. They prayed together several times a day. They went to church together. As she came to enjoy an ever-closer relationship with God, her panic attacks subsided. She felt His closeness, and a few weeks later when she was laid to rest, she was ready.

REVEL PAPAIOANNOU

Thought: Isn't it amazing what God will do to woo us? How has He reached out to you?

The Ghan Became a Legend

No one knows the day or hour when the Son of Man will come back.
Matt. 25:13, Clear Word.

"HERE IT COMES!" The shout rang out as I strained to get my first glimpse of the train that would make history this day, February 1, 2004. Two red locomotives blasted their horns as they thundered into view, clearly identified by the name, *The Ghan*, pulling 43 silver coaches, each with its symbol of the Afghan and camel blazed midway along the side. The total length of this train was just over two thirds of a mile (a kilometer), making it the longest passenger train in Australian history.

Until today Alice Springs had been the end of the line, half the distance to Darwin. Now this legendary journey through the heart of Australia would link Adelaide to Darwin in two days, a distance of 1,850 miles (3,000 kilometers).

The previous May I had boarded *The Ghan* to travel to the Red Center on a tour of the outback. May is a good time to visit, as the days are warm and the nights cool. The desert of Australia is an arid beauty. Its sunrises and sunsets are beyond description. In the silence of night I could feel the presence of God as I gazed at the stars, bright in the heavens, for they seemed to touch earth. The majesty of the mountains left me standing in awe; they made me realize how very small we are in such vast areas of God's creation.

The Ghan, with its 400 passengers (including dignitaries and happy crew), would be passing through all this as they headed north on this historical and memorable trip. It would have been great to be aboard, but this time the tickets were priced in the thousands.

Some day the trumpet of the Lord will announce His coming to take us to heaven. I pray that I'll be waiting and watching, because unlike *The Ghan*, we do not know when our Savor will appear. On that memorable trip my brothers and sisters will all be equal in God's sight, and I know I won't need a ticket, for Jesus paid the price at Calvary.

God has been gracious in giving us a taste of His handiwork to see and enjoy while we journey on this earth; however, the beauty He has prepared in heaven will leave us standing in awe of His majesty and power.

LYN WELK-SANDY

The Eastern Brown

Deliver us from evil. Matt. 6:13.

WHEN I ANSWERED THE PHONE that Sunday afternoon I instantly recognized the voice of a very dear friend who lived some 50 minutes' drive from us. "What government department do I ring for the snake catcher?" she asked. In Australia many snakes are endangered species and are protected. Official snake catchers take them out of the cities and back into the country and set them free. I told Christine where she needed to look in her phone book, and that evening she rang again to tell me the full story.

Housework was the number one priority for my friend that day. Her husband was away for a few days, and so all morning Christine cleaned their bathroom. From the walls to the floor, the shower cubicle, the vanity, the basin—it all got a good cleaning. Just after lunch Christine went into her bathroom and noticed something brown on the floor. *What's that?* she wondered, *I don't think I left anything here.* Closer inspection gave her an enormous fright—it was a snake!

Christine fled, yelling for her teenage daughter. They quickly shut the door and jammed towels underneath so the snake couldn't escape. While waiting for the snake catcher to arrive, my friend and her daughter went outside and could see the snake angrily hitting against the sliding-glass doors, trying to get out.

The first attempt to capture the snake failed, and the snake catcher retreated into the garage to make hasty repairs to his net. He identified the snake as an eastern brown, one of the most poisonous snakes in the world. When he reentered the bathroom, he couldn't see the snake anywhere. It had slithered through slats in the bottom of the clothes basket and coiled up in there. Eventually the snake was caught, and peace replaced the panic at my friend's home.

Satan chose the disguise of a snake to deceive Eve in the Garden of Eden. These days Satan stealthily makes his way into our homes in many guises and coils his sin around us so easily. No wonder we are admonished to "resist the devil, and he will flee from you" (James 4:7).

LEONIE DONALD

Thought: In your culture or church, who would qualify as a snake catcher? Would you? Should you?

Before They Call I Will Answer

Before they call I will answer; while they are still speaking I will hear.
Isa. 65:24, NIV.

I WAS INTRODUCED TO COMPUTERS rather late in life. Not without a lot of trauma, I mastered ("learned" would be a better word) the computer. Does one ever master a computer?

For more than a decade I maintained a love-hate relationship with the computer. I used it in the same way that I use a car. I am a reasonably expert driver, but if anything goes wrong with the works, I'm done. I haven't a clue what goes on inside.

A few months ago I completed another book. To be on the safe side, I made three copies of my manuscript on a floppy disk. Then a grandson inadvertently passed on a virus. I had heard of viruses, but as we never used borrowed disks, we didn't worry about them. Like the virus of an illness, this one stealthily grew and multiplied (or whatever they do), and the only inkling of disaster came weeks later when I found that I couldn't copy an important article from a floppy disk. Never mind; I did it the hard way, line by line.

Then I had occasion to use one of the backups of my manuscript. I called up chapter after chapter, only to be faced with a blank screen—or at best a couple of disconnected lines. Horrified, I tried all three backup disks, with the same result. My whole book manuscript had disappeared—gobbled up by a virus.

It could have been a calamity to the nth degree, except that a fourth copy was in the hands of the publisher. However, I desperately needed access to one of those 35 chapters. What to do?

No, I didn't pray about it. I had done that so often during my learning stages that I concluded that God didn't work miracles whenever computers were concerned. He expected me to call in a computer expert when I needed help.

But my desperate wish must have been as good as a prayer. I sat in front of that soulless screen and dejectedly called up every chapter. Only one of them was readable; in fact, it was more than readable—it was perfect. And it was the very chapter I so much needed.

I'm sorry, Lord. Please forgive me for my lack of faith. I should have remembered that the God who cares about sparrows cares about computer Grannies, too—even before they ask.

GOLDIE DOWN

42

Put Your Feet Down

Do not be afraid. Stand firm and you will see the deliverance the Lord will bring you today. Ex. 14:13, NIV.

I WAS IN HANAUMA BAY, Hawaii, when it happened. During my second year of college I decided to be a student missionary teacher in the South Pacific for one year. That's how I found myself in Hawaii for a five-day teacher orientation. After three intensive days of training and seminars, our instructors finally granted us some leisure time to explore the tropical paradise of Oahu. With several friends, I chose to relax on Hanauma Bay's beach.

Not being a very strong swimmer, I stayed close to shore as my friends ventured into deeper waters. I stretched out on the water, tipping my face toward the sun as I allowed the gentle swell of the clear water to rock me into a drowsy state of bliss. After my leisurely float I began swimming laps parallel to the shoreline, but this exhausted me, and I soon decided to head back to dry land. I glanced toward the shore. It seemed awfully far away. Had I drifted into the deeper water? I couldn't tell, but I began swimming toward shore anyway.

My progress was slow and tiring. Panic crept in and mounted with each new stroke. The shoreline seemed so far away that I didn't dare put my feet down to gauge my depth for fear of what I might discover. Yet I knew I couldn't keep swimming forever. I had to do something—anything— quickly. I flapped in the water for a few more desperate moments before panic surpassed pride and I screamed, "Help! Help!" Nobody moved. *Oh, no!* I thought, horrified, *they're all experiencing that crowd mentality thing— nobody does anything because everybody thinks somebody else will.* I yelled again. This time one of my friends sized up my dilemma and drawled, "Grace, just put your *feet* down!" I mechanically followed her orders and lowered my feet. Sweet relief flooded over me as I stood up in about four feet of water.

So often I have grown discouraged or fearful and felt abandoned by everyone, including God. But invariably when I cry out for help God is there, gently reminding me to put my feet down and realize that He has not called me to stand in waters above my head. Nor has He called me to do any task that I cannot accomplish with His help. I need only to trust Him and have enough faith in His promises to stand.

A. GRACE BROWN

A Class With a Blessing

Man plans to do all kinds of things, but what the Lord plans will ultimately be done. Prov. 19:21, Clear Word.

ONE MORNING BEFORE A HOME BUSINESS CLASS my daughter read in her Bible, "We do not know the direction our lives will take, but the Lord knows and understands." She prayed that she would be a shining light to each of her customers. This was especially important, as a larger group than usual had signed up and she always wants these events to be restful, happy, and inspiring for her customers. She shared with me by e-mail how God answered her prayer in a special way. I had been praying for her and her family ever since they had moved clear across the country.

She and her 10-year-old daughter assistant had prepared ahead of time, so she felt confident that this would be an exciting learning session. After a nice breakfast, her husband suggested that they make a special meal for her group that evening. She thought he had to be joking. That was a lot of work to prepare for 18 people, and usually her husband is out the door at the mere thought of a houseful of women. But this time he promised to come help her at 5:00 p.m., saying, "We can do this together with the kids."

Then they discovered that the pipes in the downstairs bathroom were frozen—again. Once again her husband came to the rescue, and in zero-degree weather he thawed the pipes with a blow dryer and reinsulated them. People started arriving an hour early, one woman wringing her hands because she wasn't used to the icy roads and her car had slid into the ditch. Another came with a birthday cake, since this was the way she had chosen to celebrate her birthday with two friends. There were many special women with many special needs at the class that day.

Even the complicated meal was a great success, and when the busy day was over, my daughter sat at the table with her husband, thinking, *Was that what I prayed for when I asked to be a shining light?* Hopefully, for seven hours that day her students released stress, shared with others, remembered happy times, filled their stomachs, and went home with new energy. She felt that they had been a shining light to her also as she read again, "Man plans to do all kinds of things, but what the Lord plans will ultimately be done."

BETTY J. ADAMS

I Need a Spiritual Blessing

Blessed be the God and Father of our Lord Jesus Christ, who hath blessed us with all spiritual blessings in heavenly places in Christ. Eph. 1:3.

IT WAS ONE of those mornings that seemed to say, "I'm full of potential and will accomplish just about anything if I'm put to work." So I began. I took up my Bible just after my husband left for work. I've been reading Luke again after an elder reawakened my interest during one of his sermons. So as the morning suggested, I invigorated myself and was ready to be empowered. I feel comfortable studying my Bible lying down, so with the Bible in front of me I began reading, but there was no connection—I felt void of all interaction with God.

I realized that my thoughts were elsewhere. I felt a prompting to call a friend. To accomplish this, I had to go to the store first to purchase a Pay-and-Go card for my cell phone. However, before leaving home I blurted out to God that I needed a spiritual blessing myself.

As I approached the store, for some reason my eyes fell on a young woman I saw standing alone, seemingly unconcerned about the cares of life. I exclaimed, "Did you know that Jesus is coming, and that He's coming back for people who are prepared to meet Him?"

I proceeded to tell her that someone was praying for her to give her heart to Jesus. With a look of skepticism and surprise, she asked if I knew she would be there at that moment. I informed her that God knew and wanted me to give her that message. After some time of witnessing she told me that she was extremely thankful that I had spoken to her and that she wanted to give her life to Jesus.

I felt the Holy Spirit's presence raining down on me that morning and knew that God had given me the spiritual blessing that I desired. He sent me out that morning to plant a seed. Sometimes we worry if the person we witness to will follow Jesus right there and then, but God knows that using us is what is important for us—our blessing—and He will do the rest.

DONNA DENNIS

Thought: Could it be that the times that we are feeling empty and in need of a blessing are the very times we should reach out to others with the love of God? Maybe we already have the blessing, but can recognize it only when we use it. What do you think?

Excuses, Excuses!

"The woman you put here with me—she gave me some fruit from the tree,
and I ate it." . . . "The serpent deceived me, and I ate." Gen. 3:12, 13, NIV.

 WITH OUR FIRST PARENTS FOR TEACHERS, we've all
learned the fine art of making excuses. We have excuses for our
boss as to why we didn't get that report finished; excuses for our
husband as to why we backed the car over the wheelbarrow; excuses for our kids as to why we can't go camping this weekend.
Perhaps we're even so bold as to offer excuses to God!

Many of our excuses are logical and valid—at least in our own eyes.
Others are humorous, and some even ludicrous. We've all smiled at a
child's transparent attempt at making excuses.

Last year we invited a large group of friends over for supper and a visit.
One family brought their two young boys, as well as another whom they
were babysitting. There was pleasant buzzing and laughter from the older
children and lots of chatting among the adults. The little boys entertained
themselves just as three normal, rambunctious lads do. An occasional word
from the adult section kept them in check.

I had a bar with hanging beads draped across the open doorway to our
bedroom. This, along with our huge free-floating waterbed, fascinated the
boys. They spent their time surveying the bedroom from the loft, and then
running down the steps, through the beaded doorway, and bouncing gently
on the bed—with my permission.

Suddenly, in a fit of exuberance, little Philip, the youngest, grabbed a
handful of beads and did a Tarzan swing into the bedroom. Of course the
beads came apart from the frame, and he spent the rest of the evening trying to put them back together.

But it's what Philip said to his dad that still tickles me. "Dad, I barely
touched them—like this." And he gently patted a handful of the beads. And
perhaps he really believed that that was all he had done. Don't we usually
believe our own excuses?

Young Philip was trying to save his hide and keep out of hot water.
That's what excuses are all about, isn't it? But surely God must chuckle
when we give Him some of our lame excuses, just as I did at Philip's.

DAWNA BEAUSOLEIL

God's Promise of Deliverance

When thou passeth through the waters, I will be with thee; and through the rivers, they shall not overflow thee: when thou walketh through the fire, thou shall not be burned; neither shall the flame kindle upon thee. Isa. 43:2.

GOD GIVES THIS POWERFUL PROMISE to Israel through Isaiah. God did protect and deliver Israel through many tribulations, wars, and troubles, and today the devil creates many overwhelming troubles and problems for Christians to hinder them on their Christian path.

My husband passed away in the middle of the night in the hospital. When I got home the following morning and the reality of his death hit me, my faith was shaken. I felt as if someone was literally pulling my faith in God from me. That was the devil attacking my faith in God. I called my prayer partner to pray for me.

The devil then presented the difficult tasks that lay ahead of me. My husband died in Mozambique. I had to arrange all the immigration documentation and the transport of the body to Zambia. Then I had to arrange transport for my three children and me to go for the funeral in rural Zambia. I felt that this was too much for me—I felt too weak to go through all that. I felt as if I would just collapse and die too, in the middle of all these tasks and difficulties.

That night God put today's scripture in my mind. I read that scripture again and again, and as I did my faith was restored. I believed what the scripture said and claimed that promise for myself. I saw in my mind God holding me and going with me throughout the whole process. I felt God protecting me and covering me and strengthening me.

Early in the morning my husband's boss came to see me. His office took over all the responsibility of buying the coffin, completing the immigration paperwork, and paying for the transportation of the body to Zambia. Our flight tickets were also arranged and paid for. On arrival in Zambia we found the family waiting for us, and they took over all the travel arrangements, church services, and prayer sessions along the way home. I could see God's hand in the whole trip.

I thank God for faithfully carrying me safely through this flooded river. It was a rough time for me, but God was there. When problems of life threaten to destroy your faith, hold on to Jesus Christ; He will protect and deliver you.

CONISIA ANTHONY

Poor Little Bird

Are not two sparrows sold for a penny? And not one of them will fall to the ground without your Father's will. . . . Fear not, therefore; you are of more value than many sparrows. Matt. 10:29-31, RSV.

I WAS FALSELY ACCUSED of doing something I was not even aware of. To say I was upset is putting it mildly. Not being the verbally retaliatory type of woman, I thought it best to get out of the house and take a walk. That, I thought, would be a good way to "cool off."

Thoughts raced through my mind. *Why must I be blamed for everything? Why me? It isn't fair. Why, when I try to do what's right, do things go against me?*

A bird flew by as I looked up to the sky, and I said to myself, *Why could I not be a bird and fly away when troubles come?* When I was a child, I used to think how wonderful it would be to be like a bird and take flight when troubles come my way.

Then as I turned the corner, I noticed a little bird lying in the gutter. *Poor thing*, I thought. *Why are you lying here? Who killed you?* There seemed nothing I could do. My trend of thought now changed completely from feeling sorry for myself to what had caused that little bird's demise.

Our verse in Matthew 10:29 came to mind. These little birds don't have much value, yet if one of them falls to the ground our heavenly Father knows about it! He must be so sad to see one of His creatures die.

I now realized that I was still better off than a bird. I still had life and hope. The bird could not fly again, but I was still free. Not so bad after all! The bird could not sing again; I could still sing despite my disappointment. After all, we must praise God in all circumstances, even when the going is rough.

The bird could not gather food anymore for its family; my heavenly Father provides for me still. The bird lay alone in the gutter, but I still have family and friends who love me, and a roof over my head.

"Fear not, [put your name here]; you are of more value than many sparrows." Thank your heavenly Father right now for loving you so much.

PRISCILLA E. ADONIS

Your Name

But thou, O Lord, knowest me: thou hast seen me, and tried mine heart toward thee. Jer. 12:3.

IN 1974 WE LIVED IN THE BEAUTIFUL CITY of Nova Lisboa, the queen of the Angolan high plateau (now named Huambo).

One day, while I played with my son, I put my ear to his chest and said, "Son, your heart is not saying my name!" With his 3-year-old wisdom he took on an afflicted attitude and asked me, "But Mommy, tell me then, what is your name?" And slowly I began to tell him my name—Maria Costa Sales Cardoso—and he repeated it with me. He asked me to say it again, and he continued repeating it. When I thought that he knew it well, he said, "Mommy, listen now and see if my heart now knows how to say your name." While I put my ear to his chest again, he held my head with his little hands and whispered my name quietly so that his heart could say it and I could hear.

As I remember this episode I imagine the Lord saying, "Daughter, so many times your lips have said My name, but your heart is not always available to pronounce it. What is going on with you? I left you a letter, and you need to read it. You will find something special in it that I have dedicated to you. When you walk in the midst of nature, when you look at the starlit sky, when the rain falls or you see a sunset, when you travel by land or by sea—there are so many messages that I send you. What do you think of joy, laughter, pain, or the tenderness of a friendship that is shared? When you look at your children, what love is this that lives in your heart? And your grandchildren? Do you understand what I want to tell you when they run to you, when they kiss you and embrace you, or when they just remain in silence at your side or lie sleeping on your lap? All of these messages of love are Mine! I have so many blessings to give you, and I expect so much of you. I know that the path is difficult. There are detours and shortcuts that you still have to take, but you need your heart to always say My name so that you do not falter!"

And as I imagine the Lord talking to me in this manner I want to ask Him to teach me everything about His name, because I want to keep His name in my heart forever. I want to speak to Him, to say His name, every day.

MARIA SALES

He Never
Abandons His Children

I was young and now I am old, yet I have never seen the righteous forsaken or their children begging bread. Ps. 37:25, NIV.

RIGHT AFTER WE WERE MARRIED, my husband and I worked in a rural mission school in the south of Brazil. During the two years there we learned much and worked together with wonderful people who helped us immensely. Our small apartment was near the social room, the church, and the local cemetery. In this cemetery rested great men who had taken the gospel message of Jesus' return to this region.

My husband took college classes at night and taught classes in the school during the day. Many nights I stayed alone with our little son and prayed until my husband returned, because he had to walk five miles (eight kilometers) to our apartment from where he got off the bus. Sometimes, when it had rained, he couldn't return because the river had overflowed, and no one was able to cross. At these times he spent the night on the other side of the river in the home of friends who kindly took him in.

At the end of each month we experienced financial difficulties because by that time our salary had been totally used. These were days of doing without, when we prayed a lot for God's help and His protection. He never abandoned us. We often experienced the fulfillment of His promise "The angel of the Lord encamps around those who fear him, and he delivers them" (Ps. 34:7, NIV).

One day someone who lived in the neighborhood visited us and promised to give us a basket containing enough food to last us the rest of the month. The only condition that he placed on us was that we were not to tell anyone about his donation. Faithfully we fulfilled this promise. After all, he was the "angel" whom God had sent to help us. And on the set date he came very early with a lovely basket filled with food. Among the things he brought was even a package of cookies for our son.

I praise God because at the times of greatest need He used His children to help us and to make us strong workers for Him.

You can always trust in God; He never abandons His children who are faithful to Him.

MARLENE ESTEVES GARCIA

The Gift Bag

But seek ye first the kingdom of God, and his righteousness; and all these things shall be added unto you. Matt. 6:33.

 SHE WAS AT THAT DELIGHTFUL CHILD-WOMAN STAGE, this niece of mine, when everything could be perfect one moment and absolutely horrible the next. In one of those moments, I'm not sure which it was, she told me in no uncertain terms that she wanted only money for her upcoming twelfth birthday. "No gift certificates; no cute gifts. Nothing but money. And Auntie, can you tell that to my family?"

A few nights later she came for a sleepover. "Oh, what a cute camera," the budding photographer enthused. "I'd really like one just like this for my birthday. Is it very expensive?" The question was thoughtful. When she heard it wasn't, the other question I knew was coming followed. "Will you get one for me?"

"But Takara—"

"I know what I said, but I would buy one anyway with your money. So . . ." Her shrug said it all. "And would you get it in another color, please?"

I searched the stores for cameras in various colors. I began to think her original idea was more perfect than we'd realized. Four stores later, with her gift camera in hand, I spotted a pretty little beaded gift bag in the tangerine and fuchsia colors that were the current craze. It was in the clearance rack and cost less than a dollar. I had to pick it up.

When her birthday arrived, the envelopes rolled in. Then she spotted my gift. "Oh, that's such a pretty bag. It's even nicer than the gift." Her smile took the sting from her words.

"But Takara—"

"I really do like the camera, Auntie. But the bag is so cool."

I wondered if that was how I regarded my heavenly Father. Was my Christianity no more than an attractive, outward show of the real thing? Was I really treasuring His expensive kingdom? Did I really want to attain it? Was I actually putting Him first in all of my life?

Dear Father, I prayed, *help me to put You at the real center of my life. I give myself, my thoughts and actions, completely over to You.*

GLENDA-MAE GREENE

Our Future in His Hands

Your eyes saw my unformed body. All the days ordained for me were written in your book before one of them came to be. Ps. 139:16, NIV.

 FEBRUARY 18, 2004, was a completely normal day, just like all other days. When the phone rang at 11:00 p.m., I had already gone to sleep. My husband answered the call, and on the other end of the line my brother revealed to him the news of a tragic accident that had taken my youngest sister's life.

I could not believe the news was possible. It did not make sense. It could have been another person. I began to cry, and asked my husband to kneel with me to pray for her, for my parents, for my brothers and sisters, and for everyone who was suffering.

The next morning we traveled to my family's home to attend the funeral. The following days were filled with great anguish and much pain. I contemplated my parents, and I understood the pain that they felt, because I too am a mother. My anguish only increased as I looked at the situation from their point of view.

Special things brought back many memories, and photographs began to appear. We remembered and shared her life, her words, her gestures, her beautiful smile, without really understanding why this had happened. She was only 29 years old and had so many dreams—a whole life ahead to be lived.

Today, looking with the eyes of faith, I understand that God knows the reasons, and I am certain that one day we will understand also. I know that she sleeps, unaware of our pain, tears, and feelings.

When we are born, God already has our days and His purposes written; they belong only to Him. But those who are faithful to Him have their life hidden in Him, and He will certainly return it as He has promised.

Lord, help each father, mother, brother, or sister, son, or daughter who may be experiencing the pain and suffering of losing a loved one. With Jesus Christ in our life, may these losses of today in this sad and painful world be transformed into beautiful and joyful reunions in Your kingdom in the near future. Amen!

JEANINE XAVIER NÁZER LATIF

Troubles Come, Troubles Go

For He [God] Himself has said, "I will never leave you nor forsake you."
Heb. 13:5, NKJV.

LIFE IS FILLED WITH CHANGES. Some we like, many we don't—especially those that cause us to leave our comfort zones. Yet they say that change is the one constant in life. Or is it? As I think back over my life it does seem as though the one constant was change. Moves from one home to another or from one country to another; friends that came and went, depending on where we lived. School changes for the kids. Changes in my size over the years (now, that one I'd prefer to forget, especially my efforts to lose unwanted weight). Change in hairstyles (and there have been many) from long to short.

My husband, Joe, and I were married in 1979, and over the years we have experienced many changes, both personally and as a couple. Some changes came easily, some were unexpected, and many were against our will. But they still came.

Yes, it does seem as though change is life's one constant. But that's not true. As a Christian I have found that the only one unchangeable thing in my life is God. He never changes. He is always the same—yesterday, today, and tomorrow. Our text reminds us of that fact. And this one fact, more than any other, has comforted me through all of life's changes.

No matter what happened in my life, whether we moved to a new country or lost old friends—even when we lost our firstborn son many years ago—the one constant in my life was that God was always with me. Even when I could not feel Him, sense Him, or hear from Him, I knew He was there. That is a real Valentine's Day message for today—or any day.

I don't know what changes you are going through in your life today as you read this, but I do know the one thing that will not change, that you can depend on no matter what happens, is that our Friend and Savior, our Father and our Creator, will never leave you nor forsake you.

On this Valentine's Day, take heart, my friend—God is with you. Remember the disciples in the boat in the storm. Jesus was fast asleep while they battled their storms. They could neither hear Him nor see Him at work to save them, but He was there. One lesson that life has taught me is that God may be silent, but He is never absent. Praise God.

HEATHER-DAWN SMALL

The Touch of an Angel

Before they call I will answer. Isa. 65:24, NIV.

MY HUSBAND AND I were teaching a group of pastors and their wives in Romania. We adjusted our seminars as we learned about the different needs of the people. We spoke mostly through translators, and stood up as we presented. We were passionate about our topic and enjoyed the challenge of teaching in a very different culture from our own. During breaks we counseled, talked to people, or prepared for the next presentation. With so much happening (and probably so much adrenaline coursing through my body), I didn't realize how tense my body had become and how tight my shoulders were. But Lily had noticed, and she had an idea.

Over a cup of fruit tea Lily came to speak to me. She was a pastor's wife who had learned how to do massage in Norway. "I have a special gift that I will give you tonight after you have finished speaking. I will come to your room and give you a back, head, and face massage. You are getting very tired and stiff, and when I have massaged you, you will feel much better."

Late in the evening Lily came to our room and gifted me with the most wonderful massage, kneading into my tight shoulders, loosening my scalp, and soothing my face. As I lay there, feeling the wonderful relaxing movement of her hands, it was as if I were being touched by an angel, as if what she were giving me was a gift from God, as if her hands were showing me the love that God wanted me to experience. By the time she finished I was almost asleep, pleasantly and deeply drowsy.

Her gift was the perfect gift for me. I didn't even know that I needed such a gift, but she had seen me through different eyes, eyes that could see the tension in my body and that cared enough to minister to my need.

In a situation in which we were giving so much it was just what I needed: to stop for a few minutes and receive something from someone else. The memory of Lily's gift will stay with me always and soothe my heart, even when she isn't there to soothe my body. Through her gift I was touched by an angel and loved by God.

I wonder how God will use me today to touch someone with His love. May He use me to bless someone by meeting a need they have, even before they are aware of it themselves.

KAREN HOLFORD

I Will Persevere

Praying always with prayer and supplication in the Spirit, and watching thereunto with perseverance and supplication. Eph. 6:18.

I WANTED TO GO into selling real estate, but there was a test I had to pass before I could be licensed. I spent a long time in prayer, then took the test. Eight times.

The first time I tried to take the Florida real estate exam I forgot my eligibility slip. No one is allowed to take the test without it. By the time the school faxed over the slip, the test had begun, so I failed. I failed the second time, too, but I didn't feel bad, because only about 25 percent pass on the first try. After the fourth failure, however, I couldn't help crying. I had studied so hard and thought I really knew the material. I yearned to give up, but I kept remembering a line I'd once heard. "One of the requirements for answered prayer is perseverance." I vowed to persevere, and I claimed two Bible texts: "All things work together for good to them that love God" (Rom. 8:28) and "If any of you lack wisdom, let him ask of God" (James 1:5).

I asked God for wisdom to pass the test, but still I failed. When I failed the seventh time, I told the test supervisor, "I will not be back." But a voice whispered, "Trust God even when you don't understand. He is trustworthy."

Two nights later I lay in bed, exhausted. Suddenly I had a compelling urge: "Get on the computer. See if there is a cancellation for tomorrow's test." I didn't want to obey. I had checked the day before, and the earliest opening was three weeks later. But I couldn't get rid of the thought. Finally, minutes before midnight, I checked. There was an opening in Ormond Beach for the next day. This was the place everyone had urged me to try. It was a relatively easy-to-get-to site. But this test would be different. Then I heard God say, "Take the test." I really started praying then. Too wound up to review my notes, I simply prayed.

The drive to Ormond Beach the next morning was beautiful, and the test seemed easy. When the exam was complete—it takes about a minute for the computer to print the results—I got the good news. I had passed.

Thank You for increasing my faith. Because of You, I will never give up.

NORMA HOWELL

The Invitation

Wake up, Deborah . . . ! Wake up, . . . and sing a song! Judges 5:12, NLT.

THE HOLY SPIRIT instructed me, "Do not be concerned about what it costs to distribute the letters you are inspired to write, and the little ornaments you make. Just do it—pretend you are a millionaire, sharing from the treasure-house of your own heart!" Oh, what a totally outrageous invitation I accepted from God years ago!

I believe that Jesus has given me a personal ministry, "Dimensions of Love," as an avenue to share His love and to tell others about Him. To get attention, one often needs to use something unique, so I place dimes on the ornaments I make and the pages I write. People ask, "Why the dimes?" This gives me a golden opportunity to share my faith in hopes of encouraging others to seek a personal relationship with Jesus.

Recently I realized that there was a deeper, subconscious, spiritual reason I was inspired to use dimes in my ministry. In 1971 Daddy had surgery for stomach cancer. I spent a month in Oregon with my family. Then he and Mom drove me back to my home in Canada. On the way I was thinking and praying. About one mile from the U.S.-Canadian border, while still on the American side, I said, "Daddy, I have something I need to tell you. When I was in second grade I stole money from your overalls while you were sleeping so that I could buy candy at the Kiddy Corner across from West Park School. I'm so sorry; will you please forgive me?" (Of course he did!) I had stolen *dimes*—and later Jesus turned my confessed sin into a ministry for His glory!

Daddy passed away at age 44, three months before my daughter, Andrea, was born. I was 20. From the very first word to the last, "Dimensions of Love" was—and is—being written in loving memory of my father, William Robert Bailey.

I wrote my first devotional in anguish many years later. I had willingly laid my mind upon the altar of sacrifice. The cross I'd been given to carry (my son, Sonny, is mentally challenged with psychomotor retardation and autism) was just too heavy. This article gave birth to my writing/prayer ministries. I feel my life is blessed by prayers. God is often able to turn a bad experience into a blessing. We just have to be willing to accept His invitation to work with Him. Will you join me in doing that today?

DEBORAH SANDERS

Deliverance From Guilt

He shall call upon me, and I will answer him: I will be with him in trouble; I will deliver him, and honour him. Ps. 91:15.

MY LIFE SEEMED TO BE EBBING AWAY. The thought of how I'd messed up tormented me. It felt like claws were holding my neck in a tight grip. Every time I thought of the event, I cringed, and embarrassment and shame stared at me. I pleaded, "Lord, please help me put this nightmare behind me." I thought of the song that included, "All your anxiety, all your care, bring to the mercy seat—leave it there; never a burden He cannot bear, never a friend like Jesus."

It all began after I served as the emcee at my friend's wedding reception. It seemed everything went well until I reached home. Somehow I convinced myself that I'd messed up, and guilt began to plague me. The following day my husband and I traveled to California for our vacation. I was miserable on the plane.

We arrived safely at our friend's home, but during the night I felt sick to my stomach. After my husband fell asleep, I knelt by my bed and prayed, "Lord, forgive me; I didn't mean to mess up. Deliver me from my guilt." We are blessed to serve a gracious and compassionate God who is always available and willing to lift us out of our dungeon of guilt and give us hope, healing, and restoration. He's never on vacation, and we don't have to listen to a voice mail saying, "Jesus is busy helping other sinners; please hold," or "Take a number and stand in line." Instantly we have direct access to our Father's throne room.

A few days after returning home I called the bride and apologized for messing up. To my utter amazement, she responded that I hadn't messed up and that they had enjoyed themselves. So many hours I had wasted worrying about nothing! That's what Satan does. He makes us believe we've messed up, and we walk around carrying a heavy load of guilt that robs us of our joy and peace of mind. "Yes, Jesus took my burden I could no longer bear; yes, Jesus took my burden in answer to my prayer; my anxious fears subsided; my spirit was made strong, for Jesus took my burden and left me with a song."

If you're weighed down with guilt, call upon your heavenly Father. He has promised to deliver you. He will quiet your raging sea and give you peace, sweet peace.

SHIRLEY C. IHEANACHO

Looks on the Heart

Let Us make man in Our image, according to Our likeness. Gen. 1:26, NKJV.

 WE DECIDED TO REMOVE THE CARPET in the family room and install hardwood flooring in the high-traffic area. My husband and son moved the piano into the hallway, but chipped one of the legs in the process. I was not impressed! Finally the room was put back in order and the piano—and its chipped leg—was returned to its place.

Whenever I looked at the piano, all I saw was the missing wood. I was so conscious of the imperfection of the piano that I tried to cover up the flaw. I felt as though everyone noticed it. That chip did not impact the way the piano played or sounded. Everything about the piano was fine, except the leg.

Sometimes we put too much emphasis on external appearances. Have you ever had a pimple on your nose, or a cold sore on your lip? You think that whenever people look at you, all they see is the big zit or the sore you are trying to cover up.

I am so glad that God does not see as people see. People look on the outside, but God looks on the heart. When we interact with each other, we focus on the external, the things we see. We put a lot of emphasis on beauty, size, height, skin color, length of hair, and other things that, when you really think about it, really don't matter. Just as the chip on the piano leg made no difference in the way the piano functioned.

What counts is who you are inside—which will be reflected on the outside. Your personality, your heart, the way you treat others. Your relationship with your heavenly Father! By their fruits you shall know them. Now that I am getting older, when I look in the mirror I reframe the gray hairs to life experiences. I look at the love handles at my sides and reflect on the four children, including the twins, that the Lord has blessed me with.

In all things give thanks. You are beautiful because God made you. You belong to His family, and He loves you. Love yourself, too. You were chosen by Him, and He loves you unconditionally. He invites you to come to Him just as you are, imperfections and all. We are Shekinah glory in clay jars. Let God mold and fashion you after His will so that you can become beautiful, inside and out. After all, He made you in His image.

SHARON LONG (BROWN)

What About Eve?

Adam lay with his wife Eve, and she became pregnant and gave birth to Cain. She said, "With the help of the Lord I have brought forth a man." Later she gave birth to his brother Abel. Gen. 4:1, 2, NIV.

IT WAS A THRILL FOR ME to be in the delivery room when Elise was born. When she let out that first lusty cry, I started to cry too! It was all so incredible. This beautiful new baby girl was the daughter of the one who had been my own baby girl.

Later, while still in the delivery room, I had the opportunity to hold Elise, and I began to muse about Eve. Elise was helped into the world by an obstetrician and an experienced labor and delivery nurse. There was a medical student there to observe, and she even helped a bit. And if all that had failed, Elise's father is a physician's assistant. She was in good hands!

But what about Eve? No one had ever even witnessed a human birth before. Did God tell Eve what to expect, or what was happening? My daughter and son-in-law had read all kinds of books—they knew more than I, who had given birth twice! But who told Eve? Who served as a midwife? An angel? Who told her when to push? Who told her or Adam how to cut the umbilical cord? Or massage the uterus back into place? Who coached Eve on breast feeding? Do you suppose Cain ever had colic? How did Eve know what to do? Oh, I have so many questions!

I believe that Eve, fresh from the hand of God, probably had an easier delivery than anyone since, but I do hope that angels were there to give the advice and support that women now value from their sisters. I am sure God did not leave Eve frightened and clueless, because our text indicates that the Lord helped her. Likewise, I believe God takes care of women in a special way even today, whether or not they have children.

Women give birth to more than babies: ideas, ministries, services, and products. It all started with Eve, but it didn't end with Eve. These are sometimes new, untried, unknown. That can be scary and daunting. But even these can be achieved "with the help of the Lord." Peter says that if we have the character qualities of faith, goodness, knowledge, self-control, perseverance, godliness, kindness, and love, "they will keep you from being ineffective and unproductive [barren] in your knowledge of our Lord Jesus Christ" (2 Peter 1:8, NIV).

ARDIS DICK STENBAKKEN

God Always
Does What Is Necessary

Delight yourself in the Lord and he will give you the desires of your heart.
Commit your way to the Lord; trust in him and he will do this. Ps. 37:4, 5, NIV.

IT WAS 1997 when I passed through the gates of Brazil Adventist College in São Paulo to get a degree in mathematics. Heart beating fast, joy stamped on my face—which was marked by smiles and tears of gratitude to God for a dream come true—all these feelings were mixed with homesickness because of the family and friends I had left behind.

Accustomed to the facilities of home and the protection of my parents, I now had a totally new and challenging life before me. Who would take care of me? Who would hold me in their arms when things became difficult? Where would I find someone willing to listen to me when sadness tugged at my heart? Faced with all of these questions, I knew one thing was certain: I was not alone. Since the first moment, even when everything that I was experiencing was just a desire, I could feel the powerful hand of God guiding my life.

During the four happy years that I spent at that institution, I felt God's presence as a loving father who cared for each detail of my life. From the room where I lived (and my roommates who shared the same space with me), to the area where I worked, to my dear bosses and the friends I made, and the church I attended—in all these things, in all these people, I could feel the hand of God.

Today's Bible verse followed me very closely during the entire time that I spent there, and it had a special meaning during that time of my life. I never took a test in college without reading this verse and asking God to fulfill it in my life. I attempted to do my part, and God always was faithful to fulfill His promises.

Every day I meditated and sought strength from God. He fulfills His promises when we call out in prayer. If we leave everything we are going to do in His hands and make Him our great joy, "He will give you the desires of your heart," and He will do everything that is necessary for you.

Thank You, dear Father, for fulfilling the promises of Psalm 37 in our lives.

JANAÍNA V.C.B. PORTES

Signed, Sealed—
Then Delivered

I know whom I have believed, and am convinced that he is able to guard what I have entrusted to him for that day. 2 Tim. 1:12, NIV.

DARIUS WAS IN A QUANDARY. His own pride and arrogance had gotten him into an unenviable position. He had allowed himself to be flattered into signing a foolish decree about worship by the satraps and administrators without thinking the consequences through. If he tried to revoke his decree, he would lose all credibility, and could even lose power. If he did not revoke it, he stood to lose his best advisor. What was he to do?

Many times we find ourselves in situations in which we are facing the bitter consequences of speaking or acting before we've had time to think. Whatever we do, the end is going to be uncomfortable, or even horrible. In such a situation, what can you do?

Even though Darius was the author of his own trouble, as we so often are in our own situations, he knew that Daniel's God was not limited by what had been written.

This is what the Lord says: "Is my hand shortened at all, that it cannot redeem? or have I no power to deliver?" (Isa. 50:2). "Do you not know? Have you not heard?" (Isa. 40:21, NIV). "Behold, the Lord God shall come with strong hand" (verse 10), "For he that toucheth you toucheth the apple of his eye" (Zech. 2:8). When the king came to inquire after Daniel, he called to Daniel in an anguished voice, "Daniel, servant of the living God, has your God, whom you serve continually, been able to deliver you from the lions?" (Dan. 6:20, NKJV).

Was He able? Daniel replied, "My God hath sent his angel, and hath shut the lions' mouths" (verse 22). The apostle Paul was able to echo Daniel's faith: "For I know whom I have believed and am persuaded that He is able to keep what I have committed to Him until that day" (2 Tim. 1:12, NKJV). Was He able? Of course He was able! He still is able to help us, if only we ask Him.

"He who dwells in the shelter of the Most High will rest in the shadow of the Almighty. I will say of the Lord, 'He is my refuge and my fortress, my God, in whom I trust' (Ps. 91:1, 2, NIV). Signed, sealed, delivered—you're God's. Is He able in your life?

JUDITH PURKISS

The Wedding

Let us rejoice and be glad and give him glory! For the wedding of the Lamb has come. Rev. 19:7, NIV.

SHE WAS BEAUTIFUL! My only daughter, dressed in white, entering through the church doors. So much emotion for a mother! So many thoughts go through one's mind at such a special moment as this! The joy of being able to share in dreams, plans, and the happiness of your daughter! The difficulty in accepting the fact that your so dear and dependent daughter has grown up, become independent, and now shares her secrets with the groom, who will soon be her husband, and no longer with Mommy.

My mind went back to the recent months of shopping together, buying the last items for her new home and the remodeling of their house. While we worked hard to get everything ready, I heard her talk with enthusiasm about her fiancé, their promises, and their plans. The decorations in the house, the church, and the party; the minute details of the dress, the cake, lodging for guests, groomsmen, bridesmaids, the Bible boy, the flower girls, the hairdresser, the musicians, the singers, the honeymoon—everything was now done according to the good taste of the bride and groom.

As her mother, I could see the final product: everything was ready and perfect. They had done it! Now was the time just to enjoy all of the emotions, without any concerns.

There is another wedding feast that is to take place. Since I don't know the exact date of this event, I could be caught unprepared. Will I, like my daughter and her fiancé, have taken care of all of the last details? Do I have my clothing ready, as "fine linen stands for the righteous acts of the saints" (Rev. 19:8, NIV)?

And most important, does the Bridegroom see me as a pure bride who is faithful and honest to Him? Have I chosen to share my life completely with Him, as my daughter chose to do with her bridegroom? Is the Bridegroom the most important person in my life, and the one with whom I most enjoy talking?

Lord, on the day of Your wedding feast may I be joyful with a sense of mission accomplished so that I may just enjoy the long-awaited moment for which I have prayed and prepared.

SÔNIA MARIA RIGOLI SANTOS

One of the Least of These

For whosoever shall give you a cup of water to drink in my name, because ye belong to Christ, verily I say unto you, he shall not lose his reward. Mark 9:41.

MY OLDEST GRANDSON, Tyler, delights to have his grandmother take him fishing in a particular stream in Pisgah Forest named Davidson River. There are many cool streams rushing over their rocky beds, a perfect place for trout to abound. He appears at our house clad in his old clothes and shoes, his tackle box in hand. After our breakfast, we put our supplies in the trunk—an old lawn chair, blanket, some reading material for me, and his beloved tackle box. Then we happily drive the few miles to his favorite fishing spot.

One morning Tyler had waded upstream some distance, leaving me to watch the stringer to which was attached his precious rainbow trout. He was gone longer than expected. The noonday sun had pierced my shady spot, and I was getting hot and thirsty but didn't dare leave his precious fish unattended.

A brown Buick pulled up right beside my resting spot, and the door opened. An elderly gentleman lowered his feet to the ground but remained seated in his car. He asked if I had caught any fish. I explained that I was guarding my grandson's catch. He laughed and said he used to love to fish, but because of health problems he could no longer participate in his favorite sport. I told him I was sorry he couldn't fish anymore. He stood up and asked if I was thirsty. I hesitantly nodded. He opened the back door of his car to reveal a large, clean cooler filled with ice and bottled soft drinks—free. He reached into the cooler, pulled out a bottle of orange soda, and handed it to me. I gratefully accepted it. When I expressed my thanks for his acts of kindness, he laughed and said he did this every day. He said since he couldn't fish anymore, he was trying to bring joy to those who could. He smiled, got back into his car, and drove off.

After he left, I recalled several texts in the Bible about giving a drink of water to "the least of these," and how it is the same as doing it to Jesus. In my heart I determined to look for—and see more clearly—opportunities given to me each day to bring refreshment, affirmation, and comfort to those around me. I hope that my random acts of kindness will help others see the love of Jesus more clearly.

ROSE NEFF SIKORA

Obstacles Along the Way

God is our refuge and strength, an ever-present help in trouble. Ps. 46:1, NIV.

THE FIRST PLACE my husband and I pastored was a small town with a population of about 3,000. Living there was very nice because we lived in the midst of nature. The stress of the big cities with the noise of cars, pollution, dangers, and evil that infiltrates the large metropolitan areas was not to be found. We enjoyed only the songs of birds, pure air, and a calm country life.

We were especially happy one Sabbath because the previous day we had returned from a marvelous vacation trip during which we had had the opportunity to see our relatives and friends. On this beautiful and pleasant morning we were on our way to visit our local congregation that anxiously awaited the return of their pastor.

On our return home from church, however, an unexpected situation arose. Since it had been raining quite a bit, obstacles had fallen onto the highway, our only way home. We stopped the car. Immediately a city administrator, who also could not continue on his way, told my husband, "Don't worry; we've already called for help. The machines are on the way!"

Some time later the machines arrived, and we continued waiting for an hour and a half more for the men to finish the work of removing the obstacles and all the mud so that the cars could continue. While we waited, we had the opportunity to reflect on the numerous obstacles that we face in our daily life.

On the paths of this life we come upon many different kinds of barriers. There are small and large obstacles, sometimes insurmountable and immovable. We aren't able to overcome these obstacles through our own efforts.

It is time, then, to ask for help from the Leader of our life, our Refuge, who is Jesus Christ. Like the machines that cleaned the obstacles from the highway on that Sabbath so that we could reach our house, He also cleans the obstacles from our life and removes the mud of sin so that we can continue our journey in the direction of our eternal home!

Thank You, Lord Jesus, for being our help, for removing the obstacles from our life and allowing us to walk in safety and be sustained by You!

ELAINE APARECIDA DA SILVA

Running Out of Gas

I will provide for their needs before they ask, and I will help them while they are still asking for help. Isa. 65:24, NCV.

WE WERE RETURNING on the freeway from an appointment with my eye surgeon, happily chatting. My friend, Romana, who was driving my car, noticed that the low fuel warning light had come on. We were approaching the Port Man Bridge out of the Vancouver area, so I said, "Well, if it has only just come on, we have enough gas to get us over the bridge, and we'll take the first exit after the bridge. There's a gas station nearby."

As we approached the last exit before the bridge Romana cried, "Oh, no! I'm losing power! We are out of gas." We were in the left-hand "multiple occupancy lane." To make it off the freeway and onto the off ramp, we would have to cross three lanes full of traffic. Romana put on the flashing emergency lights and very skillfully managed to get the car off the highway and onto the exit ramp before the engine died completely. That in itself was a miracle.

We stopped, half on the road still, but at least we were not on the bridge, where a stalled car would have caused major traffic problems. We both said a brief prayer: "Lord, help us as we don't know what to do now." When we looked up, a face was at the driver's window.

"What seems to be the problem?" asked a friendly voice.

"We've run out of gas," answered Romana.

"That's no problem," the man said cheerily. "I'll push you with my truck to the top of the off ramp, and then you can coast down to where there is room at the side of the road to park safely. I have a tank of gas and will put enough in for you to get to the gas station."

He did as he said, and after he had put in some gas he came again to the window. When I asked, "How much do we owe you?" he answered, "Oh, nothing."

"Are you an angel in disguise?" Romana queried.

The man laughed and replied, "I don't think so. Have a good day." Then he returned to his truck

Following his instructions, we were able to get to the gas station, fill up, and find our way back onto the freeway and safely home. God had answered our prayers before we had even prayed. What a God we serve!

RUTH LENNOX

God's Laws

Thou hast made known to me the ways of life; thou shalt make me full of joy with thy countenance. Acts 2:28.

IT WAS SUMMERTIME, and I sat in the cool of my home discussing old flames and the pursuit of happiness within the romantic relationship realm. I had filed for divorce from my husband and had been daydreaming of how different my life could have been had I married someone more willing to serve God—maybe someone friendlier, someone more in tune with me as an individual. Before I knew it, I was envying someone who used to be married to someone with whom I had once gone out on a date.

Envy is a barricade on the road of happiness. Satan's angels chose Satan over God, much as a person can choose a lover over God's plan. We can make a choice to worship someone or something more than our Creator. Satan coveted God's power and glory, God's throne, and I had been coveting someone who wasn't mine. Ephesians 5:5 warns us, "For this you know, that no fornicator, unclean person, nor covetous man, who is an idolater, has any inheritance in the kingdom of Christ and God" (NKJV).

If we're not prayerful, envy can threaten our souls and have a power over us that is evil in its very nature. "For where envy and self-seeking exist, confusion and every evil thing are there" (James 3:16, NKJV). In Matthew 27:18 it says that Jesus had been handed over out of envy. I realize now that no matter whom I would have married, I still would have had to struggle through some devastating experiences so that I could grow spiritually the way I needed to. God uses our personal choices to teach us to lean on the wisdom in the Bible, to lead us, and to develop faith. "For this is commendable, if because of conscience toward God one endures grief, suffering wrongfully" (1 Peter 2:19, NKJV).

No matter what our situation, Acts 2:28 reminds us that as God makes known the ways of life, the Lord will also make us full of joy in the Creator's presence. That's something to definitely claim and look forward to, as well as to encourage. "But may the God of all grace, who called us to His eternal glory by Christ Jesus, after you have suffered a while, perfect, establish, strengthen, and settle you" (1 Peter 5:10, NKJV).

MELISSA WILSON

A Taste of Heaven

And God shall wipe away all tears from their eyes; and there shall be no more death, neither sorrow, nor crying, neither shall there be any more pain: for the former things are passed away. . . . Behold, I make all things new. Rev. 21:4, 5.

I HAD THE PRIVILEGE of growing up on the Nebraska prairie, a descendant of a large, close family that met for annual reunions. My great-grandparents emigrated from Norway and raised their children near Elm Creek. Great-grandmother Sarah was a widow and single mother at a young age and raised 14 children to be responsible and respectable adults.

The reunions dwindled after Great-grandmother died in 1973, and I had not seen many of my relatives since the funeral. But in 2005 we all met in Kearney, Nebraska, for a Johnson family reunion. More than 70 family members gathered for a weekend to reminisce and rejoice in fellowship. It was a joyous occasion, seeing aunts and uncles and cousins after many years, and there were also many spouses and children I had never met.

Sadly, many were missing from the gathering. My great-grandparents have been dead for many years, and most of the children, and even some grandchildren, have been laid to rest. On Friday evening we visited the small church and cemetery where many family members are buried. The weather was beautiful, and as the sun slowly set over the nearby sand hills, we sang songs and listened to stories of how we had come to be here in this time and place.

This short time spent together was a little taste of heaven. We laughed and cried at stories shared. We looked at yellowed photographs and items that are important because they belonged to or were created by our ancestors. Through the miracle of technology we watched videos made many years ago of family members now gone. We talked of our hope in the coming resurrection. It was a time of looking back, but also a time of looking forward, and when we parted we made plans to meet again, if not on this earth, then at the soon coming of Jesus.

I thoroughly enjoyed myself that weekend and plan to attend any future reunions if possible. But I'm longing for that glorious final reunion, at which I'll see not only my family but friends and loved ones who are now sleeping in their graves. And most important, I'll see Jesus, my Savior, who died on the cross so that I could be there. Won't you join me?

Fauna Rankin Dean

A Still Small Voice

And behold, the Lord passed by, and a great and strong wind tore into the mountains and broke the rocks in pieces before the Lord, but the Lord was not in the wind; and after the wind an earthquake, but the Lord was not in the earthquake; and after the earthquake a fire, but the Lord was not in the fire; and after the fire a still small voice. 1 Kings 19:11, 12, NKJV.

SEVERAL YEARS AGO I began buying the daily devotional books in the series you are now reading and have enjoyed them so much. In 2001 I wanted to buy one for a friend. Her mother had died unexpectedly, and she was having a hard time dealing with that. When I gave her the book she commented on the name, *Fabric of Faith*. She thought it was really neat, since she owns a fabric store. I had not even thought about the title until she mentioned it; but it was at that point that I knew it was God who had put the thought in my mind to buy the book for her. She really enjoyed it.

Each year since then God has led in my buying and giving the books as gifts. In 2002 I bought three books and was impressed to give one to my boss. I had no idea what I would do with the other one, or even why I had bought three of them. My boss really liked her book, and a few weeks after she had received it she called me and wondered if I could get another one. A friend was going through a really difficult time, she said, and she felt it would help her. The title of this book, *Alone With God*, really meant a lot to my boss's friend, as she needed that time alone with God. God knew all along there was a woman in need.

The Lord is so awesome! He never fails to amaze me. In 2003, as I ordered the books, I wondered whom the Lord would have me give them to. I never know the title of the books when I order them, and I never know whom the Lord wants me to share them with. This year the Lord directed me to my neighbor, married a year, who had been having marital problems. I had been trying to help her and her husband. They had separated, and she was really going through a bad situation. When I went to the church to pick up my books, I began to cry when I saw the title, *Bouquets of Hope*. You see, her name is Hope.

Our God works through many ways to reach those in need. So when you feel impressed to do something for someone, don't hesitate. It may be that still small voice.

DONNA COOK

Daddy's Death

He will swallow up death in victory; and the Lord God will wipe away tears from off all faces. Isa. 25:8.

I WAS PREPARING FOR CHURCH when I got the long-distance call. Daddy had been rushed to the hospital, unconscious. I immediately started praying. "No, Father," I pleaded. "Mercy, Father. Spare his life and save him." I loved my dad dearly, and I couldn't stand the thought of not having him now or in eternity. I couldn't remember my dad ever being confined to bed or admitted to a hospital, so it was really unexpected news for me. When he regained consciousness, he said, in his typical optimistic manner that I expected of Daddy, "Don't worry; I'll be all right."

Many telephone calls and hours online later, I felt reassured of his recovery and decided to take a nap. No sooner had I gotten into bed than the phone rang. My sister was on the phone, and she was in tears. I heard her breathe the words, "Brenda girl, you know Daddy died!"

I reeled from shock. My first thought was "He said he'd be all right; so what happened?" He either thought—or hoped—he'd be all right, but only God can predict the future.

I traveled to my homeland for the funeral and dreaded meeting my siblings—I knew my facade of strength would crumble. I met one of my brothers at an airport transit, and indeed, we completely fell apart. Because we all live in various parts of the globe, it had been a little while since we had been together in one location. When we arrived home, it was a bittersweet reunion as we spent time together grieving and reminiscing about the fun we had in "the olden days."

After we separated I began thinking, *What will it be like when we all get together in heaven? Will there be some surprises?* We often think that there is no life in eternity for some persons because of their lives here, but do we know? What about those genuine deathbed conversions—such as the thief on the cross (Luke 23:42, 43)?

Today we grieve and mourn our loved ones who have gone to sleep, but a time of rejoicing is coming. That great reunion in heaven will be a time of rejoicing only if we are prepared. And now is the time to prepare. Preparation means allowing God to take full control of our lives so that everything we do is directed by His Spirit. Welcome Christ today and every day.

BRENDA D. OTTLEY

Be Ye Kind

Be kind and compassionate to one another. Eph. 4:32, NIV.

 "THANK YOU FOR BEING NICE TO ME," she said as the plane touched down. The flight had taken only an hour and 15 minutes, but for this young woman, who had not flown in 17 years, it had been a long ordeal.

I first noticed her while having breakfast with my daughter-in-law and grandchildren at the airport lunch counter. Spiky hair, piercing around her eyes, dressed all in black, she was hard to miss. All too soon it was time for me to say goodbye to my family and board the plane.

I had an aisle seat, so I didn't buckle up, because no one had come to occupy the other seats. Then I heard a voice: "Excuse me." To my surprise—and almost shock—it was the young woman in black. "I'm really scared," she said as she sat down and adjusted her seat belt. "I haven't been in a plane since I was 3." I told her I often made this flight and was certain everything would be all right. In fact, I had flown this same flight only two days after September 11, 2001.

As the plane took off, she took a two-liter bottle from her backpack. It was filled with chocolate milk, not soda, as I had expected. She drank from it and snacked on chips. *Perhaps this is her breakfast,* I thought. I don't always make conversation with those around me, but this time I did. I asked where she was going and why. She was going to attend a funeral, she said. I told her about my visit with my grandchildren that had come to an end all too soon.

I noticed a change in the sound of the engines of the plane that was an indication that we would soon be landing. As I tucked the magazine I was reading back into my pack, she turned to me and said, "Thanks for being nice to me." She caught me by surprise, because I didn't think I had said anything of great importance. I began to wonder if I had not been placed there for a purpose.

VERA WIEBE

Thought: Had you been in Vera's place, what would you have thought, done, and said? Does a contact have to be religious to be meaningful? How do we find and make the most of these opportunities? Read all of Ephesians 4:32 (today's text is only the first part) and see if it tells you something further regarding how and why we should be kind.

Patience Has a Chance

When the way is rough, your patience has a chance to grow. James 1:3, TLB.

I SAT ON A HOSPITAL BED, waiting more than an hour for an ambulance to arrive to take me home. Earlier I had gone down a small step, and a drain hole in the corner had caught my right heel and held it while the rest of me catapulted forward. Both ankles were now embedded in plaster, and I was helpless to move without assistance. Nothing to read, no pen and paper to write with, nothing to do except wait. I was very frustrated. It was then that an identification sheet on the wall behind me caught my attention:

Patient *Peggy Mason*

I laughed to myself. *Oh, no, I'm not, Lord! Not at all patient. A room to redecorate, a plane trip to take, gifts to make for Christmas, spring bulbs to plant. No, I certainly don't qualify for a patience award!*

But in the two months that followed, largely confined to a wheelchair before I was out of the casts and had two workable ankles again, I thought a lot about patience. I thought about John describing the patience of the saints, Paul listing it among the fruits of the Spirit, and Peter's warning against impatience while awaiting Christ's return. They all reminded me of my own inadequacy in this area. Waiting—waiting for people to arrive, waiting for plants to grow, waiting for plans to materialize and prayers to be answered—all part of my experience.

Here my thoughts began to crystallize. I thought of my own little mission field, all those I pray for by name—family and many friends and their needs—and those who have wandered away. How I long for them to come back, to meet Jesus on the road, and recognize how much He loves them and has missed them. Paul tells us that God called him from his birth (Gal. 1:15). How long God must have waited for him before the Damascus road experience. I was reminded of God's patience in waiting for each one of us to "come to repentance" (2 Peter 3:9, NIV), and how patience is one of the many good and perfect gifts He wants to give us.

I want to open the door of my heart to receive that gift so that my patience may grow and have her "perfect work" in me (James 1:4, NKJV).

PEGGY MASON

Thought: Read all of James 1:4 in several Bible translations. It is a real challenge!

God's Care

Give thanks to the Lord, for he is good. His love endures forever. Ps. 136:1, NIV.

 OUR CAR DIDN'T HAVE A POWERFUL ENGINE, neither was it the latest model. But we were happy with it and kept it in good working order, because it was all we had to go on short trips and outings. We also used the car for our work. In other words, we depended on that car for our survival.

The mountainous region in which we lived made the road rather steep, with curves and dangerous drop-offs along the edge. If this was not enough, the dust was intense, because the road was not paved. This caused visibility to be very difficult for drivers. It was rather risky and dangerous to travel in this region.

One Friday as my husband returned home, the car slid on a curve along the road and, after flipping over several times, tumbled down the embankment below the level of the road. Only the tires fit on a ledge that seemed to have been made especially for that car; and only a few inches separated my husband from becoming a fatality.

The following day I visited the location, and I can verify that God was great and merciful to my husband. Besides his life being saved the previous night, he had arrived home very grateful to have only a cut on his foot.

Someone commented that the car seemed to have been placed on the ledge by an invisible hand. Yes, I firmly believe it was the hand of the Lord who had placed it there. The car was removed by a tow truck—only the top had been damaged. The car still ran with no problems, so the repair bill was not so expensive. We used the car for several days before we took it in to be repaired. This gave us the opportunity to witness to the wonderful manner in which God had saved my husband's life.

How good it is to look back and see the wonders that God has provided for us in the past to witness of His care, and through our joy to reflect Jesus to those who are around us. Even in adversities may we always remember the loving manner in which God has guided us—and will continue guiding us until the day that we are together with Him in our heavenly home.

MARIA MOREIRA DE ALMEIDA RIBEIRO

Ancestors in Heaven

And God shall wipe away all tears from their eyes: and there shall be no more death, neither sorrow, nor crying, neither shall there be any more pain. Rev. 21:4.

THIS PAST YEAR I was introduced to genealogy. As I became more involved, I began to think and wonder about my ancestors. Will I find some of them in heaven? How many of them were Christians? How many were waiting for the Lord to come?

I discovered one family in which the father died in the Civil War, as so many did while fighting for either the North or the South. Next the mother, Abigail, lost her 1-year-old baby girl in June, and Abigail herself died that September, leaving behind three parentless little boys, ages 2, 9, and 10. Someone later applied for a Civil War pension for the boys, and six years later, according to the 1870 census, the three boys were all living with other families who may or may not have been their relatives. Another family also lost their husband and father in the Civil War. Again, two little children, a boy and a girl, were left fatherless.

War, including the Civil War, had never really interested me, since I believe wars to be senseless evils that seldom accomplish much. Now that I'm seeing the impact of just one war on my ancestors, wars are becoming more real to me. I'm glad we have a God who sees the overall picture and is in control.

What a grand reunion it will be in heaven when we will be able to see many of these people in person. We will be able to ask them questions for which, in this time period, there are no answers. I remember teaching our children that one day we will be able to see and speak with the Bible characters we have read about, and ask them questions regarding their lives. Only recently have I thought about our immediate ancestors ("immediate" compared to biblical people) and wondered what it will be like to meet them: how many will be there, how many may be lost eternally, what questions I will ask? What's even more important is the question, Will I be faithful and also be there?

My prayer for myself and for those who are reading this today is that we all remain faithful, true, and obedient to Jesus and the Father, and that we invite the Holy Spirit each day into our lives to finally save us in that heavenly kingdom.

LORAINE F. SWEETLAND

Our God Loves Relationships

And the God of all grace, who called you to his eternal glory in Christ, after you have suffered a little while, will himself restore you and make you strong, firm and steadfast. 1 Peter 5:10, NIV.

THE BEAUTY CAPTIVATED me one sunny spring afternoon as I drove across central Florida. For miles the rolling terrain adorned in verdant grass because of the recent rains, interspersed with the waxy green leaves of the orange groves, drew my attention. Then, without warning, I came upon an unsightly area of dead, brown grass and scorched tree trunks. In a few hours the fires of a planned burn had turned the area into a patch of earth unpleasant to the human eye and foreign to the little creatures that lived there. Driving on past the burn, I again enjoyed the beauty nature provided.

Taking time daily to commune with God makes our lives vibrant, like living vegetation after a recent rain. In addition to Bible study and prayer, there are other ways to interact with our Maker. Partaking of the beauties of nature affirms God as our Creator. Enjoying an article or book that exalts Him and inspires us to be more like Him has drawing power. These experiences and many others keep our spiritual juices flowing.

What about the times in our lives when we neglect to commune on a regular basis with our Creator, Redeemer, and Sustainer? The demands of family, job, and even church work may create a busyness that allows no time for one-on-one encounters with the One who is supposedly our best friend. Don't these times leave us spiritually parched?

Failure to tap the Living Water when life becomes hectic and challenging makes life harder. Negativity creeps in, and an I-don't-care attitude often crops up. It doesn't take long for our lives to become like the ugly brown area caused by the planned burn.

Praise God, when life becomes overwhelming or circumstances arise over which we have no control, there is hope. God is always there, waiting with arms wide open. With rain and sunshine the burned area becomes green and beautiful again. Likewise, when we return to those habits that knitted our relationship to God in the first place, our joy is complete.

Dear Lord, help me day by day to make You the green and growing center of my life so that I may radiate Your beauty in every situation that life holds for me. Amen.

MARIAN M. HART

Through the Valley

Yea, though I walk through the valley of the shadow of death, I will fear no evil: for thou art with me. Ps. 23:4.

I CAN'T BREATHE! my mind screamed in panic. My eyes popped open, and my hands began to claw upward. I saw three surgically masked faces looking down at me with surprised eyes.

"Intubate!" someone ordered.

Rational thought stopped my grasping hands from grabbing out in panic. *They are taking out the breathing tube,* I thought. *That's why I can't breathe.*

I passed out, then awoke later in post-op, the same three pairs of eyes, now unmasked, clustered around me. I tried to speak, but the intern with his finger on my wrist said, "Shhhh! We're taking your PRT [pulse, respiration, temperature]." I repeatedly awoke for a few seconds the next few hours and gathered from the snatches of conversation between the two nurses and the intern monitoring me that the minor outpatient surgery for which I had checked into the hospital that morning had been a success. However, they were concerned about my irregular breathing—normal while awake, but dangerously shallow when asleep. They refused to release me until I breathed as normally asleep as awake.

Several years later a chance remark from my doctor clarified that incident. I had died on the operating table, only to awaken after the doctor "called it." That was why I couldn't breathe. The command "Intubate!" was an order to insert the breathing tube, not, as I had thought, to remove it. Like guardian angels, the intern and those two nurses stayed by my bedside for several hours, coaxing me to breathe, guiding me back safely to the world of the living.

While I was legally dead, did I find myself floating on the ceiling, watching the surgery team and my body below me as the doctor called out the time of my death? No. Did I see a bright light at the end of a tunnel? No. As the Bible says so plainly, I knew nothing during that time.

Today I marvel at the glimpse into the reality of God's Word that I have been granted. God put me to sleep, then woke me, to prove a point to me and anyone else who wants to know about death and the truth about His enduring love and protection through "the valley of the shadow of death."

DARLENEJOAN MCKIBBIN RHINE

Lessons From a Rose

For without Me you can do nothing. John 15:5, NKJV.

ON INTERNATIONAL WOMEN'S DAY I received a lovely rose and felt motivated to do everything possible to conserve its beauty for as long as possible. I put it in a vase with water and salt and left it on the counter in my kitchen so that I could look at it more closely.

When my little son, Gabriel, saw the rose there, he asked me why I had put the rose in the water. I explained to him that I wanted to preserve it as long as possible because I knew that it would soon wilt otherwise. The days went by, and he came to tell me that the rose was wilting.

I explained to my son that the rose was wilting because it had been cut from the rosebush where it had received the necessary nutrients to make it beautiful during its life, and that after being cut from the bush, it would soon die. As I explained this to him, I remembered how much we also need to be connected to Jesus, the True Vine, so that we may have life.

John 15:5 is very important to me. As soon as I was baptized, I experienced serious trials. My husband, for various reasons that I was not able to understand, asked for a separation. I knew only that he was facing a crisis of depression. Our home was crumbling, and I didn't know what to do.

As I questioned God, doubts came. One night, in the midst of despair and still on my knees, I about gave up on everything. However, within me a voice spoke: "Where are you going? There is no other God; there is no point in wanting to flee." I returned to the corner where I pray and asked for forgiveness, and I was able to sleep the rest of the night.

The following morning I read this verse in my daily devotional: "For without Me you can do nothing." I praise God for helping me stay connected to Him. Like that rose far from the rosebush, when we are separated from the True Vine we do not receive the life-giving connection that restores us. Only in Jesus can we be brought to life and obtain His power that sustains us.

God restored my family, returned health to my husband, and made us come alive and bloom to His honor and glory.

ANTÔNIA RODRIGUES N. MESQUITA

Thought: How do we stay connected to the Vine? What are you doing to stay connected?

Frustration

Where can I go from Your Spirit? Or where can I flee from Your presence? If I ascend into heaven, You are there; if I make my bed in hell, behold, You are there. Ps. 139:7, 8, NKJV.

THE TRIP BEGAN WITHOUT INCIDENT. I took the scenic route to avoid traffic on the interstate and was well on the way to my destination. The trip had been planned for weeks, and I was eager to see my "sustah-friend"* and her family. The weather was perfect, and as I cruised down the road it was as if I were attending a live nature show with featured artist Jesus Christ, Master Designer.

As I continued on my journey there were signs indicating that I was almost to my destination. I pulled out my hurriedly written directions as I continued on my way. Almost without notice the skies began to darken, and incredibly large drops of rain began to pound on my car. I was now sitting at attention at the steering wheel and having difficulty seeing. Everything looked gray. As I struggled along the interstate, now wondering why it was taking so long to find the exit toward my friend's house, it finally become obvious that I had missed one instruction in my directions. I had failed to merge onto the proper connecting interstate. Because of this significant mistake, I found myself in another state! I was tired and frustrated. My anticipated five-hour journey had now extended to nearly seven hours!

The rain showers slowly began to abate, the clouds cleared, and the sun slowly set. Instead of focusing on my frustration, I remembered to pray. As I asked for God's direction and sang several hymns, I paused to whisper yet another prayer: "Lord, lead me to the right exit." As I ended with "amen" and raised my attention to the sky above, I saw a rainbow. But it wasn't just a rainbow—it was a double rainbow! Just as quickly as I noticed the rainbows, the green sign ahead indicated that my exit was less than a mile away. Double rainbow, double blessings!

I arrived safely at my friend's house and had a wonderful weekend. As I made my way back home on Sunday, it was with a renewed awareness of God's presence and watchcare. That double rainbow reminded me that God brings showers of blessings to us and that He is with us in any situation. If we pause and ask Him to help, He never fails us. He is always there for us, whether in time of peace or in the midst of our frustration.

TERRIE E. (RUFF) LONG

*A friend who is like a sister

Finders, Keepers

Ask, and it shall be given you; seek, and ye shall find. Matt. 7:7.

 I AM NOT GOOD AT FINDING THINGS. I'm better at losing them. Even if the item is within easy reach, I still don't see it. Often when I exclaim in despair, "I can't find my _____," my husband comes to the rescue. Things just seem to present themselves when he appears.

My glasses are the most frequent lost-and-found article. If I manage to secure them safely on my face, then the spectacle case disappears. The other day I contrived to lose my cell phone. Now, that really hurt. I felt as if a part of me was missing.

Just as I was beginning to suffer from a wave of hopelessness, Jesus gave me some encouraging words. I do not have to be afraid of not finding my possessions. My eyes will be anointed with eyesalve (Rev. 3:18). If I keep searching, I will find. "Seek, and ye shall find." Therefore I don't have to give up in desperation. Nothing in my life can be hidden so snugly that it escapes the eyes of God. Hagar, rejected and alone in the wilderness, had the assurance that her heavenly Father took note of her. Like Hagar, I can calm my frantic heart with "Thou God seest me" (Gen. 16:13). And He celebrates the recovery with me.

There was someone else who trusted in God's ability to uncover things—Daniel. "But there is a God in heaven that revealeth secrets" (Dan. 2:28). For my God, who reveals national and international secrets, the revelation of a lost watch, misplaced keys, or mislaid glasses is really a small matter.

Even in Bible times people lost things—and people got lost too. Think of the parables of the lost coin, the lost sheep, and the lost boy. In fact, the concept of loss is of major concern to Jesus. He does not want us to be lost. "For what is a man profited, if he shall gain the whole world, and lose his own soul?" (Matt. 16:26). God sent His only Son to die for us to avert our losing eternal life.

Yes, Jesus can help us find anything we desire, including eternal life; but we must desire Him first. Think of the wonderful promise: "Ye shall seek me, and find me, when ye shall search for me with all your heart" (Jer. 29:13).

Thank You, dear God, that my search for You will never be in vain.

GLORIA LINDSEY TROTMAN

The Great Race of Mercy

Set your minds, then, on endorsing by your conduct the fact that God has called and chosen you. . . . If you live this sort of life a rich welcome awaits you as you enter the eternal kingdom of our Lord and saviour Jesus Christ. 2 Peter 1:10, 11, Phillips.

IT WAS 2:00 IN THE MORNING. My sister, her husband, and I excitedly bundled into Alaskan winter clothing. The fire whistle had just alerted the whole town that the first dogsled team of the 1992 Iditarod trail race was only two miles from Nome.

The Iditarod race covers more than 1,000 miles of frozen tundra, and is run in memory of a life-or-death race. In 1925 two Inuit children died of diphtheria. An epidemic threatened. The town's only doctor called for help over the radiotelegraph. Anchorage had 300,000 units of antitoxin serum. The governor asked if the best dogsled teams would relay the serum to Nome. The weather held steady at -60° F—when the wind didn't blow. Even so, 20 dog-team drivers volunteered. A railroad carried the precious 20-pound package one third of the way, and mushers and their dogs rushed it the remaining 674 miles through raging windstorms, over a sea of ice, and through the night, arriving in Nome in less than six days. The town was saved. Joe Redington, an old-time musher, who was afraid people would forget about the Great Race of Mercy, and Dorothy Page organized the Iditarod trail race in 1967.

I was visiting my sister in Nome, and now the big day (or night) had come. We joined the throngs pressing the rope fences that lined each side of the winner's chute, eager to catch a glimpse of the headlamp Martin Buser would be wearing to light his way through the night. Yes, Martin, our favorite musher, would race under the burl arch first. He'd done it in only 10 days.

As we clapped and shouted, another scene popped into my mind. I was racing down the winner's chute toward the gates of heaven. A great shout went up from the angels, and Jesus was standing at the archway, welcoming me to live with them forever.

Tears came to my eyes as I realized how thrilled all heaven will be for each one of us who choose to run the race and enter in through the gates into the Holy City. And just as I had no idea what Martin Buser had just experienced, the angels will admit they have no idea what it is like to be redeemed from a world of sin.

LANA FLETCHER

No Woman Is an Island

For we are members of one another. Eph. 4:25, NKJV.

AS I DROVE ALONG TO WORK recently I noticed that it was one of those rare times traffic flowed evenly. Cars went in and out of various lanes as necessary without difficulty. Everyone seemed to cooperate for the good of the other. There were no horns honking, no disgruntled, anxious drivers. As I exited the freeway, proceeding down the street, I thought to myself, *I'm doing well today.* I seemed to make all the traffic lights in the one area that I think of as "stoplight city." I began to boast privately.

Then it struck me: *I'm not doing this alone.* The other drivers, cognizant or not, are cooperating. I was not operating in a vacuum, for I could be driving the speed limit, using my signals, and doing everything right, and still be involved in an accident if someone else was not watching out. I was depending on those other drivers to pay attention and watch where they were going. In fact, I had been involved in an accident just weeks earlier. I was headed home after a wonderful day of worship. I wasn't speeding and was being careful when another driver, who was speeding and not paying attention, plowed into the rear of my vehicle. I had been doing "everything right," and still it had happened. I was the one who ended up in the hospital while the other driver was fine. I thank God that I sustained no serious injuries.

No! No woman is an island. In most aspects of our lives we, of necessity, depend on each other. For the food we eat we are dependent on farmers, processors, truckers, and grocers. For the clothes we wear we depend on the fabric manufacturers, tailors, and clothing stores. For transportation we need cars, buses, trains, planes, and boats. For reasonable health, be it physical, emotional, or otherwise, we look to doctors and specialists. And the list goes on, a constant reminder that we indeed are not self-existent or self-sufficient. We are not little islands independently doing our own thing, unaffected by those around us. We are part of an interdependent whole because that's how the Lord made us. Only He, the Almighty, can function without us. And even He chooses and longs to be a part of our lives—but He will not force us. He invites and implores us to cooperate with Him, the Omniscient, Omnipresent, and Omnipotent One, to accept His invitation for our own benefit. He loves us that much.

GLORIA J. STELLA FELDER

Nothing to Chance

Now thanks be unto God, which always causeth us to triumph in Christ, and maketh manifest the saviour of his knowledge by us in every place. 2 Cor. 2:14.

SINCE I LIVE only 10 minutes away from the hospital, my normal routine is to pull out of my subdivision and head down a one-lane country highway just in time to begin my shift. One particular afternoon I found myself scurrying out of the house with the realistic goal of making it to work in eight minutes—tops. *Just do the speed limit,* I said, *and pray that there are no delays.* But as I drove, the unexpected happened. A school bus pulled out in front of me and began making its usual afternoon drop-off of children, house after house. The bus driver was gracious enough to let another bus driver onto the roadway. Befuddled, I determined not to stress over my situation. I shut out the delay and patiently waited. I said to myself: *What are the chances of this happening again?* However, a few days later the same thing did happen. This time a utility truck drove down the road at 10 miles per hour. On another day an elderly couple leisurely cruised down the highway without a care. Needless to say, my patience was tried and tested.

I paused for a moment to ponder my situation and asked myself, *What spiritual lesson is God trying to teach me from these experiences?* I sought the Lord in prayer for an answer, and He revealed to me a very important spiritual truth. I recalled several quotes from the devotional book *That I May Know Him:* "Abundant provision has been made that all who desire to live a godly life may have grace and strength through Jesus our divine Redeemer" (p. 92). "The divine Author of salvation left nothing incomplete in the plan; every phase of it is perfect. . . . The plan of redemption provides for every emergency and for every want of the soul" (p. 96).

As I remembered these words, I realized that nothing God allows in my life is by chance or coincidence. The plan of salvation is perfectly complete, and every provision for every trial, every test, every temptation, and every experience, no matter how minute or insignificant, has been designed for spiritual growth, development, and character building. So God permits something as simple as getting stuck in traffic, that I may overcome as He overcame.

I thank You, Father, for the provisions You have made for me to triumph in Christ Jesus and for not leaving even the minutest trial in my life to chance.

CHERYL D. COCHRAN

Living Beyond the Checklist

Create in me a pure heart, O God, and renew a steadfast spirit within me. Ps. 51:10, NIV.

This is the covenant I will make with the house of Israel after that time, declares the Lord. I will put my laws in their minds and write them on their hearts. Heb. 8:10, NIV.

MY JUNIOR YEAR IN HIGH SCHOOL was my first year away from home. I attended a boarding school and, for the most part, enjoyed it. One of the things that took a little getting used to was having to be at work at 6:00 a.m., Monday through Friday. Because of my work schedule I had to fix my own breakfast at the school cafeteria because I needed to eat and be gone before most of the kitchen staff arrived.

Being young helped, but so did being stubborn. Unwilling to give up my morning worship time, I got up at 4:30 and quietly slipped out of my dorm room so as not to awaken my roommate. I would take my shower and get ready, then sit in the hall and study my Bible. I mostly read through the Psalms that year, and it was very spiritually enriching for me.

But it was also the year that I discovered I was using a spiritual checklist. You see, every night as I went to sleep I reviewed the day and checked to see if I had broken any of the Ten Commandments. Some were very easy to cover—no other gods, taking the Lord's name in vain, idols, keeping the Sabbath, killing, stealing, adultery. No problem. Lying, coveting, and honoring my parents required a little more thought.

As you might imagine, with regular Bible study and daily reflection I soon curbed my creative story-enhancing tendency, and many nights went to sleep thinking that I hadn't sinned that day. Was I wrong!

It was only after hearing a series of sermons that discussed the do's or don'ts that are in the Ten Commandments that I realized my mistake. I was never really sinless. But I also saw that trying to obey the commands of God felt natural instead of something that I had to work at.

That's where today's scripture comes in. God was creating in me a clean heart. He was writing His law in my heart—not just my head. That made it possible for my actions to reflect more of Him than of me. May God bless you today as He helps you also to put aside the checklist and embrace the wisdom of living by His will.

JULI BLOOD

Inseparable Friend

Train up a child in the way he should go, and when he is old he will not depart from it. Prov. 22:6, NKJV.

MY GRANDDAUGHTER, NATÁLIA, IS A SWEET CHILD. Whenever possible, she spends several days with me during her vacation. When she was 7 years old, she came to stay for a week at my house. We strolled through the streets in my town, we ate delicious ice-cream cones, and we enjoyed unforgettable moments together.

One afternoon we were seated in the living room when she stated, "Grandma, it seems like you never feel lonely!"

"Why are you thinking about this?" I asked.

"Because I see that you have a very special Friend who loves you and keeps you company. When your children are far away, He always is by your side, even though He is invisible."

I was touched to hear such an affirmation from my granddaughter. I felt very happy to learn that she could see the presence of God reflected in my life, and that His presence was also reflected in this little girl who was also blossoming to life. I told her of the joy that I felt in having a granddaughter and that her life was very special to me. I also expressed my happiness in seeing her grow and that she thought like this.

Since that day I have thought about her words and have attempted to feel God's presence in my life. However, in the difficult and lonely moments, when my children return to their "nests," I feel the presence of God even more closely in my life.

Children get married and leave. They make their homes in other places, and we, their parents, are left alone, just as when we began our lives together. What a joy it is to be able to have our grandchildren on our laps! They become an extension of our lives. What a joy to see that what we have taught our children about the love of God has been cultivated in our grandchildren! In turn, these little ones come to our home and help us to understand more completely the blessing of a Christian home in which children are taught the ways of the Lord.

Thank You, loving Father, for the certainty that You give us of Your presence in our life.

JOANA VIEIRA DE AQUIAR RAMOS

One Fateful Step

My steps have held to your paths; my feet have not slipped. Ps. 17:5, NIV.

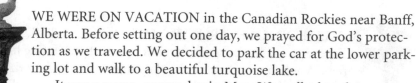

WE WERE ON VACATION in the Canadian Rockies near Banff, Alberta. Before setting out one day, we prayed for God's protection as we traveled. We decided to park the car at the lower parking lot and walk to a beautiful turquoise lake.

It was a warm, sunny day in May. We walked to the upper parking lot and across to the lake. The view was magnificent, and we were exhilarated by it. Coming back another way, through the woods, we found a little snow on the pathway where the sun had not reached. When we got back to the lower parking lot, we found that there was a pile of snow all around that end that had previously been snowplowed. The snow was only about two feet high, and the rest of the group jumped over it without any trouble.

I viewed it with concern. *Could I make it safely over?* I could walk around the parking lot to the other side and then come in that way. Because of some weakness in my legs, that would have been the safer thing to do. But I chose to go over that snow. I strode onto the snow—and realized my mistake. I wouldn't be able to make it safely down the other side, nor could I go back. So I called to my husband. "Help!" He was too far ahead to hear, but our daughter and her husband heard and turned to see what was wrong. I made yet another wrong decision and tried to make one more step over the snow. The next thing I knew, I was landing on my back on the hard tarmac, and then the back of my head hit the ground—hard.

To our amazement, I was not seriously hurt—just a bruised back and head, but no broken bones. If I had landed on my side I would almost certainly have broken my hip or shoulder with the force with which I fell. I got up with help from my husband and daughter, and we carried on with the vacation.

I learned—or relearned—some important lessons that day:
1. Even when we make wrong decisions, God still cares for us and answers our prayers.
2. While God does protect us from serious harm, He still allows the natural outcome of our actions to occur, to teach us important lessons.
3. When we ask for help, it is better to wait for that help than to go ahead alone.

RUTH LENNOX

Flowers for the Living

Whatsoever ye do in word or deed, do all in the name of the Lord Jesus, giving thanks to God. Col. 3:17.

RECENTLY A WOMAN in our church started a ministry. Anyone can tell her of a good deed done by a church member. She types out the situation on beautifully flowered paper and posts it, along with other notes of thanks, so that people can read of the good deeds and loving helpfulness of so many caring people. It is a loving thing to do, making others feel warm and worthwhile.

My father, a landscaper, grew many flowers, blossoming trees, and rosebushes. He often gave the customers an extra bonus with their purchase. He had the philosophy of giving flowers while people could see them and smell them. Often he expressed displeasure at funerals when viewing the many beautiful floral arrangements that would never benefit the deceased. Almost every week my siblings and I could be found taking bouquets to the shut-ins we knew.

Our son was 2½ years old when my father died, but he developed his own version of the same thinking. Sometimes his gifts included delicious home-baked desserts or other goodies, hand-delivered to friends who really appreciated them.

Many flowers of appreciation are due the many friends and people who helped me after an accidental fall in front of the learning center. Somehow my right ankle twisted, and both feet went right while my body turned left. Watercolor supplies, brushes, paints, and paper scattered into the bushes and all around.

My friend Debbie, a nurse, was one of the first to arrive. She got control of the situation and determined that there were no broken bones. Someone came with ice, and Pastor Jim was there to assess the whole situation, and Sally and Ken picked up the scattered supplies. After everyone determined it was OK for me to get up, Pastor Jim took my left arm and Ken took my right arm to lift me up and get me back on two feet. Jim and Dixie heard the commotion and came out to see if they could help too. I was safely delivered to the watercolors class, and everyone wished me well. So many caring people deserve those lovely flowers!

I want to thank God and everyone for their kindnesses in a meaningful way, don't you?

LILLIAN MUSGRAVE

The Potatoes Are Ready

But the fruit of the Spirit is love, joy, peace, patience. Gal. 5:22, NIV.

IT WAS SPRING, and one Sunday the entire family got together to plant a vegetable garden. We planted corn, red peas (kidney beans), and sweet potatoes. At the end of the day we inspected our day's work and felt proud of our accomplishment. There were rows of peas and corn and patches of sweet potatoes.

The days and weeks that followed included watering the tiny plants and keeping the garden weed-free. It was a joy to watch our garden grow. Our girls were thrilled to see the tiny shoots turn into mature plants and were eager to see what would happen next. The red peas were reaped first. It was fun opening the pods and counting how many seeds there were in each one. Next came the corn. We plucked and shared it with our neighbors and friends.

What had happened to the sweet potatoes? We knew that they would take longer than the peas and the corn to mature, but months went by and they were still not ready. What signs do you look for when sweet potatoes are ready? Maybe the leaves will dry up. So we waited and waited.

One day, after waiting for what seemed to be a year, a member of the family decided to pull up the potato plants. There was some resistance, so he pulled a little harder. Behold, a big sweet potato clung to the potato slip! Excitedly we continued to dig and found more and more sweet potatoes.

There is an object lesson in this story. We talk to our loved ones, friends, and family members about God. We pray for them and live an exemplary life. Sometimes we wait a long time but can't see any evidence that a positive spiritual impact is being made on them. We are anxious and fret ourselves about the length of time it is taking them to show evidence that they are developing a relationship with God. Yet unknown to us, God is working in them, and they have become close friends with Him. Like the sweet potatoes, they were silently developing their relationship with Him, but we couldn't see.

Do you have a child, a spouse, friends, or family members for whom you've been praying for a long time? Are you beginning to lose patience? Don't give up. The seeds have been sown. When the time is right, you'll know that the fruit is ready.

GLORIA GREGORY

Saved to Serve

The angel of the Lord encampeth round about them that fear him, and delivereth them. Ps. 34:7.

MY HUSBAND AND I decided to celebrate our fortieth wedding anniversary with several activities. The first was a marriage retreat in Cohutta Springs, Georgia. I was excited because it would be my first time there, and we'd missed out on many such opportunities while living in Kenya the previous six years.

It was a beautiful spring day, and many people in our group, including our youngest son and his wife, decided to go canoeing. I watched their 1-year-old son as he enjoyed feeding the geese at the edge of the lake.

When my son returned, his wife asked him to take me for a canoe ride. My son, his best friend, and I got into the canoe. I sat in the middle with one of them at either end, paddles in hand. Somehow I felt uncomfortable and held to the sides very tightly. Suddenly, without warning, the canoe capsized and landed on top of us. I found myself unable to touch the bottom of the lake and frantically fought my way to the surface. I was immediately grabbed by one of the boys. We were all wearing life jackets and I could float and swim, but I panicked. By this time my son was holding me, but I ignored all his instructions to float, swim, or relax. I just held on to him while he was desperately trying to support both of us. He was getting tired, and we were both terrified.

Just then I looked toward the bank and noticed a canoe approaching. A female voice called, "Just be calm; I am coming to get you." Those were the most comforting words. The woman rowed to us, calmly told us to hold on to the sides of the canoe, then rowed us to safety.

We thank God for so many blessings of that day. This woman, who was not one of our group, later said she was sitting on the bank reading a book. She looked up, knew we were in trouble, and came to our rescue in a canoe that happened to be available. The entire incident happened before we rounded the bend, so we were still in full view of those on the bank. I am convinced that the woman was an angel sent by God to save us from that watery grave. God saved us for service, and He wants to use us for His glory. Each day I ask Him to show me where He wants me to serve, and I will praise His name forever. Do you do that too?

LYDIA D. ANDREWS

Who's Watching?

The eyes of the Lord are upon the righteous, and his ears are open unto their cry. Ps. 34:15.

 WHEN I WAS GROWING UP, no matter where my brother, sister, and I were going, our parents never failed to give us their favorite advice: "You children be on your best behavior, for you never know who's watching."

"Who's watching?" is a valid question, for it is a fact of life that people are watching, whether they are in their workplace, the shopping mall, church, school, or home. In my neighborhood, as in many others, one can even see signs posted that say: "Neighborhood Watch."

One morning I was unknowingly under the watchful eye of my husband as I struggled with the vacuum, trying to get the bag on. He came over and asked what I was doing. Having watched me, he decided it was time to see if he could be of help. (He was!)

During my working years a coworker and I had the same scheduled playground duty. One day while on duty she came over to my area and surprised me when she asked how many coats I had. Before I could respond, she smiled and said she'd been watching me each time I was on duty. I've concluded that people are watching, regardless of their gender or circumstances.

I'm reminded also of the morning I sat listening as a dear friend of mine began telling me about an experience she had had one Thursday evening as she completed her grocery shopping. She was thinking about getting home after a day's work. While pushing the cart through the parking lot to her car, she heard someone say, "Give me your purse." Standing in front of her was a young man holding a gun. She yelled at him, "Get out of here!" He turned and ran away.

My friend and I work together in the beginner and kindergarten departments of our church, so we discussed her ordeal and talked about one of our favorite songs we often sing with the children: "Angels are watching over me; I am glad, I am glad. Angels are watching over me; thank God for angels bright."

Without a doubt my friend and I know who was watching over her that Thursday evening in that parking lot, and we thank Jesus so much for sending His angel.

May our faith in Him continue, and may we believe His promise given in Psalm 91:11: "For he shall give his angels charge over thee, to keep thee in all thy ways."

Annie B. Best

Clear Vision

Now we see but a poor reflection as in a mirror; then we shall see face to face. Now I know in part; then I shall know fully, even as I am fully known. 1 Cor. 13:12, NIV.

SLOWLY MY EYESIGHT HAD DIMMED through the years. The good doctor told me it was because a cataract had formed and caused my vision to become cloudy. When he determined it was the right time to remove the cataract, the surgical procedure proceeded without any complications. A new lens was implanted and the eyelid taped shut. Within a half hour the anesthesia had worn off, and I was free to go home. Five hours later I removed the tape and found that I could see, even though everything was blurry and out of focus. There were no stitches, so I didn't feel any pain or irritation.

As the days went by, those things within my field of vision became much clearer. Patience was the name of the game, but I was rewarded as my eyesight improved. With a new lens in my eyeglasses, once again I'm able to see clearly. I cherish my clear vision.

Associating with other people sometimes dims vision. We look only on the most obvious behavior patterns or the person's outward beauty or lack of beauty. Failing to take the time to really get to know another person, we misjudge them and attribute various undesirable character traits to them. We look at them through eyes that are clouded with cataracts caused by our lack of perfect vision. If we would truly try to understand these same individuals, we would find that within everyone there is something good. We might even come to look upon humankind with a new perspective and find a precious pearl who could become a true friend.

We often let our vision become dim and fail to allow time and circumstances to have a part in the transformation of each individual. How often we misjudge one another and then never try to set things right again. In a very real sense we walk around with cataracts upon our eyes. We are not able to get beyond our original snap judgment and see others in a positive light.

Our families and friends are the most precious people on this earth to us, and we should make every effort to understand who they are and why they do things in a certain way. The love that exists when we have clear vision will always be forgiving and will not allow anything to destroy our precious relationships.

EVELYN GLASS

Unexpected Incidents

*For he shall give his angels charge over thee, to keep thee in all thy ways.
Ps. 91:11.*

MOTHER WAS VISITING FROM AUSTRALIA, so we decided
to enjoy Easter in the highlands of the tropical island. We set out
late Thursday afternoon, planning to spend the night at our mission college, where a friend would join us for the trip.

The narrow gravel road wound around the sides of the hills.
As we negotiated a tight bend, the car's wheels lost traction on the loose
gravel in a flash, giving me no time to right the vehicle as it started over the
embankment. The car came to rest on the edge of the road, with one front
wheel suspended in midair. As she looked down upon the tops of the vine-
covered trees, Mother muttered, "If we had gone down there we wouldn't
have been found for days."

As my car was a front-wheel drive, all my efforts to reverse it failed, so
we had to stand helplessly by the side of the road. Soon a passing vehicle
stopped, and two strong local men lifted the car back onto the road. They
offered to follow us for some distance in case we needed any further help.
My mother spent the night reliving the incident in her dreams.

Next morning, mindful of God's protecting care the evening before, we
set out for our destination. Just before the main ascent to the highlands, we
drove over many small hills. At one particular place guava trees, loaded with
large yellow fruit, attracted my friend's attention. We stopped, and she
climbed the bank to gather some of the fruit. She seemed to be gone a long
time, so I decided to help her. While climbing the bank, I turned and saw my
car, with mother in the back seat, begin to roll down the hill. I let out a
scream, jumped out of my thongs, and ran the race of my life, not even noticing the sharp gravel piercing the soles of my feet. I caught up with the car, and
all ended well.

Two incidents in two days, the only two I have ever had in the car, left
my usually calm and placid mother in a state of shock. As we reviewed the
incidents that could have ended in tragedy, we thanked the Lord for angels
who indeed are constantly by our sides to care for and to protect us from
harm and danger.

JOY DUSTOW

Thought: God does't always send His angels. How do you explain that?

Could It Be Reversed?

I, even I, am he who blots out your transgression for my own sake, and remembers your sins no more. Isa. 43:25, NIV.

WHEN I WAS AT THE WINNEBA COLLEGE OF ART, I was the nursery Sunday school teacher. One Sunday I taught the Easter story, using pictures showing Jesus on the cross. Time did not allow us to talk about His resurrection.

The next day I met my painting lecturer, who confronted me about how I had confused his son. Atsu went home and climbed tables and chairs to remove all the pictures of Jesus from their living room. When asked why, he said, "My teacher said in church that Jesus is dead. If He is dead, He cannot take care of us anymore."

I was very disturbed, but I apologized and left without an explanation, as I didn't know what to do. I went to my cubicle and prayed that God would forgive me and guide me to reverse the harm that I had done to many innocent little children.

Sometimes our ways of life and attitudes discourage, mislead, or put off others around us. At times some even lose their faith and leave the church. But do we realize that? If we do, do we try to reverse it with apologies and a change of attitude? That reminds me of one preacher who said some of us don't realize that we are wearing masks, spiritually, that frighten others from the church.

I met my class the next Sunday, well prepared, and God led me to continue my story with the help of pictures. I explained to them how Jesus did not stay in the tomb. The risen Christ visited His disciples. I told them about how Thomas wanted to see and touch His wounded hands. Atsu listened quietly with a smile.

On graduation day my lecturer shook my hand and said, "Congratulations, Mabel; you did it—you reversed it. Atsu hung all the pictures back up and said, 'Jesus was resurrected, and He will be with us always.'"

Thank You, Lord, for coming to die to blot out my transgressions. Please make me new so that my life and utterances will lead others to Your cross at Calvary. And even if I err, help me to be able to realize it and reverse it.

MABEL KWEI

No Cliques in Heaven

But when He saw the multitudes, He was moved with compassion for them,
because they were weary and scattered, like sheep having no shepherd.
Matt. 9:36, NKJV.

WHEN I WAS A YOUNG FRESHMAN GIRL in college many years ago, there was a clique of girls from a large boarding high school who looked down upon our little group of girls from a small country high school. We were scorned by them for our simple country ways and clothing. It made us feel unloved and ignored. In wonder, we watched the popularity of those girls and wished we could be as well liked by the others. But we eventually got over that and went on with our studies, even becoming friends with special, kindly fellow classmates, who, like us, later became church workers in various places.

I'm afraid some of those women may still belong to their clique! My dictionary defines a clique as "a small exclusive group of people." It's more than just that. I think the dictionary should say, "a small group who think they are exclusive."

I am reading the book *In the Footsteps of Jesus,* by Bruce Marchiano. As I read, I reflected on that long-ago life of Christ. Bruce reminds us how Jesus treated people with compassion, regardless of their background. Bruce was hired to play the part of Jesus in the movie *"Matthew"* some years ago. He tells how he was greatly changed by the task of portraying Jesus, His character, His words, His compassion for all people.

Telling of one scene he played, Bruce wrote that Jesus saw "a sea of people living lives in ways He didn't plan. People living lives away from His love, away from His care, outside of His goodness, His embrace, His plans, purposes, and hopes for them" (p. 116). It made the actor weep in his portrayal of Jesus.

I am sure that there will be no exclusive cliques in heaven. I long for that time.

Thank You, Lord, for Your compassion for all kinds of people. Help me today to look at people through Your eyes and love them as You would.

BESSIE SIEMENS LOBSIEN

Thought: Read Matthew 22:16 and think about how Jesus treated people. What would make them say this? Could they say the same about us?

The Coach's Voice

My sheep hear my voice, and I know them, and they follow me. John 10:27.

I HAVE THREE NEPHEWS who have been wrestling for the local school district throughout their high school years. They started wrestling with their dad as soon as they learned to walk. After all of these years of practice they are very good at it. It is considered quite an honor if a wrestler can make it to the state competition by his senior year. My nephews made it by their junior year, and each of them has their name written on the wall in the gymnasium, in the section where those holding school records are posted. The country newspaper even did a full-page story on them.

I enjoy watching and cheering my nephews on from the stands. During one particularly exciting match the entire crowd was screaming and yelling. Everyone, including me, was yelling advice from the stands and cheering with all their might. The boys won their match. Afterward I asked all three of the boys separately if they could hear us cheer. They all said no. The only thing they could hear was the voice of their coach. They had been listening to him during practice. They were used to his voice. They trusted his advice; they listened to no one else.

What a lesson there is to learn here! We are all in a "game," a "conflict" called the great controversy—the struggle between good and evil, between Christ and Satan. We all have "matches" that we encounter every day. We have a coach, the very best. His name is Jesus Christ. In fact, when His instructions are followed, He has never lost a match. He gives us instructions in the Bible. He promises that He will stand behind us and tell us to turn to the left and turn to the right. He tells us that His people hear His voice (Deut. 5:32; Joshua 1:7; Isa. 30:21).

The question is Do we practice listening every day by reading what He has to say? Do we obey what He tells us immediately and get in the practice of obeying at once so that when we are in the tough spots we can "hear and obey" and become victorious? Will we have our names written in the hall of fame, which is the book of life? I guess it all depends on whom we choose to listen to.

SUSAN BERRIDGE

God's Loving Care

Are not two sparrows sold for a farthing? and one of them shall not fall on
the ground without your Father. . . . Fear ye not therefore, ye are of more
value than many sparrows. Matt. 10:29-31.

TODAY WAS AN EXCITING DAY! The little Carolina wren had built her nest in the same place she had built it last year. (Or am I imagining that it was the same mother?) I watched as she sat on her eggs, day after day, rarely leaving the nest. Then one day I could see two little mouths. Mother Wren was faithful in making untold trips back and forth with tidbits in her beak. How could she tell which baby she had fed last?

I can remember when my twin sisters were born. I was the oldest of four siblings before the twins, so sometimes my poor mother would be so tired and distraught she would accidentally give one baby two bottles and the other baby none.

But this morning I spent more time than usual looking through the window into the storage area where the bird family lived. When our women's prayer circle met, I told them about what was going on with the bird family. Then, after everyone left, I sat very still and watched. To my utter amazement, not two but four babies flew off the nest and fluttered to the ground. "Oh, no, don't stay *there*!" I warned them. "Something will eat you!" But as I watched they flew back up close to their nest, and Mother Wren faithfully went back and forth to feed each one. After I called my husband to watch, they flew up and down and finally flew into a tree. While I watched this scenario I sang to myself, "His eye is on the sparrow, and I know He watches me."

The next morning as I was telling a friend my bird story, she had one of her own. She and her husband had a box trailer. One day when they needed to make a trip, they discovered that a bird had built her nest between the wheel and the trailer body. Since they had to make the trip, they decided not to disturb the nest. Sure enough, when they returned it was still intact.

The next time they needed to use the trailer for a longer trip, the baby birds went along for the ride. Since they were going to be away from home a few days, my friend and her husband found worms and fed the babies. Once they returned home, the mother bird resumed the responsibility of feeding. I thought this was an incredible story of God's care for His creatures.

RUBYE SUE

Cyclone!

The Lord Almighty is with us; the God of Jacob is our fortress. Ps. 46:7, NIV.

ON MARCH 26, 2004, my husband and I, along with three other people, made a trip to offer a training course in a neighboring city. Before we left home we prayed to the Lord, asking Him to provide us with a safe trip and to take care of our family who would remain behind. I left my 5-year-old daughter with my sister, and we traveled trusting in divine care.

The next day my sister telephoned because she was concerned with the radio and TV warnings that a cyclone had formed at sea. Strong winds of 186 miles (300 kilometers) per hour were bringing it landward toward where our family lived. At first the news was hard for us to believe, because the incidence of cyclones in the southern region of Brazil was practically unknown. My sister was crying, and the seriousness of the problem became apparent. I attempted to calm her, but when the phone conversation ended, I felt apprehensive. So I knelt and prayed to the Lord, asking that He extend His powerful hand over all who were in danger.

That night I called again, and everything was calm. On Sunday several attempts to call home resulted in frustration. I couldn't reach anyone. *Something is wrong with my cell phone*, I decided. After lunch we began the trip home.

As we traveled we began to see trees that had been uprooted, fallen lamp posts, gasoline stations destroyed, houses without roofs. A sensation of complete terror came over us as we saw all of this destruction!

The information had been correct. A cyclone had really gone through the region, but not with the force it had had at sea. God extended His hand and calmed the fury of the winds. If the winds from the high seas had reached inland, nothing—and no one—would have survived.

I am very grateful that God protected my family, my daughter, friends, neighbors, and my home.

Even today some uncertainties about what really happened exist. The information that we received was that the wind reached approximately 93 miles (150 kilometers) per hour.

At any time, in any situation, we should seek the Lord, because He is—and always will be—the great Lord who guards and protects our fortress.

ELIZETE BORGES GOULART

Shadows

Let us hold fast the confession of our hope without wavering, for He who promised is faithful. Heb. 10:23, NKJV.

 IT WAS A DREARY MORNING when we set out for Battle Creek. We stayed on the back roads to avoid the more traveled ways and found ourselves on a country road out of Mason, Michigan. The brilliance of a beautiful fall had long faded from the trees, and they loomed up gray and cold on either side of the car. The scene matched our moods. My husband and I had heard the doctor's verdict that would cast a shadow on the rest of our lives.

Bill had less than five years to live—he had Hodgkin's disease. The 5½-hour surgery on the lump in his neck verified the fact. The doctor advised him to get his affairs in order. He was only 37, just starting his own business, his dream for the future. We were silent as we rode along that morning, struggling with thoughts, trying to grasp the depth of the doctor's words. Hodgkin's disease is fatal, and there was nothing that could be done except to pray for healing.

In the gloom of the early-morning raindrops we passed one bright spot—a country schoolhouse painted pink, with a white picket fence and a mailbox inscribed "Pink School." Who dared to paint a schoolhouse such a color? It had to be someone who adored children, with a heart filled with love, someone who cared enough to dress up their "home away from home." Children are so impressionable. Such a teacher could not help instilling love in the little hearts gathered around her. The pink schoolhouse was symbolic of love, inspiration, and promise.

It inadvertently helped Bill and me to face our tomorrows when all seemed lost, out of focus, and difficult to grasp. Perhaps it was the chain of events leading up to the moment of the pink schoolhouse. Perhaps it was a glimpse of the only bright color on that country road in such a dreary atmosphere that changed our train of thinking. We could face whatever was up the road and around the bend.

God does not always promise a bright future. We will experience valleys and mountaintops throughout our lifetimes. But He does promise His constant presence to see us through the shadows and heartaches. Maybe His presence will even show up in a pink schoolhouse.

LAURIE DIXON-McCLANAHAN

The Indecisive Squirrels

And thine ears shall hear a word behind thee, saying, This is the way, walk ye in it. Isa. 30:21.

LIVING IN THE DEVELOPING AREA IN FLORIDA, one gets a close look at the wildlife and learns their behavior. We get to see the many critters and the reptiles that cross the streets on a daily basis.

The two critters that fascinate me most are the squirrels and the turtles. The turtle will stop dead in its tracks when it feels movement, but the squirrel will run back and forth until it is killed by an unsuspecting motorist, or it will narrowly escape being run over.

I remember my first encounter with a squirrel. At that time I was unaware of the squirrel's particular behavior. Early one morning I was on my way to work when suddenly a squirrel ran out in the street; I slowed down so that it could cross, but it turned to go back in the direction from which it had come. Suddenly it dashed back into the street and met disaster. Now that I know how they act, I make sure they are out of the way before I speed up.

Recently I noticed a behavior that is totally out of character for the squirrel. I was traveling on a side road when I noticed one on the edge of the road. I felt sure that it was going to dart across the road and back. To my surprise, it got on its belly and dragged itself across the road. The motorists on either side of the road stopped to let it go. I sat there thinking that it was injured. Another surprise was in store: when it got to the other side, it got up on all fours and ran away.

I am reminded daily that the devil is like a roaring lion, "seeking whom he may devour" (1 Peter 5:8). Sometimes circumstances come our way, and we act like the turtle or the squirrel—we come to a complete halt, or we run back and forth in a confused manner. We act lame, not knowing which way we should go.

My prayer is that I focus on the Lord and put all my trust in Him so that when trouble or other circumstances come my way, I can move on with confidence, knowing that my strength is in the Lord.

GLORIA HUTCHINSON

Thought: Today's text seems so clear: "This is the way." But other texts say "Wait" or "Go." How does one know what to do in the confusing times we live in? What helps you to decide?

HW-4

Teach Them Diligently

And thou shalt teach them diligently unto thy children, and shalt talk of them when thou sittest in thine house, and when thou walkest by the way, and when thou liest down, and when thou risest up. Deut. 6:7.

"TEACH THEM DILIGENTLY UNTO THY CHILDREN." What are we to teach the children?

"Bye-bye, Daddy; remember to buy me a led balala!" shouted little Daphne as her dad hopped onto the bus. Living in Meghalaya, India, the wettest place in the world, Daphne definitely needed an umbrella of her own to go to church. So she begged her dad to buy her a red umbrella, which she called a "led balala." She felt awkward being carried under her dad's big black umbrella while her friends walked to church under their own colorful ones.

While waiting for her dad to bring the umbrella, Daphne passed her time playing in the yard. When Mother checked on her, she saw little Daphne kneeling down with hands folded, eyes closed, mumbling her prayer. In fact, throughout the week she had been praying about the red umbrella in worship. She prayed, "Dear Jesus, help Daddy to get me a led balala."

That day, when shopping was done, her father stopped into one of the shops in Jowai and asked, "*Phiydon shatri khynnah?*" ("Do you have kids' umbrellas?") The saleswoman shook her head and said, "Sorry; all sold out." Not wanting to give up, he begged her to check again. Sure enough, she found one—a small red umbrella—hidden in a pile of big black umbrellas! She smiled and said, "Eight rupees, please." To his surprise, when he took out his wallet Father found only six rupees. Embarrassed, he said, "Sorry; keep the umbrella for me. I'll be back tomorrow."

However, as he waited for the bus to take him home, he spotted a note on the ground just a yard from him. He picked it up. Wow! It was a new, crisp two-rupee note! "God did it for my girl!" he whispered to himself. He immediately dashed back to the shop and excitedly blurted out, "Here is eight rupees!" The woman smiled as she handed him the small red umbrella. He paid her six rupees plus a two-rupee God-sent note.

In evening worship little Daphne prayed, "Dear Jesus, thank You for led balala!"

Today Daphne diligently teaches her two sons, Mark and John, to love God and trust Him. She knows and understands the power and love of God and has a story to share. Don't you?

ANNIE M KUJUR

Forgiven

Forgive us our debts, as we also have forgiven our debtors. Matt. 6:12, NIV.

AS A LIBRARY CLERK I can sympathize with schoolteachers who listen to such excuses as "The dog ate my homework." When it comes to paying late fines on their books and videos, some patrons come up with all sorts of reasons they shouldn't have to pay.

One woman was indignant and said she refused to pay because the calendar on her watch was wrong. Someone else said it was our fault because there was an old receipt in his book saying it was due on the tenth. I pointed out that the receipt had someone else's name on it and that the month on the receipt showed it was due three months earlier. He still maintained that he didn't owe any money because he had read only the day, not the month.

Then there's the excuse that someone borrowed the card and that it is actually the fault of the roommate, husband, sister, etc. People who don't want to pay their video fines often come up with the statement that they shouldn't have to pay because they didn't get a chance to watch them. Then there are those who firmly believe that if they put a book in our drop the morning it's due, they won't be charged, or they maintain that Sundays and holidays don't count. They do.

It is possible to get out of paying your fine if you tell a convincing story and if your record shows that you've been responsible about paying your fines in the past. You see, on the computer screen that shows how much money is owed there are several options: cash, check, cancel, or forgive. We mere clerks are not allowed to forgive fines over a dollar or two, but the supervisor is authorized to forgive fines of any amount. She can clear up a patron's record by clicking on the "forgive" option.

I often think how wonderful it would be if we could clear up all our debts with a single keystroke on the computer. Can't pay the rent? It's forgiven. Running short on your credit card bill? Don't worry; it's been forgiven.

Actually, we can be forgiven, and it's pretty simple. Jesus paid the debt for our sins on the cross. We don't have to make up any excuses. All we have to do is ask, and our record is wiped clean. Forgiven. I like the sound of that.

GINA LEE

Eternal Meeting

And this gospel of the kingdom will be preached in all the world as a witness to all the nations, and then the end will come. Matt. 24:14, NKJV.

THE OFFICE TELEPHONE rang, and the call brought news that shocked me: the death of a great friend. I couldn't believe that someone who was so full of life was gone, but time and the will of God in the lives of those who give themselves to Him are often unexplainable. Heaven alone will bring the answers.

Much reflection has happened since the initial shock and these moments of sadness. I began to feel stronger and to understand that in life it is people who are most important. We are so busy, yet we never have time, never have money, to do and think about what is really most important. We always have several excuses for our omissions; but truthfully, what is most important is people.

At the high point of my considerations and new objectives, my mother called me to say that my grandfather was in the hospital once again. On Monday, April 1 (known as the "Day of the Lie" in Brazil), another phone call came: "Grandfather passed away. The cause of his death was his most noble possession—his heart," my father said. Impossible! The only thing that I wanted was for the news to be a lie.

These losses made me feel that God was closer to me, as if He were carrying me in His arms. How elusive and temporary the beauties and commodities of modern life are! I began to understand totally why God so wants to take us to live with Him. And today, more than ever, I want heaven. I want eternal happiness. I want peace like a river. I want Jesus to come soon! I want to be reunited with my loved ones in a place where there is no more pain, no more separation, and no more death. More than anything, I want to be with our precious Jesus.

We talk a lot about preaching the gospel to the world, but what is the gospel? It is good news! Today's verse defines the type of preaching that is really effective as a "witness"—sharing good news. I want to be an efficient witness, preaching good news to those who are around me, and being a true Christian example. Don't you want to join me in this effort?

VIVIANE FRAGOSO DE OLIVEIRA

The Lord Knows What Is Best

Trust in the Lord, and do good; dwell in the land, and feed on His faithfulness. Delight yourself also in the Lord, and He shall give you the desires of your heart. Ps. 37:3, 4, NKJV.

WE HAD BEEN IN THE MISSION FIELD FOR 16 YEARS. It seemed only yesterday that my husband and I got married and left for mission service. Then one day my husband thought it was time for both of us to go back to school so that we could recharge our batteries, so to speak. Because we had tried to be faithful through His grace and empowerment, the mission leaders said we could go for our much-needed upgrading. You can imagine my joy in sharing with my fellow teachers and my students that we were going for our graduate studies. Though I wondered how I would feel being on the other side of the desk, I was excited about the thoughts of going back to school.

My happiness was short-lived. My husband came home from his office one day and said that perhaps our going would have to be postponed. I was devastated! How could I face everyone and tell them that I wasn't leaving after all? My husband comforted me and explained why we needed to wait another year. He said that the leadership in the mission was going to be nationalized for the first time. Since he was one of the few with seniority, we really needed to stay to support the new leadership. After all, if we had waited for 16 years, what was another year? So I had to swallow my pride, face my students, and explain the situation to them.

As I look back on that incident, I know God had His hand in it. Instead of going to a university in the Philippines, as originally planned, we went to Andrews University in Michigan. After our upgrading, we returned to the mission field to continue our work. A few years later we immigrated to Canada, where the only university acknowledged by the board of education was the University of the Philippines. However, because I had graduated from a university in the United States, my credentials were accepted, and I was able to teach the entire time I was in Canada.

Many times we question God when our dreams and hopes don't happen in the way we had hoped or planned. We honestly think our plans have been well orchestrated, but the Lord always knows what is best. We can always trust in the Lord.

Ofelia A. Pangan

Present from God

Behold, children are a heritage from the Lord, the fruit of the womb is a reward. Ps. 127:3, NKJV.

 THE WEATHER REPORT for that April night predicted rain. Thunder boomed, and lightning cut the sky. Above the sound of the wind, the crying of a child woke us up. We learned later that the couple who lived next door had adopted a baby girl.

It was with great joy that the couple received her, considering her truly a "present from God." After going through the adoption requirements, the parents began to have a very active life.

The little girl filled her mother and father's hearts with contentment; now they were legally her parents, who continued to give her all their love. Then several years went by, and another child was received with the same love and joy.

One day I witnessed a very touching moment that I shall never forget. One of the girls asked, "Mommy, I heard that you are not our birth mother. Is this true?"

"Yes, my daughter, but I love you in the same way, with all of my soul. When I received both of you, I promised the Lord that from that moment you both belonged to me and that I would defend you from everything and from everyone."

Immediately the girl answered, "Mommy, what happened before doesn't matter. It was good to hear this from you, and we promise to be grateful to you and Daddy until the end of our lives." Then I saw the mother and her daughters exchange a long embrace. That mother, who was very grateful, wept with joy.

I am a true witness of the blessings without measure that the Lord granted to that couple.

Lord, may other couples be able to perceive that there are so many children longing for love and protection, and may they have the courage to make this decision, if possible. May they give homeless children a place in their home, preparing them to live with You in the heavenly home You are making ready for us.

Through Your great love You made us Your children, adopting us into the family of God. Thank You, Lord!

MARIA SINHARINHA DE OLIVEIRA NOGUEIRA

Garden Weeds

Acquaint now thyself with him, and be at peace: thereby good shall come to thee. Receive, I pray thee, the law from his mouth, and lay up his words in thine heart. Job 22:21, 22.

SPRING IS ALWAYS a welcome sight after the winter fog, ice, and snow. Each spring we plant our vegetable and flower gardens. However, the unfailing blessing of spring showers produces an abundance of weeds as well as sprouting garden seeds. No one is exempt from garden weeds.

One evening I diligently hoed and pulled weeds from my flower garden. The next day I discovered that I had missed some of the weeds. My neighbor told me she spent hours each morning pulling tall weeds from her husband's used-to-be garden. Her neighbors complained, "We don't want your weed seeds blowing into our yard. You'd best get rid of them."

"I'm not a gardener, and I hate to pull weeds," she said. "My husband was the gardener. He loved to garden, but now he is unable, and the yard work and all the weeds are left to me. But one weed at a time—I'll get the job done!" And she did!

While I gloved my hands and used a hoe to rid my garden of weeds, I thought about the weeds I may find in the garden of my heart: selfishness, pride, envy, resentment, and unforgiveness. *What tools will I need to eliminate the weeds from my heart garden?* I asked myself.

In today's text Job mentions specific tools for ridding my heart of weeds. Other treasured tools I've found in, *The Desire of Ages.* I discovered these precious promises: "So long as we surrender the will to God and trust in His strength and wisdom, we shall be guided in safe paths, to fulfill our appointed part in His great plan" (p. 209). "The Holy Spirit never leaves unassisted the soul who is looking unto Jesus. . . . If the eye is kept fixed upon Christ, the work of the Spirit ceases not until the soul is conformed to His image" (p. 302). These are the tools I need in my life!

Lord, with all of the distractions in this life, I need Your help every moment. I pray that the Holy Spirit will never cease to work in my heart so that I will be ready for Your soon coming in the clouds of heaven, free from all the weeds in the garden of my heart!

NATHALIE LADNER-BISCHOFF

Speak With Grace

Let your speech be alway with grace, seasoned with salt, that ye may know how ye ought to answer every man. Col. 4:6.

IT WAS A COLD, WINDY DAY on the pinnacle of the Valley of the Moon in Bolivia. What a view! A man and his wife took advantage of the high elevation and the cold temperature to offer their warm alpaca wool scarves for sale. I stopped to look. One of the tourists advised me to wait until we got to the open market, where prices would be cheaper, but I wasn't about to quibble over $8 when I needed warmth about my head and neck right then! I looked at the woman squatting on the barren rocks, clutching a colorful shawl that shielded her from the biting wind. She needed a customer. I paid for the scarf with a $10 bill and received a priceless smile for change!

Another time, as I paid for a basket of peaches at a farmer's fruit stand, a friend tapped me on the shoulder and said, "Do you realize you're paying a dollar per peach?" I hadn't looked at my purchase that way. Rather than accepting his judgment, I replied, "But they have much better flavor than those one buys in the store, so I will pay the price."

In neither case was I seeking advice. Have you ever considered the common topics of daily conversation? Is it unsought advice or something shallow and meaningless? How often when we meet someone on the street, in the church foyer, or at our workplace do we talk about the weather? The weather seldom seems to be perfect—it's too wet, too dry, too hot, too cold, too windy, or too cloudy. Even on sunny days the sun may be too bright. I don't think we mean to complain; it's just a conversation opener.

One day my sister and I were shopping at a grocery store. We retrieved a shoppingcart by inserting a loonie (a Canadian dollar coin) in a slot, releasing it from the locked line of carts. A woman nearby complained, "We used to pay only a quarter for a cart!" What was the reason to grumble? We'd get our loonie back when we returned the cart.

Perhaps we need to give some thought to engaging conversations on a higher level. Our prayer each day should be "Let the words of my mouth, and the meditation of my heart, be acceptable in thy sight, O Lord, my strength, and my redeemer" (Ps. 19:14).

EDITH FITCH

The Angel of the Lord

The angel of the Lord encampeth round about them that fear him, and delivereth them. Ps. 34:7.

OUR CHILDREN'S PEDIATRICIAN counseled us to let them be together whenever one of the two had a contagious/infectious childhood disease, such as measles, mumps, or chicken pox, so that I wouldn't have to miss work twice for the same reason. It would be beneficial to them, too, because I could take care of both of them at the same time. When it became necessary for our daughter to have her tonsils removed, the pediatrician's counsel was to wait until our son was 4 so that the children could be operated on together. He said this would be a chronic problem throughout their lives if we didn't take this measure.

In the spring of 1975, after everything was planned, the children, the girl who worked for us, and I left our home very early, headed for the Bongo Seventh-day Adventist Hospital, about 50 miles (80 kilometers) away from Nova Lisboa, Angola, where we lived. Just as we passed a tire repair shop, our car had a flat tire. We waited for the shop to open, then the spare tire was put on. While we were placing the repaired tire in the trunk, we noticed that the other tire was also flat. It was replaced by the one that had just been repaired, and we asked for repairs to be made on that tire also. More than an hour passed, before we continued our trip. Now we were in a hurry.

We passed six different checkpoints where soldiers recently had hidden, shooting wildly at the hills or bushes on that dirt road, watching everyone who approached, and shooting everything they had doubts about.

In spite of being a little nervous, I knew that God had gone before us. Two flat tires, one after the other, in front of a tire repair shop, was not a coincidence. Nor was it a coincidence that soldiers who had been at the checkpoints earlier had left before we went by. God had, without a doubt, other plans for us, and He did not let any evil befall us.

The Lord sent His angel to free us from evil. Only He knows the reason why things happen to us. We must always entrust our life to His care! How many stories our angel will have to tell us when we meet in our heavenly home! I want to be there with all of those I love. What about you?

MARIA SALES

Out the Window

And be sure your sin will find you out. Num. 32:23.

WHEN MY BROTHER, Duane, and I were children, we occasionally got into reading comic books about Batman, Superman, and Captain Marvel. Much of the content of one of them had to do with space science. I remember hiding them on the closet shelf so Mom wouldn't find them. You see, she had warned us that reading them might give us bad ideas. "First of all," she said, "nobody can fly, and no one can get to the moon."

Well, today people have gone to the moon, but in that day comic books were not recommended by most Christians as good reading because of the violence. Our keeping them and hiding them was deceitful.

I remember one very hot day my brother and I were playing outside and strayed too far from the house without asking permission. For punishment we got banished to the upstairs bedrooms for the rest of the day. We wanted to be outside so badly that I thought we should sneak outside, and maybe Mom wouldn't check. Then I remembered that in one of the comic books someone had tied bedsheets together, anchored them to the bedpost, and then went out the window. I thought that was a neat idea, so I quickly tied our sheets tightly together, and then knotted one end around the bedpost. "You go first," I said to my brother, "and then I'll come down." Halfway down—you guessed it—the knot broke, and my poor brother crashed to the ground on top of some debris and broken glass. Of course, he cried very loudly. This brought Mom rushing outside. Flabbergasted, in her Norwegian accent she asked, "Vat in da vorld are you doing?" We explain that we had tried something from comic books, but it didn't help. "Be sure your sins vil find you out!" she answered.

My poor brother. While his injuries were superficial, I was horrified to think that he may have been severely injured—or even killed—because of my wild idea. Duane grew up to be a successful radiation oncologist and has blessed many lives. How thankful I am that he survived!

That experience was the biggest lesson of my life as to the consequences of wrongdoing. Truly, the Bible is right: "Be sure your sin will find you out."

DARLENE YTREDAL BURGESON

Spoon-fed Children

In all your ways acknowledge him, and he will make your paths straight.
Prov. 3:6, NIV.

WHEN I WAS A YOUNG ADULT, making decisions on my own was difficult. One of the first tough decisions came when I was about 23. It was toward the end of graduate school, and the summer before I had met John, a Bible worker. I well remember the day we met. That night I prayed, "Lord, I like that guy—but please don't let him know."

And he never did know until later in the summer. Then, after seeking counsel from his mentors, he asked me if he could "court" me. Knowing I was heading back to complete my studies in two weeks made it a more difficult decision, but after a brief hesitation I said, "Yes." And John said, "Praise the Lord!"

Also on the team that summer was a young pastor, Kim Johnson. He invited John to be the Bible worker in his church, and he invited me to be the health educator. (He didn't know that John and I were courting.) Back at school, I faced a major decision: Do I accept this job offer? What if it doesn't work out between us? How could I work on a job with John still there? The questions plagued me night and day. Every morning as I walked for exercise through the neighborhoods, I would frequently stop by the home of my friend Fran and lament about my dilemma and the difficult decisions ahead of me.

After many of these sessions, Fran (no doubt weary of my laments) gave me some advice that I remember to this very day: "The Lord wants us to grow up from being spoon-fed children who want God to tell them everything to do, to be mature adults who are willing to look at the providences of God and be willing to make the best decision we can, and then be willing to take the consequences if it isn't the best decision." That last phrase was the key for me—I was afraid of the consequences!

John and I married 27 years ago. It was the right decision for both of us. Now I no longer wait for that handwritten letter from God, that telephone call—even an e-mail—to spoon-feed me the right decision. Rather, I look at God's leading, His providence; I seek counsel from trusted friends, and together we make the best decision we can; and we are willing to take the consequences!

BECKI KNOBLOCH

Direct My Paths

Trust in the Lord with all your heart and lean not on your own understanding. Prov. 3:5, NIV.

"YOUR RECENT CT SCAN shows that you have a mass on your right kidney. I'm referring you to a urologist." I was making an uneventful recovery after a fairly simple surgery, and this was to be a routine visit with my doctor. There had been no symptoms of any kidney problems, so this verdict was entirely unexpected.

Several weeks passed before I got an appointment with the busy urologist. After looking at the films of my CT scan, he said in a matter-of-fact way, "Yes, you have a mass on your right kidney, and it's probably malignant. That means we'll have to remove the kidney, but it's all right—you still have another kidney." Well, I didn't feel so optimistic. In fact, I felt devastated. Two of my friends had had kidney surgery within the past six months, and I knew it wouldn't be an easy recovery. I had plans to attend my granddaughter's high school graduation in another state the following month. Also, my husband and I were going to take a trip to celebrate our fiftieth wedding anniversary. Later there was a church/family outing in the redwoods of northern California.

That afternoon as I walked the half mile to our mailbox, I talked to God about my problem. At first it was a real emotional struggle, but suddenly I felt at peace—whatever happened, it would be all right.

Two days later I had a needle biopsy to check the mass. The hospital personnel, especially the radiologist, were kind and helpful. I had to wait another 10 days before I got the official results, but I wasn't worried about the outcome. I had left it all in God's hands.

Somehow I wasn't surprised when the doctor told me that I didn't have a malignancy and that I could keep my kidney, but you can be sure I was very happy. My granddaughter was excited to have her grandma attend her graduation. Our anniversary trip gave us the opportunity to share this special occasion with friends and family we don't often see. And spending time camped among the beautiful redwoods was a fitting climax to a very special summer.

Thank You, Father, for giving me peace when I turned my plans and problems over to You, and for making my paths straight.

BETTY J. ADAMS

God's Little Creatures

And God said, Let the earth bring forth living creature after his kind, cattle, and creeping thing, and beast of the earth after his kind: and it was so. Gen. 1:24.

GROWING UP, I WAS A LITTLE CREATURE WATCHER— and admit that I still am. During the fall I enjoy watching the squirrels as they scamper up and down trees, walk along overhead power wires without falling, and suddenly decide to come down, chasing each other. It reminds me of Isaiah 40:26: "Lift up your eyes on high, and behold who hath created these things, that bringeth out their host by number: he calleth them all by names by the greatness of his might, for that he is strong in power; not one faileth."

I welcome springtime for many reasons, especially the chance to watch the birds created in their beautiful colors. There's the bluebird, robin, cardinal, and the smaller of God's creation, the little sparrow, flying here and there from tree to tree, singing their melodies until they get hungry and soar to the ground for something to eat. One morning as I sat at the breakfast table, a robin perched outside my window, singing. I sat quietly, listening and enjoying its chirping, so as not to frighten it away. Another robin stopped by; then both flew away.

During the spring of 2004 the Washington, D.C., area had an unforgettable natural event—cicadas. They were everywhere (and I admit they weren't my favorite). As I was driving one day, one decided to take a ride with me, flying in the open window, landing on my lap. How thankful I was that it wasn't one of God's stinging creatures.

Once as I walked toward the bank, a woman walked in front of me. Upon nearing the entrance, I noticed a cicada resting on the back of her blouse. My first thought was to ignore it. But then God spoke through my conscience, saying, "If a cicada was on your blouse, wouldn't you want someone to get it off?" So I said, "Excuse me; one of God's little creatures is on your back." I didn't have time to ask "May I get it off?" before she quickly turned and said, "Please, please get it off!" Surprisingly, a month later we saw each other again, and she remembered my calling the cicada "God's little creature."

Many thanks to You, dear Jesus, for including us in Your creation. All are precious in Your sight—whether big or small, You dearly love us all.

ANNIE B. BEST

The Same or Different?

Now you are the body of Christ, and members individually. 1 Cor. 12:27, NKJV.

ON THE LAST CORNER before I turn into my street, there is a rather crowded yard. It appears as if a keen gardener planted an assortment of trees in her front garden a number of years ago, without any thought for their potential size, and now they have grown until their branches intertwine. Two maples in particular have grown tall and straight and strong, and their branches combine to form a united canopy—that is, for most of the year. When fall came last year, I suddenly realized that there were, in fact, two distinctly different trees. One turned a brilliant yellow while the other remained the usual summer green, and by the time it had turned the matching shade of yellow, the other tree was a filigree of bare branches.

Now it is spring again, and the soft, light green of new leaves has completely covered the once-naked tree, while the other tree is only starting to show that the sap is rising, and that it is still alive.

I've been thinking of the two wonderful girls that my husband and I have been blessed with. In an (unsuccessful) attempt to avoid sibling rivalry, we were determined to treat them exactly the same so that we could not be accused of favoritism. My husband even went so far as to copy what he had written on the first page of a gift book for one daughter into the identical book for her sister. The problem was that he copied the name as well!

But as the years have passed, we've realized that each girl is very different in gifts and needs, and now we do our best to treat them appropriately—and differently, too.

And now, as I pass the two maple trees, I breathe a little prayer for our unique girls; then I add: *Lord, give me discernment to know how to love and reach each individual I meet with a special, fitting message from You. And please give me acceptance and tolerance of those who might praise or worship or relate to You in ways that are different from mine.*

ROS LANDLESS

Thought: How often we think that people, events, needs, or ideas are the same, but on closer examination we discover they are quite different. How do we avoid treating people or circumstances in an inappropriate way because of a previous experience? Can you think of any Bible stories that illustrate this?

The Silent Killer

The Lord shall preserve thy going out and thy coming in from this time forth, and even for evermore. Ps. 121:8.

I THANK THE LORD daily for good health and strength to do my own work. I think of many women my age who suffer from various illnesses.

Last week as I went to do my usual grocery shopping at the mall, I saw a woman sitting at a table, and some women standing in a line. I inquired what it was about. The woman was from the Heart Foundation and was giving free checkups for high blood pressure (hypertension). I decided to join the line.

When it was my turn to sit and be checked, the woman told me my pressure was too high—170/95. I couldn't believe it! She asked me to finish my shopping, then return for another checkup.

An hour later my pressure had actually escalated to 194/104. She asked me to see a doctor as soon as possible. This really was a shock for me.

I rested all afternoon before going to the doctor that evening, thinking it would decrease the pressure. The doctor checked my blood pressure three times. It was still at 194/104. The doctor, who has my case history, was just as shocked as I was. Now I have to take medication for a lifetime.

The doctor told me it was a godsend that I had decided to be checked out. I felt the same as I usually do (or thought I did), so I never expected anything like this would happen to me. I'd always had a good, normal blood pressure. The doctor told me that I could have had a stroke if I had gone on much longer. High blood pressure is known as the silent killer because there are rarely visible symptoms. Two out of three people with high blood pressure are unaware of the condition.

I can only thank the Lord for the woman who "just happened" to choose that venue at the time I would pass by, and for leading me to that table.

I appreciate the words of the psalmist recorded in today's text. *Thank You, heavenly Father, for again sparing this life that You have redeemed and prolonged.*

PRISCILLA E. ADONIS

Warnings

But as the days of Noah were, so also will the coming of the Son of Man be. Matt. 24:37, NKJV.

 SCIENTISTS AROUND THE WORLD predicted that the 2005 hurricane season would be extremely active. We heard the warning, but life went on without preparation. It seemed faintly similar to what we'd been hearing for 10 years; but we said, "The 'big one' will not be this year."

Prior to the season, engineer experts and computer models predicted that if a hurricane in the Gulf of Mexico struck New Orleans, Louisiana, it would be disastrous. They predicted that 200,000 people, or more, would be unwilling or unable to heed evacuation orders, and thousands would die. They said that people would be housed in the Superdome, and that aid workers would find it difficult to gain access to the city, as roads would be impassable. In July 2004 Hurricane Pam, a five-day simulation, was conducted. Federal, state, local, and volunteer organizations participated in this imaginary disaster. However, despite the predictions and computer simulations, when Hurricane Katrina struck, authorities were still unprepared, and the predicted became a reality.

Disaster preparedness is not something modern. Noah preached, warned, and prepared for the impending disaster that was to come upon this world. People participated in the preparation, but because they had never seen rain, they failed to prepare themselves for the eventuality of the flood. Unfortunately, of the thousands of people living then, only eight family members were saved. What a disaster!

Our text for today issues the warning that people are still basically the same. Just as it was in the days of Noah, so shall it be in our day. The Bible gives us adequate warning signs of the end of this world in Matthew 24. These are accurate predictions that should not be ignored. Because an event like this is beyond our imagination, the warning signs are largely ignored by the majority, and the impending doom will catch many unprepared.

I pray today that as we go about our busy lives we will take the time to sound the warning and encourage our family members, friends, loved ones, and strangers to be prepared for the second coming of Christ.

ANDREA A. BUSSUE

How to Be Content With a Mansion

I am not saying this because I am in need, for I have learned to be content whatever the circumstances. I know what it is to be in need, and I know what it is to have plenty. I have learned the secret of being content in any and every situation, whether well fed or hungry, whether living in plenty or in want. Phil. 4:11, 12, NIV.

"I WANT TO WAIT FOR MY MANSION IN HEAVEN!" I told my husband. I had grown up with a frugal father. So when I found myself married to Ed, a more-than-generous man, I felt he was careless, extravagant, and wasteful. Ed had grown up with poverty and misery, so he determined that his family would have the best. He worked hard to make that happen. He always returned tithe, paid the bills, and gave generously to charities. But he used the rest to be generous with himself and his family. After a few years he insisted on building a house that seemed like a mansion to me.

Ungratefully, and in a tone that implied that he was less than righteous, I let him know, "I want to wait for my mansion in heaven."

One morning as I did my prayer journaling, I told God I was sorry about the house, but I had no control over my poor husband, who just didn't understand. Now I can almost hear God's chuckle at my self-righteous attitude as He graciously reminded me, "I have asked you to be content in whatever situation you are in. Please read Philippians 4:11, 12 in the Amplified version."

So I did. Paul says: "I have learned how to be content (satisfied to the point where I am not disturbed or disquieted) in whatever state I am. I know how to be abased and live humbly in straitened circumstances, and I know also how to enjoy plenty and live in abundance." God continued with His tactful rebuke: "When Ed was in dental school, he made the decision that you would not work, since you had a new baby. Then you were content to live simply and had fun watching Me supply your needs. Now I am asking you to be content with plenty as your way of obeying Me. I want you to accept graciously the gift your husband is giving you. It's not Ed giving it to you, anyway—I'm the one. You are really complaining against My goodness."

I praised God for showing me His truth and His reality so that I could apologize to my husband and begin enjoying God's and Ed's generosity.

LANA FLETCHER

Reliable Directions

In all thy ways acknowledge him, and he shall direct thy paths. Prov. 3:6.

 WE NEED HIGHWAY SIGNS. They keep traffic moving and alert us to everything from rest areas to food and overnight accommodations. They warn us of trouble, demand we halt, merge, yield, or proceed with caution. But not all signs are equal. Even uncomplicated directions can be confusing from behind the steering wheel, especially in the dark. Some signs are big and bold, making decisions easy. Some lurk behind trees and even other signs. Others hide in a tangled jungle of arrows, warnings, and instructions, creating nightmare confusion.

One rainy evening I had to drive to Philadelphia from New Jersey. I was new to the area, but the Internet directions sounded simple: a couple of major highways, a few turns—no problem. Step 1: "Take Interstate 295 North." As I eased onto the highway, I noticed the road was headed in a westerly direction, with the setting sun dancing on the moist windshield. Concern turned to confusion a few miles later at the sight of a prominent sign "I-295 North/I-95 South." Even a directionally impaired driver like me knows one can't travel north and south simultaneously. My mind reeled. If Philadelphia was southwest, why did the road signs read north and south on an east-west highway? I feared it would be impossible to arrive at my appointment before daybreak.

I needed help. The familiar glow of an always-open convenience store illuminated the next exit. Studying their big multifold map, I realized that Interstate 295 is a circular highway connecting to Interstate 95 for a short time. I could clearly see that if I continued to follow Interstate 95, ignoring the directional notations, I would arrive at my destination.

Today lots of voices are giving life instructions. Some say "Get all you can"; others advocate meditation and austerity. Some believe in prelife, afterlife, and multiple life. There are God-believing moralists, and moralists with no known foundation. Some yearn to earn salvation, and others believe that nothing they do will block heaven's doors. The myriad of directions can send the searcher reeling back and forth, wondering if anything can lead to the peace and happiness they seek. Looking at God's big picture eases the confusion. Only in Christ do we give up to gain, kneel down to lift up, and surrender to win, when we allow God to direct our path.

SHIRLEY KIMBROUGH GREAR

Just One Day Away

Blessed are they that mourn: for they shall be comforted. Matt. 5:4.

IT WAS A 2001 CALENDAR BOOK with headings labeled "Thanksgiving." At the bottom of each page were two other headings: "Requests" and "Answers." On April 16 I wrote: "Thank You, Lord, for my mother's 85 years. Although she is fine physically, her mental state is weak. . . . And please, Lord, don't let my mother suffer." In the bottom section I wrote, "Please keep Judy and George in good health so they can continue to care for others as they serve you."

The next month Mother moved to California with Judy, her caretaker. Though we would be miles apart, I knew the kind of loving care she would receive. Judy and I talked often, and Mother adjusted to her new home. She attended church and went on short trips with Judy.

In August we were packed and ready to leave for California on a Thursday morning, anticipating seeing Mother. On Wednesday night I received a call from Judy about a slight problem with Mother. About 10 minutes later Judy called back. "Oh, Marie, she's gone!" Thinking she meant to the hospital, I asked, "Gone where?" There was a pause; then I knew immediately that my mother had died.

My heart was broken because I missed seeing my mother by just one day. I found out that Mother went peacefully to sleep. She did not suffer. God had answered my prayer.

The Lord has placed many good Christian friends in my path, many that I, an only child, consider my sisters, for they have walked this path with me. The prayers of my Christian family buoyed me up.

This experience teaches me never to doubt God, for His promises are true. It's never easy to lose your mother, no matter how old she is, but God wraps His arms around us to comfort us. He knows what it is like.

I grieve, but I have hope in the coming resurrection. I grieve, but I will be comforted. Christ says so, and He does comfort.

My greatest wish is to be among those who, along with our resurrected loved ones, will meet the Savior around His throne, where there'll be neither death nor tears, and where we will live forever.

MARIE H. SEARD

Chosen Soil

He is a chosen vessel unto me, to bear my name before the Gentiles, and kings, and the children of Israel. Acts 9:15.

I LOOKED AT THE VIOLET that usually greeted me each morning—delicate, rich, royal purple velvet petals with golden-centered middles. The leaves drooped over the edge of the pot. I was sure that the plant was dying. I looked closely and realized that my precious plant had outgrown the pot. The soil could no longer provide the nutrients necessary for its growth.

I found a bigger pot, large enough to accommodate more soil for my loved plant. Shovel in hand, I trekked to the garden, searched for the right spot, and cleared it, removing the leaves, sticks, stones, and grass. I then thrust my tiny shovel deep into the rich red soil. Satisfied that I had chosen the right soil, I filled the new pot, ready for the transplant. Sure enough—a couple weeks after the transplant, my violet was smiling with me again. Its succulent petals reached for the sky, as though in an act of praise.

The soil did not choose itself; I chose it. It was disturbed from its cozy resting place and crammed into a restrictive pot. The soil gave freely of its nutrients to the plant that could not survive without it. It could have resisted and decided not to give of its nutrients to the violet, but it did not.

How much are our lives like that of the soil that I chose for my African violet! God has chosen you today. He recognizes your abilities and asks you to give freely to those who are in need. You can continue to be a strong tower of strength to those who are weak. He values your ability to put others at ease. He commends you for your kindness, even when you are in need. He appreciates your willingness to nurture those around you and to comfort those who mourn.

God has chosen you as His rich soil. You are His hands. You are His feet. You are the one who can make a difference for those around you each day as you give of yourself. You can carry good tidings to those you will reach for Him—today.

GLORIA GREGORY

Thought: Perhaps you have never likened yourself to dirt before, but just think for a few minutes about all the things we would not be able to enjoy if it were not for good soil.

Angels

Praise the Lord, you his angels, you mighty ones who do his bidding, who obey his word. Ps. 103:20, NIV.

I BELIEVE IN ANGELS, DON'T YOU?

When my younger daughter was a college student near Washington, D.C., I went to visit her one Sunday. Living on the Eastern Shore in Maryland, I am used to less traffic than I find on the beltway around that city, so I am very nervous driving there. A few minutes after entering the beltway, I heard a noise and felt a bump. I had a flat tire! Lord, help me! All this traffic is going by, and I don't know what to do. A minute later a Cadillac stopped, and a well-dressed man got out and asked me if I needed help. Seeing the tire, he deftly removed it, and in no time at all he had my spare tire in place. I rolled down the window to thank him and offer to pay, but he was already driving off into traffic.

One afternoon my daughter and I went to a park. There were a few people there also enjoying the warm spring weather. As we got ready to leave, I realized that I had locked my purse and my keys in the car! What could we do? There were no phones or houses nearby. Quietly we offered a prayer. God always knows where we are and when we need help, and has told us to call on Him. A young man we hadn't seen before came to our rescue. With a thin piece of metal he unlocked the door. As quickly as he came, he left; we didn't see him again.

Last week my daughter and her daughter drove to a mall a half hour away. As they neared the mall, they heard a strange noise, and the car engine sputtered—they were constantly afraid it was going to stop. They sent up an urgent prayer and got to the mall only to find total darkness. The electricity had been knocked out by an accident nearby. "Lord, please get us home safely; help the car to keep running." They got home safely and sent up a prayer of thanks.

The next morning my daughter had trouble getting the car started. When it finally did, she headed to the car dealership instead of school. She was told there was a serious problem—the man couldn't understand how she had driven it the few blocks. When she told him about their hour trip the night before, he shook his head and said, "It was a miracle." Yes, it was. She believes an angel was at the wheel all the way home. I believe in angels, don't you?

NELDA BIGELOW

Life's Giants

You come to me with a sword and with a spear and with a javelin; but I come to you in the name of the Lord of hosts, the God of the armies of Israel, whom you have defied. 1 Sam. 17:45, RSV.

HAVE YOU EVER NOTICED how much all children like stories? And they not only enjoy new stories, but are very pleased to hear the same ones again, the stories that they've already heard many, many times. They like to have the stories read even after they've memorized the words. My children are no different. They really enjoy stories, especially stories from the Bible. Among these stories are some that we always have to repeat.

My 5-year-old never tires of hearing, seeing, and watching the story of David and the giant Goliath. In spite of the fact that we already own several videotapes with this story, and also an assorted number of books, each time he discovers something new with pictures that are different he asks us to buy it for him.

As I read this story to him again, I began to think of little David and his gigantic faith. David did not need to become involved with the war that was taking place; however, he could not tolerate the insults that Goliath made toward his people, much less the insults being directed toward his God. Without hesitation he courageously decided to face Goliath, and was victorious.

This episode makes me think of our daily activities. Many giants appear along our way that we must face, and if we don't have faith in God, we do what Saul's army did. We will not fight, and we will end up being overcome. On the other hand, if we have faith like that of David, the Lord will give us victory.

These giants, which present themselves to us in the form of financial problems, problems at work, unemployment, accidents, fears, and problems with our spouse or children, will be overcome, one by one, when we have God on our side. We should not forget that trust in God was the main weapon used by David. Without this trust he would never have reached his objective.

Certainly David was a young man who had a true personal relationship with God. Let's follow his example, and with Jesus, the Lord Almighty, we will be victorious over all the giants that we shall face in this war between good and evil, even while we are still on this earth.

LUCIANA RIBEIRO DE MATTOS

What Was Lost Is Found

Or suppose a woman has ten silver coins and loses one. Does she not light a lamp, sweep the house and search carefully until she finds it? And when she finds it, she calls her friends and neighbors together and says, "Rejoice with me; I have found my lost coin." Luke 15:8, 9, NIV.

WHILE A STUDENT MISSIONARY IN NORWAY I visited Denmark to meet some relatives for the first time. To my dismay, when I arrived I discovered that the bag I had packed with my computer and digital camera cables was missing. I felt sick—now I couldn't show the photographs of my family on my laptop. Nevertheless, we enjoyed the visit.

Returning home the following week, I experienced more dismay when the bag was not there either. I must have left it at the place I visited before my trip to Denmark. I called to see.

"I don't remember seeing it, but I'll look when I get home!" my friend promised. But her e-mail said the bag was nowhere to be found.

I despaired. They would cost so much to replace! Where else could it be? I entreated my Best Friend, and He reminded me where else I had opened my backpack: the Oslo-Copenhagen ferry, the Skodsborg School of Physiotherapy, the train in Denmark, and downtown Copenhagen.

I began calling. The woman at the ferry sympathized as she rummaged through lost items. "I'm not the only forgetful one?" I joked.

"Oh no—there are all kinds of things here," she said. But neither her search, nor the school's, nor the train's, yielded anything I wanted.

That evening at church I announced, "I have a far-fetched prayer request—but isn't that what God is best at?" The congregation groaned as I listed my lost items and asked for prayer.

Later I was going out—had already left, actually, but returned to get something—when the phone rang. "We have your computer cables," a man from the ferry said.

"Thank you so much! I have been praying fervently!" I exclaimed spontaneously.

He chuckled, promising to mail the bag the next day. I received the bag nearly three weeks after losing it, and everything was there.

If God cares about my computer cables, trivial things soon to pass away, how much more He will provide for my essential needs!

EMILY THOMSEN

I Saw My Guardian Angel

See, I am sending an angel ahead of you to guard you along the way and to bring you to the place I have prepared. Ex. 23:20, NIV.

ONE DAY MY WORK PARTNER became ill, and in a moment's time I had to travel alone from Huaraz to Pomabamba, in Peru, to deliver the books we were selling.

That morning I went to an intersection where I had to wait for a bus that was headed to Pomabamba. If the bus came at the expected time, 3:00 or 4:00 p.m., I would arrive at 11:00 or 12:00 the following morning. But the bus didn't come. What should I do? I became frightened, thinking that I would have to spend the night along the highway. About then a truck appeared with a driver and his helper. When they told me that they were going to Sihuas, I asked if they could take me to where there was a family that I knew. They assured me that this was possible. Then they went to a small roadside stand to buy some food.

I was still afraid and thought, *How can I travel alone with two men I don't know?* I began to cry. Immediately a police officer approached me. I don't know where he came from because I hadn't noticed him before. He asked me where I was going and what type of work I did. When I explained that I sold religious books, he complimented me on my work and recommended that I should take my books to another province.

He inspired me with so much confidence that I asked him to suggest to the truck driver that he should take me to Pomabamba. "Right away, señorita," he answered, and quickly went to the roadside stand. Then I thought, *How could I have asked him to suggest this to the driver when I don't know him and he doesn't know the driver?*

But I am certain that my guardian angel presented himself to me in the form of the police officer to encourage me. God had sent that truck especially for me, because the driver changed his plans. He not only took me to Ponabamba but also to Piscobamba, a nearby town where I had to deliver books.

Coincidence? No! We have a wonderful Father who attends to our needs. I invite you to give your life and your plans to Him, and He will do wonderful things for you, too.

MARGOLÍ SAAVEDRA PANDURO

The Marks of Friendship

If someone asks him, "What are these wounds on your body?" he will answer, "The wounds I was given at the house of my friends." Zech. 13:6, NIV.

WHEN OUR GOD CREATED PEOPLE, He knew, in His infinite wisdom, that a person could not live alone. People soon realize the necessity of another person. In this context we are able to consider not only the creation of Eve, but also the true friendship of God with Adam and Eve. They talked with God. It was a relationship between friends—Father and child.

Only through constant and sincere relationship is it possible to discover someone's necessities, and truly the first bonds of friendship began in Eden between God and Adam and Eve. God did not create the human being as an island, to live alone and be isolated. We were all created to live in society, in the company of others and, better yet, to have friends.

Friendship extends throughout all of history, and in the Bible we find the examples of Moses and Aaron, David and Jonathan, Naomi and Ruth, and Jesus and Lazarus.

Friendship is beneficial because it was instituted by God, and when it is developed in a sincere and loyal manner, it is something precious. Whether it is between brothers and sisters, relatives or friends, it elevates us and provides the potential for a life of complete harmony.

When Jesus lived on earth, He was almost always in the company of others, sometimes with a group of people, at other times with a multitude. He chose the twelve, His disciples, to be His best friends, however. At other times He took time to stay alone and pray for His friends.

There is no greater treasure than true friendship, and among all of our friendships we should consider Jesus as our best friend. Lazarus chose Jesus as His best friend, and the result of this friendship was life; Jesus, who is life, returned it to Lazarus. Let's follow Lazarus' example. Let's chose Jesus as our best friend.

Each day tell the Lord Jesus, "Even though I have many friends, You will always be my best friend, because I want to embrace You and thank You personally for the marks that seal our friendship—friendship proven by the nail scars in Your hands."

MARICÉLIA DE ALMEIDA SILVA

Thought: Sometimes it is hard to make friends—harder for some people than for others. How do you make Jesus your best friend?

Role Model

Every way of a man is right in his own eyes: but the Lord pondereth the hearts. Prov. 21:2.

WE NEVER KNOW WHAT OUR INFLUENCE on another person may be. What we say or don't say, what we wear or don't wear, what we read, what we watch, what we eat—all are part of our influence. We may be a role model for someone without even realizing it.

I remember a ninth-grade teacher who took the time to counsel me when I became unruly in another teacher's class and was sent to the principal's office. It happened several times. The principal would shake his head, then tell me to wait for the bell before I went on to my next class. I found the class boring, and the principal didn't want to deal with me. When the vice principal, my ninth-grade teacher, found me outside the office, she instructed me to come and see her after school. I found myself visiting her for 10 to 15 minutes for five very long afternoons. She would tell me that I could do better in class and that she didn't want to see me sent out of class again. Then she would send me on to basketball practice, or glee club, or one of the other extracurricular activities I was involved in. I didn't want to listen to any more lectures, and I never was sent out of class again. I also knew that she really cared about me and cared about my actions. She took the time to show her concern and show me a better way. I never forgot that. Eventually I went on to college and to graduate school. She was one of my role models. She cared and took the time to show it.

We don't live in a vacuum. I still remember when certain things were going on in our church and a young couple told me, "We trust you to tell us the truth." I was head deaconess, and it put me in a difficult position. I had to be very careful not to damage other people's reputations or betray confidences, and yet find a way to encourage this young couple to keep their faith and trust in their church. It was the first time I actually realized that I was a role model for someone else. Even when we don't realize it, people are watching us, and we have influence.

My prayer for each of you, dear readers, is that you will consciously be the Lord's role model to someone today.

LORAINE F. SWEETLAND

Thought: Titus 2:1-3 admonishes older (not old) women to mentor younger women. How are you doing that?

Being a Professional Christian

He who says he abides in Him ought himself also to walk just as He walked.
1 John 2:6, NKJV.

WHILE DRIVING HOME the other day via Oregon's Interstate 5, I got stuck behind a big rig laboring up a steep hill. In an effort to diffuse my growing irritation over this unexpected delay, I read all the signs on the back of the truck, starting with the license plates and moving on up. Plastered somewhere in the lower left quadrant of the rear trailer door was a blatantly posted notice. It not only caught my eye but also gave me pause for reflection.

It stated, "I'm a professional driver. My conduct and driving skills are on display. If you have any comments, please phone [and 800 number followed]." When I finally had the opportunity to pull out into the passing lane in order to get around him, I chose not to. Instead (since the posted notice had invited me to do so), I stayed where I was for the next seven miles in order to assess this driver's "conduct and driving skills." In that distance the driver of that rig did nothing to suggest that he was anything other than a seasoned professional with courteous motoring conduct and precautionary driving skills.

I suddenly reflected that whenever I am out on life's "highway," I too am on display as a Christian. The apostle John states that if we say we abide in Christ—in other words, if we claim to be "professional" Christians—then we will walk (or drive) as Christ did (see today's verse). Christians should reflect the attributes of Jesus. There are many, but let's review just a few:

Contentment for whatever blessings we have (2 Cor. 12:9, 10; Phil. 4:11-13). Faith that trusts God to supply all our needs (Phil. 4:19; Eph. 3:20). Loving forgiveness toward those who have wronged us (Luke 6:27; 1 Peter 4:8; 1 John 4:7). Praise instead of anxiety and worry (Phil. 4:4, 6; 1 Thess. 5:18). Assurance that He is bigger than any fear, problem, or enemy (1 John 4:4; Isa. 49:25; 59:19; Prov. 1:33; 29:25; 2 Tim. 1:7-9). Moderation in, or elimination of, life practices that harm us physically or morally (Eccl. 3:1; Phil. 4:5, 8). Are you confident that your "conduct and driving skills" rightly represent your walk with God, or do you need help? When we ask God to help us represent Him aright, He will answer our prayer (Phil. 4:13, 19)! We will then be the professional Christians we want to be.

CAROLYN RATHBUN SUTTON

No More Aching Feet!

And your feet shod with the preparation of the gospel of peace. Eph. 6:15.

 "TAKE CARE OF YOUR FEET; they're all you have to get around on," said Grandad. As a child I thought this to be quite funny, but as I matured I realized it wasn't funny at all. I never forgot his words.

All was well until I ordered a pair of nursing shoes that didn't fit my feet properly. It was then that I learned that you don't break shoes in—the shoe should fit comfortably the first time you try it on. If it doesn't fit, keep trying on shoes until you find a pair that does. I now understand why Mother had me try on several pairs of shoes when buying new shoes for me. Size doesn't matter, neither is it important. I came to this conclusion after noticing a small aching knot sitting on the side of each of my big toes. It appeared that I thought more of the shoes than I did my feet. What a valuable lesson to learn!

Since that time I've come to realize that I have plenty of company. Most adults, regardless of their ethic background, gender, or culture, complain of some kind of discomfort regarding their feet. Some suffer with swollen ankles, spurs, corns, bunions, arthritic toes, calluses, ingrown toenails, bouts with ringworms, pigeon toes—the list goes on and on. Some problems are due to carelessness, and some to natural causes, but all are problems.

It doesn't matter if you're walking on tile, hardwood, concrete, asphalt, cobblestone, unpaved roads, or carpeted floors—nothing makes one feel more defeated than a pair of hurting feet. We become distressed and adamant about going to the podiatrist. We know long before we get there that chances are we'll feel much worse before finding that comfort we so desperately seek.

It's imperative that we use our feet, as well as whatever other means we're given, to carry the gospel from one end of the earth to the other. "How beautiful on the mountains are the feet of those who bring good news, who proclaim peace, who bring good tidings, who proclaim salvation" (Isa. 52:7, NIV). I often think of Granddad's words, but I tend to focus more on the day that I will be given wings with which to fly—and a new pair of feet. What a glorious day that will be!

CORA A. WALKER

Where Two or Three Are Gathered

For where two or three come together in my name, there I am with them.
Matt. 18:20, NIV.

I WORK FOR A HOSPICE in the Appalachian Mountains. Hospice is a special way of caring for people who have a terminal illness and for their families. One of the questions that we ask patients and their families when they are first admitted to hospice care is "What has helped you in the past to deal with difficult situations?" Their answer to that question gives us an idea of how they have handled emotional pain in the past and what support they will need during this difficult time in their lives.

Sometimes people answer, "I have a large supportive family who is always there for me." Or: "Music helps me to relax." Or: "I cry and cry—my life has been so hard." But when they say, "I pray," or "I have a deep spiritual faith," we breathe a sigh of relief because we know that they already have some effective emotional skills that we can help them develop even further to enable them to grieve in a healthy manner.

Three separate families told me the following story within a period of several months as a result of this question. The families were not related, but they lived in the same community. The story took place in the 1940s during World War II.

At that time rural families in these mountains were large. Each of these families had several boys in their late teens and early 20s, as did their neighbors. Eight young men from this close community were drafted into service for their country. Eventually, all eight saw active overseas duty. The mothers grieved—so many young men never returned home. The women resolved to support these families by meeting daily at the community church to pray for the safe return of the young men.

So for the duration of the war these dear women walked to church every morning for their special prayer service. They didn't cancel the meeting when they were busy, or when the weather was bad. They walked every morning, many of them several miles, through the rain, snow, cold winds, planting season, heat, and harvest. They carried babies and toddlers. They prayed, and they didn't stop praying until each of the eight young men returned home—alive and unharmed.

CLARICE TURNER MURPHY

The Cross and the Crown

If any man will come after me, let him deny himself, and take up his cross, and follow me. Matt. 16:24.

Be thou faithful unto death, and I will give thee a crown of life. Rev. 2:10.

SIMON, A CYRENIAN, hastened toward home after several weeks of absence from his family. He was eager to get back, and he hoped that the crowd he could see in the distance would not delay his progress. As he gazed on the boisterous, angry crowd drawing closer to him, his sympathy and compassion was aroused. He realized Jesus was too weak to carry the cross, and his heart was touched with pity for the suffering Savior. Although Simon was not a follower of Jesus, he had heard about Him from his sons, and now he was convinced that Jesus did not deserve this cruel treatment.

As the Roman soldiers observed that Simon showed sympathy for Jesus, they were happy for the opportunity to take the cross from His bruised and fainting form and roughly place it on the shoulders of Simon. This solved their problem, since it was obvious that Jesus was falling and could no longer carry the cross to Calvary. None in the mob would voluntarily bear the humiliating load, and the Jewish leaders would not even think of that—the defilement would prevent them from participating in the feast of the Passover.

In commenting on this incident, my favorite Bible commentator, Ellen White, notes: "The bearing of the cross to Calvary was a blessing to Simon, and he was ever grateful for this providence. It led him to take upon himself the cross of Christ from choice, and ever cheerfully to stand beneath its burden" (*The Desire of Ages,* p. 742). I would like to imagine that Simon will wear a special crown in heaven for having carried the cross of Christ.

Today Jesus calls you and me to take up our cross and follow Him, and He promises us a crown if we are faithful. Each one must carry their own cross. Your cross might be illness, financial difficulties, unemployment, job complications, marital problems, family crisis, or even scholastic difficulties. Whatever the trial, dear friend, Jesus promises in today's text, "Be thou faithful unto death, and I will give thee a crown of life."

Dear Jesus, Thank You for bearing the cross for me. Please make me worthy to bear my cross and eventually to wear a crown.

OLGA I. CORBIN DE LINDO

Attitude Is Everything

A merry heart doeth good like a medicine: but a broken spirit drieth the bones. Prov. 17:22.

HAVE YOU EVER HEARD STATEMENTS such as "I could never do that" or "I will never be like that"? I was one of those people. I couldn't carry a tune in a teapot, couldn't knit or crochet. I wasn't a writer or a poet and couldn't paint anything more than a stick man. I didn't have a career and couldn't cook. My father always said, "She can even burn water." Neither could I ski or skate, and I was clueless about computers. I admired people who mastered at least one of these things. My sister had the longest fingernails, and I was not pretty!

In the mid-1980s three people gave me positive statements that changed my life. One was my husband, who said jokingly, "That's why I married you—you know a little bit about everything." The second person was a painter who observed me over a period of time that I came to watch and admire the people painting pictures in the mall. "You can do it," he said. I decided to take him up on his statement. And the third person was my mother-in-law, who said, "I will teach you," when I admired her knitting and crocheting. So I decided to learn and master or succeed at something and focus on extracting any hidden skill that I might have.

I've learned something about a lot of things, accomplished some, and mastered a few. I can sew, knit, and crochet, and I have won ribbons for my paintings. I can run a computer and have even written poetry. I am a Sabbath school superintendent, work in women's retreats, and have given a few sermons. My career now is being a wonderful grandma and a good person. I am remodeling my home, and I have floral design, first aid, and child safety certificates. I'm a good-at-crafts person, and have taken life skills, speech, and writing courses.

I still can't carry a tune, and I can burn water. But slowly I have come to like me. I have come to realize that by taking on things—even if I thought I couldn't do it but was willing to learn—I can become a more positive person. And you can too.

I know the Lord will take my talents and use them for His glory. And now, as you can see, I am also a published writer!

VIDELLA MCCLELLAN

Thought: Many women lack confidence to take on new things. Look up 2 Corinthians 3:4-6—it gives the secret of confidence.

Untie My Knots

Turn, O Lord, and deliver me; save me because of your unfailing love.
Ps. 6:4, NIV.

 I HAVE BEEN BLESSED with three beautiful children. They are bright, busy children, and our home is never boring. One of the joys of having children is watching them grow, develop, and learn to do things for themselves. My youngest is 2 now, and one of his favorite expressions is "Do it myself!"

When my daughter was about 5 years old, she worked hard in learning to tie the laces on her sneakers. She had become independent enough that she wanted to do it herself—no help from Mom, please! At times I wanted to step in and do it for her, especially when we were hurrying to go somewhere. What was a struggle for her would have been so easy for me. One day she worked for more than 15 minutes putting her shoes on, then trying to get the laces untangled and tied. The more she struggled with the laces, the more tangled and knotted they became. Finally admitting defeat, she looked at me with her big brown eyes and said pitifully, "Mommy, untie my knots." My heart melted! I love my little girl so much, and I was happy to step in and untie her knotted shoelaces and put things right again.

This simple experience caused me to consider my relationship with God. My independent nature sometimes causes me to rush ahead and try to do everything myself. It's easy for me to forget to slow down and let God walk ahead in my life. What usually happens is that I mess things up and spend a lot of time and energy trying to untie the knots I've made of my life because I failed to turn it over to God in the first place. I'm so thankful that when I tearfully turn back to my heavenly Father, He always responds in love when I cry, "Father, untie my knots!"

May you be reminded today that God's love for you is unfailing. He wants to lead and guide in every aspect of your life. When life is difficult, when things don't go as you plan, when you've made mistakes, when the knots and knocks get bad, He is always there, waiting for you to turn to Him for help. Trust Him to untie your knots!

Sandra Simanton

Thought: Many Bible women also made a mess of their lives. Make a list of as many of them as you can and note the results. Do we now think of her positively, or negatively? What made the difference?

My Best Friend

There is a friend who sticks closer than a brother. Prov. 18: 24, NKJV.

MY BEST FRIEND knows everything about me. She knows the lines on my face and the sparkle in my eyes. She knows what hurts me, she knows what annoys me, and she knows what brings joy to my heart. We've been best friends since we were little girls. We've shared many of life's experiences, and we share our joys and our sorrows. She laughs with me and cries with me. She's a very positive person who always looks for the good in others. She comforts me, advises me, and, most of all, she loves and accepts me just as I am, warts and all. She's an amazing inspiration in my life. Her love for our heavenly Father shines through in all that she says and does. We chat often, and it brings me so much comfort and joy to know that she is willing to talk to me any time of the day or night.

I miss my best friend. I long to see her more often—to see her smile, to hear her laugh. You see, I've seen my best friend only twice in the past 24 years. We live on opposite sides of the world—an expanse of ocean separates us. Circumstances and time make it difficult to visit each other, but she is always in my heart and is still my best friend. I wish I could share her with you so that you could enjoy her friendship too.

That may not be possible, but there is another best friend I can share with you. Jesus is the ultimate best friend. He knows everything about you. He knows every line on your face and the sparkle in your eyes. He knows what makes you smile and what brings you joy. He feels your pain and shares your tears. He longs to hold you in His arms and tell you how much you mean to Him. Psalm 139 tells us that God knew you before you were born. He watched you being formed in your mother's womb. He knows when you sit and when you lie down. He planned every day of your life. He is always willing and waiting to talk to you any time of the day or night. He misses you, just as I miss my best friend. He longs for you to share everything about your life with Him, your joy and your pain. He longs to comfort you. He accepts you just as you are because He loves you and He created you. There is nothing that separates you from Him. Most of all, He has promised that one day you will be able to see Him face to face! What a best friend! Won't you make Jesus your best friend today?

DEBBIE STEYN SYMES

God's Peace

You will keep him in perfect peace, whose mind is stayed on You, because he trusts in You. Isa. 26:3, NKJV.

I'M SO GLAD I don't know the end from the beginning! But I'm also glad that God does know.

I enjoy my work, I thought, as I finished massaging one of my patients. *Besides, it's nice to have people to talk to, and I feel good— although I know I'll have to retire someday, maybe next year.* About an hour later one of the company owners came into the office. After greeting several people, he turned to me. "I need to speak to you privately, Mildred."

We went to a side room, where my boss began telling me how valuable I had been throughout my years of working with the company, and how much everyone—staff and patients—loved me. Then came the *however.* "I have decided to get a full-time therapist to cover this office instead of the two part-time people I am using presently. It's hard to tell you this, but he will be starting the second Monday of next month. You will stay through his first week to get him oriented, and your last day will be on the fifteenth."

I was in shock! Only a few minutes before I'd been thinking about how much I enjoyed my work. How could this be happening? Yet I could sense God's still small voice whispering, "I have never forsaken you, and I will not forsake you now." That reassurance was keeping me outwardly calm.

My boss stood up to leave as he continued to tell me how valuable I had been and how sorry he was to bring me such bad news. Sensing he was fighting back tears, I reached out and gave him a hug.

The company gave me two termination checks and a retirement party that included my family. I was able to enjoy the festivities because God had given me some of His perfect peace. I'm learning to have less money and much more free time, but I'm so grateful for God's sustaining power. I'm also learning that when God allows one door to be closed, He opens another one. What a wonderful God we serve! May we trust Him today and every day, knowing that whatever happens, He loves us and is taking care of us in the way that is best.

MILDRED C. WILLIAMS

Faith of a Little Child

Faith that doesn't lead us to do good deeds is all alone and dead. James 2:17, CEV.

I COULDN'T SLEEP. Lots of unpleasant thoughts flashed across my mind. I felt lonely. My children were in different places of responsibility and study programs, and my husband was on his usual itinerary. I closed my eyes and lay still for a long time. Wild thoughts attacked me, and sleep was very far away. I thought, *What if . . . my son is not careful when he drives to his workplace . . . my daughter neglects her cold and fever till she becomes worse . . . my youngest one doesn't get a proper place to stay? And what if my husband sleeps too long, because he is tired, and misses the next train connection?* Never-ending thoughts. I prayed, *Lord , give me peace of mind that I may go to sleep.* But I received neither sleep nor peace.

Morning came with its routine business. I got up with a heavy body and a heavier mind. I called my children first thing. During the course of our talk, I expressed my worries about them. They listened patiently and tried to comfort me with soothing and encouraging words. The comment of my youngest son stopped me: "Mom, you have so many blessings to be thankful for, and you don't have enough faith to trust in God." How true it was. It took my son, younger in years and experience, to teach me that great lesson. It was a rekindling thought for me.

Yes, I am grateful to the Lord, so I thanked Him for a happy married life with a very loving and understanding husband, and for three lovely children. I thanked Him for supportive parents and siblings and helpful in-laws, who accepted me as their own. I thanked God for friendly neighbors and colleagues. I thanked God for the very life that is granted to me.

Further, I understood that if I had faith as little as a mustard seed I could have slept like a mountain. From now on, as best as I can, I will leave my mountain of worries with my Lord and request that little mustard seed of faith.

And you know what? Every night since, I've slept with that mustard seed of faith, and I've slept well—like a mountain.

MARGARET TITO

Thought: All of us have times we can't sleep, sometimes from worry. There are several good Bible texts regarding worry that you might want to memorize. One is Philippians 4:6, 7.

Emerald Hunting

Whatever is true, whatever is noble, whatever is right, whatever is pure, whatever is lovely, whatever is admirable—if anything is excellent or praiseworthy—think about such things. Phil. 4:8, NIV.

MY HUSBAND AND TWO SONS were looking around the field and caves by the edge of a lake in Norway. All around them were coarse, ugly rocks piled in untidy heaps. Nathan kicked at a stray rock. It looked like dried mud to him, useless and boring. But as it rolled away from him, something sparkled in the sunlight. When he turned the rock over, he saw clusters of tiny emeralds hiding underneath. What had looked like mud was really treasure!

When we look at other people we often see only the mud and not the emeralds. But I've never yet met a person who was only mud! When I look hard enough, I've found that I can always find some emeralds. Here are some emerald-hunting tips:

Put yourself in other people's shoes for a while. Think about others until you are filled with wonder at how they manage their life so well, considering all their circumstances.

Make a list of everything that the other person does well. Turn any characteristic you see as negative upside down, and find a different way to describe it. For example: Kate finds it hard to plan ahead, but she could also be described as choosing to be spontaneous.

When someone does something that unintentionally disappoints you, reframe their actions positively—find different ways to describe what they are doing. (The slow driver in front of you could be described as someone who is preventing you from getting a speeding fine!)

Whenever you catch yourself thinking a negative thought about someone, stop yourself, pick up the thought, and turn it over until it becomes something positive. When you're tempted to say something critical about someone, stop and find an appreciative thing to say instead.

Develop a sense of humor. Finding the gentle humor in a situation can help you to think positively about others. And when you are talking to people, highlight their emeralds by asking questions that will help them to look for positive qualities in themselves and others.

When you begin to look for emeralds in other people, you'll be amazed at what you'll find! And you'll begin to see people as God sees them. We're much more precious than emeralds in His eyes!

KAREN HOLFORD

Whom Shall I Send?

As my Father hath sent me, even so send I you. John 20:21.

LET ME TELL YOU about two outstanding experiences that I've had in praying for non-Christian friends.

As a young Muslim widow, Manosha and her two girls said goodbye to fly to Iran. I asked when they would come back to Delhi. "In a month, but we will come back by train," she replied. Shaking my head, I told her it was not safe by train. Rape is common on the train. I urged them to come back by air, but Manosha said in a sad tone, "I do not have money to fly back." Clasping her hands, I said, "I will be praying to the God that you know, the God of Abraham, to help you fly back." She smiled and said, "Thank you, Annie."

When it was time for Manosha and her girls to return to Delhi, her father was ready to book the train ticket, but Manosha stopped him. "Wait, Dad, because Annie is praying for us to get the money to fly back."

A few days later the postman handed a registered letter to Manosha's dad. Inside was a check for $2,000 as a royalty for a book he had authored 11 years earlier. He had actually given up ever getting the royalty.

My little Hindu friend Survi shouted with joy, "Grandma, guess what happened to me in school today?" Little Survi and I had been praying for two months about the ugly growth on her forehead. Her parents had gone to many doctors to have the growth removed, but they refused to perform the surgery. So Survi wore her hair in a fringe to hide the ugly lump.

I'd been talking to Survi about the living God, who can do what is impossible. Daily, with Survi by my side, I prayed about this ugly lump. And with that faith in God, I also did some work. I tied the lump at its base with a sewing thread. Looking up to me, Survi said, "I wish this lump would drop off before my birthday." On Survi's birthday something did happen. As Survi wrote a test in school, she suddenly noticed the ugly lump on her paper. As she broke the news, I clasped her hands and said, "God did it!" She repeated, "The living God did it!"

My prayer, Lord, is "Use me today to be a true witness to the dying world."

ANNIE M. KUJUR

Seasonings

Let your conversation be always full of grace, seasoned with salt, so that you may know how to answer everyone. Col. 4:6, NIV.

 THEY WERE GROUPED AROUND THE TABLE on the patio. Adolescent lunch. A step up from the tea parties of yesteryear. I watch the three of them. Suddenly my reminiscing was shattered by the crash of chairs. And screams.

Hurrying from the family room, I saw Melissa doubled over with laughter, tears squeezing from her eyes because she was laughing so hard. Nell, on the other hand, was standing in the middle of the table, her arms wrapped around the umbrella pole, screeching her head off. Daisy was off to one side, face red, veins protruding on her neck, hands fisted.

Nell stopped screaming, and Daisy's voice broke the silence. "Way to ruin a perfect meal!" Her words bit through clenched teeth. "A mouse! Yuck!"

I had the picture. In no time the mess was cleaned up, Nell pried from the umbrella pole, and peace restored. Over pink lemonade the talk turned to why each girl had presented such a different response. "Probably because your brain is a sack of hormones," I mused. "Think of it as a pot of stew. Now, metaphorically dump in a tablespoon of chili powder. What will happen?"

"It will taste very hot, of course, and I'd need to be careful not to burn my mouth," Melissa offered.

"You might have to remove your sweater if you ate a lot," added Nell.

"And if you added sage or a bay leaf instead?"

"An entirely different taste . . ." Melissa's voice trailed off in comprehension.

"Think of your thoughts as seasonings to the stew that is your brain," I continued. "If you want hot, eye-tearing behavior, add rage. For a different response, choose a different seasoning."

It was such fun chatting with the girls about how our thoughts can alter the chemicals in our brain. And how, because of the close and continuous chemical messenger service between the brain and the body, the chemical changes to the brain impact every cell in our body.

"It would appear," said Melissa in her most grown-up voice, "that the seasonings we dump in our brain stew show up as behaviors." She was right. I prayed that they would make good seasoning choices.

ARLENE TAYLOR

God's Protection

For it is written, "He will give angels charge of you, to guard you."
Luke 4:10, RSV.

I WAS GOING TO MY FRIEND'S GRADUATION, and my shoes were torn! I sat down, wondering where I'd get other shoes, when my husband came in. "Honey, here is some money to use while you're away." I stared disbelievingly at the 1,000 Kenya shillings. It was as if he knew that I had a problem. I just didn't know how to thank him! I whispered a short prayer thanking God for His wonderful care and asking Him to guard me throughout my journey.

I boarded a bus as soon as I reached the station, but the bus didn't leave. I became very anxious about the delay, since traveling at night was no longer safe. I felt powerless, unable to control the circumstances.

We arrived very late in the night. Fear filled my heart, as it was very dark; only vehicle lights gave a small glimpse of light. I felt even more concerned as I heard people talking about the danger of the next junction. I whispered a short prayer: "Lord, I'm in a dilemma; do not forget me. Let me not make wrong decisions. Send Your holy angels to protect me from danger."

I constantly reminded the driver to drop me at the next junction. He stopped at that junction, but my heart almost skipped a beat as I saw drunkards staggering along the road. In addition, the road to the college was impassable after a heavy rain. I didn't know what to do. A woman in the back seat said, "Don't dare get off here!" I made up my mind to continue on the bus. The money that my husband had given me that morning gave me confidence that I would be able to pay if I could get a hotel.

Soon we were at another small town. The conductor went to find out about the hotel, but something inside me told me that it was not a safe place. A woman seated behind me said, "In the town ahead there are good hotels. Please be calm; I'll show you."

At the last destination she took the time to escort me to a cheap, safe hotel. The driver assisted me to the place without any extra pay. I sincerely thanked each one of them for the kind actions. I'll never forget to praise God, who was my shelter and my stronghold that day. God's presence was seen and felt in the difficult incidences. God sent His angels to guard and protect me. The torn shoes provided the extra money needed for a hotel that night, and I managed to continue my journey safely the next day.

MARGRET NYARANGI BUNDI

Final

But they that wait on the Lord shall renew their strength; they shall mount up with wings as eagles; they shall run, and not be weary; and they shall walk, and not faint. Isa. 40:31.

LAST WEEK I RECEIVED A PHONE CALL from a friend of mine. She told me that her mother had suffered a stroke and had been rushed to intensive care. She asked if I would take her to see her. So after work she and I, along with two other friends, headed to the hospital. As we entered the small room, I stared at the equipment surrounding the bed. The electronic beep of the heart monitor provided an immediate reality check to the seriousness of the situation. Judy lay in the bed, unconscious and unresponsive. I encouraged my friend to hold her mother's hand, and watched as she gently combed her hair, then wiped her face.

Minute melted slowly into minute, and for some reason I found myself drawn to watching the heart monitor. My friends chatted easily with one another, trying to sound more cheery than they felt, but still I watched the monitor. At first I thought I was imagining it, but slowly I realized that Judy's heart was slowing down.

Silently I slipped out of the room to find the nurse on duty. As we reentered the room, it grew still. The nurse checked each machine carefully, and then looked at her watch—and then we knew. She was making a note of the time of death. Looking up at me, she quietly said, "I'm so sorry." It took just a moment—but the answer was final. Judy was gone.

At home once again, I wrestled with the realization of how frail we humans are—here today and gone tomorrow. A question pounded in my mind: *Where is my relationship with my God?* I thought of my constant busyness at home, at church, and at work. Was it to the neglect of deepening my relationship with my God? In my haste, was I missing the truly important things in life? Somewhere along the way I had forgotten how much God desired to commune with me.

Dear Lord, thank You for the hunger You place within me for more of You. Slow me down so I don't rush past You. Keep me still so I don't miss Your whisper, breathing new life into my weary heart. May I feel Your touch today and know the calm assurance that whatever may be happening around me or within me, it can be well with my soul—because You are there!

CORDELL LIEBRANDT

In My Father's Arms

I sought the Lord, and he answered me; he delivered me from all my fears. Ps. 34:4, NIV.

CRACKING THUNDER AND FLASHING LIGHTNING are frightening and cause fear, especially in a little 5-year-old girl.

I was scared to death of this spectacle of nature. I wanted to hide under the bed when a storm came, or better yet, snuggle up in my father's strong arms. When he was beside me, I was not afraid. I felt safe and protected; however, he was not always nearby when there was a thunderstorm. There is, however, a Father who is always present on all occasions, and it was to Him that I turned when I was very little, because I already understood the kindness of His love.

The afternoon was dark and gloomy. It seemed the world was going to fall on my head. So in my innocent and childlike faith I offered a fervent prayer: "Lord, I am afraid. I want to ask something special. I'm asking that it never rain hard again—with lightning and thunder."

From that moment on I felt an immense peace, and I realized that I was in the arms of my Father and that I was well protected. Of course, the rain, thunder, and lightning continued—and they will continue to happen, but never again like those earlier frightening storms. Now I realize that I found rest and am no longer afraid of these phenomena. Jesus did more than what I had asked for—He removed my fear.

Our conception of God's care is very narrow. We don't claim the power of the love and presence of the Father, who is waiting and wanting us to ask. We need to exercise faith and claim these blessings.

Whatever may be causing a storm in our life, whatever may be causing us to hear thunder and feel the dark clouds that are leaving us in gloom, we can be certain that God always gives us a promise for each trial. He is ready to extend His hand to us. Serenely protected under His wings, we do not need to fear. Under His wings we are safe. We "find refuge in the shadow of your wings" (Ps. 36:7, NIV).

Let's hide ourselves in Him, overcoming the clouds of fear that surround our lives, rising up to the elevated heights of an innocent childhood faith.

NELCI DE ROCCO LIMA

Our Ugly Dog

The angel of the Lord encamps around those who fear him, and he delivers them. Ps. 34:7, NIV.

MY DAUGHTER CALLED OUT TO HER SON, Marc, as I set the table for lunch. After several minutes of no response, she asked, "Where's Marc?" I remembered seeing him in the front yard with Butch, our big part-this-and-part-that ugly dog. A sweeping look over the front and back yards found no boy or dog. A check with the neighbors confirmed that the two were not there, either.

I made a frantic call to the police to report a missing 3-year-old. The dispatcher on the phone encouraged us to stay calm. He assured us that an officer was on the way and advised us to stay close to the phone. My daughter was in near panic by now.

After what seemed an eternity, the phone rang. The dispatcher had received a call from a family reporting that a little boy was sitting in their front yard with a big part-this-and-part-that dog who was snarling at anyone attempting to approach. The dispatcher gave me the name of the street. It was more than a mile away! My daughter and I jumped into the car and arrived at our destination at the same time as the police cruiser.

In the front yard a dozen people were standing around watching. Three-year-old Marc sat on the grass with absolutely no fear in his face. Butch sat on his haunches two feet away. His eyes carefully watched the crowd with a ready snarl, showing teeth at any movement toward the boy. These people knew that this was a dog they dared not challenge.

As soon as Marc saw us, he smiled and waved. Butch wagged his tail with gusto. We walked over and sat down on the grass beside the two of them. Butch licked our faces, as if to say, "Well, where have you two been for the past hour?" He then walked over to the car and patiently waited until I opened the door for him to climb in.

Marc, safely in his mother's arms, told her that he and Butch had gone for a walk and gotten tired. We thanked the people for their concern and for the call they placed to the police. The officer expressed relief that this missing child report turned out favorably.

On that summer day was Butch more than just an ugly dog? Our hearts were full of praise and thanksgiving to the Lord for Butch, and that Marc was found safe.

MARIANNE TOTH BAYLESS

Fishing Trip

Simon answered, "Master, we've worked hard all night and haven't caught anything. But because you say so, I will let down the nets." Luke 5:5, NIV.

LUKE 5 TELLS THE STORY of a fishing trip. Jesus' disciples had been at sea the entire night and had caught nothing. At sunrise Jesus arrived at Lake Gennesaret and saw two boats, one of which belonged to Simon, His disciple. The crowd was near the lake to hear Jesus speak. He asked Simon to pull away from the shore so that He could preach to the multitude while seated in the boat. When He finished speaking, Jesus told Simon to throw the nets into the water. Simon replied that they had spent the entire night at sea and had caught nothing, but because of the word of Jesus, he would throw out the nets again. As he pulled them in, the nets were full of fish. Simon motioned to his companions in the other boat to come help him. Soon both boats were so full of fish that they almost sank.

Many times we struggle the entire "night" of our life, seeking to obtain answers to our problems. As the sun of a new day arises, we return, tired, with empty nets. The Master finds us cleaning the nets, giving up on everything. How many times have we thrown out our nets into the gloomy seas, looking for peace, happiness, and satisfaction, only to bring in nothing but old shoes, pieces of glass (which cut the net), and other junk? We continue to be empty, and even our empty nets have been ripped in places. We are wounded fishers who are tired and longing for peace.

Why not listen to the voice of the Master, and even though discouraged say, "Lord, the whole night we struggled. All night long we tried to solve problems, attempting to find solutions, and we were not able. However, on Your word we will throw out the nets." Then our life, like the nets that were cast into the sea by those fishermen long ago, will return to us full of peace, with marvelous answers, and we will be so blessed that our nets will overflow to the lives of those around us. We will be ready to hear the call of Jesus to be fishers for His kingdom, using the nets of the good news of His Word, bringing light and joy to the lives of others.

IANI DIAS LAUER-LEITE

Thought: How and when do you know to throw out your net? And can this net catch anything other than people?

Who Is My Mother?

Let the little children come to Me, and do not forbid them; for of such is the kingdom of heaven. Matt. 19:14, NKJV.

WHEN I WAS A CHILD AND TEENAGER, Mother's Day was a day to honor my mother. With our dad's help, we bought, or made, lovely gifts, and even tried to cook breakfast for Mommy. It was all about her and all she did for us. On this special day I also think of other women in my life who have been mothers to me. Mother's Day has become a day to honor any woman who has in some way mothered me, and there have been many.

I remember Sister Gabriel. What a wonderful mother she was to me! We chatted on the phone from time to time, and she always left me with words of wisdom for my life. I learned much from her about hospitality.

Then there was my aunt Ethlene, who was never a mother herself but who mothered so many. From childhood right into adulthood she was a mother to me. I remember learning my first Sabbath school songs and Bible stories at her knee. She instilled in me a love for children that even now encompasses my own children, and any and all children, wherever I go.

I can list many mothers who have influenced my life and showed me that a mother's love extends beyond her own children. It has to do, not with what I've done, but with who I am.

One of the most important examples we have of mothering is Jesus Himself. Remember when the mothers brought their children for Him to bless? He was tired; it had been a long day. Knowing this, His disciples didn't want Jesus to be disturbed by the playfulness of children; He had more important things to do. But like a true mother, Jesus looked beyond His own feelings and needs and saw only the expectant faces of the children; He felt their love and desire to be with Him, and that was all that mattered. He called them to Him and loved each one.

That is a mother's love, a love that reaches outside oneself and one's own needs to embrace another with the love of God. Are you a mother? Even without children the answer is yes. For God has called each woman to show His love, unconditionally, to those who need it most. That is what mothers do. Who is a mother? A mother is every woman who has God's love in her heart.

HEATHER-DAWN SMALL

Untraceable Ways

Oh, the depth of the riches both of the wisdom and knowledge of God! How unsearchable are His judgments and His ways past finding out! Rom. 11:33, NKJV.

HAVE YOU EVER BEEN LED BY GOD on mysterious, unpleasant, or difficult ways, ways that in the end you saw were in fact the most appropriate, the most favorable, for your spiritual life? For some time, as I have been at the Lord's feet, I've read the scripture in Romans 11:33. Each time, together with Paul, I have admired the riches of God's wisdom, being aware of human meanness and helplessness.

It's not easy to trust the ways and plans of God, but it brings the peace of Christ that passes all understanding. This peace I experienced fully in March 2003. It was a Saturday night, and my husband and I, in worship, were trying to bring God an acceptable offering through study, hymns, prayer, and especially our hearts. After a total surrender into God's hands, my husband fell asleep quickly. Not long after, I noticed he was in a coma, and had blood on his mouth.

I was alone, and I was frightened, not knowing what to do. I fell on my knees and asked God to show me what to do. Then I phoned Gabi, a neighbor and sister in the Lord. She came immediately and called an ambulance.

In a short time we reached the hospital. On the way to the ward, as by a miracle, my husband improved and began talking. After two days we were sent to the neurosurgical hospital in Bucharest for further tests. We stayed there several days, together in a semiprivate room with another patient, who was being taken care of by his mother and daughter.

The first night, the two women watched us when my husband and I prayed, and seemed interested. It gave us a wonderful occasion to witness for God. Mrs. Geta, Marta, and Petre, acknowledged that only God had made our encounter possible. We were able to spend time talking about God and His love, and by the end of the hospital stay all three of them promised me that they would be baptized.

Then I understood divine love once more, and I found the answer for the "why" that came from my husband's illness. Again I surrendered to God, asking Him to lead me in His ways—whether they are traceable or untraceable by me!

LIDIA FLORICEL

The Power
of Intercessory Prayer

Ask and it will be given to you; seek and you will find; knock and the door will be opened to you. Matt. 7:7, NIV.

MY MOTHER WAS A VERY SINCERE CHRISTIAN who always sought to be an example to her family. Ours was a large family of 10 children, a typical family living in the interior of south Brazil, making a living exclusively by farming and raising a small herd of animals.

My mother developed Christian fidelity, returning her tithe and offerings, praying every day to God, and asking for the Lord's blessing on her family. I saw her asking God that her children remain united and faithful to Him in whatever circumstance they might face.

Grandma Jeorgina, as she was lovingly called by her grandchildren, faced many trials and challenges in her life. She was aware that life was not always a bed of roses, and she always reminded us of the words of Jesus: "In the world you will have tribulation; but be of good cheer; I have overcome the world" (John 16:33, NKJV).

On one occasion when we had moved in search of better chances for work and new opportunities in life, Mother faced serious problems with her health. One Friday night she began to feel sharp pain in her kidneys—a kidney stone. In her anguish and suffering, she remembered that in front of our house lived a faithful Christian man, and she requested that we call him.

He kindly came and read the Bible and prayed earnestly, comforting my mother, stating that soon she would no longer feel any pain and would sleep calmly because Jesus had cured her. It wasn't long until her pain disappeared. She did sleep in peace, with immense gratitude in her heart for the healing that Jesus had accomplished in her life.

She never again had pain in her kidneys. The miracle was complete. Jesus' promise was fulfilled in her life. "Praise the Lord, O my soul, and forget not all his benefits—who forgives all your sins and heals all your diseases" (Ps. 103:2, 3, NIV).

If you are experiencing problems and struggles in your life, place them in the hands of Jesus. Ask someone to pray with and for you. There is power in intercessory prayer! Trust in this Father of love, and miracles can take place in your life.

MARLENE ESTEVES GARCIA

One Hand Clapping

Carry each other's burdens, and in this way you will fulfill the law of Christ.
Gal. 6:2, NIV.

THERE'S AN OLD PROVERB about understanding that goes like this: You will never have wisdom until you can hear the sound of one hand clapping. I've always thought that was stupid. I mean, you can't clap without two good hands. At least, that's what I thought—until I met Teri.

I had a part-time job when I was a teenager working in the nursery of a local church on Sunday mornings during the adults' worship service. I've always loved kids, but it was very hard for me to be around Teri. She was an average 5-year-old girl except that she was missing a hand. Where her right hand should have been, there was only a little stub of a wrist. I was careful to treat her the same as I treated the other children, with one major exception—I never looked at where her hand should have been.

Then it happened—not a major catastrophe, but one of the little crises that a child's life is full of. Teri and another girl were squabbling over the rights to a popular coloring book while a third party stood by and badgered her with questions about what had happened to her hand.

I resolved the conflict by removing the coloring book and suggesting they play with something else. Soon Teri's two adversaries were happily rummaging through the toy box, but Teri was not so easily comforted. I still had one very unhappy little girl to deal with.

"What do you want to play?" I asked her.

"I want to play beauty parlor," she told me. "Can I brush your hair?"

I produced a hairbrush from my purse and handed it to the girl. The budding beautician took her work seriously as she industriously brushed with her left hand and then smoothed down my hair with her right arm.

"Now you look beautiful," she informed me in an overly sophisticated adult voice. She handed me a doll's mirror to view the results. "If you come in next week, I'll give you a touch-up." Then in her normal voice she whispered, "How do you like it?"

"It's beautiful, just like you." I reached out my two good hands and grabbed her left hand and right arm to pull her closer for a quick hug. After meeting Teri, I learned that it is possible for a person with one hand to clap. All that is needed is for a friend to lend a hand.

GINA LEE

Except You Be Like Little Children

I tell you the truth, unless you change and became like little children, you will never enter the kingdom of Heaven. Matt. 18:3, NIV.

MY NEPHEW LEON IS 40, but his mental retardation places him with a mental age of about 7 years. In spite of his mental disabilities, I am surprised by the many beautiful lessons he has taught us.

His capacity to love and express his affection is immense. Every day, sometimes three or four times a day, he gives his mother, sister, or me a kiss and says, "I love you, Mother; I love you, Glory; I love you, Tia." He'll shake his brother's hand, saying, "I love you, Ernesto."

After one of these incidents, I thought how good it would be if in our families we would express our love to each other more often. Many times we don't think it necessary to tell our children, our parents, our husbands or wives, that we love them. How beautiful our world would be if we expressed our love to each other all the time, as Leon does, and not only on Valentine's Day or birthdays or Christmas or other special occasions, such as Mother's Day or Father's Day. How we could cheer the hearts of our loved ones if we met them with a smile and an "I love you!"

Not only should we express our love more often to our families and friends, but what about our God, who bestows such boundless love to us? I like to think our heavenly Father would be pleased if His earthly children would say, "My Father, I love You." We sing "My Jesus, I love Thee," but do we stop during the day to tell Him of our love? Do we even say "I love You" during our regular prayers?

In reality, we all can use more love in our lives. Perhaps today you could begin by telling Jesus how much you love Him. And yes, you might gladden the day for your husband, wife, son, daughter, or parents right now by a sincere "I love you." And tell them often.

Dear Lord of love, we pray that You fill our hearts with Your love, and help us to pass this love on, to bless someone else today.

OLGA I. CORBIN DE LINDO

Thought: Why does it seem easy for children to say "I love you," but difficult for adults? How does God tell you He loves you?

Forgetting Words

I can do all things through Christ which strengtheneth me. Phil. 4:13.

SINCE THEY WERE SMALL my two children, Carlos and Carla, weekly memorized Bible verses. In this way they easily repeated the verses in their classes. My son was a sweet child and timidly held the microphone while he slowly repeated from memory the verses he had learned during the week. At times he looked at me; other times he glanced at his teacher, who afterward gave him a big hug for being able to recite all the verses.

Now my daughter, four years younger, was learning the art of public speaking. I was surprised at the uninhibited manner in which she held the microphone and looked firmly at those in attendance as she recited all the verses in order. One day she stumbled over one of the verses. She could not say the word correctly. Nervously I whispered a little louder so that she could remember it and continue on. After attempting to say it once or twice, she stopped, looked at me, said, "I don't know this one, Mom," then continued reciting the rest of the verses without being concerned with the laughter coming from everyone present.

We often falter in our lives. Embarrassed, many of us give up, sit down, and say, "I don't know, Lord. I can't do it." But Jesus continues to look at us, encouraging us and whispering, "Go ahead! I am beside you! I can help you!" Faced with laughter, ridicule, or disapproving looks from others we give up, sometimes never to try again.

When I was still young, I was invited to recite a poem in my church. I stumbled on some of the difficult words. Frightened, I panicked. This was enough for me to forget the entire poem. I promised myself I would never again memorize verse. When I was a teenager, the first presentation of our girls' trio was no better. We were not able to harmonize correctly. We left the church crying, affirming that we would never sing again.

These were just some of my errors; however, as I matured, many others—some even more serious—occurred. I had to choose either to give up or go on, but I always chose to go on instead of sitting still and crying about the circumstances. When you falter, remember that we all stumble at times. No one can say, "I have never failed." And the best part—the only One who never failed is always there to help you!

SÔNIA MARIA RIGOLI SANTOS

Love in Details

Can a mother forget the baby at her breast and have no compassion on the child she has borne? Though she may forget, I will not forget you!
Isa. 49:15, NIV.

I HAVE TWO CHILDREN, and I remember very well when my oldest was 5 months old. I needed to return to work, and leaving her for another person to care for was very difficult for me. My desire was to be with her all the time. My mother love was like a magnet that attracted us to one another.

The saddest moment came during the morning that I went to work for the first time after she was born, and the time for her nursing came. My body, which was already in the habit, had begun to prepare to furnish the precious milk that she needed so much. At that moment the sensation for me was total agony. There was absolutely no way I could forget about my daughter.

When I read today's verse in Isaiah I consider how impossible it was to forget about my precious little daughter, and I see that God promises that even if this were to happen, He would not forget her—or you or me.

What a marvelous God this is who is always concerned about us, even in the smallest details of our life! If we are sleeping, or if we are at our work, everything will come out right—whether we are happy, sad, or even worried.

These precious words are from Ellen White: "He who numbers the hairs of your head is not indifferent to the wants of His children. . . . His heart of love is touched by our sorrows. . . . Nothing is too great for Him to bear, for He holds up worlds, He rules over all the affairs of the universe. Nothing that in any way concerns our peace is too small for Him to notice. There is no chapter in our experience too dark for Him to read; there is no perplexity too difficult for Him to unravel. . . . The relations between God and each soul are as distinct and full as though there were not another soul upon the earth to share His watchcare, not another soul for whom He gave His beloved Son" (*Steps to Christ*, p. 100).

It is comforting to know that we are always under the watchcare of our dear God. I live very happily knowing this. What about you?

LUCIANA RIBEIRO DE MATTOS

Mail on Angel's Wings

Cast thy burden upon the Lord, and he shall sustain thee. Ps. 55:22.

IT WAS MAY, and Tyler, my grandson, was graduating from twelfth grade. Terry and Nancy, his parents, were planning an open house for him in June. Nancy decided it would be nice to do up a creative memory photo album of Tyler from when he was a baby until graduation. She called me on a weeknight for the things she thought she would need to make this book. I told her, "No problem." I would get the things together and mail them the next day. I got everything put into a box, ready to mail. When I left in the morning, I put the box in my car.

I had a very busy schedule that day. At 7:45 a.m. I dropped Ashley, my granddaughter, off at her school, then went on to work myself. I got to work at 8:00—no time then to mail the package. When I got out of work at 4:00, I had a doctor's appointment. I figured right after that I would mail the box. Well, I got held up at the doctor's, so I had to rush right on to the student I tutor! When I arrived at my student's house, I opened the side door on my van to get my teaching things—and there was that package! I knew I had needed to put it in the mail that day for Nancy to get it in time to complete the album. Now it was too late. I told God, "I put this all in Your hands."

The next day I headed into my busy schedule again, dropping Ashley off at school and on to work to grade school tests till 4:00. Then I headed for the post office, where they asked me when I wanted the package to get there. "Yesterday!" I said. Everyone laughed. It always takes several days to get even a letter up north to Nancy, and now it was 4:45 p.m. the day before she needed it. I said another prayer.

All the next day I dreaded calling Nancy to tell her the package probably wouldn't arrive until a day—or even two days—after she needed it. So with faith in my heart I didn't call her. The following morning Nancy called to thank me for the package—it had arrived around 2:00 the day after it was mailed. I said, "Praise the Lord!" then proceeded to tell her all that had happened. I know that package went on angel's wings. God is good!

ANNE ELAINE NELSON

Thought: What if the package had not arrived on time? Would God still be good? Why?

Waiting for the King of Kings

At that time the kingdom of heaven will be like ten virgins who took their lamps and went out to meet the bridegroom. . . . The bridegroom was a long time in coming. . . . Therefore keep watch, because you do not know the day or the hour. Matt. 25:1-13, NIV.

MY MOTHER AND I flew to Canada to visit my sister. On our way to their home from the airport in Calgary, my brother-in-law asked, "Would you like to see the queen?"

The queen was coming for the Alberta centennial celebrations on Victoria Day. Of course we wanted to see her! The celebration would be in the Commonwealth Stadium in Edmonton, which seats 35,000 people, and you had to have an invitation and an entrance ticket. My sister phoned. She was told there were 35,000 people on the waiting list! But she knew somebody who worked at the office of a member of the Legislative Assembly who could get us tickets.

On Victoria Day the weather forecast promised rain and cold. So we dressed up fit to meet the queen and took a couple of umbrellas—just in case. With every mile toward our destination the weather got worse. The rain pelted the windshield. We thought maybe we shouldn't go, after all, as our mother was 89 years old. We didn't want her to get sick, but we didn't want to miss the opportunity of seeing the queen, either. In Edmonton the weather got worse and worse. We gave up trying to look worthy of seeing the queen, turned up our collars, wrapped up in blankets, and tied a scarf around Mom's head. We looked like rag dolls. It was icy cold, and the rain and wind whipped into our faces. Even our seats were wet. Soon our hands and feet were numb because of the cold. My mother's lips turned blue, and she was shaking.

The program started at 2:00; the queen was to arrive at 3:00. After an endlessly long time, they announced that the royal couple would be a bit late. We had to wait a bit longer.

Finally we saw the royal limousine. The queen was there! I saw her in person, not on TV. I will never forget it. Soon there will be another celebration. We're not waiting for the queen of England but for the King of kings and Lord of lords. Have we bothered to get tickets? They're free. Are we prepared to wait long hours in the storm and rain? Will we become discouraged? When the King comes, I want to be there!

HANNELE OTTSCHOFSKI

Night to Sunlight

I remembered God, and was troubled: I complained, and my spirit was overwhelmed. Ps. 77:3.

"YOU SAVED ME from an impending crisis. I had almost lost my way. I had lost my trust in God, and had been questioning Him: 'What have I done? Where did I go wrong that You have punished me with one disaster after another?' My experience in the recent past has been overwhelming. First my two grandchildren died. Then my husband died in an accident. Next, one of my sons died. Worst of all, our motor-tricycle was highjacked, and another of my sons, who was driving it, was murdered. Because of this I planted in my heart untold anger and deep-seated hatred. This caused me sleepless nights thinking of revenge toward the killer of my son. I looked for someone to assist me in hunting down the killer. I was worried that my third son might be the next victim. I found somebody I could pay to kill."

I listened to the woman in wonder. Her tragedies were hard to comprehend. Then she said, "Your team came just in time. You brought a message of hope in Jesus. I realize that it would be wrong for me to act on what I had thought and planned. Thank you so much, dear friends, for saving me from disaster. You brought sunshine to our town."

We had been holding gospel meetings in this woman's village. We had told of Jesus' death, which can save us from sin and punishment. This woman had been touched with the love of Jesus. She continued, "Now that you are leaving, we will be far from each other. I trust that you will reach your destination safely. Please remember us always in your prayers."

We build up new hope in the hearts of others. Our friendships will continue until the day of Jesus' return, when there will be no more tears, no more pain, no more sorrows, and no more death. God, our Creator, will be with us, and there will be peace forever.

My happiness in this new friendship is overflowing. I have every reason to believe that our visit in her town was all planned by God. Sharing God's love is rewarding. His promises never fail. Only believe and follow His lead.

A few verses after today's text the psalmist writes, "Thou art the God that doest wonders: thou hast declared thy strength among the people" (verse 14). That changes night to sunlight.

Esperanza Aquino Mopera

It's Not Fair

For God so loved the world, that he gave his only begotten Son, that whosoever believeth in him should not perish, but have everlasting life. For God sent not his Son into the world to condemn the world; but that the world through him might be saved. John 3:16, 17.

BABIES SEEM TO ARRIVE with an instinct for justice. They know what is just and what is not fair. Though these are usually not the first words a toddler lisps, they are understood and said early in a child's life, particularly if there are siblings.

"It's not fair; his apple is bigger than mine!"

"It's not fair; you bought her new shoes and didn't buy the baseball cap I wanted."

It continues right through school days. Nothing is fair; favors are not equally divided, punishments are not justly meted out, advancement is not properly assessed.

Teenagers even direct a few of their complaints upward: Why couldn't I have been born with blue eyes instead of brown? I wish I had her figure—she eats anything and doesn't put on weight. It's not fair! Look at me—I only need to smell chocolate and I gain ounces."

Then the mating game begins, and with it the old saying "all's fair in love and war." The mousiest-looking girl gets the most handsome man; the sweetest, most talented girl makes the poorest choice. It's not fair!

And on through life—nothing is fair. The profligate prospers and enjoys perfect health, while the pure has poor health and little else. The honest woman is despised, the cheat admired.

I'm sorry, ladies, but that's the way it is. *Life is not fair!*

We might even be tempted to think that God is not fair. He sends rain and sunshine on the just and the unjust, the deserving and the undeserving. He offers His salvation free to all, the rich and the poor, the worst and the best. "For whosoever shall call upon the name of the Lord shall be saved" (Rom. 10:13).

The thief on the cross beside Jesus made a last-minute decision, and he will be in heaven as surely as the martyrs who gave their entire life to His service and died a horrible death. It's not fair, God; it is just not fair!

But oh, how wonderfully unfair if that thief had been my child!

GOLDIE DOWN

Much More
Than Built-in Closets

Now to him who is able to do immeasurably more than all we ask or imagine, according to his power that is at work within us. Eph. 3:20, NIV.

AS A MINISTER'S WIFE in Brazil, I have moved to many different cities, as well as to various houses and apartments. Often our furniture doesn't fit into the new housing. When we moved from Londrina to Maringá, in the south, we had to do away with our large wardrobe because our new apartment had built-in closets and kitchen cabinets—there was no room for the wardrobe.

Two years later we received an unexpected call to the city of Blumenau. We were pleased with the call, but we soon realized that we had a big problem: we did not now have wardrobes for the bedrooms, and we didn't have kitchen cabinets. What if the new home didn't have these items? We didn't have the money to buy new ones.

In Blumenau we began searching for a house or apartment, praying that we could find a place with built-in closets and cabinets; however, housing with built-in closets and cabinets was not common, and our options were few. We looked at some rentals, but they weren't satisfactory, and we were somewhat discouraged. However, we trusted that because God knew of our necessity, He would provide.

At the end of the day we visited an apartment—and it was just what we needed. We still live there today.

Now, as I take time for my devotional, I am grateful to God for the additional blessings He has granted us. Both the front and the back of our building are surrounded by trees, so I begin and end my day with a true bird symphony. I can sleep with the window open, viewing the moon behind the trees. From where I am seated to meditate, I see the mountains and trees covered with flowers.

I am grateful to God for all He has provided. And to think that I wanted only built-in closets! How right Paul was when he said that our God would do infinitely more than we ask for or can imagine.

Thank You, Lord, for loving us—and many times You give much more than we ask for.

REGINA MARY SILVEIRA NUNES

It's a Small World

But our citizenship is in heaven. And we eagerly await a Savior from there, the Lord Jesus Christ. Phil. 3:20, NIV.

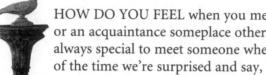 HOW DO YOU FEEL when you meet a family member, a friend, or an acquaintance someplace other than your own territory? It's always special to meet someone when I am far from home. Most of the time we're surprised and say, "Isn't it a small world?"

I flew to Loma Linda, California, recently to attend my nephew Harvey's eighth-grade graduation. The next morning, with Linda and Ate Dinah, I drove to Fresno, where my sister Luda lives. While there, we met several people we'd not seen for a long time. Small world!

After Harvey's graduation we drove back to Loma Linda to attend a friend's graduation. That Sunday I was bored, all alone in my room, so I decided to take a walk. Who would think that during my walk in this new place I would meet friends? The Macayas, from the Philippines, were also visiting. Again, a small world!

During the graduation I squeezed through the crowd of people who were trying to get a good spot to take a picture. It was tight and awkward, so who would think that in the midst of the crowd I would meet Russell, another friend? We were both surprised to see each other. Another small world!

Then it was time to go back home to Maryland. While preparing to board my plane, I couldn't believe another surprise—there was Lowell Cooper, my boss and colleague at work, who was also waiting to board the plane. Truly, a small world!

As you read this devotional this day, you're probably relating to my experience of the surprise of meeting people in places and at times we don't expect. But have you thought about how it will feel when we get to heaven and greet, or are greeted by, a long-lost friend, an acquaintance, or a family member? It will be a thrilling experience, and I think I will have tears of joy. Oh, how I long for that day!

Lord, help me today to look forward to meeting You. Help me to share my love for You with others. It would be a small world if we would all share Your love!

JEMIMA D. ORILLOSA

Circumstances Can Break or Make You

And he said, Hearken ye, all Judah, and ye inhabitants of Jerusalem, and thou king Jehoshaphat, Thus saith the Lord unto you, Be not afraid nor dismayed by reason of this great multitude; for the battle is not yours, but God's. 2 Chron. 20:15.

Be still, and know that I am God: I will be exalted among the heathen, I will be exalted in the earth. Ps. 46:10.

CIRCUMSTANCES IN OUR LIVES are sometimes unfair, unjust, and undeserved. The sum of our past determines who we are today. We can allow the injustices of our past to make us bitter and resentful. We can decide that life has been unfair, so we take our frustration out on those closest to us. No one said that life would be fair or just, or that we'd have life the way we wanted it.

You may say, "You don't understand my life. I've had more than my fair share of life's troubles." Perhaps you were abused as a child or are in an abusive relationship now. It's possible that you, or someone close to you, is fighting a losing battle with a terminal illness. Maybe it seems as though you've lost not only the battle but the war.

Don't despair; there is good news! You don't have to fight the battles life throws your way. Today's first verse reminds us that "the battle is not yours, but God's."

I've asked God why I have the struggles I do, but He remains silent. When I fight and struggle to figure it out, I feel alone and desperate. I'm learning to wait on Him, accepting that maybe not in this lifetime—but someday—I'll understand. He commands us to "be still" and to "know" Him (Ps. 46:10). He is God, and He is in control.

Everything comes down to choice. Will I choose to obey God, no matter what comes my way? Will I put Him first in every circumstance in my life? Can I lay down my burdens of guilt, resentment, bitterness, and hatefulness and allow the Spirit to take control and bear fruit? Wouldn't experiencing joy, peace, goodness, faith, and kindness be more fulfilling then holding a grudge? God is not the cause of our troubles, but He can use it for good if we ask Him to. Allow God to transform us into who we will become tomorrow!

KATHLEEN SOWARDS

This Little One Is Mine

But now . . . the Lord who created you says: "Do not be afraid, for I have ransomed you. I have called you by name; you are mine. Isa. 43:1, NLt.

DEAR DIARY: *Here I am, officially a missionary out in the field. Who would have thought I would be writing from the other side of "my world"? Yes, He surely did. Almaty, Kazakhstan—beautiful snow-covered mountains. I love it! Here I am, Lord; thank You for bringing me here!*

Not even a week after my arrival, and here I sit on a bench in a park, crying my heart out. Lord, what am I doing here? I don't understand them, and they don't understand me! How am I supposed to teach them anything this way?

My eyes full of tears, I prayed to God, asking Him all these questions. When I opened my eyes, the first thing I saw were two sets of dirty, tiny hands. Right there in front of me were two little ones with dirt not only on their hands but on their feet and even in their chopped hair. Both of them were saying, *"Tenge, tenge pozhalsta, tenge pozhalsta."* Tenge is their money. I had no money with me. So with my limited Russian, and using English and Spanish, and even trying to see if sign language would work, I told them, "No money." They seemed to understand but wouldn't leave, wouldn't stop begging for money. They were so persistent. After about five minutes I said "Oh! OK, I know! I don't have money, but I'll sing a song for you." And I started singing, "Jesus loves the little children, all the children of the world."

Wow! It was like magic. They were quiet, and only when I stopped would they speak. "Please, again!" And so I did—once, twice, again and again. Their mother had to drag them away when she noticed they were not making money.

Later: My roommate and I were walking when a dozen refugee kids surrounded us, begging for money. A little tenge here, another one there, and there, and a little hand kept pulling me down. When I turned to see who did this, I noticed the little girl with dirty chopped hair, one of the little ones from the park! Her eyes opened wide as she started humming, "Jesus loves the little children, all the children of the world."

A year later: Flying back from Almaty, I understand everything now. I thought I was sent to teach and show them things. Instead, I have learned the greatest lesson of all from them—we are all precious in His sight.

SAYURI RUIZ

Ask, Seek, and Knock

Ask and it will be given to you; seek and you will find; knock and the door will be opened to you. Matt. 7:7, NIV.

THE HUMAN BEING is expert at asking. When we are babies, we cry to ask for food, to have our diaper changed, or even because we cannot reach a toy. As time goes by, we learn that it is not by crying only that we obtain what we desire. Sometimes it's by smiling, negotiating, or making exchanges. Some go further, using even half apologies to obtain what they desire.

Today's verse is a marvelous promise. At first glance it seems to us that we need only to ask, and God will give us what we want. We just need to cry like spiritual babies, and we will get what we want. However, we soon realize that this is not how it works.

In this small text there are three actions: ask, seek, and knock in order of increasing spiritual action and faith.

Ask: This is a simple action; it doesn't require much effort. Simply, we talk to God, expressing to Him our request. We use our thoughts and our ability to talk.

Seek: Here is a more complex action. It depends on our willingness, time, and disposition. This is reading the Bible. We need to look for and seek revelation in His Word. We use our thought and vision to read, and our reasoning to reflect on what we have read.

Knock: In this stage there is total utilization of our faculties: movement, unselfishness, understanding, and faith. It is the moment of action and giving up of self. It is the time to become humble; to ask, knock, and take a step in faith so that the blessing can be poured out and the request answered.

This does not always mean that by following these steps we receive what we want. Many times we ask and do not receive. Perhaps our motives are selfish, or we haven't asked according to God's will. Other times, we seek and do not find because we have searched in the wrong place, knocked at the wrong location, and consequently we don't see the door opening. What is important is that we grow in faith and leave behind the things of selfish children. The secret is daily communion to know God and His will. Only in this way will we be capable of asking according to His will and seeking and knocking in the right place.

DENISE MÚCKENBERGE LOPES

Who Was More Blessed?

It is more blessed to give than to receive. Acts 20:35.

MY 92-YEAR-OLD MOTHER AND I had just completed her shopping for vitamins at our favorite nutrition center when I realized she was looking pretty tired. I was thinking of buying just one item, but I took her out to the car to rest as soon as her transaction was completed.

When I returned to the store to ponder my purchase, there was a gentleman at the counter with a large number of items, two of which were the very ones that I was thinking of purchasing. We fell into conversation, and I asked him about the product, a simple little plastic shaker mixer. He assured me they worked very well. Assuming it would work just as well for me to mix up our powdered soy milk, I brought one to the counter.

As soon as the clerk had the man's purchases totaled, the man started frantically looking through his wallet for his gold card. (This card entitles the bearer to a 20 percent discount on all products at this nutrition center during the first 10 days of every month.) He finally shrugged his shoulders and explained that he couldn't find his card. I could see he was distraught, because he had more than $100 worth of merchandise.

Then it hit me. "Hey," I said to the clerk, "can you use my gold card to save him on his purchases?" She replied that she could, and I handed her my card. I didn't really think that much about it—it wasn't going to cost me anything at all—but I wish you could have seen that man's face! He turned to me with tears in his eyes and said, "You are the sweetest lady! I appreciate this so much!" Then he picked up my little shaker mixer and told the clerk he was going to pay for that, too—it was the least he could do for me. I told him, "No! It's OK; you don't owe me anything." But he insisted. When he left the store, his face was absolutely glowing.

I truly do not know who was more blessed, but every time I mix up my powdered soy milk in that little shaker mixer, I remember that day and how the Lord brought such a blessing into both my life and the life of a total stranger.

ANNA MAY RADKE WATERS

Thought: Have you thought that giving something had to cost you? What can you give today?

Weapon Against Temptation

It is written, Man shall not live by bread alone, but by every word that proceedeth out of the mouth of God. Matt. 4:4.

I WAS GETTING READY to have my devotions one morning when I noticed a large black spider on the floor nearby. The closest "weapon" was my Bible study guide. So I grabbed it and swatted the spider. Immediately I had guilt feelings. How could I use the precious Scriptures to kill a spider?

Then I reflected on what Jesus said to Satan at the time of His temptation on the mount. To every invitation of Satan Jesus replied, "It is written." Every day we are faced with temptations. The evil one never takes a vacation! And I must keep my mind filled with ammunition against his attacks. Every morning I pray to hear a voice behind me saying, "This is the way, walk ye in it, when ye turn to the right hand, and when ye turn to the left" (Isa. 30:21).

As I walk to work, am I not blessed to be able to walk in the country instead of driving in the chaotic traffic of the city? I am reminded of God's great creative power by the colorful flowers along my path, the majestic trees, the sweet songs of the birds welcoming the morning, the warmth of the sunshine, the gray and brown squirrels that run across my path.

Arriving at my office, I remember with dismay my fruitless efforts to recover from my computer whole chapters of a book that I had spent endless hours typing. I am tempted by the evil one to be overcome with feelings of frustration and helplessness. Then the voice behind me says, "There is a reason for this. Perhaps you need the message of the book to be reviewed once more in your mind."

You see, for 25 years I worked as a transcriber for court reporters in Atlanta, Georgia.

There are many things that go on in court that are not profitable for one's mind. Over these years I learned to type material that came from the transcription machine to my ears, then on to the typewriter, without really letting it lodge in my mind. As a result of this practice, I must now make a concentrated effort to be sure that good things reach my brain.

Another Scripture comes to mind: "Let the words of my mouth, and the meditation of my heart, be acceptable in thy sight, O Lord, my strength, and my redeemer" (Ps. 19:14).

RUBYE SUE

157

Oops!

These commandments that I give you today are to be upon your hearts. . . .
Talk about them when you sit at home and when you walk along the road,
when you lie down and when you get up. Deut. 6:6, 7, NIV.

THREE OTHER WOMEN and I were visiting inmates at a women's prison. I'd been there before and had reviewed the four pages of rules and regulations for admittance—what colors can be worn, no under-wire undergarments, no flip-flops.

Upon arrival, I filled out the admittance form with the inmate's name. Oops! I'd forgotten to bring her ID number. That had to be looked up. Next the guard examined the contents of what I was taking in, displayed in a locking plastic bag, and saw a $20 bill. Oops again. She changed the $20 for dollar bills and quarters, and I sat awaiting entry.

After I was called, everything on me was carefully noted—glasses, watch, wedding band, cat pin. As I proceeded through the metal detector, it buzzed. I was instructed to go back and try again. It still went off, so I removed my glasses. Then the cat pin. It still went off. That's when I remembered that I was wearing a strictly prohibited underwire undergarment. Oops again! The guard instructed me to hold my hand tightly over the hook and eyes, but the detector still buzzed.

I was sent to another building where stashes of clothing were stored for visitors who failed to comply with the rules. I tried on a black thingy that didn't work, and giggled as I pulled out a daring red velvet number. Strictly Victoria's Secret style! When I eventually joined my friends, we had a good laugh over what was hidden under my black pantsuit.

AForgotten@ rules. We'd been delayed because of my forgetfulness and lack of attention to prison rules. And there was no admittance without strict adherence to every rule.

God gives us 10 rules, the Ten Commandments, as a standard to live by. If I faithfully adhere to His standards in my everyday life, I will gain entrance to heaven. If I don't, I will be denied entrance, just as I was almost denied entrance on my visit to the prison. Merely abiding by His standards won't save me, but if I follow today's text and rely on God's grace and power, I can be assured of admittance to my heavenly home. Obedience to His standards does matter.

NANCY VAN PELT

Errant Golf Balls

If anyone does not stumble in word, [she] is a perfect [woman], able to bridle the whole body. James 3:2, NKJV.

MY MORNING WALK took me parallel to a golf course. At some points there were only a few feet between my path and its green lawns. One morning I stopped short and stared at a new sign placed at one of these spots where the public path and the golf course almost meet. "Watch out for errant golf balls," I read. I chuckled that the word "errant" was applied to golf balls. That confirmed what I had always suspected: golf balls have a mind of their own.

In the early years of our marriage I tried to get enthusiastic about golf, since it was a game my husband enjoyed. He coached me patiently, and after a while not so patiently. It seemed that no matter how I stood, bent my knees, and swung the club, the golf ball did not go where I intended it to go. Instead of heading straight down the fairway for the little flag on the distant green, it headed for the woods or the pond or the sand trap.

"I can't help it!" I defended myself to a husband who just stood there, shaking his head. "I told it to go straight!" It seemed every ball I used was errant. It went wherever it wanted. After more than my share of errant golf balls, I chose to pursue my hobby of bird watching, while my husband continued to pursue golf balls. Fortunate it was for cows, cars, and other golfers that I stopped before any of my "errant" balls did them damage.

As I moved on in my morning walk I couldn't get that sign out of my mind. How many times my words have been as "errant" as stray golf balls. So many times I've opened my mouth and sent a word flying that ended up hurting someone unintentionally. I thought of the words: "Boys flying kites haul in their white winged birds, but you can't do that when you are flying words." I now paraphrased it to be in tune with my thoughts about golf. "When Dorothy hit errant golf balls, she found most of them where they had landed and put them back in her golf bag; but she couldn't do that when she was hitting words."

Lord, help me to think twice before I send words flying today. Should they be "errant," they could hurt someone deeply. Let the words of my mouth be straight today, and not errant; helpful, and not hurtful.

DOROTHY EATON WATTS

For I Desired Mercy and Not Sacrifice

Come, and let us return unto the Lord. Hosea 6:1.

DO YOU REMEMBER a childhood sickness or a touch of pneumonia that made you sick—with the potential for something even worse? In the long feverish night you would awaken from a half sleep to see in the soft glow of the night light your mother or father sitting in a chair beside your bed. Just so, in a figurative, human sense, God sat by the bedside of a sin-sick world as satanic darkness began to deepen in the centuries after the Flood. The Lord was not going to leave the bedside of His world unattended, not with it in such dire need.

At the time of Hosea's ministry, the Israelite nation was professing loyalty to God but having secret, illicit liaisons with Satan. Israel was not sincere in their commitment to their Creator. "O Ephraim, what shall I do unto thee? . . . O Judah, he hath set an harvest for thee" (Hosea 6:4-11).

If ever we needed to divorce the adulterous gods of lust, lewdness, and murder in the way of consent, as in Hosea 6:9, 10, it is now. This is the horrible thing, the whoredom of Ephraim, the superficial goodness of Judah that Hosea prophesied about.

Sabbath after pitiful Sabbath we call on the Lord to come to us, to pour out the latter rain upon us, to give us a double portion of His Spirit, but are we really ready to receive it? It will not happen until we first come together in unity with God and our spiritual brothers and sisters. We must put away the idolatrous gods of jealousy, hatred, pride, envy, coveting, gossiping, witchcraft, and indifference to God's Word.

Believe it or not, God is a sentimental God. Little things mean a lot to Him, little tokens of appreciation such as wrapping your arms around His lost children, picking them up, and carrying them to safety. He's thrilled when He's not being ripped off in His tithes and offerings. He really does like these sorts of things.

Yes, we are spiritual Israel. Despite the punishment that God promised, there is a strong attitude of hope evident throughout Hosea. Just as Hosea bought back his unfaithful wife, Israel will be redeemed by God in the last days, for the Lord says, "Come, and let us return unto the Lord: for he hath torn, and he will heal us; he hath smitten, and he will bind us up" (verse1).

CEREATHA J. VAUGHN

The Tree Is Known by Its Fruit

And seeing a fig tree by the road, He came to it and found nothing on it but leaves, and said to it, "Let no fruit grow on you ever again." Immediately the fig tree withered away. Matt. 21:19, NKJV.

THE SPRING AFTER MY HUSBAND AND I MOVED to the new house God provided for us, we decided to plant fruit trees in the backyard instead of building a swimming pool, as nearly all our neighbors did. We figured that before long we would taste some fruit from those trees. We planted two navel orange, two grapefruit, one mandarin orange, three persimmon, two cherry, one pear, one lemon, one Asian pear, four apple, one plum, one apricot, one nectarine, and one peach. Later, we added a white peach and a white nectarine. Before long the trees began to bear fruit. It was wonderful to eat and to share with friends and neighbors.

But something wasn't right with the apple trees. Year after year we looked forward to seeing some blooms and fruit from those four trees, only to be disappointed. The same was true with the pear tree. My husband and I aren't farmers, but we tried to follow the recommendations in our horticulture books, as well as suggestions from people who had succeeded in raising fruit trees. One day I was aghast when I found that my husband had cut down the pear tree and one of the apple trees. The following year he cut down another apple tree. I said it was too bad that those three were good for nothing, although I felt bad to see them go.

The following year when we were looking at all the fruit-bearing trees, my husband looked at the apple trees and said, "If these apple trees don't bear any fruit next year, I'll cut them down." Maybe these trees were teaching us a lesson in patience, because the following season that fuji apple tree was loaded with fruit, although the other apple tree didn't bear much.

God has never been impatient with His people—and certainly not with me. What a lesson my husband and I learned from the apple trees!

Dear God, You never get tired of listening to me and answering my requests. Please help me to be more patient not only with the fruit trees but with my loved ones and fellow sojourners.

OFELIA A. PANGAN

Thought: Does God have limits to His patience? If so, how should I evaluate my fruit bearing?

Healing

At once Jesus realized that power had gone out from him. He turned around in the crowd and asked, "Who touched my clothes?" Mark 5:30, NIV.

A FRIEND OF MINE periodically brings a group of disabled people to our church. One week the foyer was a-bustle with them waiting to go into the church service. I casually waved at one of the women sitting in the corner. She was expressionless, and I didn't think she had been aware of the gesture. As I stopped briefly in the sanctuary to look for my husband, I felt a body pressing close to me. Turning, this same small stranger giggled and said, "I'm Bonnie." Turning to her caretaker nearby, she pointed to me and said, "I want to sit with her." She was so wonderfully childlike and honest—she was a delight! Her caretaker winked at her and told her to behave. Giggling, she followed closely behind me as we sat down in my usual pew.

Bonnie snuggled close to me; she smelled of soap and freshness. She leaned over, chatting to my friend sitting beside me, commenting that all three of us had hair the same color. "We are all alike," she said, smiling broadly.

My friend whispered, "But there is one big difference." I knew she was referring to the fact that she and I both had extra pounds and Bonnie was a "string bean." "The neat thing is she doesn't even notice that," I assured my friend.

Standing for the opening song, Bonnie giggled again, saying she liked to sing. She could not read, but when the music began she sang her choice of words with great gusto. I loved her and was so happy she had chosen me. She was a special blessing, refreshingly needed in my tired life. I'd been ill for a number of years with an autoimmune disease, and most days are a challenge for me. Bonnie's childlike warmth was a gift, an indescribable touch of healing.

When the pastor knelt for prayer, those who had special prayer thoughts knelt at the front of the church. "Sweet Hour of Prayer" filled the sanctuary. Bonnie said, "I want to go up there; will you go with me?" When I nodded, she grabbed my hand and nearly ran to the front of the church. Hand in hand, Bonnie and I knelt at the altar.

Thank You, Jesus, for the power of healing through simply being touched. Oh, for the revival of a childlike love to fill our hearts!

JUDY GOOD SILVER

Graduation Day

Delight yourself also in the Lord, and He shall give you the desires of your heart. Ps. 37:4, NKJV.

THEY WERE GOING to celebrate the graduation of all the members of our church who had received certificates, diplomas, or degrees that June. All the celebrants seemed excited. But I wasn't. Every time I thought of graduation, a bittersweet pang sent a dagger through my soul.

Although I've earned three degrees, one diploma, and a teacher's certificate, I had attended only my first graduation (as a teacher) in Jamaica. I had never marched to the majestic strains of "Pomp and Circumstance." A vacationing professor's error prevented my second graduation. When I received my bachelor's degree, my responsibilities as a single mother made graduation impossible. My graduation for my master's degree conflicted with my daughter's high school graduation celebrations. Finally, I had to fly to Jamaica to bury my mother instead of my last graduation.

I had never worn a cap and gown. I had never heard the crowd's applause when I received my degree. I felt that familiar pang as I heard some of my friends at a singles' ministries lunch discuss the upcoming graduation. I sighed. I mentioned to one of the women that graduation was not something I wanted to hear about. "I'm too old for that sort of thing," I said. It was a lame excuse. Suddenly she exclaimed, "Denise, you graduated in January. Why not put your name on our list? We definitely want you to march."

Adjusting my cap that Sabbath morning, I smiled. I can wear this crown! My despair had given way to delight. My tears were transformed into joy. I had achieved, and everyone in the church would know it. Marching down the aisle, I thought of another graduation we all can participate in, another cap we can don, and the song "I will wear a crown in my Father's house." I know that my eligibility is assured. God is on my side. All I have to do is listen to Him and follow. I shared my story the next day when I was selected to give the valedictorian's address. I saw many jubilant expressions—and even moist eyes. Several declared that my testimony had reignited the flame within them. They would act on their dreams. I smiled—my grief had not been in vain.

DENISE MALCOLM

Accept a Helping Hand

If ye then, being evil, know how to give good gifts unto your children: how much more shall your heavenly Father give the Holy Spirit to them that ask him? Luke 11:13.

WHEN TRIBUTES ARE GIVEN at community banquets or funerals, one learns a lot about the individual being honored. Often there's one special, endearing characteristic that makes that person stand out in one's memory. Such was the case at a funeral I attended for one of our senior church members.

The man's son, Des, gave a moving tribute to his father, whom we all knew as a kindhearted, gentle soul with a dry sense of humor. I listened with intense interest as Des told of an experience with his father 20 years before.

Des had bought a piece of property in town and built a house on it. The lot was now ready for landscaping, but before sod could be laid or grass planted, numerous rocks needed to be picked up. Des's father helped him do this backbreaking task. At the end of the day the father looked at the pile of rocks and said, "Let's load them on the truck and haul them to the landfill site."

"No," Des said, "we've worked hard enough for today. I'll do that another day."

However, Des had a hunch his father would do the job the next day while he was at work. To prevent his dad from overdoing it, Des moved his truck down the street early the next morning, trusting that his dad wouldn't find it. To be on the safe side, he then took the keys to work so that if, perchance, his dad found the truck, he wouldn't be able to move it in front of the house and load the rocks.

When Des came home the next day, the rock pile was gone! He went to get the truck and was aghast to see the box full of rocks. His dad had carried the rocks, pail by pail, to the truck.

Do we ever make it difficult for our heavenly Father to do a favor for us? Do we feel that we can handle a situation without His help? Our heavenly Father is willing to carry the "rocks" in our lives and haul them to the dump. But do we make it more difficult for Him to lighten our burdens by placing distance between us and Him? Let's leave our "truck" parked conveniently for God to remove the "rocks" in our life today.

EDITH FITCH

Sudden Destruction

When they shall say, Peace and safety; then sudden destruction cometh upon them. 1 Thess. 5:3.

MY HUSBAND AND I were traveling by train from Bangalore to Goa in India with Mae, my 87-year-old sister-in-law from Canada. A young man, the manager of a corporation, was in the same compartment. The four of us were comfortably seated in the air-conditioned sleeper and making small talk. The train was making good time when suddenly we heard clanging and grating noises from under the train. Scared, we looked at each other, wide-eyed. "The train is falling apart!" Mae exclaimed.

The terrible noise continued over the chugging of the train. I noticed that the young man had a frightened look on his face and asked him if he was scared. He admitted he was—all of us were scared.

Then, as suddenly as it began, the noise subsided. The train was still in one piece and moving along. The train attendant told us that he had reported the noise to the ticket collector. Then the noise started all over again and continued, on and off. We were uncomfortable, and whenever the noise reappeared, we would stop whatever we were doing and listen in tense silence.

At the next station a team of mechanics checked out the coach. They didn't seem to find much wrong, but secured the nuts and bolts, and there was no noise thereafter. We were then told that the train had hit and killed three buffalo that had been grazing on the track. Oblivious of the danger, they had strayed from the herd and wandered onto the tracks. The train could have easily been derailed, causing injury and death to the passengers. But God kept His promise and sent His angels to keep the train on the tracks (Ps. 34:7).

We are living in the time of the end. Many of us will be eating and drinking when the sudden destruction comes. Today's text says, "When they shall say, Peace and safety; then sudden destruction cometh upon them." It will be like the tsunami of 2004 that caught the world unaware, or other disasters that seem to be happening more and more frequently. The same fate lies in store for those who do not watch for the second coming of the Lord.

Let us watch and be ready—His coming is very near!

BIROL CHARLOTTE CHRISTO

Three for the Doctors

But my God shall supply all your need. Phil. 4:19.

 I HAVE BEEN SO BLESSED to participate in a study at Mayo Clinic for circulatory problems for heart and lung disease. For two years my faithful sister has accompanied us to the tests to help care for my husband, who has multiple sclerosis.

On my last visit, when I was in my last appointment of the day, a police officer came into the room and said, "Your sister has been taken to St. Mary's Hospital by ambulance." She told me that my sister was still in the emergency room waiting area. As soon as my appointment ended, my husband and I waited 35 minutes for the shuttle bus to take us on the 15-minute ride to St. Mary's. It was a very cold, windy day, and the bus dropped us some distance from the entrance. I could see that my husband was having trouble, and just as I grabbed his arm he pitched forward and crashed onto the concrete about 15 feet from the emergency room entrance. He was knocked out cold, his face cut up badly and bleeding. I stood there in shock while someone else ran inside for help.

Soon he was in the emergency room, hooked up to monitors and oxygen, and, thankfully, he was conscious. We learned that he'd had a heart attack. They admitted him and did the necessary stents and angioplasty. The bottom of the heart, they said, was not getting enough oxygen, causing him to collapse.

My sister was released after several hours. It was determined that a medication interaction had caused the dizzy spells she'd had while at the Mayo library.

What a day! If it hadn't been for my sister's medication problem and the 50 minutes it took us to get from one hospital to the other, we would have been well on our way home, out in the middle of nowhere, at the time that my husband had the heart attack.

The Lord uses many ways to protect us. Everyone said, "You never could have picked a better place to have a heart attack than at the emergency room entrance of a hospital." He got the best and immediate care.

Praise the Lord for always knowing exactly what we need!

DARLENE YTREDAL BURGESON

A Heavenly Wedding

O Lord, you have examined my heart and know everything about me. You know when I sit down or stand up. You know my every thought when far away. You chart the path ahead of me and tell me where to stop and rest....
Such knowledge is too wonderful for me, too great for me to know!
Ps. 139:1-6, NLT.

LIFE HAD TAKEN SOME VERY HARD TURNS, and the past year found me in the darkest valley of my life. My marriage of 20 years had ended despite my hopes of a better day.

One day I drove to the city with divorce papers on the seat next to me, my estranged husband following behind in his vehicle. We were going to a process server to proceed with the next step of the divorce, a word I've come to hate. We had just started out when I was once again overcome with grief at the death of the marriage and the shattering of hopes and dreams.

I quickly called a close friend on my cell phone. She knew what I was facing that day, and amid tears I asked her to pray for me. I had completely lost my composure and needed to be strong to face what was ahead. I knew she would drop everything and pray.

I took a few deep breaths and waited for Jesus to speak "peace" to my soul. I had a new CD in the car stereo, and a song came on that I'd not really listened to before. I heard the group sing, "Is that wedding music I hear?/The bride's adorned and ready to appear./There's heavenly preparation for the wedding celebration./Is that wedding music that I hear?"

As the song continued I became acutely aware that God had been using these dark days and deep valleys to prepare my heart and soul for this great heavenly celebration. The words of that song and the prayers of my friend took me to a whole new spiritual level. I could lose sight of what I was leaving behind and fix my eyes on what was to come: a beautiful wedding celebration of Jesus to His people—and I would be one of them! Suddenly I was overwhelmed by God's grace and the knowledge that I too would stand on that day, adorned and waiting for my Groom to open the doors and welcome me in.

By the time I arrived at my destination the only thing on my mind was Jesus and the wedding celebration that was being prepared. I am looking forward to that day, and anything good that happens between now and then is bonus.

DALRY DEAN

Ask and You Will Receive

Ask of me, and I will make the nations your inheritance. Ps. 2:8, NIV.

WHEN YOU DECIDE to ask the Lord for something, remember that He sometimes responds in an unexpected manner. This is what happened to me, and I'm certain that God was there.

My family was ready for a vacation. I sighed, "How I would love to go to a beautiful, magnificent hotel where I'd be served, and I wouldn't have to make the beds, and the food would be very delicious!" And the Lord heard my wish.

We left very early, and as always, we prayed for the Lord's blessing. When the sun rose, we were in a beautiful tourist city, where we stopped to read the morning devotional and thank God for the care we had received. Listening to religious music, we continued our trip. Some six miles (10 kilometers) later a car unexpectedly crossed in front of us, and our car skidded into the middle of a field. We were stuck—without a telephone or any type of assistance nearby.

How I wished to be in any other situation! *Why, Lord?* I thought. *We've done everything according to what You want. Why did this happen to us?*

Suddenly, from nowhere, our "angel" appeared. A stranger kindly helped us through each detail. Since nothing like this had ever happened to us before, we didn't know what to do. He indicated a garage that we should call from his telephone, and within an hour our car was being fixed.

The insurance company immediately called us to indicate where we needed to stay. Since no one was seriously injured but we were all tired from the ordeal, we were taken to a hotel. To my surprise, it was the best hotel in the city! We contacted a doctor for our minor injuries, and everything that I had dreamed of regarding a hotel was coming true.

In three days our car was like new; we had spent an unplanned mini vacation in a tourist location, just as I had wished for—and without having to spend a cent!

God is so merciful, although at times we don't understand the reasons for what happens to us. He wants the best for us. He wants to give us everything we ask for—and at times in ways that we do not imagine. We must remember to ask God for what is best for us, and nothing more.

NANCY CANO DE ZIEGLER

Are You a Peach or a Prune?

Each man should give what he has decided in his heart to give, not reluctantly or under compulsion, for God loves a cheerful giver. 2 Cor. 9:7, NIV.

PEACH? PRUNE? I'm not talking about physical fruit. So if you hate peaches and love prunes, please don't be offended. What I'm talking about is our attitudes.

There was once a common saying that was used when someone did something nice: "You're a peach." If something was good, then the phrase might be "That's peachy."

The opposite was also true. If someone had a bad or negative attitude, the saying went something like "What did you have for breakfast—a bowl of prunes?" or "You can be such a prune."

So what are you? On average, would you say you're a peach or a prune? Do you go about your daily life being sweet and kind? Are you smiling, and sharing the love and joy of your salvation with all those you meet? Or is your Christian experience drying out and getting bitter? In other words, are you becoming a prune? How can you really tell? Take a look at this short example.

Here's a common situation one might face as often as once a week. You're standing in line at the grocery store with a cart full of all the things that you and your family need, calmly waiting your turn. Turning, you see someone come up behind you with a gallon of milk, a box of cereal, and a loaf of bread. What do you do? Do you do anything? I mean, you were there first, so it's completely fair simply to wait your turn and then be on your way. But you could also let the other person go first. After all, they'd most likely be done in the time it would take you to unload your cart.

The most common scripture that I've ever heard used in asking for an offering is today's verse. I believe this text, but I have a question: Since when has God cared only about our money?

As you go about your day today, remember that money isn't the only thing we can give. God wants our hearts, our lives. How you give will partly indicate whether you are a peach or a prune. But whatever you give, "cheerful" is the key.

JULI BLOOD

Like a Blooming Cherry Tree

Behold, thou art fair, my beloved. S. of Sol. 1:16.

I HAD KNOWN THEM 19 YEARS BEFORE. They lived in a village on the Vrancea hills of Romania, and they were the same age as my parents. It was a pleasure for my husband and me to visit in the house of these faithful and thrifty people.

Time went by, and when we were passing through the area again we heard that the woman was ill, so we visited them. She lay in her bed, weak and just managing to say a few words with difficulty. The long suffering had marred her face but not her confidence in God. Every time she had the opportunity to intervene in our conversation or in the prayers, she approved, and praised God by brief words or gestures.

That she kept her faith in spite of being confined to bed for so many years didn't surprise me too much. I knew the relationship between the man and his wife. As a consecrated man who keeps the promises made to God and before God, he took care of his wife with love and devotion. And he did it with faithfulness and love.

Meanwhile she, who had never led an easy life, felt his fondness and care. She thanked him, she smiled at him, she prayed for him, she praised God because she had him.

Enough! Stop it! you probably think. *What else could a woman in her position do?*

Well, dear friends, she was doing more than that. She was doing more than many of us are doing when we are passing through sunny days or the valley of shadows: she practiced and modeled the art of appreciation.

"Do you know what she told me not long ago?" her husband asked us. "She told me that I am, for her, like a blooming cherry tree."

"Like a bloo-ming che-rry tree," she repeated, pronouncing each syllable in her own way but with conviction.

Until then I had managed to hold back my tears, but now I rushed out of the house for a while. There, in front of her window, stood a beautiful cherry tree, full of fruit.

Have you said nice words to your husband, your family, or to those around you? It is an art to show appreciation. *Be with us, God, and teach us the art of living beautifully!*

SILVIA DIMA

Revenge Is the Lord's

*Beloved, do not avenge yourselves, but rather give place to wrath; for it is
written, "Vengeance is Mine, I will repay," says the Lord. Rom. 12:19, NKJV.*

WHEN SOMEONE WRONGS US, the first thing we want to do
is—hug them?

Not!

Our first instinct is to *punish* them. We want to hurt them
with the same kind of words with which they have hurt us. But
Proverbs 6:16-19 tells us that gossip is one of the seven things God hates.

I hired a church member to work in my place of business. She really
needed the work, so sympathy for her situation clouded my judgment and led
me to ignore the Holy Spirit's leading. Even though she seemed grateful at
first, she repaid my kindness by spreading lies that threatened to ruin my business. Everyone who knew the situation offered all kinds of opinions and advice. But I chose to leave the revenge to God. Retaliation would profit no one.

The Lord wants us to follow Him always; not just when we want to, but
all the time. You never know who is watching you or taking notes. At times,
however, I wanted nothing more than to do to others as they were doing to
me. I would reassure myself by thinking that those who knew me would
not listen to the lies. My mind kept replaying the cartoon from my childhood in which the devil sits on one shoulder of the character and an angel
sits on the other. That memory represented my spiritual struggle. But after
much prayer the real me won out: I would melt them with kindness. I knew
what my heavenly Father expected. I could do no less. I surely hope I made
Jesus proud. One day in heaven I'll know for sure. I do know that I feel
good about the choices I made. Vengeance didn't belong to me.

If you're ever in similar circumstances, remember today's verse, espe-
cially the part that says, "'Vengeance is Mine, I will repay,' says the Lord."
No matter what people do to you, or how they make you feel, choose
God—He chose you.

TAMMY BARNES TAYLOR

Thought: The Bible has several references on this topic. Here are some
texts that you may want to study: Exodus 21:22-25; Matthew 5:11, 12, 38-
48. Read them in several versions.

Ungrateful? I Guess!

Share each other's troubles and problems, and in this way obey the law of Christ. Gal. 6:2, NLT.

HE LAY THERE ON HIS BACK at the side of the pavement, still and silent. As I topped the rise in the road, I saw him and braked to a stop. I moved toward him guardedly. As I got closer I saw his leg move ever so slightly, and then his neck moved almost imperceptibly.

"He's still alive!" I said to my husband, Laun, who was riding with me.

We scanned him and the surrounding roadside for blood or other signs of injury, but found nothing. Cautiously Laun nudged him with the front wheel of his bicycle. Instantly the four legs of the snapping turtle came to life, the long, sharp claws on his feet angrily flailing the air. We both jumped back, startled, and then smiled with relief that this amazing creature would be OK—with a little help. We were unwilling to leave him to his inevitable fate, so Laun nudged the snapper again—hard—and flipped him over. The indignant beast immediately rose to his full height on all four legs, whirled around to face us, opened his three-inch mouth wide, and hissed loudly and menacingly at us. We stepped back respectfully.

"Ungrateful? I guess!" we laughed as we watched him deliberately turn his back on us and slowly amble into the surrounding woods toward the nearby pond. We were grateful we could have a part in assisting him to safety.

Sometimes we've become discouraged when someone we've tried to help has shown no appreciation for our efforts, or has made us feel like an intruder into the inner spaces of their lives. Or maybe we've ungratefully displayed "turtle appreciation" when others have tried to assist us. How many times have we, because of the circumstance in which we found ourselves, hissed angrily at God when He has reached out to sustain us?

Regardless of the reactions or ingratitude an individual may display, God has asked us to share the burdens and troubles of others, to reach out to those in need. Our reward is not the thanks or accolades of people. Knowing we are doing what God has asked us to do is enough. How difficult is it to give 30 minutes of our time to listen, to share a few cookies or a loaf of bread, to sit by the bedside of someone who is ill, to prepare a meal for a needy family, or to pray with someone? When we do those things, we are doing the will of Christ. And our reward is "out of this world."

BARBARA J. HORST REINHOLTZ

How Great Thou Art

I will instruct thee and teach thee in the way which thou shalt go: I will guide thee with mine eye. Ps. 32:8.

I ALWAYS FEEL HAPPY when I sing the hymn "How Great Thou Art." My mind flashes back to a European tour that took us through the Alps and the Dolomites. I silently sang it then and praised God for allowing me to have this wonderful trip.

Then 10 years later, while doing volunteer secretarial service in Pakistan at a hospital in Karachi, I was able to go on a trip to the north. First, we visited the mountainous area of Murree, Patriata, and the Khyber Pass. Again, "How Great Thou Art" was predominantly in my mind. A year later, on a trip further north, I saw Rakaposhi, the mountain of the legendary Shangri-la, and the golden peaks of Galmut. We traveled along the Silk Road that Marco Polo traveled. (It's now tarred and called Karakoram Highway.)

It was June, and cool. We walked over a mountain pass on five feet of glacier ice that had slipped down from the mountain during the night. Again the words of the beautiful hymn were continually in my mind. "Then sings my soul, my Savior God to Thee, how great Thou art!"

We have a well-known mountain here in South Africa. When planning a holiday trip, besides visiting family we make an effort to take the cable car up Table Mountain in Cape Town. We've also traveled near the Drakensberg Mountain in the Natal area and admired the beauty and majesty of the tall peaks. God's greatness is seen in so many places.

Another aspect of nature that always fascinates me is the sea. Oceans are enormous and important around the world. I'm fascinated by the large variety of sea life in aquariums. Family and friends know how I love pictures of fish. I even have a framed jigsaw puzzle with fish shapes and water and sea plants. Recently I was fortunate to receive a beautiful clock built on a frame of two blue fish, one over the top and one underneath. I also have a collection of shells. Although I don't know much about them, they fascinate me, and when I'm curious about something I see, I look for them in some of my books that have lovely shell pictures. What a God of love to have given us so much variety to enjoy! How great Thou art!

PHYLLIS DALGLEISH

Daddy's Little Girl

And so we know and rely on the love God has for us. God is love. Whoever lives in love lives in God, and God in him. 1 John 4:16, NIV.

AS WE SAT EATING IN A RESTAURANT, I noticed a daddy with his little daughter. The face of the child was angelic. The drinks they ordered had been served, and as they waited for their food their interaction intrigued me. While sipping happily, they chatted. Then they began playing a little game that brought much laughter from the little girl. Her daddy ended it by smothering her with kisses. Both were obviously enjoying each other's company immensely.

Their food arrived, and they began to eat, often sharing food from each other's plate. She held her fork in the proper manner, an indication of earlier training in etiquette. Suddenly she began crying. After a bit she sobbed, "I miss Mommy!" As the crying continued, her daddy took her from her chair and held her on his lap, enveloping her in his arms and gently rocking her. Soon she stopped crying and appeared sufficiently comforted. She then sat back in her own chair and the meal continued.

What loving acts that daddy demonstrated! As a result, there was no sign of tension or fear, only a mutually joyous relationship between them. Our heavenly Father longs to have such a relationship with us. He is eager for us to spend time with Him and to find joy and satisfaction in that communion. Never too busy, He is always there, waiting for us to come to Him. In His Word His invitation is given in many different ways—when we are burdened, joyful, sad, thankful, or lonely. He says, "I have loved you with an everlasting love; I have drawn you with loving-kindness" (Jer. 31:3, NIV). There is nothing that can separate us from that love.

There were times, I am sure, when that precious little girl was naughty and had to be disciplined. If my guess is correct, even during those times that daddy disciplined in love. Our precious Father knows what is best for us and sometimes has to bring tough reality or consequences into our lives to get our attention. That loving discipline can save us from eternal disaster. He always does so in love. He wants our characters made ready to spend eternity with Him. I want to respond to that kind of love, don't you?

MARIAN M. HART

My Daddy's Girl

Love is patient, love is kind…. It always protects, always trusts, always hopes, always perseveres. Love never fails. 1 Cor. 13:4-8, NIV.

I REMEMBER BEING DADDY'S GIRL. My favorite part of going shopping with my father was Daddy paying the cashier. I don't know if he ever had change in his pocket, because he always paid with big bills. When the cashier handed Daddy his change, Daddy always gave me the coins. It never failed to make me smile. I never knew that we could use the extra money—I thought he had the second job of pumping gas at the corner gas station on Sunday for fun. I remember taking Daddy his dinner on Sunday afternoon. With Mommy watching, I would walk the half block to the end of our road. Then Daddy would cross the intersection and walk me across to the gas station. As I watched him eat and work, I remember being so in awe of him. I remember telling Daddy that when I grew up I wanted to be just like him.

Somewhere after puberty my relationship with my father changed—I can't remember when or even how. Somewhere I forgot that I was Daddy's girl, and my heart broke, longing for the relationship. When I was a teenager I remember receiving a plaque during the induction into the honor society and seeing my parents' beaming faces. Yet when my plaque disappeared the next day I found it hard to believe that my father had taken it to work. When I asked my mother why daddy had the plaque, she replied, "Because he is proud of you, and he loves you very much." Somehow I couldn't see that my father even liked me, much less loved me.

Unfortunately my relationship with my heavenly Father has been the same. As a child I found Him, and my love for Him grew. My greatest desire was to be like Him. Somehow my focus changed, and my heavenly Father took a back seat. On some level I knew He still loved me, but it was difficult to feel His presence in my life—much less allow Him to lead.

Over the years my relationship with my Father has changed again. I cannot say that it is as it was when I was a child; nevertheless, I can say that I am my Daddy's girl. I know he doesn't agree with every decision I have made in my life, but that doesn't matter, because he loves me; his love supports me. My earthly father has shown me what my heavenly Father wanted to teach me. I learned that love is long-suffering, love is kind, and love never fails.

TAMARA MARQUEZ DE SMITH

The Colors of Love

And it shall come to pass, when I bring a cloud over the earth, that the bow shall be seen in the cloud: And I will remember my covenant, which is between me and you. Gen. 9:14, 15.

IT WAS THE END OF THE SCHOOL YEAR. For Vlad, my eldest son, it was the end of the eighth form, and he was to participate in the farewell prom that marked the finish of the year. Until then all had gone well.

Almost a year before, I had started to unravel the mysteries of a new great love—knowing God. I was in the baptismal class and living a new, wonderful experience: father, mother, and the two children were together in church!

But that Friday afternoon I looked into the schoolyard and saw a great commotion: many children, professors, congratulations, flowers—a celebration atmosphere. However, the heart of my 15-year-old son was troubled by a dilemma: Should he go to the banquet or not?

When he came home, in a shy tone he told me, "My form teacher asked me once again to come to the banquet."

"What do you say, Vlad? What do you choose?" I asked him quietly.

Silence. Moments of pressure. We both knew that the atmosphere at the prom would be totally unsuitable for a child of God. The last preparations to leave for the banquet were taking place in the schoolyard. We decided to pray together, to speak with God. We knelt down in our usual place. When we stood up, my son decided not to go to the banquet! We walked together to the window. During the few moments of fellowship with God a few crystalline drops of rain had fallen from a clear summer sky. And then across the whole sky suddenly shone two brilliant, divine rainbows. God was there, together with us. We remembered His words: "And it shall come to pass, when I bring a cloud over the earth, that the bow shall be seen in the cloud: And I will remember my covenant, which is between me and you."

Through the colors of His love God bent over us, spoke to us, and gave us strength. I understood that my son's decision was viewed by God as an acceptance of His covenant. I felt the presence and acceptance of God too. This was a new experience of the peace of Jesus, so sweet and so different from the peace that the world tries to offer us.

DOINA NICOLAE

Oh, He Touched Me

Then Jesus, moved with compassion, stretched out His hand and touched him. Mark 1:41, NKJV.

WE HAD JUST EATEN AT OLIVE GARDEN that Sunday night to celebrate my brother's graduation from Alabama Agricultural and Mechanical University in Huntsville, Alabama. My dad suggested that we go for a drive so that he could show my aunt some of the beautiful houses in and around Mount Sano. As we headed for the mountain, my 21-month-old daughter, Guielle, began to get cranky. Being new to parenthood, I had no idea what she wanted. Several family members made suggestions, and each one was tried to no avail. As my father drove on, we realized that Guielle was tired. I reached out and touched the right side of her face. In that second my daughter became calm. I kept patting the side of her face without saying a word. Minutes later Guielle was fast asleep in her car seat. Talk about the power of touch! My touch!

God's touch can be the leathery hands of a father who works with his hands, or it may be soft, like a mother's. His touch can soothe and calm your fears.

The Bible has so many references to Jesus touching people. Jesus' touch cleansed people of leprosy. Both Mark and Matthew talk about Jesus healing someone by using the power of touch: "Then He took the child by the hand" (Mark 5:41, NKJV). "Then Jesus put out His hand and touched him" (Matt. 8:3, NKJV). Jesus' touch reaches out to us when we falter: "And immediately Jesus stretched out His hand and caught him" (Matt. 14:31, NKJV).

One day Jesus will put my hand in His and take me home to be with Him forever. Oh, to feel that touch! You and I can experience it today, as well as look forward to feeling His touch for eternity. Won't you allow Him to touch you today? Be comforted by His touch!

Dear Lord, please help us to accept Your touch. Help us to realize the power that is in Your hand to heal us. Make me whole today, Lord, through Your touch.

DANA M. BEAN

Thought: God touches us in many ways. He reaches out to us through His Word as we meditate. Sometimes He touches us through the kindness and healing of others. Sometimes the touch of a friend feels like the touch of God. And you can give that touch to someone today.

A Blessing in Disguise

Consider it pure joy . . . , whenever you face trials of many kinds.
James 1:2, NIV.

OUR FRIEND, BILL, had been getting ready to move into a new office he was remodeling, but his planned opening date of July 1 had to be delayed a few days because of a problem getting the carpeting in. The building next door was a small, nondescript place that had been used for many years by a local thrift store for their furniture, books, and odds and ends.

Then one night there was a fire that involved both buildings, but the thrift shop building suffered more damage. Even though Bill had to postpone his opening for several months while the fire damage was repaired, he was thankful that he hadn't moved all his furniture and supplies in before the fire. And the transformation of the little building next door was the most amazing. The burned store was torn down and replaced by a neat office building that housed a medical practice. Yes, those were trials, but they turned out to be a blessing in disguise.

Even though I have passed my threescore and 10 years, my health had always been good. Then, rather suddenly it seemed, I began to have many problems. For several months I was in and out of the hospital, had all kinds of tests and blood work, and saw several specialists. None of them could find anything wrong with me, even though I knew I didn't feel up to par. Finally one of the specialists suggested that I have a routine procedure. It really didn't have anything directly to do with my symptoms, but just seemed like a good idea.

The results of that procedure showed that I had several precancerous polyps, which were removed at once. If it hadn't been for my sick spell, I would never have thought to have that test. Gradually my health improved, and once again I was able to see a blessing in disguise.

Thank You, heavenly Father, for these blessings in disguise. And help me to consider it joy when I face trials instead of complaining, because testing of my faith brings perseverance.

BETTY J. ADAMS

Thought: Blessings in disguise . . . You may want to study carefully the entire first chapter of James. There are many thoughts there worth memorizing.

Gifts and Talents

Having then gifts differing according to the grace that is given to us. Rom. 12:6.

I ENJOY CASUAL STROLLS through my daughter's yard and garden. Row upon row of beautiful flowers and plants of all kinds and colors are a constant reminder of her devotion to her talent (plus a lot of the hard work). Patti has a special gift for utilizing all sorts of outdoor memorabilia along with the flowers. She has varied trellises, stone-lined paths, and walkways. She displays so effectively old garden tools, birdhouses, baskets, and even old ladders and benches.

She inherited none of that talent from me; in fact, flowers and plants in my care usually wilt and die. The few flowers I did plant in front of her house and around the lamppost are on their own, except for some help from nature.

I always felt frustrated when my flowers looked so puny compared to others in the neighborhood. Then I read an article on natural talents and spiritual gifts that convinced me that we can't all be gardeners any more than we can all be singers or teachers.

When I recall some of the jobs I've held, I think that perhaps I was looking for my talent back then. I've cared for both preschoolers and teens in my home, cleaned houses, and worked in a cafeteria. I've sold Christian literature from door to door, and was a telephone operator for several years. Then at age 38 I went to school to become a licensed practical nurse. I really enjoyed my years as a nurse and was sure I'd found my niche, but after only five years I became ill and didn't return to my job after I recovered.

None of us have all the gifts, but we each have at least one, and I am responsible for that one gift that God has given me. I may not be able to be a nurse again, but I can be hospitable to those I meet each day. I may not be able to go door to door to sell Christian books again, but I can speak for my Lord from time to time. Perhaps I can't do as much as someone else might, and I may not be as effective as another person, but whatever I do will be unique with me because no one else can do it in the exact same way.

My prayer is that I may glorify my heavenly Father in whatever I do.

CLAREEN COLCLESSER

Thought: Look up 1 Corinthians 12 and Romans 12. With which of these gifts has God blessed you? Are you using them to His glory?

Daffodils

The winter is past, the rain is over and gone; the flowers appear on the earth.
S. of Sol. 2:11, 12.

 THE YOUNG PEOPLE FROM A NEIGHBORING CHURCH walked into Bethesda Retirement Home one weekend recently, bringing dozens of bunches of daffodils. The elderly residents were thrilled to be given the golden trumpet flowers. Vases soon appeared, and the dining tables were lavishly adorned with daffodils. I think that of all of God's beautiful flowers, daffodils are truly special. The sight of golden daffodils bravely withstanding chilly winds is a sure sign of spring.

I'll never forget the time my husband and I were on a narrow metal road on the east coast of New Zealand. As the car rounded a corner, my breath was taken away by a glorious sight. On the side of a hill were hundreds and hundreds of daffodils! No houses were in sight—not even nearby. Just the hillside literally covered with glorious, golden flowers heralding spring. I thanked God for His handiwork and that I was able to enjoy it.

For many years I lived in a much drier, hotter climate, where growing spring bulbs was virtually impossible. Instead God gave me the joy of flowers found in vivid subtropical colors. In October the jacaranda trees were covered with purple flowers. In December the flame trees were just that—aflame with red flowers. But I did miss the signs of spring.

I'm now back in the cooler climate of New Zealand. I can look out of my kitchen window and see a mature plum tree in my neighbor's garden that is literally covered with white blossoms. Spring is everywhere, in every garden I see. Tiny pale-green leaves appear on my clematis plant as it comes to life under the warming sun's rays. I enjoy seeing trees lining the edges of roads, awash in pale-pink blossom.

But my favorite? Golden daffodils. I have the joy of seeing them every day at this time of the year. It is spring.

Jesus told a parable of the fig tree: "Now learn this lesson from the fig tree: As soon as its twigs get tender and its leaves come out, you know that summer is near. Even so, when you see all these things, you know that it is near, right at the door" (Matt. 24:32, 33, NIV). As certain as the fig tree showed that summer was near, signs in the world today tell me that Jesus is coming soon. Let us all be ready!

LEONIE DONALD

Sound Advice for Scary Times

And now I have told you before it come to pass, that, when it is come to pass, ye might believe. John 14:29.

ON A RECENT AIRPLANE TRIP I noticed a passenger in the seat ahead of me reading *The Wall Street Journal*. One subhead identified an article on that page as a book review for a new tome about how to make safe investments in financially shaky times. The article's title promised "Sound Advice for Scary Times."

That brought to mind another Book that is chock-full of sound advice for scary times: the Holy Bible. The Bible offers invaluable advice about how to stay spiritually balanced during these times in which we live. I've been amazed at how God speaks to my innermost personal needs almost anywhere I turn in the Bible for devotional reading. For example, here is what I found in a superficial skimming of three random chapters.

- From the Old Testament: Psalm 103 addresses issues of fear, children, health, guilt, pain from the past, anger, low self-esteem, who God is, obedience, and trust.
- From the New Testament: Luke 4 discusses how to overcome any kind of temptation; how, and when, to keep the Sabbath; our duty to others; faith; spiritual warfare; the power of Christ; and balance in personal ministry.
- A random chapter from the book of Proverbs (chapter 14) addresses the following: how to be a wise woman, how to choose one's words, integrity of action and speech, a critical tongue, laughing at sin [think about the content of most sitcoms on TV], heavy hearts, controlling anger, relationships with our neighbors, planning good things for others, how to cooperate with God in order to have safe sanctuary, politicians, envying others, even how to avoid looking stupid in public!

Jesus told His disciples that if they paid attention to His words He would prepare them for whatever difficult, shocking, or tragic events might occur in their future. He wanted them to understand that notwithstanding human appearances, God was still in control of what goes on in this world. How much time each day are you spending in the only Book that can give you truly sound advice for the scary times in which we live?

CAROLYN RATHBUN SUTTON

Morning Joys

He wakeneth morning by morning; he wakeneth mine ear to hear as the
learned. Isa. 50:4.

 I AWAKE TO the singing of the birds at the very beginning of
dawn. I look at the clock and read the bright numbers: 4:30. A
full chorus of birds are performing now. I wonder, *Are they hav-*
ing a committee meeting, greeting each other and assigning the daily
duties, or are they having worship and singing praises? It is glorious
music to listen to as I stretch out comfortably in my bed, knowing that I
don't have to get up for some time yet.

A cool breeze blows in from the open window. I shiver a bit and turn
on the electric blanket, luxuriating in its coziness, especially as I remember
the cold winters of North Dakota from childhood. We used to stand
around the stovepipe coming up through our bedroom and undress
quickly. Then we made one fast leap into the center of the bed and bur-
rowed down under many quilts to wait for our body's heat to warm the
bed. Today a flick of the finger, and the heat is here.

Sasha, my charming blue mink cat (her registration papers call her that),
begins the night at the foot of the bed, appearing to be a watchwoman to guard
and protect. As the night cools, she comes up to lie as close as she can by my
body. I am a cat lover forever, and when I wake during the night it feels good to
have the warm little body against me. (My husband gets a little provoked if she
plops her little body on top of him. He doesn't think it's so little when he
awakes to her weight.) This morning she is still snuggled warmly against me.

I awake again at 7:00. I don't have any appointments this morning. I
can eat a leisurely breakfast while watching the morning news. I have a fas-
cination with the local weather report because we live in a temperate zone.
Best of all, I have plenty of time for my morning worship. I'm studying
from my German Bible and also reading a book on the life of Jesus. I come
away with added knowledge, refreshed and encouraged. What a blessing
when I have time for a long worship period instead of grabbing something
as I run out the door to catch the subway!

Maybe these aren't important joys in the whole spectrum of life, but I
rejoice in them.

Thank You, God, for the singing birds, the electric blanket, the sleeping cat,
and the wonderful Words You have given us. Thank You for my morning joys.

DESSA WEISZ HARDIN

Where in Your House Is Jesus?

If they obey and serve him, they will spend the rest of their days in prosperity and their years in contentment. Job 36:11, NIV.

MY SISTER, INGIE, loves to tell me stories. She shared a story with me of a Christian woman who admitted Jesus to her house and put Him in her guest room. It wasn't long after Jesus took up residence in that room that Satan visited her. The devil waged war in her house day after day. The woman couldn't understand how Jesus remained comfortable in her guest room and allowed the devil to cause such destruction to her home. So she decided to take Jesus to task about the situation. She went up to the guest room and, sure enough, Jesus was there, as peaceful as ever.

"Jesus," said the woman, "how could You be up here and not do something about all that the devil has been doing in my home? Everything is destroyed!"

Jesus replied, "I can work only where you put Me to work. You see, I have stayed where you invited Me to stay. You confined Me to your guest room—you didn't ask Me to take full control of the entire house."

The woman saw her error, apologized to Jesus, and gave Him full control of her home. When the devil arrived that evening and knocked on the door, Jesus answered. Upon seeing Jesus, he said, "Sorry! I have the wrong address!"

How important it is for us to give everything to Jesus! Withholding anything from Jesus can only be to our detriment.

According to biologists we have one heart with four chambers. We need to be sure that Jesus is in control of all four chambers of our hearts. What love would permeate our whole being and overflow to those around us if Jesus and His love resided in the chambers of our hearts!

Today I am recommitting everything I own to Jesus.

I now give You, dear Jesus, all of me—my dear husband, my children, our home, and all that we possess. I give You, Jesus, my hopes, my fears, my challenges, my frustrations, my joys and my sorrows, my health, my all. I give You, Lord, my relatives and friends, my job, my enemies, and anything else that I have forgotten to mention. Please take these as well, and then please live out Your life within me. Amen.

JACKIE HOPE HoShING-CLARKE

What Am I Doing Here?

Whatever your hand finds to do, do it with all your might, for in the grave, where you are going, there is neither working nor planning nor knowledge nor wisdom. Eccl. 9:10, NIV.

MY GALLBLADDER WASN'T FUNCTIONING, and the doctor's decision was final—surgery. "You don't need the gallbladder anyway, especially if it's not working. It's blocked with numerous gallstones," he said, looking at the results of the pelvic ultrasound. As I weighed the pros and cons of surgery, I thought, *This gallbladder is not a problem to me right now. Do I truly need to take it out? Couldn't I just quietly ignore it since it is obviously giving no distress signals?*

"It could become a problem later on," warned the surgeon, obviously reading my mind. "Then we would have to remove it with your body in a compromised state." Was this good advice? A second and third opinion confirmed it, so we proceeded to surgery.

Recuperation provides time for reflection. In the painful days that followed, days of not lifting anything heavier than a teacup, climbing steps slowly and heavily, I had time to ponder, to think about the things that really matter.

"Not functioning. Remove it." Could that be me? Was I "just there" in my spiritual life? Now I realized that "just there" was actually dangerous. A stalled vehicle "just there" in the middle of a freeway could be a real problem. If I was "just there," if I existed, I needed to understand my function and perform it. Gallbladders store bile, not gallstones, and they assist with digestion. Writers write. Teachers teach. Auditors audit. Witnesses witness. You get my point. What did the Lord want me to do—what was my function? What am I, a Christian, doing here on this earth? Am I "just here," sitting in church every Sabbath in my usual spot on the cushioned pew, my heart filling up with gallstones of malice, covetousness, gossip, and anger? If so, I need surgery, spiritual surgery.

Lord, lift me up to see my assigned task in Your vineyard. Let me not just sit here, doing nothing, looking pretty with my matching bag and shoes and with my hat tilted just right. You have a task for Your daughter. Help me to do my job because You created me to accomplish just that, or help me to be ready for surgery.

ANNETTE WALWYN MICHAEL

Fighting an Alien Power

For we wrestle not against flesh and blood, but against principalities, against powers, against the rulers of the darkness of this world, against spiritual wickedness in high places. Wherefore take unto you the whole armour of God, that ye may be able to withstand in the evil day, and having done all, to stand. Eph. 6:12, 13.

HAVE YOU EVER WATCHED *STAR TREK*, the TV series about the starship *Enterprise* and its odyssey through space? If so, perhaps you saw the episode in which an alien power invades the ship. This power is very disruptive and thrives on strife and discord. The crew and passengers learn how to get along peacefully with one another, and their good behavior eventually becomes their "shield," preventing this unwelcome alien power from taking over the ship, and finally banishing the power.

We earthlings are in the middle of an odyssey—our life's journey. We belong to the federation of planets that God placed in our universe. The crew on the *Enterprise* couldn't leave their ship to escape their enemy. Nor can we leave our "ship," Planet Earth, which has been invaded by the unwelcome alien power of Satan and his angels. They thrive on our disharmony.

The more we yield to the influence of those invaders, the easier it is for them to gain control of us and eventually make us their slaves, thus wrecking our lives. We may find it even more difficult to banish these evil beings than it was for the occupants of the spaceship to get rid of their enemy, for we can't do it by ourselves. However, we aren't without hope in this seemingly one-sided cosmic conflict between good and evil.

God has promised to help. He says, "Fear thou not; for I am with thee . . . ; yea, I will help thee; yea, I will uphold thee with the right hand of my righteousness. Behold, all they that were incensed against thee shall be ashamed and confounded: they shall be as nothing; and they that strive with thee shall perish" (Isa. 41:10, 11).

When the alien power tries to sneak back into our lives, we can keep our shields in place by staying close to God. Nothing makes these enemies tremble more than seeing us reading our Bibles or hearing us praying. With God helping us, we will win this war! God is stronger than the devil. The Bible says so!

BONNIE MOYERS

Mrs. Job, II

God shall wipe away all tears from their eyes. Rev. 7:17.

 MY FRIEND ODLIE WENT THROUGH A PERIOD of trial similar to Job in the Bible. Every six weeks, for a full two years, she was buffeted by one disappointment, loss, or crisis after another. The time was so traumatic for her that, in self-defense, her mind blocked the entire second year from her memory. She has no recollection of it at all.

It all began when her car was stolen while she and a group of children were watching the finish line of the Los Angeles Marathon. At six-week intervals after that, her brother died, she suffered a life-threatening emergency operation, and her father died. She sent her youngest son away to a boarding high school to remove him from the dangers of their gang-infested neighborhood. Her eldest son and his family immigrated to England. Odlie missed her two sons and her grandchildren and constantly worried about and prayed for them.

Her 15-year marriage to a cruel and consistently unfaithful husband finally disintegrated. Odlie took—and failed—the C-Best, a test she was thoroughly prepared for. (The C-Best is a test one must pass to teach public school in California.) All through those two horrible years Odlie persisted in taking and failing the C-Best every time she became eligible to do so. Her poor, battered mind simply would not function above a survival level.

At the end of those two years her divorce came to trial. Her unemployed husband petitioned the court for alimony. The divorce was granted, but the judge pointed to Odlie's near-poverty-level income and refused the alimony request. A week later Odlie took—and passed—the C-Best and was immediately hired as a fourth-grade teacher at a substantial salary. Had she passed the test earlier and been working as a teacher at the time of the court hearing, she would have had to pay alimony.

Now, nearly 20 years later, Odlie, like Job, has seen her trials end with an outpouring of God's love and blessings. She is retired from a rewarding teaching career and married to a Christian man who is loving, faithful, and totally committed to God and to her. All her children and grandchildren live nearby. She serves her loving God at church as a deaconess and as the leader of the women's intercessory prayer group. God has wiped away her tears.

DARLENEJOAN MCKIBBIN RHINE

The Least of These

The second is this, "You shall love your neighbor as yourself."
Mark 12:31, NRSV.

I HAVE A CHILDHOOD FRIEND who is a minister. Our families were reunited a couple years ago when they visited Canada. I was thrilled to learn that he has dedicated a large portion of his ministry to the service of the less privileged in various parts of Africa. I was moved to action when he described his work, his relationship with the people, their gratitude, their response to the gospel, and the miraculous ways that God has blessed. His passion leaves me with a burning desire to have some hands-on involvement.

At times like these, making a financial contribution seems terribly inadequate, but then I am jolted to the reality that my experience and limited skills may not be as effective as those of a teacher, gospel worker, tradesperson, or health-care professional. Does that mean that people like me cannot become involved in a tangible way? I think not!

It is my belief that God wants to use us just where we are. Often it is not our ability but our availability and willingness that makes the difference in whether or not God can use us. As a judicial officer, I must be impartial in my decisions. I am prohibited from bringing religion to the forefront. I can, however, apply Christian principles to my decisions and interactions with the people who come before my court. Although my work setting is based on an adversarial model, compromises are often made, and justice becomes tempered with mercy. It is beyond heartwarming when a mother meets me and tells me that "Johnny" or "Suzie" has straightened out his or her life and is now making better choices and is no longer involved in the criminal justice system. Or the young people, whom I faintly recall, who seek me out to report that they are now in college and are doing well at their studies because of a mini lecture from me or because they were given a second chance.

If, like me, you too yearn for the opportunity to make a more direct and significant impact on your fellow travelers on life's journey but feel you are coming up short, be patient. Maybe you need to ask God to use you where *He* sees fit. You might be surprised at just how effectively God can use you to bless others when you make yourself available. Your field of service might be much closer than you think!

AVIS MAE RODNEY

The Awesome One

But the Lord is with me as a mighty, awesome One. Jer. 20:11, NKJV.

Great is thy faithfulness. Lam. 3:23.

THE SOUTH ISLAND OF NEW ZEALAND has some of the most majestic mountains and lakes to be found in the world. As I drove along the long roads, the scenery all around me was majestic. Dark, brooding mountains towering above the lakes sought their reflections in the still waters. Snowcapped peaks touched the sky, and there was space all around. I called out to God, *The Lord is with me as a mighty, awesome one! Thank You, God.* I wept with joy and sang, "Great is thy faithfulness."

I had decided to take some days to drive to a women's retreat, to stop off at quiet spots, and to work on papers and overdue e-mails between two busy weekends in the southern part of the country where I was born. I prayed that God would lead me to quiet places where I could meditate and pray, as well. I had no idea of the grandeur that awaited me on this trip. The contrasts in the country were glorious—snowy jagged mountains; thousands of sheep and deer; farms dotting the slopes of the high country; trees and mountains reflected in mirror-like lakes; jagged rocky outcrops covered with moss; and wide, stony rivers rushing out to sea. Then I drove out to the coast and was surprised to find even more beauty awaiting me. My cabin on the cove had the largest glass window I had ever seen that overlooked a huge coastal bay where I could watch the sun set, and then watch it rise the next morning. On that morning I heard the gentle hopping of the birds on the tin roof. I hadn't heard that sound for many years, and I was delighted. Then I found native bush-clad hills right down to the sea's edges along the lonely coast where I could collect the beautiful turquoise paua shells, so famous in New Zealand. On that beach three long-legged birds performed a unique (to me) dance and song just for me.

God touched me again with His faithfulness. I could only praise Him and say that these three days were some of the best I had experienced in a long time. Life had been too busy with papers, meetings, schedules, and strategic plans; this was time to regain a sense of calm. The beautiful scenes have been here a long time, but even though this was my home country, I had never had time to see them before. I decided I would come back to this land where "God was with me as a mighty, awesome one."

JOY BUTLER

For the Rest of My Life

And Jesus said unto him, No man, having put his hand to the plough, and looking back, is fit for the kingdom of God. Luke 9:62.

AN E-MAIL WAS SENT TO ME with the final answer: "The number of steps the guard takes during the walk past the Tomb of the Unknowns." All players missed it.

I did some research and learned that there are a number of rules for these guards, and also a number of myths or rumors about them. One rumor is that they must commit two years of their life to guard the tomb, must live in a barracks under the tomb, cannot drink any alcohol on or off duty, and cannot swear for the rest of their lives.

The truth is that the average tour at the tomb is about a year. The sentinels live at Fort Myer, the nearby Army post, or off base, if they like. They do have living quarters under the steps of the amphitheater where they stay during their 24-hour shifts, but if they are of legal age they may drink anything they like, except while on duty. After nine months guards are given wreath pins that are worn on their lapels, signifying that they have served as guards of the tomb. If they disgrace the tomb, the wreath is taken away. Before soldiers are allowed "a walk," they must memorize seven pages of history on Arlington National Cemetery and then recite it verbatim. They must study the manual of arms, the guard-change ceremony, and the intricacies of military ritual, and the guard candidates are required to memorize additional information on Arlington Cemetery. They also must spend time preparing their uniforms for duty.

I had to think of my commitment to Jesus Christ. Not taking other gods before Him? Not making something an idol over God? No swearing? Keeping the Sabbath? Honoring parents? Not killing? Not committing adultery? Or stealing, lying, or coveting? (Ex. 20:1-17). God says that most important, people will know that I belong to Him by the love I show. What is my commitment?

The *Jeopardy* question/answer is "What is 21 steps?" It alludes to the 21-gun salute, which is the highest honor given any military or foreign dignitary. For our recognition of faithful service, Jesus will give us a robe, a crown, a victor's palm, and a mansion.

TRUDY DUNCAN

An Offhanded Prayer

If we are thrown into the blazing furnace, the God we serve is able to save us from it, and he will rescue us from your hand, O king. But even if he does not, we want you to know, O king, that we will not serve your gods or worship the image of gold you have set up. Dan. 3:17, 18, NIV.

THE DIXIE CHICKS SING A SONG entitled "Wide Open Spaces." It's about a girl moving out on her own for the first time, needing "room to make her big mistakes." Relocating to Oklahoma from California in my early 20s was my way of finding wide-open spaces. But as I settled into my first house, I discovered I lacked some of the things such a step requires—a washer and dryer, to name two. Working at a self-supporting mission institution required the accumulation process to be a gradual one!

That summer Pastor Mark Finley from the television show, *It Is Written,* led us each day in an in-depth study of the book of Daniel. One day, as he retold the story of Shadrach, Meshach and Abednego in Daniel 3, he pointed out verses 17 and 18. Shadrach, Meshach and Abednego told Nebuchadnezzar, "Our God is able to save us from the fiery furnace. But even if He does not, we'll still trust Him." That phrase reechoed in my head throughout the day. I had never heard it put that way before.

When I talked to my mom on the phone that evening, I told her how much I disliked going to the Laundromat to do my laundry. We both spoke wistfully of how nice it would be if I had my own washer and dryer at home. Our conversation turned to other things, and then ended moments later. I was lying on my stomach on my living room floor, and when we hung up I stayed there for a moment. Somewhat offhandedly I said to God in my mind, *God, I'd sure like to have my own washer and dryer. But even if I can't, I'll still trust You.*

The next day at work I ate my lunch with a friend and fellow worker. Excitedly she told me how she had just gotten a new washer and dryer. Would I like her old set?

I looked at her, and my eyes began to fill with tears. "What's wrong?" she asked.

I told her the prayer I had just prayed so casually the day before, and we hugged in exultation of our God's greatness and His interest in our personal wants and needs.

Thank you, Melinda—and thank You, God!

EMILY THOMSEN

My Hero

God is faithful, and he will not let you be tested beyond your strength, but with the testing he will also provide the way out so that you may be able to endure it. 1 Cor. 10:13, NRSV.

IT WAS MY SON BENJI'S SIXTEENTH BIRTHDAY. To celebrate, my three children and I took a raft trip down the American River—a calm floating/swimming/floating adventure. It was awesome! At one point, however, things changed. We encountered some very fast rapids, and I found myself on the outside of the raft. Although I was standing in water only above my knees, I couldn't get myself back in. It didn't help that there were three boys on the shore, laughing themselves silly at my less-than-graceful attempts. The current tugged the raft out of my hands, sweeping it downstream with my three cherubs aboard.

The 43-year-old me thought, *I'm too young to die, and if I don't die I will be in great pain if I bang over rocks.* My adventures these years tend to be tempered with an assessment of the pain potential.

I decided to make my way over to a calmer part of the river and swim down to meet my family. By now the boys watching from the shore were holding themselves up to keep from rolling on the ground laughing. I just grinned at them and hoped they were enjoying the drama.

Fighting the very strong current to get out, I walked on very tender feet over hard, mossy rocks. Partway to the little island separating the tumultuous waters from the navigable ones, I spied my son—my hero—wearing his tennis shoes, beating a path to my rescue. He walked out to me, slipped his own shoes onto my feet, and led me out to deeper water, assuring me that the rapids were deep enough to bodysurf down without pulverizing myself.

When did my children start protecting me instead of me protecting them? I wondered.

My heart both swelled with pride at my son, my protector, and cringed in dread at the realization that not only were they getting older—so was I.

I saw a poignant parallel in my experience that day. I have another Hero, a heavenly one, who also rescued me from the tumultuous currents. He bore the pain of the cross and the mockery of the onlookers. He did it all for me. And He, like Benji, never said a mumbling word.

PATRICIA CALAHAN MUÑIZ

Unbelievable

In my distress I called to the Lord; I cried to my God for help. From his temple He heard my voice. Ps.18:6, NIV.

ABOUT FIVE YEARS AGO I noticed a small lump in my left breast. I contacted different doctors, and they all said it was nothing to be worried about. A year later I met Dr. Mosquida at Cooper Memorial Hospital in Monrovia, who did a fine lumpectomy on my breast. Because he is not an oncologist, we sent the lump for a pathology test in Gambia, and I was put on Tamoxifen.

I visited England six months later and went for the final checkup. Unbelievably, I was diagnosed as a stage 2 breast cancer patient. Though I was surprised and frightened, I wasn't discouraged. So when my doctor invited me to ask questions, all I said was "'He is the Lord; let him do what is good in his eyes' (1 Sam. 3:18, NIV)." I then bowed down my head and prayed silently. Even though there was a long line for mastectomies in England, I was told there and then that I would be operated upon within two weeks. Isn't our God awesome?

Our God works; He never fails us whenever we call on Him. The surgery was successful, even though it was difficult and landed me in the intensive-care unit. After a day of blood transfusions my health improved.

I was worried about how I would be able to pay my hospital bills, but my name was put under the National Health Service, so I was discharged without charges—another miracle! This was unbelievable, because sometimes others are charged as much as $19,500 (£10,000). How come I was not charged even a penny?

I don't know how God does it, but He has ways that are beyond human understanding. After I was discharged from the hospital, God touched so many brothers and sisters from different churches to help me. Some came bringing gifts of all sorts: food, cards, pamphlets, books, and even money. Some volunteered to drive me to the hospital for my chemotherapy and radiotherapy appointments, as my husband was away on missionary work in Gambia.

Though I am still under a doctor's care, I know that the Lord will see me through this ordeal just as He did for the Bible woman with the issue of blood. All I need to do is trust Him and hold on to His promises—He never fails.

MABEL KWEI

Just Trust Me

Behold, God is my salvation; I will trust, and not be afraid: for the Lord Jehovah is my strength and my song; he also is become my salvation. Isa. 12:2.

MY HUSBAND AND I were planning to leave in a few days for our vacation in Barbados to visit my 88-year-old mom and other family members. One night I lay in bed, imagining all kinds of what-if scenarios. I worried that I would experience a severe allergic reaction to cologne or alcohol on the plane, and that I would become sick and the flight attendant would have to give me oxygen. Fear petrified me. As these crazy thoughts raced through my head, I tossed and turned. Sleep evaded me. Oh, what peace we often forfeit when we don't take our concerns to God in prayer.

Before daybreak I went to the bathroom and looked out the window. A large, brilliantly lit moon with a cross glowing from it appeared to be right outside my window, within touching range. It was incredible! How can the moon have a shape like a cross emanating from it? I looked at it in disbelief and felt impressed that God had seen my fear and anxiety and was reassuring me. He said, "My child, why are you worrying so? I gave My only beloved Son to die on a cross for you because I love you. Don't you know that not one sparrow falls to the ground without My notice, and that even the hairs on your head are numbered? Don't be afraid; I'll take care of you."

I thought to myself, *God, You really care about little ol'me.* He reminded me that He had cared for me for 63-plus years as I traveled to faraway places on land, sea, and air. Why was I doubting that He could do it again? My fears abated, and I returned to bed and slept soundly.

My cardiologist had cautioned me not to sit for more than two hours at a time because of a blood clot in my right lung. But on the trip from Miami to Barbados I was not assigned an aisle seat. I asked the woman sitting next to me if we could exchange seats. She disliked sitting in middle or window seats, but was willing to let me have hers. Just as we were about to move, she saw vacant seats and volunteered to move. This left me with an extra seat on which to rest my legs.

We had a great time visiting my family and friends and arrived home safely. God has shown His love to me in so many ways. Hasn't He done the same for you?

SHIRLEY C. IHEANACHO

Forty-four No's, One Yes

Pray without ceasing. 1 Thess. 5:17.

INDEPENDENCE DAY IS MY SMALLEST DOG. At 55 pounds, she's my little runt puppy. When she was born she fell on the floor, still in her birth sack that had torn. Her little tiny yelps woke me up. A fine "canine midwife" I turned out to be! Midgie, her mother, was just as worn out as I was. It took a while to find Indy on the floor, behind the bed. Indy turned out to be one of 10 puppies born during the wee hours of July 4.

Around her fourth birthday Indy had an epilepsy seizure. At first I had no idea what was happening. After consulting with Doc, my vet, we decided to let things go and see what would develop. She didn't have the seizures on a regular basis—every 30 to 60 days at the most. Because of the infrequency we didn't medicate her.

A year later I had told her how proud I was of her for not having a seizure for 90 days. Within 30 minutes she had a seizure, followed by another, and then another. Over the next four days she had one seizure after another, 30 to 60 minutes apart. Doc sent me some medicine, but unfortunately nothing seemed to stop the horrible seizures. It is one thing for a human to have a seizure; it is quite another for an animal to have one. I was alone, and it was difficult to deal with completely by myself.

With every episode, I would pray, "Please, God! Help me! I can't take much more." Then I would feel horrible. Poor little Indy was having a harder time than I was! My other three dogs weren't really dealing with this situation either. After a really bad episode, I asked Indy if I should put her down. She reached up and nipped my nose.

Finally, as mysteriously as they began, the seizures stopped. She had had 45 seizures in four days. It took nearly a week for her to return to health, and she had absolutely no side effects. Today Indy is healthy, happy, and as normal as she can possibly be. There have been no ill effects from the seizures, nor has she had any since. It really is a miracle. I had prayed 45 times. I am thankful I got a yes to one of those prayers. I'm thankful God cares for pets as well as humans.

MARY E. DUNKIN

A Protecting God

The Lord will keep you from all harm. Ps. 121:7, NIV.

AFTER A FOUR-DAY VISIT TO THE ETOSHA NATIONAL PARK in Namibia, we thought that it would be good to spend part of our vacation there again. Our children were studying in Portugal, so we agreed that when they came home during the next vacation period, we would visit the park again. And so we did.

After being in the park for several days, we drove by car on the same roads that we had driven previously and visited the same watering holes at which the animals congregate. At the edge of the road we saw a female elephant with her small calf, resting behind a tree. With the windows and doors closed, we stopped at a distance to film her.

As we watched, we noticed a park ranger's Land Rover coming in our direction. He backed up and stopped in the weeds, ready to take off. We all thought this was strange. Then, looking in one of the side mirrors, I saw an enormous elephant behind us, silently waving his huge ears, while a herd slowly neared us. I realized that the vehicle that had stopped at some distance was ready to take off and seek help—if this was necessary. I don't know how long we remained there in fearful silence, waiting to see what would develop while we requested divine assistance.

Finally the smaller elephants, guided by their mothers, slowly crossed the road in front of us. The mother elephant we had filmed with her calf went with the herd. The big chief of the herd remained behind us. We counted 39 elephants. When all of the elephants were some distance away, the big elephant went into the brush beside us, returned to the road waving his huge ears, and trumpeted. He stamped the ground, stared directly at us, then calmly went on his way.

It was then that the park ranger continued on his journey and passed by us, smiling. The danger had passed, and we thanked God! We imagined what could have happened if the Lord had not been there and if we had not understood that the chief elephant was just protecting his herd.

Have you stopped to think how your life would be if you didn't have God as a protector? How great and marvelous is our God, and what wonderful experiences we can have with Him each day!

MARIA SALES

Space Flight

And if I go and prepare a place for you, I will come again and receive you to Myself; that where I am, there you may be also. John 14:3, NKJV.

 THE CAPTION READ "U.S. Millionaire Heads 'Out of this World.'" How fortunate that a seemingly ordinary citizen can join a cosmonaut and an astronaut on their space trip to the International Space Station for a weeklong stay—for a hefty price tag of $20 million! Mr. Gregory Olsen is a wealthy businessman and can afford the ticket. For an island girl like me who lives to fly, space travel is too costly and will never be like air travel. Surfing the Internet and comparing ticket prices online is one of my favorite pastimes because I love to travel, and I love great deals.

I thought about life on the spaceship—the cramped space, the different apparatus that must be correctly connected, the space suit, the computers and other gadgets, the dehydrated and floating food. Then my mind quickly thought of the space trip that will take place one day if I am faithful. I will fly through earth's atmosphere and on to God's dwelling place, a seven-day journey, without the aid of a heavy space suit, computer stations, or scientists monitoring my ascent. I won't need to cross my fingers, hoping that nothing goes wrong, because Jesus Himself will escort me, along with the millions of other people, through space. And the trip will be free! That means that I don't have to worry about investing on Wall Street and saving every dime to make this trip possible. A trip that cost Mr. Olsen approximately $2 million a day will be absolutely free for me as along as I accept Jesus into my life. It doesn't matter what my socioeconomic status is. I can't even imagine what the bill would be to spend 1,000 years with my Lord if I had to pay—trillions of dollars!

Mr. Olsen said that some day space flight will be as routine as air travel is today. I most certainly agree. But the trip I am going on will be even more spectacular. Imagine being in a place where God lives and reigns! No more heartache, sorrow, or pain. My mansion will be tailor-made for me, with all the amenities. No mortgage, no termites, no taxes. There will be no returning to earth after a mere 10 days. One thousand years in Paradise! I want to be ready for that space trip. Don't you?

ANDREA A. BUSSUE

Through the Flood

When you pass through the waters, I will be with you; and when you pass through the rivers, they will not sweep over you. Isa. 43:2, NIV.

BY THE TIME I GOT OUT OF BED the storm was at its height. Strong winds blew through the trees, and the rain pelted against my windows. *God, You are going to have to stop that rain so that I can get to work.* But He had another lesson prepared for me. The rain didn't let up; in fact, it got worse just when I had to leave for work. Because I had forgotten my umbrella at the office, I used an old jacket to cover my head and wrapped my 2-year-old in towels. I arrived safely at my mom's house and dropped off my daughter. Now all I had to do was to get to work.

It was raining so hard that I could barely see. Aware of how quickly roads flood in Panama City, I took another route, trying to avoid the streets in my neighborhood that usually flood. Everything seemed fine until I reached the main road. Here the cars were moving extremely slowly, and then they stopped completely. I tried to see what had happened, but it was hard to tell. *Hope it's not an accident,* I thought nervously. I wanted to detour as some of the other motorists were doing, but I wasn't familiar with the connecting streets. It seemed as though the street was so flooded that some of the cars were having mechanical problems.

I decided not to panic, although the cars that were stalled seemed to be much better vehicles than mine! *Lord, I don't really know any techniques for getting a little old car through high waters. You're going to have to take me through.*

I watched wide-eyed as some motorists bravely advanced. In some places the water became as high as mid-door. Then came my turn. I whispered another prayer and stepped on the gas. *Lord, I really hope that verse in Isaiah 43:2 can be taken literally!*

Huge waves formed at the sides of my car as I drove by a half dozen "good" cars that had simply stopped running. I said a little prayer for those stranded in the storm and then realized that God had taken me through the flood! *Hallelujah! Hallelujah!* I said over and over as I drove to higher ground.

No matter what you are called to face today, be encouraged—God will take you through the flood and the fire. He'll be standing by, and in the end everything will be all right.

DINORAH BLACKMAN

197

Unknown Danger

The Lord watches over you . . . ; the sun will not harm you by day, nor the moon by night. . . . The Lord will watch over your coming and going. Ps. 121:5-8, NIV.

A WARM EARLY-SUMMER NIGHT beckoned me as I laced my jogging shoes and snapped the leash on Sheba, my Doberman. Eager for a walk, she wagged her stubby tail and pranced, her eyes gleaming in eager anticipation. I too looked forward to our evening walks.

Trees and pretty yards greeted us as we jogged out of my driveway. We trotted a few blocks, then slowed to a walk. The moon hadn't climbed the sky yet, and the only lights were streetlamps and the usual traffic. I felt the breeze and smelled the new spring orange blossoms.

Then in the distance behind me I heard a siren. *An ambulance*, I thought, as I turned to look. But it wasn't an ambulance. A huge, dark truck and trailer, its headlights off, barreled down the street at a high rate of speed. A car was driving toward me in the opposite lane of the small, two-lane street. The truck slowed slightly, then raced forward, squeezing between the car and my side of the sidewalk.

It happened so fast! I could only stop and stare—no time to run. I could have reached out my hand and touched the truck, it seemed so close. Yet the wheels didn't come up on the sidewalk. The truck rushed by, followed by a police car with siren blasting. Both ran the stop sign up ahead and sped on down the once-quiet street.

When I got to the stop sign, I looked down the street to see it barricaded with roadblocks, police cars, and red lights.

The morning's newspaper told the story. A teenage boy had stolen a truck and horse trailer (fortunately no horse was in the trailer) and given the police a wild 10-mile chase before the truck was stopped by a tack strip thrown in front of its wheels. To avoid the police, the driver had run stop signs and red lights, swerved around cars, and driven on sidewalks, sending people scurrying out of his way, the paper said.

I breathed a prayer of relief and thanks to God for keeping the truck off my sidewalk as it passed the other car, and for keeping everyone involved from injury that evening. We never know just how close we are to eternity.

EDNA MAYE GALLINGTON

Victory Park

And this is the victory that has overcome the world—our faith.
1 John 5:4, NKJV.

IT WAS NARROW AND STEEP, and it was winding. That road appeared to have been hewn from solid rock, and our tour bus proceeded cautiously. Then suddenly it made a sharp turn to the right, and we passed under an impressive sign: "Victory Park."

Victory Park is situated on a narrow plateau. Guardrails provide safety from returning unexpectedly to that road below! To our left we saw an array of weather-beaten war planes. Our host explained the virtues of each plane, including when and where it had been utilized. He also provided a moving eulogy for the loyal pilots who had won glorious victories for the nation.

Next we paused before a war memorial, a 25-foot statue of a woman holding a child's hand. The little girl clutched the folds of the woman's peasant skirt. Other children played about her feet. The inscription declared: "She did what she could. She gave her children." What heartaches accompany war!

Then our host pointed to the highest peak in a range of low mountains. "That," he said, "is Mount Ararat." Mount Ararat? I hadn't expected to see Mount Ararat from this location (Gen. 8:4)! I walked a few steps toward the wall at the end of Victory Park, gazing silently at the snowcapped mountain, significant for its place in Judeo-Christian history. A myriad of thoughts and emotions tumbled through my mind.

Noah, God's messenger for the pre-Flood world, is described as "just" and "perfect" (Gen. 6:9). Undeterred by indifference, ridicule, or doubt in a world characterized by corruption and violence (verse 11), his unwavering faith in God established him as an heir of righteousness by faith (Heb. 11:7). Jesus, speaking of our time, said it would be like that of Noah's (Matt. 24:37-39). But John encourages us with the assurance that there will be victory, by faith, that will overcome the world (1 John 5:4)!

Yes, Victory Park, there will be victories. There will be millions of them, including mine, not won by war planes but by faith which will overcome the world.

These victories, by faith, exonerate God, Sovereign of the universe.

LOIS E. JOHANNES

Do You See What I Sea?

Brethren, I count not myself to have apprehended: but this one thing I do, forgetting those things which are behind, and reaching forth unto those things which are before. Phil. 3:13.

I ENJOY TV PROGRAMS that tell the story of experienced divers who search the ocean floor for treasures. The determination involved in this process is obvious from the tedious work required to retrieve treasures or information. The remnants of tragic events continually perpetuate an interest in dredging up these treasures and reliving the past. Although the world attempts to uncover history, God is in the business of covering some of it up.

Micah 7:18, 19 reads, "Who is a God like unto thee, that pardoneth iniquity, and passeth by the transgression of the remnant of his heritage? he retaineth not his anger for ever, because he delighteth in mercy. He will turn again, he will have compassion upon us; he will subdue our iniquities; and thou wilt cast all their sins into depths of the sea." I revel in that promise! In watching these nautical programs, I can see how far down the depths of the sea really are and the importance of God's use of the word "sea" in this verse. This verse brings two issues to mind that I battle with on a regular basis.

First, I wonder how much dredging of people's past I have done to my friends, family, and/or myself. Maybe I need to stop the dredging of the ocean floor of others and toss back into the "sea" what I found in that search.

Second, I ask myself if I really believe that I've been forgiven for something that I've gone to God about. This is especially true when Satan brings to mind a particular iniquity, or the effect it has had on someone. It's to my benefit to trust God's Word. Again and again He promises to forgive our sins if we rely on Him: "To open their eyes, and to turn them from darkness to light, and from the power of Satan unto God, that they may receive forgiveness of sins, and inheritance among them which are sanctified by faith that is in me" (Acts 26:18). It seems so simple—all I have to do is ask. Yet that seems like a monumental task.

MARY M. J. WAGONER ANGELIN

Thought: Have you thanked God recently for burying your sins so deeply? Is there some past sin—even forgiven sin—that you dredge up from time to time? What do you want to do about it today?

Old Dog—New Tricks

You were taught, with regard to your former way of life, to put off your old self, which is being corrupted by its deceitful desires; to be made new in the attitude of your minds. Eph. 4:22, 23, NIV.

AFTER A BUSINESS appointment I headed home, nothing special on my mind. A glance in my rearview mirror and the sight of a flashing blue light confirmed my worst fear—a police officer. I immediately pulled to the side of the road. "Not again!" I muttered, as dreaded thoughts flooded my brain.

The not-too-friendly officer demanded my driver's license and registration. He had clocked me at 53 miles an hour in a 40-mile-an-hour zone. I pleaded for mercy. "Lady," he quipped as he wrote out the ticket, "if I give you mercy, I have to give it to everyone else I've issued tickets to today."

Getting a speeding ticket is never a pleasant experience, but this ticket was worse. After more than 30 years of never having a speeding ticket, this ticket made two in one year! To keep the first one off my record I went to traffic school—online. Anything online challenges me. But this turned out to be a triple challenge. Only perseverance, ingenuity, and prayer got me a passing grade. The thought of traffic school again threw me into a tailspin!

Later I analyzed why I was in this speeding pickle. Why was I speeding? Because I always squeeze more into any given time frame than can possibly be accomplished. I am time-oriented. I talk fast, walk fast, type fast—and yes, drive fast. When I'm driving, I feel competitive, as if I need to pass everyone on the road—to be the first one out of the starting gate when the light turns green. It's my habit, part of my nature. For many years, I thought it was "cool."

No longer do I think that way. Habits are difficult to break and are sometimes cherished. Two tickets in one year have convinced me (the fine helped) that I must slow down. Every time I'm on the road now, I attempt to drive the exact speed limit, or one mile an hour under. Occasionally the old habit takes over, and the speedometer creeps up. The second I see it, I slow down again. I was forced to become aware of a bad habit, made a conscious effort to change—and did. Who said you can't teach an old dog new tricks?

NANCY VAN PELT

Sitting Still With Jesus

They listened to Him, and then they began going out, conscience-stricken, one by one, from the oldest down to the last one of them, till Jesus was left alone, with the woman standing there before Him in the center of the court. John 8:9, Amplified.

THE WOMAN WAS POSSIBLY A PROSTITUTE. Respectable people ostracized prostitutes, religious leaders condemned them, but Jesus forgave them.

I have always read this woman's story and experienced two emotions—embarrassment for the woman, and anger with those who thrust her into the presence of the holy Jesus, especially because they were the ones who encouraged her to sin. But recently that anger has changed to pity. I feel sorry for those who demanded her stoning. I feel sorry for them to be in the presence of Jesus, to have their sins revealed (even if only to themselves), and to walk away before they hear Jesus say, "Neither do I condemn you." It must be one of the loneliest experiences of life.

The beauty of this story is that the woman sat long enough in Jesus' presence to experience forgiveness for her sins, freedom from guilt in her heart. Now, I wonder whether we are quiet enough, when we are in Jesus' company, to experience release from guilt, cleansing from the evil that seeps through our hearts and minds? Are we still enough to know without any hesitation that there is no sin, intentionally performed or unconsciously committed, that God will not forgive? Do we really know that God longs more than anything to give us His forgiveness and acceptance?

For many years I have taught an intercessory prayer group. In one of the sessions we focus on our sins. We ask God to reveal our sins. We then confess to God and ask for cleansing.

When I first did this I was shocked at the sins God brought to mind—not obvious things, but attitudes, thoughts, and emotions that I hadn't been aware of. As these sins came to mind, I spent time with God, asking Him to cleanse me. What amazed me was how peaceful I felt within! I also experienced an increased desire to do right, not just outwardly but inwardly. I wanted to rely on God, to serve Him, and to worship Him more.

Sit down with God long enough that He can show you your sins. Let Him bathe you with His forgiveness. Sit still, listen to God's words of acceptance, and live in His peace.

MARY BARRETT

Where Beauty Lies

She is a woman of strength and dignity, and has no fear of old age. When she speaks, her words are wise, and kindness is the rule for everything she says. Prov. 31:25, 26, TLB.

THE GATE IS PUSHED OPEN AND SWINGS WIDE, giving off a metallic sound as it clangs noisily against the fence. It's 4:30 p.m., and although the women gathered there are talking together and laughing, each has her eye on the gate in anticipation of being one of the first into the pool. I watch as they hurry through the gate, carrying their trendy bags and towels decorated with fishes and seashells. Many will disappear into the restroom, emerging moments later clad only in their swimsuits. They laugh and kid each other as they walk toward the ramp and make their way into the pool.

Their dimpled arms and thighs are made more obvious by the unforgiving rays of the sun. Many have large distended bellies that protrude downward, and sagging breasts and buttocks. Some wear suits with skirts to hide fleshy thighs that rub together. Many of these women have legs mottled blue with varicose veins. Others are just big, well-proportioned women, and some are slender. Most of them are in their 60s, 70s, and even 80s. All are regulars at the water aerobics class.

I watch as these beautiful women in their stylish suits enter the pool. And as each one slowly submerges into the cool, clear water, gone are the ravages of time, gravity, childbirth, motherhood, and years of putting others ahead of themselves. What remains are the lovely faces of different women, each one made beautiful by the vast experiences of a life unique to her.

The water feels wonderful, and for the next hour we laugh and joke as we exercise and enjoy this time for ourselves. And for that hour I watch and learn and look forward to that time when I reach that stage of my life, their time. Though I will eventually lose what in society's eyes is considered youthful beauty, by doing my very best to accept and fulfill my role as a daughter, sister, wife, mother, grandma, as a woman, I will give honor to my Creator as I grow more beautiful in His loving eyes.

TERRI CASEY

Thought: Western culture does not honor age as does some other cultures. What do you think you can do to honor the women in your community who deserve this respect and honor?

Doing the Impossible

For with God all things are possible. Mark 10:27.

IN 1975 WE WERE IN OUR FIRST DISTRICT, pastoring three churches in Quitman, Mississippi, a small town with a population of 2,000. I was 37 weeks into my fourth pregnancy. We lived in an old plantation house with 10-foot-high ceilings and four huge white columns on a porch that stretched from one side of the front of the house to the other. On one side of the house an empty field went all the way to the corner on the main street in town. A huge, very old pecan tree in the backyard supported a rope and tire swing suspended from a high, fat branch.

Our car was old and the engine blew, so my husband, whose hobby is auto mechanics, used a branch of the old pecan and a come-along to lift the engine out of the car. He was able to get the engine out by himself, and he rebuilt it on top of my chest freezer in the family room. But when he went to put it back in, it became a challenge to line up the transmission and the engine without a second person to help him. So when he told me of the problem, I did the only thing I could to help. I volunteered to climb up on top of the car and work the come-along while he guided the engine into place.

I put my 20-month-old toddler outside in the playpen under another tree about 30 feet away where I could still see him. I told his two brothers, 4 and 6 years old, to watch him and to stay out of the way of the car.

I must say that as I look back on that day, I wonder what people thought as they drove by that corner and looked over and saw me, huge belly and all, up on top of the car helping my husband. I don't know how we did it, but I'm sure our angels must have been helping us. I'm sure they were probably amused. I thank God that we have continued through 38 years of marriage to work together as a team.

CELIA MEJIA CRUZ

Thought: What kinds of teams have you worked on in your life? Marriage is mentioned here. As Christians we should be on a team working with our God and His angels. But what about other family teams? Church, community, or even national teams? Do you feel as if you are making a difference? Look at today's text and ask yourself, Why not?

Open Our Eyes, Lord

However, as it is written: "No eye has seen, no ear has heard, no mind has conceived what God has prepared for those who love him." 1 Cor. 2:9, NIV.

MY MOTHER, NEARLY 80, was having vision challenges. One morning she just could not seem to be able to read our devotional book during worship. She handed me the book to read. Later, during her hydrotherapy treatment, the therapist said, "Verena, do you know you have a lens missing?" No! She didn't know! That explained why she hadn't been able to read earlier!

Just a couple days later my mom was paying her bills in her little office. She kept asking me to adjust the light for her because she couldn't read well enough. Then she asked for me to put in a brighter bulb, which I brought and installed. Then, and only then, did I notice the problem. "Mom, do you know you have your sunglasses on?" I asked her.

"Oh, no! No wonder I couldn't read these numbers!" We laughed and laughed at these two incidents. Because of her macular degeneration, we had assumed her eyes were just getting worse, when all along it was a simple, undetected, unrelated limitation.

Sometimes we have limited spiritual vision because of the issues in life—problems in our families, our churches, our schools, ourselves; problems that consume us and cause untold anxiety and worry. How much better to start each day by remembering this: "Good morning! I am God. Today I will be handling all your problems. Please remember that I do not need your help. If the devil happens to deliver a situation to you that you cannot handle, do not attempt to resolve it. Kindly put it in the SFJTD (Something for Jesus to Do) box. It will be addressed in My time, not yours.

"Once the matter is placed in the box, do not hold on to it by worrying about it. Holding on to, or removal from, will delay the resolution to your problems. If it is a solution that you think you are capable of handling, please consult Me in prayer to be sure that it is the proper solution. Because I do not sleep nor do I slumber, there is no need for you to lose any sleep. Rest, my child. If you need to contact Me, I am only a prayer away. Have a great day!"

This opens my eyes; it helps me to see, to understand who really is in control in my life! *Open our eyes, Lord; we want to see Jesus.*

BECKI KNOBLOCH

The Cure

For I am the Lord, who heals you. Ex. 15:26, NIV.

I LIKE THE VERB "HEAL." During the past year this verb assumed a special significance to me. I experienced turbulent times in my personal life, full of pain and confusion. Suddenly I no longer believed in the God who in the past had been so near to me. I believed in His existence, but I didn't believe that He could fix my life again. I went to church, spoke to people, listened to the minister, but my thoughts were far away. Deep down I felt a thirst toward relentless self-destruction that seemed to plunge me further down and take away my will to live. Every morning I became sad as I woke up. It was difficult to live with my own thoughts. The day dragged slowly along, and I longed for night, for the unconsciousness of sleep.

Most of the time I felt sustained by my family, specifically by the prayers they offered with me and for me. I was at the edge of an abyss, and their hands maintained me. I almost didn't have strength to pray for myself. It was their prayers that kept me lucid.

I knew that my life was in pieces, and I had no idea how to put it back together. Actually, a part of me didn't *want* to put anything together, but another part knew that this was necessary for my own happiness. During these times I called out for healing. I thought that healing would come quickly and that it would not depend so much on me. I lost my patience with God. I wanted Him to answer in my way, exactly at the moment I wanted. I was wrong. The God who heals wanted only one thing from me—for me to seek Him each day, even though I didn't believe in many concepts and principles, because I was broken within.

When I understood this, I went to Him and promised just one thing: I would seek Him each day, even if I didn't want to. It was difficult and discouraging; I lacked concentration, and reading the Bible didn't interest me. But then the healing slowly began. The rebellion started to leave, belief took its place, and I began to give myself to Him. Since then I have felt confident regarding the future, even though I admit I still feel some fear. But I know that my God can do all things. My God gathers the pieces to which I was reduced, the pieces that have fallen on the floor and have been abandoned, and He remakes me in His image—a new person, better than the previous—and tells me, "For I am the Lord, who heals you." He can do it for you, too.

IANI DIAS LAUER-LEITE

Everything in Its Place

Let all things be done decently and in order. 1 Cor. 14:40.

ONE OF THE MANY LESSONS I LEARNED from Mama and Papa was "A place for everything, and everything in its place."

I was on my way to college vespers and in a hurry because I was a little behind schedule. The music coming from the chapel indicated that the service had already begun, so I hastened my footsteps. Suddenly I was distracted by an anxious, high-pitched voice, the voice of little Miss J.

"Miss G, Miss G—your skirt!"

Puzzled, I thought, *How can she see my skirt?* It was winter, and I was wearing a full-length coat.

"Miss G, your skirt is hanging from the back of your coat."

Sometimes we hear people talk about wishing the earth would open up to swallow them. Well, at that very moment I was in that exact position, wishing to be relieved of the horrible embarrassment. The soft pink accordion-pleated skirt I had been working on had somehow become securely anchored to the back of the coat I was wearing. All the labor that had been exerted to make sure that all the pleats were pinned in place was forgotten as with anxious, awkward fingers I hastily removed pins, released the skirt, and mercilessly stuffed the now-crumpled mess into one pocket of the coat.

The skirt was something I had long wished to own; it had become an object of pride. In its place it was very useful. But now, out of place, it suddenly seemed so unimportant. Also out of place were the precious minutes spent to secure the pleats. Out of place, too, was the almost iconic value I had assigned to it. But now it was nothing, for idols are nothing.

Deeply humiliated but truly grateful, I thanked Miss J as gracefully as I could for her kind act. With fallen pride and slower steps, I finally reached the chapel, where I joined the worshippers, while "Everything in its place" kept ringing in my ears.

Lord, I am thankful for the help I receive from others, but especially from You as I try to keep everything in its place.

QUILVIE G. MILLS

Sandwiched

Have faith in the Lord your God and you will be upheld. 2 Chron. 20:20, NIV.

 IT WAS 7:00 IN THE MORNING, just the right time for me to get started with my walking exercise. It was cold, and it had just rained, but I needed my exercise. With my condition, walking is therapeutic.

Although the rain had stopped, the dark clouds were hanging low, and a storm was imminent. With a prayer in my heart, I asked the Lord to at least hold the rain for an hour so I could finish my round of two miles up the hill and two miles back down to where I was temporarily living.

I fully enjoyed my walk, especially when another jogger slowed down and talked to me. He said, "This is a foretaste of heaven." Then in a duet we both said, "The difference is, there will be no more pain, no more sickness, no more tsunami, nor terrorists." Then we parted ways.

About a block away from home the fine showers started. I hurried on, and as soon as I was inside, the thunder roared, lightning began to strike, and the rain poured down "like cats and dogs."

I immediately prayed, "O Father God, how can I not believe Your promise that You will send Your holy angels to protect Your child! You have calmed the raging storms and the roaring waves of the ocean, and You created the peaceful Sea of Galilee for Your disciples. You can even create a 'weather sandwich.'"

God had created a space between the rains for me to enjoy His nature and His care. It caused me to praise Him more. David praises God this way: "For thy mercy is great unto the heavens, and thy truth unto the clouds" (Ps. 57:10). He is worthy of His name. How thankful I am for an awesome God who creates a "time sandwich."

May we, your daughters, continue to hold on to your promises. I have experienced your answers many times. I pray that we may all appreciate them each day, through sunshine or rain.

ESPERANZA AQUINO MOPERA

Thought: Today might be a good time to take inventory of your prayer experiences and answers. How has your faith been, and what are you doing to exercise it? And when you get a positive answer, do you too praise God, as did David and Esperanza?

The Good Accident

And we know that all things work together for good to them that love God, to them who are the called according to his purpose. Rom. 8:28.

WE HAD BEEN MARRIED EXACTLY 10 MONTHS when we decided to visit my husband's mother and participate in an anniversary celebration at the boarding school at which we had studied. As we neared home we remembered that there was a large hole in the highway on a long hill close to home, and that we needed to go around it so that we wouldn't run the risk of blowing a tire or causing even greater damage to the car. As we drove around the hole, another car came from the opposite direction, as though it were dancing on the road. We realized that the driver must be under the influence of alcohol. As we swerved, the other driver became frightened and swerved in front of our car. My husband abruptly turned the steering wheel, and the car, out of control, went up a hill, then flipped over—five times! The last flip landed the car on top of an old tree trunk.

While the car was still flipping, I closed my eyes. I was certain that the Lord would save our lives. I had never remained so calm when faced with such a great problem. I know that it was the Lord who gave me this calm attitude.

When the car came to a stop, we heard a loud noise, like an explosion. We quickly got out of the car and saw that it was only the boiling radiator. Thinking our little dog had been thrown out of the car, we looked everywhere, calling him insistently. He finally crawled out from under the luggage, trembling with fear.

Incredible as it may seem, nothing serious had happened to us. My husband had suffered one cut, and absolutely nothing had happened to me! When the police arrived to make the accident report, the police officer looked at my husband and asked, "Are you the owner of this car?" My husband answered affirmatively. "Look," stated the police officer, "I do not believe in God, but I am going to tell you one thing: when you get home, thank your God for saving your lives!"

After that accident our lives changed. My husband decided to work for God full-time as a pastor, making a dream that I had carried in my heart come true. As the apostle Paul says: "All things work together for good to them that love God."

WALKÍRIA VESPA S. S. MOREIRA

He Watches Over Me

*Whither shall I go from thy spirit? or whither shall I flee from thy presence? . . .
Even there shall thy hand lead me, and thy right hand shall hold me.
Ps. 139:7-10.*

AFTER SHOPPING IN A FEW STORES in town that morning, I stopped at the supermarket on my way out of town. I left my shopping bag at the parcel counter, my cubicle ticket was handed to me, and I walked into the market with the ticket in my hand.

I took a shopping cart and began picking the grocery items I needed. As I stood in front of the shelf where peanut butter and baking powder were displayed, I thought of my parcel ticket. I looked through my handbag and among the items I had already picked. I asked one of the store workers who was replenishing the shelves on the opposite side if he had seen a parcel ticket lying around. He told me to report to the parcel counter immediately and tell them that I had lost my ticket.

Just as I turned around I saw a suspicious-looking man behind me. I left for the parcel counter, reported the lost ticket, and paid a fine. I returned to pick up my trolley with a feeling of relief and thanked the store worker for his help. I noticed that the suspicious-looking character had gone. I wondered if he could really have been the one who picked up my ticket—and if I had really dropped it while shopping. I had a strange feeling, but couldn't see the man anywhere.

I paid for the groceries and collected my shopping bag at the parcel counter. I made sure that I clung to my handbag, thinking that perhaps that man might be lying in wait to rob me, since his first attempt was a failure.

Before I left for my vehicle, I silently thanked God for saving me and my belongings. When I got home, I started feeling shaky as I thought of all that could have happened.

How many times have I failed my Savior? Yet not for a moment has He not been watching over me. I then realized what a mighty God we serve. We serve a God who always sees and cares for a sinner like me.

No matter what the circumstances are, remember that God is watching over you.

ETHEL DORIS MSUSENI

Thought: Our text indicates that God is always with us. Do we think to praise Him for that when nothing frightening happens?

Many Are Called, but Few Are Chosen

For many are called, but few are chosen. Matt. 22:14, NKJV.

WHEN I TAKE MY MORNING WALK, I ask God to help me meet someone to whom I can witness. One day I met a couple with their 12-year-old son. We had a pleasant chat, and since we were going the same direction, I asked them to drop by to see our vegetable garden. They agreed. I picked a few baby bok choy to give them and said, "I hope one of these days we can get together, perhaps have lunch, and get better acquainted."

The man responded, "Oh, that would really be nice. When?"

"It's up to you," I replied.

"Shall we have it this noon?" the man asked.

Of course I agreed and started right away to prepare for lunch.

Another time I met a single woman and invited her to lunch also. (My aim is to get better acquainted with those I meet so that I can ask them to join our small group Bible study we call "Ohana" [family].) I was quite disappointed when she refused, making all kinds of excuses. Every now and then, when I met her, I would tell her she was still invited, that the rain check was there. She always made excuses, even though she said she hardly ever had a hot meal, since she was too busy with her art gallery and lived in a studio apartment, where it was very difficult to cook. Finally I told the Lord that I shouldn't be held responsible for her soul because I had invited her so many times. I remembered the "parable of the great supper" in Luke 14, particularly Luke 14:18-20.

One of the most rewarding invitations we extended was to an 82-year-old woman. She had been a community leader, yet when my husband and I invited her to join us in our Bible study every Friday evening, she came, rain or shine. She never missed an evening except when she attended her grandson's graduation in Kentucky. What a joy to have such responsive people!

Truly the Scriptures are right. Many are called, but few are chosen. I am glad the Lord God called and chose me to be a part of His royal family.

OFELIA A. PANGAN

Thought: Ofelia was intentional in sharing the gospel. Are you?

Knead or Knees

"Sir," they said, "we remember that while he was still alive that deceiver said, 'After three days I will rise again.'" Matt. 27:63, NIV.

He who dwells in the shelter of the Most High will rest in the shadow of the Almighty. Ps. 91:1, NIV.

WHILE PREPARING TO BAKE BREAD with the help of my curious young daughter, I measured out the exact ingredients. We heated the liquid to a nice warm temperature to activate the yeast, and I explained that if the liquid is too hot it will kill the yeast; if it is too cool it will not work. After careful mixing, we made sure to include every item, and then proceeded to knead the dough for exactly five minutes. Monique asked, "Why do we have to keep kneading the dough when we know that all the ingredients are in?"

I replied "If it is not kneaded, the dough will be tough." I then took out a small portion of dough and allowed it to rest while we continued to knead the remainder. I added, "The more you knead, the better the bread."

When the five minutes were over, we covered the dough to allow it to rise. After 45 minutes we punched it down flat, then rolled it out on a board, cut into shapes, set it aside, and allowed it to rise again. After baking, the bread was nice and light. But the unkneaded portion we had put aside was hard and tough.

Sometimes we Christian women are buffed about, kneaded, needled, punched down, rolled out, and cut up—stressed out every day. Nevertheless, we come back better after each session and rise higher because we have spent quality time in the knees-bent, body-bowed position, asking the Lord for guidance for our families and loved ones.

When we keep an attitude of prayer, no matter what life throws our way, we will rise above it. The devil tried to stop our Lord when he caused Him to be crucified, but Jesus rose with all power.

The devil cannot hurt a praying sister—he just tries harder.

Lord, thank You for Your watchful care. Please keep us under the shadow of the Almighty to protect us from hurt, harm, or danger. We will be so careful to give You all the praise, honor, and glory. Amen.

BETTY G. PERRY

Free at Last

And ye shall know the truth, and the truth shall make you free. John 8:32.

WHEN WE WERE NEWLY MARRIED we used to roam all over the hills. We loved the evergreen trees, cool streams, waterfalls, and wildflowers. One day we saw an unusual bunch of yellow orchids, more beautiful than others. With great difficulty my husband uprooted it from the tree. We brought it home and planted it in a wooden box and hung it near our doorstep.

When my husband studied in the Philippines, he sent me plastic orchids that looked so real and beautiful. I treasured these for many years. In those days even plastic flowers were rare in India and not as beautiful as those from other countries. Many times I find it difficult to differentiate between the real ones and the artificial ones if I don't look carefully. Oh, but there is nothing like the ones God has created for us!

My neighbor once owned many rubber reptiles. Those snakes and lizards were detestable to me, so she took great pleasure in frightening me. I knew they were artificial, but I could never keep from screaming. They could never match God's beautiful creatures, either.

In college I watched a film about a nurse on the front line of a battle helping wounded soldiers. This nurse was very kindhearted and crossed over to the enemy camp to help their wounded. I was shocked when the nurse was arrested and prosecuted. When we went back to the dorm, I went to the shower room, where I would not be observed, and there I cried for that nurse. Later on I realized that it was silly to be overcome by emotions when the actress was not even the real person. I also learned that most of the film was made up for the sake of entertainment and to make money, though based on facts. After that I lost interest in watching films or reading fiction.

My favorite author, Ellen White, wrote: "There is no influence in our land more powerful to poison the imagination, to destroy religious impressions, and to blunt the relish for the tranquil pleasures and sober realities of life than theatrical amusements" (*Testimonies*, vol. 4, p. 653). I read in Revelation about those who will be outside the City of God. The last part says "whosoever loveth and maketh a lie" (Rev. 22:15). It's important that we fill our minds with the true and pure (Phil. 4:8). As we cherish truth it will lead us to the City of God, and we will be free at last.

BIRDIE PODDAR

Long Skirts, With Love

And my God shall supply all your need according to His riches in glory by Christ Jesus. Phil. 4:19, NKJV.

WHEN WILL I EVER USE THESE SKIRTS? I asked myself. Although they were very pretty, I didn't have much interest in the five long skirts (that were just my size) when I received them in a bag. I always considered long skirts very formal and used them only for more solemn occasions. Then I altered them to meet my fashion taste: knee-length. I imagined that I could alter these, too, when I had time. But when I looked at them again more closely, I saw that I would ruin them, because I'd have to remove the beautiful details around the bottom. It would really be such a waste. I thought that perhaps they could be used for some special presentation or on a more formal occasion, but soon I lost interest in the skirts. So they ended up in the back of my closet, and I forgot about them.

Sometime later I had a medical examination. My many varicose veins were becoming very serious. My physician indicated that vascular surgery would be necessary because some of the veins needed to be removed. Everything went well with the surgery. The doctor said that I should not expose my legs to the sun for at least three months, because sunlight would cause permanent spots on the surgery incision.

My mind immediately went to the closet where I had placed the beautiful skirts I had received. "Doctor," I replied, "I have a heavenly Father who is omniscient and provides for me. Before the surgery was even scheduled, He already knew that I would need long skirts, and He provided them for me."

At that moment the disregard that I had felt for those skirts was transformed into love. When I arrived home I tried them on, one by one, finding them more beautiful than I had remembered. What a lovely present God sent me!

Once more, thank You, Lord. Forgive me for the times that I am concerned and worried in the midst of the trials that come to me. Help me always to remember that You are in charge of my life. When my burdens are placed at Your feet, You carry them for me.

MARIA MOREIRA DE ALMEIDA RIBEIRO

Joy Comes in the Morning

If you do not stand firm in your faith, you will not stand at all. Isa. 7:9, NIV.

SOMETHING AMAZING HAPPENED! I am speechless. I've been waking up every morning at 3:00, so I said to God last night, "OK, God, if You do not speak—and I see no reason You are waking me up—please stop this. I don't want it anymore. You aren't caring for me (at least I don't feel as though You are), so don't bother calling me at 3:00." And this morning I woke up at 8:00! But as I quickly prepared myself to go to work, I missed Him. "Hello, God? Where are You?"

Nothing! My heart felt so sad. Now I had really done it—I had pushed away the only One I could trust and count on. I tried to pray, but it really felt as if He were gone for good.

As I drove, I checked my cell phone. I had one missed call from a 323 area code—Los Angeles. I knew only one person there, and he didn't have my phone number. A man answered the phone, and I identified myself. When I told him that someone from this phone number called me, he said, "Oh? It wasn't me."

"How strange," I said.

He quickly responded, "No, it's not. I don't believe things like this happen without a reason. Listen, I'm a minister, and I believe in God. Let me ask you something: Are you OK?"

Of course not! I thought. *What kind of question is that? I haven't been OK for months now, and I lost my Best Friend this morning.* "No," I said. "I'm not."

"OK, Sayuri, let me just tell you that God loves you and He is right there, right next to you. Would you like to talk?"

I told him that I was driving and that I had to pull over—I would call him back. When I did, he said, "I just noticed that I was supposed to call someone with the same phone number you have, except with a different area code. I dialed your number by mistake! And listen, I have been waking up every morning this week at 3:00. I always think that when that happens it's God, wanting me to pray for someone. This week, though, it just wasn't clear. I asked God this morning to please allow me to know whom I was praying for. I believe it was you, Sayuri."

Thank You so much for not leaving me. I love You! Thank You for hugging my heart today—and for our 3:00 a.m. appointment. Yes, joy comes in the morning.

SAYURI RUIZ

Complete Knowledge

Our knowledge is incomplete and our ability to speak what God has revealed is incomplete. But when what is complete comes, then what is incomplete will no longer be used. 1 Cor. 13:9, God's Word.

God's divine power has given us everything we need for life and for godliness. This power was given to us through knowledge of the one who called us by his own glory and integrity. 2 Peter 1:3, God's Word.

THERE WAS MUCH EXCITEMENT AND RELIEF where I worked, because we were getting a database. At the click of a button we would be able to access information and reports. After numerous meetings with a computer technician to determine what information would be inputted and the links needed to set the database up properly, the database was finished.

A few months later the database became my responsibility. I attempted to get a report from information stored in the database, but I couldn't retrieve it. I tried many times with no success. Thinking that perhaps I didn't have an adequate understanding of the database, I took some classes. But that didn't help me get the information either. I spent some time trying to find how the information was linked together (something I learned in class), and discovered that there didn't appear to be any links. So I had to type the information into the database and later copy and reformat that information in a word-processing document to have any report I needed. Days, hours—even weeks—of extra work were spent doing this, all because of the link problem and a database that was incomplete.

Five years after the database was set up, a new computer team supervisor dropped by to determine what our departmental needs were. After consultation he assigned a newly hired technician to work with me in revising the database. I explained what our needs were and the type of reports that were necessary, and together we looked at the setup of the database. A few weeks later he delivered my "new" database. Wow! The links worked, and I could obtain the reports I needed. His complete knowledge and understanding made all the difference!

Lord Jesus, I want to know You and to be linked up properly with You. I know that I need the knowledge and understanding that only You can give to generate the right report—that I am a loving, caring, serving Christian. Help me today to seek that complete knowledge.

Iris L. Kitching

Black Bear Bounty

Before they call I will answer. Isa. 65:24, NIV.

TWILIGHT . . . THAT ETHEREAL TRANSITION between day and dark. The rental car hummed along the two-lane ribbon of cement stretching between Jasper and Banff, the only other reminder of civilization. I had already slowed for four small herds of wapiti, even stopping for a young buck as he wandered unconcerned onto the road, framed by majestic mountains. For the first time in decades my eyes were drinking in the beauty of the Canadian Rockies, their magnificence undimmed.

The road sign announced that I had left the "wild animal crossing" area. As I gradually accelerated to the speed limit, it happened. A black bear, the size of the PT Cruiser I was driving, galloped onto the highway directly in front of the vehicle. "Dear God, save the bear!" I breathed in prayer. It would happen any second now . . . It was absolutely unavoidable . . . The beast would flip into the air, land on the hood, and slam through the front windshield . . . There would be no human help for who knew how long, if I even survived the impact. My cell phone had not picked up a signal for the past hour. There had been no other vehicles coming or going. The next gas station was 75 miles (120 kilometers) away. I was alone in the Canadian wilderness.

And then smoothly, in a fraction of a second and yet in slow motion, my car was suddenly in front of the bear. Logistically that wasn't possible! I heard a thump, felt a substantial bump. Glancing in the rear view mirror, I saw the bear loping off into the bush on the far side of the road. We were both alive, but the car must be a sight!

Several miles later I pulled onto the shoulder of the road and, trembling from postincident adrenaline, got out to survey the damage. At the very least I expected to find the entire side of the rental car caved in. What I discovered was a small spot of grease and a couple of black hairs where the bear must have grazed the back bumper in its headlong dash to the other side of the road. The back bumper. A small spot of grease and two black hairs!

Leaning against the car, weak with relief, I had a chat with God. I expressed my thankfulness and marveled anew that His cell phone works 24/7—anywhere in the universe.

ARLENE TAYLOR

You Can Depend on Me!

Nevertheless I am continually with You; You hold me by my right hand.
Ps. 73:23, NKJV.

OUR CHURCH WOULD BE CELEBRATING its anniversary the next day. We had to attend an extra choir rehearsal. Although I was feeling a bit rushed, I still decided to give a call to my mother. If I called early, I might be fortunate enough to catch up with her before she departed on her errands. I still needed to go to the bank, but I thought I could say a quick hello anyway. When I called, though, I was notified by my father that I had just missed my mother. I inquired about my siblings, because they sometimes come past the family home place, where we'd all grown up. I told my father that my call was not in vain. "At least I got to talk to you!"

He calmly replied, "You can always depend on me!"

That really helped to calm me down. I was rushing and not enjoying the real beauty of the day. After hearing those words from my earthly father, I was reminded that the heavenly Father also is dependable. He is with us when it appears that others have forgotten about us. He is present when others go in different directions. We can depend on Him!

I attended the rehearsal. My timing was good. I had become more lighthearted. I found great joy in that subtle reminder from my earthly father. It is interesting how God speaks to us when we allow Him to do so.

Later in the day I was blessed to talk with my mother. The choir rehearsal had been good. The day was beautiful. Just as my earthly father has been with me at critical times in my life, my heavenly Father has been with me through my trials and the hustle and bustle of life. God will hold your hand and lead you when you think you just might fall. You will have peace with Him in you! God gave me peace that day, and He will continue to do so—for me and for you. Hallelujah!

Thank You, Lord Jesus, for loving us so much. You are always there. You are dependable beyond our own understanding. Remind us to look at the peacefulness we can acquire only from knowing You. In Your name, amen.

PATRICE HILL TAYLOR

Thought: In all honesty now, on what (or on whom) do you depend?

Carry Each Other's Burdens

Carry each other's burdens, and in this way you will fulfill the law of Christ. Gal. 6:2, NIV.

"IT'S FOR YOU," MY HUSBAND SAID as he handed me the phone. Kay, a single mom from church with two young children, was on the line. "I just had a phone call from my little girl, and she's in tears. She's been away for two and a half weeks visiting her father and is really homesick. Her brother seems to be handling it better." She went on to explain that her car was in desperate need of repair and not at all roadworthy. It would be a four-and-a-half-hour round trip, and the temperature was -40° F. .

I told her that I would call her back after talking with my husband. I suggested that perhaps the children's father could meet us halfway, making it shorter for all of us. She called me back after a quick call to him to let me know that he had agreed to the plan.

After a hurried breakfast, I drove over to Kay's house. We had a quick prayer for protection and safety before heading out on the highway. Kay had had a quiet Christmas with the children away. It allowed her to recharge her emotional battery. "That's the only break I get, when they go to their dad's," she confided. Knowing that one of her children was autistic, I could see it was no small job. Arriving at our designated location sooner than anticipated, we had a chance to visit while we waited. Finally the familiar van pulled into the parking lot, and the children jumped out, thrilled to see their mother. They put their bags into the trunk and took their places in the back seat.

"Thanks for coming to get us! I'm really sorry that my clothes smell of smoke," Kay's son said as he buckled up. The little girl kept reaching for her mother's hand. It was obvious that she too was happy to be reunited with her mother. Kay promised her children that after a time of snuggling on the sofa when they got home, she would take them out for lunch to celebrate their homecoming. That brought shouts of joy from both of them.

Hearing their joy and seeing the smiles on their faces made this early-morning drive in subzero temperatures all worth it.

Lord, there are so many needs around us. There are so many single mothers and fathers, and they seldom ask for help. Please help us to be aware today of how we can help carry each other's burdens.

VERA WIEBE

A Bottle of Shoe Polish

There hath no temptation taken you but such as is common to man: but God is faithful, who will not suffer you to be tempted above that ye are able; but will with the temptation also make a way to escape, that ye may be able to bear it. 1 Cor. 10:13.

WHEN THE MANAGER OF THE CAR REPAIR SHOP informed me that my car would not be ready for more than two hours, I mentally planned how to best use the wait time on such a hot, humid afternoon. Trudging across a six-lane highway, I safely made it to an air-conditioned store. After locating a shopping cart, I negotiated each aisle while carefully comparing prices. It felt so relaxing to shop with the knowledge that I had more than two hours. One of the items I wanted was a portable canopy tent for an upcoming party in my yard. What a blessing it was when I finally found one the right color and size on sale!

As the cashier scanned the items in my cart, she saw the large box protruding out of the cart. She leaned forward to scan the box, as it was too awkward to lift it out of the cart. As I exited by the store's security guard, he asked to look at my receipt. After I showed it to him, I asked him to please watch my cart while I walked to get my car.

I loaded all of the bagged items into the back of my car. When I lifted the large box containing the canopy, I discovered one more item that had been hiding under it at the bottom of the cart—a small bottle of shoe polish. I immediately realized this bottle had been overlooked when paying the bill. The security guard by then was not paying any attention to me, and I could have easily driven away. Besides, after spending more than $200, what difference would the $1.29 cost of that bottle make? There was the slightest temptation to let it go, but I knew God saw it even though no one else knew.

I parked my car. Just as I opened my door, I felt the Holy Spirit tell me to look at the receipt once more to be certain the bottle wasn't already paid for. As I scrutinized each item, one by one, I was shocked to discover the canopy was listed two times for $49.99.

The manager verified my claim, gave me a refund, and I bought the bottle of shoe polish.

I thank God that I did not give in to the temptation. He gave me an opportunity to escape the temptation and receive a financial rebate immediately. What a faithful God we serve!

CHARLENE M. WRIGHT

How Great Thou Art

Even though I walk through the valley of the shadow of death, I fear no evil, for you are with me; your rod and your staff, they comfort me. Ps. 23:4, NIV.

OUR FAMILY OF THREE and some close relatives decided to go to Haridwar, a historical place in India. A light drizzle was falling, and the afternoon was quite humid. As we approached a bridge, a car speeding from the opposite direction suddenly tried to overtake another car. In the process the fast-moving car hit the side of our vehicle, pushing us into a big ditch on the side of the road.

My younger son, who was at the wheel, lost control. He tried to apply the brakes, but it didn't help much. Our vehicle was already over the edge of the road. The wheels caught in the rain-soaked soil and we overturned, rolling over with a big thud into the 15-foot-deep ditch near the fast-flowing river. Fortunately, the car landed on the wheels after tumbling twice.

My two sons, Punit and Aditya, and I yelled for each other. Behind us in another car was Punit's fiancé, Soniya, and her parents. They were aghast at seeing the accident and quickly came to our rescue. They all tried hard to pull us out of the car. We could barely walk because of shock. Everything happened so fast that we were left in a daze, finding it hard to believe that we were still alive.

Surely the angels of our Lord took charge over the three of us. Not even a bone was fractured, and except for some minor bruises we came out uninjured. Everyone who saw the accident found it hard to believe that there were any survivors. It was that horrific. Indeed, what a great God we serve!

Within a few minutes we were rushed to the nearest hospital for first-aid. My blood pressure shot up to a whopping 180/130, and I had to be kept under observation for a couple hours until my blood pressure returned to normal.

I often dream about the accident, and each time it leaves me with sleepless nights, thinking of all the things that could have happened—it could have been much worse.

This incident has changed my sons' spiritual lives dramatically, and I thank God for taking us through the valley of the shadow of death to guide us toward eternal and everlasting life. "The Lord is close to the brokenhearted and saves those who are crushed in spirit" (Ps. 34:18, NIV).

TARAMANI NOREEN SINGH

The Master Planner

You did not choose me, but I chose you and appointed you to go and bear fruit—fruit that will last. John 15:16, NIV.

 PLANS WERE FALLING INTO PLACE for me to serve as a student missionary the year after I graduated from Southern Adventist University. I still didn't know where I would serve, but I wasn't worried. There was still time. During spring semester aspiring missionaries take a special class to prepare for service in a different culture, and part of the class was the annual student missions retreat at a summer camp about 45 minutes from the college.

My final semester of college was by far the most stressful time in my life. I registered for 18 credit hours and worked at least 20 hours a week at three different jobs—two of them part of my own business as a massage therapist. Most days were scheduled to the minute from the time I woke up to the time I went to bed—and I still didn't always fit in all the things I needed and wanted to do. On top of this, it was a period of tremendous emotional stress outside of work and school. I looked forward to getting away for the retreat.

As it turned out, the retreat was scheduled for the same time two good friends of mine would be out of town for 10 days, and I was to be "mom" for their three teenage kids. How would I be able to go? Could the kids go with me, their mom wondered, or could I just spend the days at the retreat and return home at night? The student missions director did not favor either idea, so we were left to brainstorm some more.

Hardly necessary; Someone Else had it all taken care of already. The oldest son would be away on a school trip that weekend. The younger two were to go on a Pathfinder campout the weekend before the retreat, but rain rescheduled the campout for the weekend of the retreat!

A friend and I drove to the retreat together. We vented and encouraged each other over our families' similar reactions to our going overseas. The beautiful north Georgia country setting and shining spring weather offered quiet rejuvenation that soothed my soul. While short, the overnight retreat provided just the peace and relaxation I needed.

Once again, God affirmed my dream of serving Him as a missionary, this time by arranging circumstances so that I could be blessed in my efforts to prepare.

EMILY THOMSEN

Put Your Hope in God

Why are you downcast, O my soul? Why so disturbed within me? Put your hope in God, for I will yet praise him. Ps. 42:5, NIV.

WHEN A CRISIS COMES IN MY LIFE, I cling to God and pray for more faith and trust. I remember years ago when a friend told me how a challenge in her life kept her on her knees. Now I understand more fully what she meant.

Recently, when my husband had a slight heart attack and I looked at his pale face and how he was shaking, having tightness in his chest and some difficulty breathing, I thought, *Oh, God, help me through this sadness.* The doctors and nurses were efficient and kind, but I didn't dare *not* to pray. I prayed a lot.

A few days before he was to have surgery, they found internal bleeding and needed to give him blood. I prayed more earnestly. They scoped his chest and found a bleeding ulcer, but were able to take care of that problem. It was a relief to have them find the problem and fix it—all in one day! Then, several days later, came the quintuple bypass operation. Oh, how I prayed that he would be all right!

Many were praying—even the children in the primary Sabbath school. But the most touching was having a woman call from Iran, wanting to know how he was doing and assuring me that she was praying earnestly for him. We had become acquainted with her when two of her daughters were educated here at the University of Oregon. They all expressed concern, as did many of our local church members and neighbors. I know many others were praying, too, and it was a comfort, as was the anointing service as described in James 5:14.

There are so many blessings in life, even when the challenges come. It is helpful that we can put our hope in God.

We were very grateful for our helpful adopted daughter, who lives nearby and helped us in many ways. She said she was adopted for such a time as this. A lovely thought!

Thank You, God, for helping us thorough the very hard times in life. Help us always to trust You—even when we wish we had a greater faith, hope, and trust. Please help our faith and trust to grow. In Jesus' name, amen.

FRIEDA TANNER

The Lord Cares for Us

Cast all your anxiety on him because he cares for you. 1 Peter 5:7, NIV.

 EVERY MORNING I HAVE OBSERVED a couple birds from where I work. They sit on the screen around the sports field for some time, seemingly unconcerned about their food or what might happen to them during the day. I believe they must have a nest in a nearby tree, because I see them there every day. They seem to have just awakened, and they stay there for some time, close together. Then the two of them fly off. Before long, one of them returns, filling the air with his joyful, sweet chirping.

My imagination tells me that he is singing joyfully because he has his mate beside him. His shelter and food are certain. Then I remember the anxiousness that people begin their days with.

Getting up quickly, eating rapidly, and rushing to their tasks, human beings are often concerned with many things, many of which are unnecessary. I say unnecessary because we have a heavenly Father who is concerned about us and says, "Come unto me, all ye that labour and are heavy laden, and I will give you rest" (Matt. 11:28).

God is willing to attend to the daily necessities of each one of His creatures. He provides food and shelter for all living beings. We need to claim this promise and live with less anxiety and more trust. How many times we carry an unnecessary load! How many times we are afflicted with fears that never happen!

I remember a small poem that illustrates a conversation between a swallow and a canary: "'I only wanted to know why people, so anxious, are always in a hurry,' said the canary to her neighbor. 'I believe that it is because they do not have the good heavenly Father who cares for you and me!'"

Let's always remember that nothing escapes the control of our God's omnipotent hands. He knows of the sparrow that falls and the number of hairs on our head. There is no problem for which He does not have a solution. This God, who sustains the universe, is the same one who cares for the insignificant details of our life. Let's place everything, big and small, in His hands and await His loving-kindness.

Why do we attempt to carry the weight of life if we can give Him all of our anxieties?

NELCI DE ROCCO LIMA

The Best Is Yet to Come

For I know the thoughts that I think toward you, saith the Lord, thoughts of peace, and not of evil, to give you an expected end. Jer. 29:11.

IT'S NOT OFTEN that a single mom and her three adult children have the opportunity to attend college at the same time and at the same institution. But this is exactly what happened to us. God sent me to join my three adult children who were already enrolled at a Christian college about 400 miles away. My oldest daughter was an instrument in God's hand as she overlooked my skepticism and proceeded to process my application for school. So determined was she that I was coming, she even inquired around campus for a job for her mom, who would be arriving shortly. "We prayed that you would come!" my daughter exclaimed. "I asked everyone to pray that you would come, and God answered our prayer."

After the unexpected ordeal of giving up my house, putting my furniture in storage, and staying with a local family in the church, the idea of going off to college was a God-sent blessing. I asked God to help me, and even yearned deep inside for an arrangement whereby I wouldn't have to pay housing expenses. Little did I know that God had already worked out a plan. Every detail began to fall into place as I interviewed over the telephone for a dean's position in the women's dormitory. God's providence was awesome! I had met the director of the women's dormitory a few months before when she paid a casual visit to my church. So as far as she was concerned she already knew me! Praise God! Not only was I hired, but I was given an employee package that enabled me to live in the residence hall, get paid, and attend school at the same time.

After five years of sacrifice and an abundance of miracles, my children and I all finished college. God worked mightily on our behalf, and the experience of college life was life-changing. That portion of God's plan has been fulfilled in my life, but the best is yet to come! God sent His best in the person of Jesus Christ that we might receive the abundant life He came to give. The ultimate plan is still in the making—the perfection of character, being like Jesus when He comes, and living with Christ and the Redeemed forever. It is truly worth the wait.

Lord Jesus, thank You for saving the best for last! The blessings are many, but I know eternity awaits us—and all who endure until the end. Amen.

CHERYL D. COCHRAN

Tie the Knot Tighter

The wise woman builds her house, but with her own hands the foolish one tears hers down. Prov. 14:1, NIV.

 WEDDING BELLS RING IN SUMMER. Family members and friends are invited to share in the joy of a new home being established. Much work is done to prepare for the special day. The bridesmaids look beautiful in their special dresses, the grooms-men are handsome in their tuxedos. The pianists and organists have practiced long hours, and the vocalists have spent time with their accompanists to perfect the songs they will sing. The minister has spent hours preparing the wedding sermon. Food and drink are prepared in readiness for the reception.

We were privileged to attend a wedding in which all these components had been arranged to perfection. During his wedding sermon the pastor mentioned that both the grandfather and the grandmother had asked him if he was going to tie the knot tight. He said he could tie the knot tight, but it was up to the couple to work at tying the knot tighter as they go through their married life. The building of a strong foundation was stressed. Without this foundation, the marriage would crumble. The beginning days, weeks, and months are the time this foundation is laid.

Speaking of a picture he had of the groom, taken several years before when he was skiing, the minister stressed the bride's need to see her groom from the right perspective. The perspective from which she chose to view him would make a difference as to which path their relationship would take. He also included the same advice for the groom.

These two pieces of advice are so important for every married couple who spends the needed hours and effort in planning the wedding day, because after the wedding ceremony and the reception comes the marriage. Consciously working at tying the knot tighter is the secret to having a home in which peace, joy, and love remain. The words husbands and wives speak to each other have the power either to build or to destroy.

Commitment to the marriage vows necessitates that both partners continue to treat each other with respect, kindness, and tact. Little things mean a lot, and performing the little acts of love strengthens the relationship. Those couples who continue to pull the strings that tie the knot tighter are the ones who will have homes that are "a little bit of heaven on earth."

EVELYN GLASS

Not Yet

Being confident of this very thing, that he which hath begun a good work in you will perform it until the day of Jesus Christ. Phil. 1:6.

AUGUST 6, 2003, FOUND MY HUSBAND AND ME aboard our flight to Maui, Hawaii, where we would enjoy our best vacation ever. And it was all that we had dreamed of and hoped for.

Before leaving Hawaii, we browsed a shopping plaza, picking up a few souvenirs. Then I noticed a packaged plant that looked like little more than a soft stick. It was about eight inches tall with a tiny, tiny green tip at the top. The package boasted that if instructions were followed, in time I would enjoy the wonderful fragrance that filled the air of Maui. It didn't cost much, so I bought one. I had to purchase sand, gravel, and topsoil, and use them in certain proportions to plant my soft, green-tipped stick plant. I even prayed over it as I followed the instructions.

Now it was time to just watch and water as necessary. Days and weeks passed; I saw no change. In fact, months passed, and I decided that maybe I should just throw it out and forget about it. After all, by now it had been nine whole months. I had followed the instructions to the letter—watered it, then kept it in a sunlit spot in the living room. Still I saw no change. Then one day I went over to look at it, and there was a tiny sprout shooting from the top. Two days later there was another, and then another. To my surprise, in a matter of two weeks there were three large leaves. My plant was suddenly growing at an unbelievable rate. I became so excited and banished the idea of throwing it out. Within three or four more weeks three more new leaves appeared. No, as I write there aren't any blossoms yet, but I see hope now where before there had been none.

Sometimes we're tempted to write people off because we don't see progress. "There's no use," we may say to ourselves. "They're hopeless." And we abandon them, sometimes spiritually, physically, or emotionally, because we feel they aren't worth the effort. My plant forced me to think a second time about giving up on people, be they friends, family, church members, or someone I may be studying with or praying for. Just as God was doing His unseen work on the inside of my plant, so He works with people in ways that may not be readily apparent. And yes, He does the same work in you and me. He says, "I will not give up—not yet," so that one day we too will blossom and give off a beautiful fragrance.

GLORIA J. STELLA FELDER

Dream House

For thy Maker is thine husband. Isa. 54:5.

THE HOUSE WAS FINALLY SOLD, and I found myself living in a cramped little apartment with my daughter while I looked for a house to buy. I knew what I wanted in a house. In fact, I had a whole list. Some of the items on the list were must-haves, while others were negotiable. Being a newly single parent wasn't easy. But it seemed that one of the most confusing parts for me was to know what price range I should be looking in for a house. I didn't want to buy a house that would keep me financially strapped.

I read in Isaiah that the Lord promised to be my husband. I decided to take Him at His word, and prayed fervently, "Lord, You said You would be my husband. If I had a husband on this earth, he would tell me what price range I should be looking in. Please help me know." At that point I felt impressed about a certain number, not a range of numbers. I dismissed this impression and kept on praying. During the next couple weeks this impression grew stronger. I finally surrendered in prayer to the Lord that I would look for a house close to that number.

After four months of looking, I found a wonderful little house, but it was above "the number." I decided to pray again. If this was the house the Lord had picked out for me then I knew I would get it at that number. If not, I would keep looking. I made an offer below the number. There was a counteroffer above the number. I gave my real estate agent an offer at the number and told her it would be my final offer. She assured me I would not get the house, and begged me to be more reasonable about my final offer. I explained to her about my prayer and said I would be content with the outcome.

The next day she called me in amazement to tell me that my offer had been accepted. The bank appraised the house at considerably more than I was paying for it. It had everything on my list, including the negotiable items. But just as an added gift, the Lord provided the things I didn't ask for but really wanted: lilacs, raspberries, and asparagus. He exceeded my expectations. He "is able to do exceedingly abundantly above all that we ask or think" (Eph. 3:20). If He can do that for a house, can't He surely do that for other things as well?

SUSAN BERRIDGE

God Is Concerned About Your Problems

And the Lord said, I have surely seen the affliction of my people which are in Egypt, and have heard their cry by reason of their taskmasters; for I know their sorrows; and I am come down to deliver them out of the hand of the Egyptians. Ex. 3:7, 8.

AFTER JOSEPH DIED IN EGYPT, the new kings who came after him had no concern for the children of Israel. They severely oppressed them and ill-treated them as slaves. Israel groaned under the yoke of Egyptian bondage. They cried to God until God heard their cries and sent Moses to deliver them out of bondage.

When Jane completed her Bible school training, she found herself without a job, which she urgently needed to recover from the financial drain of school bills. Jobs were a rare commodity back home in Zimbabwe, and Jane sent application after application with no response. As the days turned into months she became desperate. Every day she prayed, until it became hard for her to pray. So she just went before the Lord and cried.

One sleepless night she read Exodus 3:7, 8, and new light came to her heart. Her heart leaped with joy as she suddenly realized that God had not forsaken her at all. She realized that God actually saw her need for a job, that He heard her cries and her prayers, and that He knew the details of her case. The part that really excited her was that God is not simply a passive observer but that He does something about the problem. She understood that God had a plan of action for her unemployment, a plan to deliver her from it and to prosper her. She started smiling and praising the Lord in the middle of the night instead of groaning and sighing, praising God and thanking Him for the job and for His plan for her life.

Amazingly, within the next few weeks Jane got the job of her dreams. She says with a beaming smile, "Surely God saw my need and has delivered me. He is my deliverer!"

God sees your problems, your afflictions, and your perplexities. He sees the tears rolling silently down your cheeks in the middle of the night; He hears your cries. When you are hemmed in by problems and don't know what to do, God sees that. When you call His name in prayer, God hears you. God has an action plan concerning your problems and afflictions to deliver you. God executes the plan of deliverance. Just believe!

CONISIA ANTHONY

Little Oily Bird

He gives strength to the weary and increases the power of the weak. Even youths grow tired and weary, and young men stumble and fall; but those who hope in the Lord will renew their strength. They will soar on wings like eagles; they will run and not grow weary, they will walk and not be faint. Isa. 40:29-31, NIV.

I WAS FORTUNATE TO HAVE FRIENDS with a cozy lakeside home in the country where I could stay a few days and have a personal retreat while they were away on an extended trip. My husband and I had separated only two weeks earlier, and I was feeling on the verge of an emotional breakdown. A friend suggested that I could benefit from a getaway for a few days.

For much of my three days of solitude I cried and wrestled with God in grief, heartbreak, failure, fear, and guilt. I desperately prayed for peace and searched the Bible for an instant answer from God. But the peace didn't last, and there were no instant answers. It was an emotional roller-coaster ride. Finally, on the last morning I resigned myself just to go back to my regular devotional material. I was reading in the book of Romans when I was once again overwhelmed with discouragement and fear. I realized that only the devil would send those messages, so I mustered up courage and rebuked him out loud.

Immediately I recalled a Bible promise that a friend had given me earlier. The words "they will soar on wings like eagles" rang clear in my mind. I went limp and wept bitterly to God, saying, "I am anything but flying." Just then I recalled the images I had seen on television years before of little birds that fell victim to the terrible oil spill from the oceangoing tanker *Exxon Valdez.* I remembered their frail frames struggling under the weight of their oil-soaked feathers. I sobbed, "Yes, Father, that's me. I will never soar like an eagle!" A still small voice inside me spoke gently and said, "Yes, that's you. You are this bird, but you *will fly.* You are in the worst of it right now, and I want to carry you and clean you off, but you need to let Me."

God gave me a promise in a poignant word picture that caused my fears and anxiety to vanish. It's been more than a year since that morning, and God has remained true to His promise, but the work has been done only when I've let go and allowed Him. He's carried me, and cleaned me, and He's teaching me to fly. The really beautiful part is that I'll never fly alone!

DALRY DEAN

Does God Really Care?

Trust in him at all times; ye people, pour out your heart before him: God is a refuge for us. Ps. 62:8.

I'M AN ANIMAL LOVER, so when I heard that my friend's cat had four kittens I couldn't wait to see them. I held each one, admiring how sweet and tiny they were. I gave each one a kiss before giving them back to their mother, who was watching anxiously from her bed on the couch. When I picked up the last one, I noticed something different about it. As I examined it closer, I could see that its back leg was deformed. It nearly broke my heart to see its foot completely curled up by its leg. We tried to gently straighten it, but it wouldn't budge from its awkward position. We began to sadly discuss how we could help it to walk when it got older, from having surgery to building roller skates for it. We knew that no one would probably want a deformed kitten that couldn't walk, so we figured that my friend would have to keep it and care for it each day.

As I went to look at the precious little kittens one more time before I left, I held the deformed one in my hands and said a quick prayer to God to somehow fix its leg. As I went home I continued to pray, and said a special prayer for the kitten before I went to bed that night. As I was drifting off to sleep, I wondered, Does God really care? With all the big problems people face each day, such as cancer, tornadoes, hurricanes, and death, would He really take the time out to put His hand on this little kitten? It seemed like such a small problem in comparison to everything else. Then my mind turned to Luke 1:37: "With God nothing shall be impossible." I kept that verse in my mind that night.

The next morning I awoke with anticipation. I couldn't wait to find out if God would answer my small prayer. When my friend said that the kitten's leg was completely normal, I couldn't believe my ears! I had to see for myself. Sure enough; the little kitten was totally healed—in one night! It was a loud answer to my question. Yes, God cares! Even about the little things.

Don't feel as though your burdens or requests are ever too small to bring before our Lord. He finds great joy in answering even the smallest of our prayers. Take courage in knowing that yes, our Savior cares!

KATHERINE A. SMUTKA

Drifter or Angel?

And my angel will go before you. Ex. 32:34, NIV.

TRAVELING ON FRIDAYS is something I don't like to do. I prefer to dedicate myself to organizing my home, preparing clothing, and leaving everything tidy and in place on Fridays so that I can celebrate the Sabbath with my family. But that Friday was different. We needed to go to town. The day was very busy, comparing prices and shopping. We rushed from one place to another, struggling against time, until we finished everything on our list.

Our hurry was such that we didn't even eat lunch. I quickly bought some sandwiches for us to eat on the trip back home so that we would gain time and arrive before sundown. My husband, oldest son, and I were finally in the car, ready to return home.

Before leaving the city, as is our usual custom, we asked God to protect us during our return trip. We were traveling down the highway when a man who looked like a drifter suddenly appeared along the route and motioned for us to reduce our speed.

We didn't know if we should heed this caution sign. What official status did he have? But he continued waving insistently, so we decided to heed his warning. A short distance ahead we discovered the reason for his advance notice—there had been a serious accident on an overpass.

If we hadn't paid attention to that man, we would certainly have been involved in that accident too. God intervened by sending that man to warn us. Instead of being involved in the accident, we had the opportunity to offer first aid to the victims. We don't know whether that drifter was a man or an angel, but certainly God sent him to warn us.

Our trip continued, and our hearts were grateful for the divine protection that we had received. God had sent His angel ahead of us to care for us along our way. What a marvelous God we serve! All we need to do is put our life in His hands, and He is willing to send legions of angels, if necessary, to protect His children here on earth.

May we always trust in this powerful God who does everything to free us from evil.

MARIA ODETE D. DE ALMEIDA

Reunion and Answered Prayer

And it shall come to pass, that before they call, I will answer; and while they are yet speaking, I will hear. Isa. 65:24.

MY DAUGHTER, LINDA, AND I attended our first international church conference in St. Louis, Missouri. It was Sunday night, and the presenter spoke on being "transformed through Christ by healing," highlighting the church's medical work. I was excited to see the huge Edward Jones Dome filled with thousands of people.

Earlier in the day I had called my brother, Edward, in California. He informed me that my sister-in-law from Panama, Lucille, and my niece, Norka, and her husband, Warner, would be attending the conference. I then called Norka's home in New York, and left Linda's cell phone number in hopes they would check messages at home, as I didn't have their cell phone numbers. I prayed to God, "Please let us meet them before the conference is over. Perhaps we could meet at the women's ministries meetings, if that's possible, Lord," I prayed.

I focused my attention on the program as a skit unfolded, telling the history of the church's medical work. When the program concluded, Linda and I went to the ladies' room. I was washing my hands at the sink when I heard an excited voice cry, "Aunt Wilma!" I turned to see Norka and Lucille. We screamed in surprise, then hugged each other. I introduced Norka to her cousin Linda—they met for the very first time. I asked if they had checked their messages at home—they hadn't. I was amazed that God had answered my prayer so quickly. "And he shall give thee the desires of thine heart" (Ps. 37:4).

Monday morning we met again at the women's ministries meeting, and every day thereafter. Linda and Norka remarked, "It took us so long to meet—now we see each other everywhere."

On Friday my eldest daughter, Sonia, and her husband, William, came for the final weekend. It was a glorious time together with family and friends. Sabbath morning the dome was filled. The sermon theme, "Transformed in Christ," and the music—all of it was a foretaste of what heaven will be like: meeting loved ones, making friends from around the universe, and, most of all, meeting Jesus and our heavenly Father and listening to Them tell of Their love for us and how They worked for our salvation. How glorious it will be at the greatest reunion ever!

WILMA C. JARDINE

The Lost Brooch

"For I know the plans I have for you," declares the Lord, "plans to prosper you and not to harm you, plans to give you hope and a future. Then you will call upon me and come and pray to me, and I will listen to you. You will seek me and find me when you seek me with all your heart."
Jer. 29:11-13, NIV.

HAVE YOU EVER LOST SOMETHING SPECIAL to you—and then found it? How did you feel?

I had been invited to go to Brazil to speak at a women's ministries convention, but I was unable to go. The director of women's ministries for Brazil made me a brooch with a white background, purple flowers, and my name written in gold letters. I treasured the pin and wore it to church one day on a purple suit. When I got home and started to change my clothing, I realized that the pin was missing. I was so upset! I asked God to help me find it, then retraced my steps of that day, searching for my brooch. After several hours I found it! I was so very happy and thanked God!

So many of us go through life in such a big hurry that we don't even realize we've left the Holy Spirit behind somewhere. We miss the blessing of real communion with God. We pass through the circle of Christ's loving presence with hurried steps, pausing for just a moment within the sacred circle, but not waiting for counsel. We have no time to remain with the divine Teacher, so we return to our work without the blessing we need.

Our society has us programmed to want everything fast—instant pudding, minute rice, one-step cameras, microwave dinners, instant oatmeal, and Pepto-Bismol for instant relief of indigestion. We see problems and murders solved in 60 minutes on TV and expect instant solutions to our problems. And we treat God and prayer the same way. But a short, quick prayer on our way out the door is not enough. We need to bask in the sunshine of His love, contemplating the price paid for our salvation.

Father, teach me today to spend time with You in Your Word, and to listen as You speak.

CELIA MEJIA CRUZ

Thought: Many women talk with God in the shower, while exercising, while driving. What do you think? Can this substitute for quality personal time, or should it be in addition to that?

Chocolate

Ye must be born again. John 3:7.

ON ONE OF OUR MANY TRIPS between North Carolina and Denver, Colorado, to visit our son, we discovered a factory outlet for a well-known candy company near a town in Tennessee. It was some distance off the interstate, and involved traveling for a few miles on winding roads, but it made a nice break and rest stop—and it provided some goodies for a sweet tooth.

Not long ago I was taking my turn at the wheel as we were traveling in that area. I took the proper exit, but from that point on my memory of the way was a little hazy. Seeing the road sign before I did, my husband exclaimed, "Chocolate Lane!" and with a quick turn of the wheel to the right that surprised both of us, I headed toward the candy store and the treats.

Since that day any sharp turn brings forth a cry of "chocolate" from both of us, no matter who the driver is. As I returned one day from an appointment, I was thinking about what to prepare for dinner. Suddenly I realized that I needed to turn almost immediately, so I made a "chocolate" turn, heading in the right direction. Now, lest you think we are wild drivers, there was no other traffic nearby on either of these occasions, and they were not unsafe maneuvers, just startling and funny when they happened.

Even as there can be sudden changes of direction when driving, so there can be different ways that change of direction happens in lives. With some there may be a "chocolate" turn with instant conversion, such as the apostle Paul experienced on the road to Damascus. With others it may be a gradual process over many months, or even years. Nicodemus visited Jesus secretly by night but became an open follower after Jesus' death. In the book *Steps to Christ* the author writes, "A person may not be able to tell the exact time or place, or trace all the chain of circumstances in the process of conversion; but this does not prove him to be unconverted" (p. 57). Whether it's a "chocolate" move or the result of finally yielding to the pleading of the Holy Spirit, conversion leads to a new life in Christ Jesus. And after all, that's what really matters, isn't it?

MARY JANE GRAVES

Thought: Spiritual growth must be continuous no matter where or how you start. How is your spiritual growth progressing?

Ambassadors for Christ

Therefore, we are ambassadors for Christ, God making his appeal through us. We implore you on behalf of Christ, be reconciled to God. 2 Cor. 5:20, ESV.

MY HUSBAND AND I were in Mongolia in 1997 when India celebrated the fiftieth anniversary of its independence. We were delighted to receive an invitation from the Indian Embassy to attend the celebratory functions at the posh Ulaanbaator Hotel. As Indian citizens, we were very excited and felt important.

Independence Day was bright and sunny. I dressed in a pink-and-green Indian *salwar kameez,* loose pants with a knee-length top, and my husband in a formal suit. When we arrived at the hotel, we presented our invitation card and were ushered into a large hall where the reception was being held. At once I noticed the well-set tables with gleaming china and glassware. I looked up and saw the beautiful crystal chandeliers all lit up. Well-dressed couples kept walking in through the entrance, and in a short while the hall was full of ambassadors from all over the world and high officials from the government of Mongolia. As we stood among them, my husband whispered in my ear, "We are also ambassadors, ambassadors for Christ!" Yes, indeed we were.

Servers in smart uniforms passed around goblets of wine to toast the prime minister. We politely declined, telling the server that we didn't drink. She suggested that we just hold the goblets in our hands and put them down after the toast. The prime minister arrived on time. After the toast and his speech, we sought out the first secretary of the Indian Embassy and told him we had to leave for another appointment.

That unique experience that God gave us is forever fresh in my memory. The next day a friend told us that he had seen our picture on the bulletin board of the Indian Embassy. We immediately walked down to the embassy, and the staff kindly gave us a copy. So we have a photograph of the event. To think that God gave us this rare opportunity to be among the elite of Mongolia is almost unbelievable. God doesn't give us only bare necessities or only what we ask for. Often He gives us more, just to make us happy. He sometimes adds frills to His blessings. At times He gives us things we could never get on our own. What a great God we have! I am so proud to be His ambassador, aren't you?

BIROL CHARLOTTE CHRISTO

Ants

The ants are a people not strong, yet they prepare their food in the summer.
Prov. 30:25, NKJV.

IT HAPPENED MORE THAN 20 YEARS AGO, but I think about it from time to time and marvel at God's sense of humor, combined with His love and concern for our welfare. However, it didn't seem humorous at the time.

We were on our way to take our younger daughter, Jennifer, to college when our heavy-duty automobile broke down. We found ourselves forced to leave the vehicle at a repair shop for several days. The only way we could get her to Pacific Union College on time was to rent a small truck.

We got very little sleep that night, but the next morning my husband and I bade her goodbye and started back to the truck rental office. After five hours of driving, we both felt sleepy. Soon we saw a sign for a rest area, and since we needed a short nap and felt we had time to reach our destination before closing time, we decided to stop.

How comfortable the cool grass seemed. However, before we could settle down, red ants started biting our arms and legs. We hadn't seen them at first, but now they were everywhere. We sighed and gave up our idea of resting and decided to get in the truck and continue on our tired way. After driving about an hour, we saw another rest area sign. "I didn't know we saw two rest areas on the way to the college," I remarked.

"I didn't either," my husband said. Then he looked at his watch. "Uh-oh!" he remarked. "We'll barely make it in time to return this truck to the rental place."

It still took another hour, and we reached the office just minutes before they closed. It was then we realized we wouldn't have made it if the ants had not chosen to help themselves to bits of us, thus making us get back on the road.

How many times God uses simple things and happenings to guide and provide for His children. There are probably many things that we're not aware of and will not know of until we reach heaven. Meanwhile, we can thank God for His watchcare, both seen and unseen.

MILDRED C. WILLIAMS

Thought: When God provided the ants, what do you suppose His ultimate purpose was? Has He ever done that for you?

Whose Convert Are You?

If you point these things out to the brothers, you will be a good minister of Christ Jesus, brought up in the truths of the faith and of the good teaching that you have followed. 1 Tim. 4:6, NIV.

THE STORY IS TOLD of the great evangelist Dwight L. Moody's encounter with a man sitting in a gutter. The man in the gutter was in a very filthy, deplorable, and pitiful condition. Before the evangelist could reach out and speak words of hope to him, he called out to Moody, "Mr. Moody, don't you remember me? I am one of your converts." To which the evangelist replied, "That is why you are in the gutter—*I* converted you."

Whose convert are you?

It is only Jesus who can really convert the soul. Only Jesus can save. Our beloved ministers and other gospel workers are simply the instruments through which the Lord works, but the work of salvation and conversion belongs to Jesus. It is so important that we understand this, because as well-intentioned as our ministers are, they are frail humans in need of salvation themselves; they are as subject to sin as the rest of us are. If we are converted by the preacher, and the preacher should ever fall into sin, we might become discouraged and turn away from the church. But when Jesus converts our soul, no matter what happens, He will keep us faithful to Himself and His church.

We have many great and powerful preachers who really do an excellent work at presenting God's words, but we must be careful not to put too much premium on them to the extent that we—and they—forget that they are not God, but God's messengers. It is no wonder that some are converted by them instead of by God.

Preachers are God's servants, and God has a very special work for them to do. He loves them dearly. We need to pray more earnestly for all our ministers so that Satan will not sift them as wheat. We need to pray that they will never become presumptuous and lose sight of their purpose. Let's pray that as God's men and women are used by God they will remain humble, taking care not to lead the flock astray.

Pray, pray, pray, and pray some more for our beloved pastors and workers in the field of God.

JACKIE HOPE HOSHING-CLARKE

Weathering the Storm

And he arose, and rebuked the wind, and said unto the sea, Peace, be still.
And the wind ceased, and there was a great calm. Mark 4:39.

HAVE YOU EVER FELT that though death was knocking at your door, God had His hand on you? My husband and I shared an experience that allowed us to see God at work.

We moved from a Northern state to a Southern state, happy to get away from all the snow. Once settled in, we began to hear talk of tornadoes and hurricanes. We didn't think much of it, because years had passed and there hadn't been anything. Then while listening to the news one day we learned that a hurricane was headed our way.

We prayed, asking the Lord to spare our lives. God answered our prayers—the first hurricane turned into a tropical storm and died. Then the alerts started up for Hurricane Ivan. Once again we made preparations with concern, because we had never experienced the magnitude of a hurricane. Ivan came as predicted, with a little wind and rain. Then the wind became very strong, making me think about the disciples in the boat on the Sea of Galilee. They were afraid, too, and woke Jesus up. He spoke, and the storm ceased.

My husband and I sat together in our home, holding hands. The windows shook, the rain pounded. And then the wind came, roaring like a freight train. Suddenly there was a loud crack, and then a bang in the other room. We both jumped up to see what had happened. Half of the big oak tree on the side of our home had fallen onto the carport, knocking it down and smashing onto our car. There was another loud crack as another tree fell across the driveway. Throughout the storm our constant prayer was "Lord, spare our lives!" Then we heard another crack. Another oak tree had fallen, missing the house by inches.

All power was lost during the storm. We had no telephones for nearly two days, no electricity for four hours, and most of our food spoiled. But through it all we never lost the power of the Holy Spirit.

Thank You, our forever Friend, for weathering us through the storm.

ELAINE J. JOHNSON

Thought: How should we prepare for spiritual storms? Or should we even focus on future trouble?

He Is Still Working on Me

As the hart panteth after the water brooks, so panteth my soul after thee, O God. Ps. 42:1.

IT WAS THE BEGINNING of my junior year in college. Everything should have gone smoothly. Instead, I lost a very big part of me.

On August 19, 2000, on my way to college with my family after the summer break, we had a fatal car accident. I lost my younger brother, whom I dearly loved. My mother was badly injured and was in an intensive-care unit for several days. My dad suffered minor head injuries, and my other brother injured his foot. I had not a single scratch or bruise.

I often asked God if He would have spared my little brother's life had I been injured, as were my other family members. Then one day I heard a still voice whisper, "Mark was ready; but Becky, I am still working on you."

You see, about three weeks before the fatality, Mark gave his life to Christ through baptism. He was an honorary member of the Adventurers Club, knew all 13 memory verses every quarter, was a member of the children's choir, and was a home school student.

It still isn't easy for me to accept the death of my beloved little brother, because, older sister that I am, he was my pride and joy. However, I know I must accept that God is still working on me so that I can live with my brother in eternity.

I still wonder how handsome he would have been, and how he would have continued to excel in this world. God had a better plan for him, as he does for me. I know that Mary and Martha experienced the same deep pain when their brother Lazarus died. They told Jesus, "If You had been here, my brother would not have died" (John 11:21, NKJV). I know exactly what they meant. Jesus gave them no explanation of Lazarus' death, but He did give them a promise. He said to them, as He says to all of us who have experienced the loss of a loved one, "Your brother will rise again. . . . I am the resurrection and the life. He who believes in Me, though he may die, he shall live. And whoever lives and believes in Me shall never die" (verses 23-26, NKJV).

God was working on the faith of Lazarus' family, just as He is working on mine. Praise God that on the resurrection morning He will fully demonstrate His power over death! Through His glory the plans for our life will be fulfilled.

REBECCA L. USOROH

Gladioli

Consider the lilies how they grow: they toil not, they spin not; and yet I say unto you, that Solomon in all his glory was not arrayed like one of these. If then God so clothe the grass, which is today in the field, and tomorrow is cast into the oven; how much more will he clothe you, O ye of little faith? Luke 12:27, 28.

GLADIOLI THRIVE IN MY SMALL FLOWER BEDS on Long Island, New York. Every year they bloom on tall, beautiful stems of sunny yellow, delicious peach, blushing pink, snowy white, and—my favorite—white edged with shades of pink. Their bright blooms last for days, as each day a new bud opens on the already-crowded stems. Such awesome beauty, yet such resilience! Perennially returning, year after year.

While I revel in their beauty, I often reflect on what my gladioli have endured since last summer. In the searing heat of August the delicate petals had shriveled to aging curls that could no longer open. Then they slowly dropped to the ground like discarded garments. By early fall I had already begun to cut away the stems and leaves that were now turning brown. Beneath the cut stems, in the still-warm earth, gladioli bulbs prepared for the long onslaught of winter—and last year was a fierce one, snowstorm after snowstorm, icy, and bitterly cold. Could my tender gladioli bulbs survive all of that?

Spring finally came. Gradually the snow melted, the days began to warm, and soon little green slivers began to pierce the brown, bare earth—gladioli returning. Through the dreary fall, past the harsh winter, they had survived. Each day I noted their progress, as the slivers grew to leafy clusters and tiny heads appeared—my precious gladioli! Now it is summer once again, and here they are today in all of their glory.

"Consider the [gladioli]," Jesus says to His children today. If God takes such good care of simple gladioli and other flowers, in spite of the heat, the cold, the wind, and the storms, will He not care for us as well?

There are days that my faith grows dim, days that I wonder if God is even listening to my prayers. Does He see the hot tears streaming down my cheeks? Then I go outside and smile. I've seen the gladioli.

ANNETTE WALWYN MICHAEL

Respecting Others

But he that doeth wrong shall receive for the wrong which he hath done: and there is no respect of persons. Col. 3:25.

WHEN I WAS YOUNG, I lived with my auntie Florence and uncle Glenn on a ranch near Caruthers, California, about 25 miles from Fresno. I just loved living with them! All week we were busy with ranchwork—livestock, chickens, the garden, and all the things that go along with running a ranch. There was a lot to do, and I loved the animals. Since my sister was in school all day, my aunt would read, sing songs, play games, and do lots of things with me. Sometimes I'd follow my uncle around while he fed the animals, and I loved riding the tractor with him as he put up the hay. The ranch was so much fun!

On Saturday night we'd all get in the car—my aunt, uncle, cousin, sister, and I—and head for Caruthers. Now, Caruthers is a very small town. We did our grocery shopping, and then Uncle Glenn usually got us a treat of candy or an ice-cream cone.

One Saturday night, after we'd shopped, Uncle Glenn parked the car in front of a store and got out. I knew he was heading in to get us a treat, so I said, "Don't forget to get me some candy!" Uncle Glenn came around and looked me straight in the eye and said, "Little girls who ask for things don't get them!" Soon he came out with treats for my aunt, my sister, and my cousin—but none for me. Did I learn a lesson that night! And I never asked anybody for things like that again.

Years later I realized how hard it must have been on my uncle to discipline me in that way. When you have your own children, you begin to realize what it really means to be a loving parent—not always doing what the child wants or expects but what is best.

That's how it is with God. He does all He can to make us happy, along with the discipline to mold our character. Sometimes I think it makes Him sad, like Uncle Glenn, to have to be strict to teach us a valuable lesson. But He does it because He loves and cares for us much more than we can ever understand.

ANNE ELAINE NELSON

Thought: God tells us to ask for things. Why do you think He does that?

Home—Divine Institution

He taught me and said, "Lay hold of my words with all your heart; keep my commands and you will live." Prov. 4:4, NIV.

IN A MARVELOUS WAY God put me together with just the one I needed to be happy in my life. Even so, I did not experience joy—I was not happy, and I made my husband miserable also. Before marrying, I had felt incomplete. But it was better for me to feel incomplete than to feel frustrated, tired, incompetent, and indifferent.

I once read that "no success in life can make up for failure in your home." But I asked myself, *If the home is so important, why did it seem so easy for me to free myself from it?* Even with things getting worse day by day, I was not able to forget that statement.

We always prayed before meals and before going to bed. We participated in church activities, and this seemed to be enough. When I was growing up, my family held worship in our home but in my own home, I didn't think it was so necessary. We were so busy. . . we didn't have time. It was only when everything seemed bad, when there was only a small ray of light, that we remembered and really turned to God.

In the midst of this situation my husband literally determined that from that moment on everything would be different, and that the first thing that we would do would be to establish family worship in our home. A time of communion with God would take place before we left the house or before going to bed.

At first it felt as if this decision was just another burden in my life. I didn't have any time left for *me*. Fortunately, what seemed to be a great burden became the best time that we spent together. From one moment to the next I realized how fulfilled and happy I felt.

My life has become a delightful threesome: Jesus, my husband, and I. The same God who instituted marriage as being indissoluble has His hands extended to guide us with safety. Only He is capable of performing this miracle that we need to structure our family and to make us completely happy. When a home has its foundation built upon the Father, life will have a royal glow, and success will be the result of this wise choice.

VIVIANE FRAGOSO DE OLIVEIRA

My God-given Friend

Many are the plans in a man's heart, but it is the Lord's purpose that prevails. Prov. 19:21, NIV.

DALY IS NOW ONE OF MY HEAVEN-SENT FRIENDS. Let me tell you about how we met. One Monday noon my friend Linda and I were trying to decide where to have lunch. I suggested we order some food and have it delivered to the office, or just eat at the cafeteria in the building, but we didn't do either. We decided to go to the Adventist Book Center and order some sandwiches at their deli.

After our lunch I lingered around the store. Then my attention was drawn to the Bible section. As I looked at the selections, I met Daly. We chatted and shared ideas about some of the books we enjoyed reading. That was the beginning of our friendship.

What's amazing is that Daly hadn't planned to be at the bookstore that day. She was on her way to her physician's office for her yearly physical and had some time to kill, so she decided to stop by the bookstore. Daly had been searching for truth, Bible-based truth, and had been praying for the Lord's leading. I, on the other hand, had been praying that the Lord would lead me to someone I could lead to Him. It is such a privilege to be able to help lead someone to Christ!

God answered both our prayers. Our meeting resulted in friendship, and not long after that we started studying the Bible together. Daly, her son, Stanley, and her daughter, Ashley, were baptized and joined my church. It was a very special moment to see her and her children accepting Christ as their personal Savior.

Today Daly is not only a friend but a sister to me. The Lord knew I needed a friend like Daly; she encourages me to be an avid Bible student. She studies her Bible intently and tells everyone she meets of her passion for Christ.

We both know that our friendship was not a coincidence—our friendship was heaven-appointed. It's so wonderful to have a God-sent friend, and I pray that today we can be a heaven-sent friend to someone else.

JEMIMA D. ORILLOSA

Thought: Have you ever prayed for someone with whom you could share God's love? What has been the result?

Water of Life

But whosoever drinketh of the water that I shall give him shall never thirst;
but the water that I shall give him shall be in him a well of water springing
up into everlasting life. John 4:14.

OUR EIGHT-UNIT CONDOMINIUM sits on a portion of the former Alberta Nursery's property. The developer retained many of the nursery's spruce, pine, and mountain ash trees to enhance the lot. We tenants appreciate the shade in summer and the windbreak in winter these trees provide.

Alas, after three years we became annoyed with the accumulation of needles and cones that littered the ground. My sister and I assumed the role of groundskeepers and raked them up and hauled them to the dumpster. Without fail it seemed a wind came up each time as we finished, sending another shower of needles and cones earthward. This became a no-win situation.

We found a partial solution when we realized that the trees were suffering from drought. A thorough drenching of the roots meant fewer dry needles and greener, bushy boughs. This observation reminded me of Jesus, the Water of Life. Only He can provide everlasting life, but we must drink of the water He gives.

I witnessed another illustration of the rejuvenating power of water one Sabbath at my sister-in-law's home. One of her guests had brought a bouquet of flowers wrapped in florist paper. When the flowers were removed, the guest was aghast to see that many of the flowers had wilted, and their heads drooped. Gem, the hospitable host that she is, assured her guest that the flowers were beautiful and hastened to put them in a clear ornamental vase on the buffet table. She snipped off the stems, added a pinch of fertilizer to the water, and rearranged the flowers. Dinner was served, and later, as the guest relaxed in the living room, Gem moved the vase of flowers to the table in front of the sofa. Everyone was amazed to see each flower standing erect, as though freshly picked.

Sometimes we feel discouraged, wilted, and drooping, Perhaps we've neglected to draw living water through prayer, meditation, and study of God's Word. Let's begin today and every day with a drink from the Word of God. May we long for the day when we shall drink from the river of life.

EDITH FITCH

Open Doors

In all your ways acknowledge him, and he will make your paths straight. Do not be wise in your own eyes; fear the Lord and shun evil. Prov. 3:6, 7, NIV.

IN MY ROLE AS A PASTOR'S WIFE I've had the opportunity to move to various cities as part of the pastor's assignment. Not being officially employed in ministry, I always obtained employment elsewhere. Therefore, upon notification of a new assignment it was automatic that I updated my résumé and references.

My inquisitive young daughter asked several times, "How do you get jobs by mail and phone?"

"The mail and phone contacts are only door openers," I explained. "It's necessary to interview and share job descriptions, thoughts, aspirations, and goals personally. It's most important that you ask the Lord for His guidance to the right job, with the right hours, and the right remunerations, because He is all-knowing."

While in the interviewing stage, there were multiple offers—some seemed better than others. I asked the Holy Spirit to lead in my selection process, and knew that He would. Sometimes the enemy tries to mislead us with his door openings: but you walk through the door only to have it swing around and hit you. When the Lord denies a door opening, thank Him, because it wasn't the best for you. When it seems as if the Lord isn't answering, be patient and continue to do your part. When the Lord had the job for me, even though there seemed to be no door, He made one, and I landed that position. Those times I was turned down for a promising position, I was hurt, but later rejoiced that it happened that way, as it could have been to my detriment. When the Lord opens a door for you, no person can close it. God sees us down here with our problems, and all He wants from us is our acknowledgment that He can do the problem-solving best. If I had done things on my own I would have been doing exactly as the enemy wanted me to do, letting him take charge of my life.

Thank You, Father, for being my provider and protector, my sustainer, my door opener, and my all in all. In all of my ways, help me to always acknowledge You first so that my path will be easier.

BETTY G. PERRY

My Cursed Back

The works of the Lord are great. Ps. 111:2, NKJV.

ONLY THOSE WHO HAVE SUFFERED from the misery that back pain inflicts can fully relate with another so afflicted. Within a week of boasting about how well I was doing, I was stricken with back pain so severe that getting out of bed took enormous effort. During these episodes I rely on my husband, Leon, to take care of my physical needs, and on my heavenly Father to give me the healing I so much desire. Sometimes our spiritual life is somewhat like my experience with back pain—when things are fine, we forget to give God the glory and honor. Thank God, however, He sometimes brings goodness out of bad situations.

Often it's when I'm laid up with ill health that I have some of my most memorable experiences. October 31, 2002, was one such occasion. I ambled down the stairs at 7:00 a.m. to say goodbye to my husband. Bright sunshine lit up the back portion of our home and reflected brilliantly on the many shades of autumn displayed on the maple trees. It warmed my spirits and lulled me into a false expectancy of a bright, sunny day. Before I realized it, the sun had said its "good morning" and disappeared to brighten someone else's day.

While eating breakfast a couple hours later, I was drawn to a large tree on my neighbor's property. Because of autumn's late arrival in Ontario, the leaves on this tree were still green. Suddenly there appeared to be a shower of not single leaves, but small branches falling from this tree. Puzzled, I moved to the window for a closer look, because it was a perfectly calm day—no rain, no wind, and no snow. I spotted a few birds perched on some of the larger branches, but they made no movement to effect the phenomenon I was observing. These clusters of green leaves slowly tumbled from the tree, as if propelled by an unseen force. Within a two-hour period the tree was stripped of 90 percent of its leaves.

Solomon rightly states in Ecclesiastes 3:1 that there is a time for everything. In this instance, nature declared that ready or not, it was time for the tree to shed its leaves, and so it did. Had I not been incapacitated with back pain that morning I wouldn't have had the time or the opportunity to witness this microscopic yet magnificent display of God's creative power. Just maybe my "cursed" back provided a much-needed blessing after all!

Avis Mae Rodney

Wendy's Faith

Now faith is the substance of things hoped for, the evidence of things not seen. Heb. 11:1, NKJV.

 WE WERE BOTH EXHAUSTED after a challenging week. In our role as geriatric social workers, Wendy and I realized we needed a break from the office. Although rewarding, giving is hard work. At the end of our day at PACE (Program of All-inclusive Care for the Elderly), our professional hats are removed, and we both put on several personal hats—whew! Just writing about all these different hats makes me tired!

On this particular day there were more than the usual work-related challenges. The day before I was to leave for camp meeting, I discovered that my car needed a new windshield. Wendy graciously gave me a ride to the auto glass shop, and as we were headed back to the office I offered to treat her to lunch, and we agreed on the time and place. The morning quickly passed, and our stomachs reminded us of our scheduled lunch date. We arrived at the restaurant and headed toward the front doors. I noticed that Wendy didn't have her purse, but before I could comment she play- fully said, "See, Terrie? I don't need my purse—I know you've got me! I must really trust you."

We both laughed, but I began to think of my faith and trust in God. I read His promises, but instead of letting go of my "spiritual purse," I con- tinue to carry my burdens with me. So often I am weighed down. So often I forfeit peace and bear needless pain because I don't carry my spiritual purse, filled with personal cares, to God in prayer. I struggle on, carrying it by myself. Wendy reminded me on that busy and stressed-filled Friday that God's "got" me. I really should trust Him. He'll never fail me or let me down.

Wendy and I enjoyed our Mexican meal, and she was right—I paid the bill. Now, that's faith!

TERRIE E. (RUFF) LONG

Thought: Someone has said that "faith is only faith when it is the only thing you are holding on to." How does that observation fit with today's reading? Check out Hebrews 12:1-3 to see what it says about struggling to carry spiritual purses.

In the Jungle

But Jesus said, "Suffer little children, and forbid them not, to come unto me: for of such is the kingdom of heaven." Matt. 19:14.

MY TWO DAUGHTERS, Barbara and Rachel, are energetic bunnies. My husband and I jokingly say that our two are like having four. We call them the "Daughters of Thunder"—not that they are vying to be the chosen to sit next to Jesus, but because of the combined noise level.

Barbara's expertise is creativity and endurance. On a regular basis I find stuff all over the house that she has "created" and left hidden for us to find. She constantly makes suggestions on how to better any process. When she was 3, she was already hiking more than three miles. From morning to night she goes, goes, and goes.

Rachel's expertise, on the other hand, is breaking the sound barrier and very powerful bursts of energy. It's not only the decibel level that she can achieve but what she says. During the church service one week she yelled out into the hushed church, "Is it done yet?" The sermon had not even started yet.

A friend who had known my husband since childhood was curious about where my children get the amount of energy they have. I really hadn't thought about it before, but it brought back fun memories. My mom once told me, "When you were younger, you didn't just walk into a room, you exploded!" H'mmm . . . I guess "thunder" does have a source.

Although my two girls are a challenge at times, the Lord has taught me a few lessons:

- *Children teach us patience and how to slow down.* Barbara has asked me an important question: "Why are you always in a hurry?" I still haven't figured out why.
- *Children teach us how to forgive.* For the most part, children forgive easily, even when we adults mess up in the same area over and over.
- *Don't forget to be a kid.* Children laugh 200 to 400 times a day. The average adult laughs only 15 times a day. We lose something in the growth process.
- *Stay fit.* It is hard to chase when one is winded.

Lord, thank You for all children, especially mine. Continue to use them in Your work and to remind us what it is like to be a kid.

MARY M. J. WAGONER ANGELIN

Boats in the Night

They took Him along with them in the boat, just as He was. Mark 4:36, NASB.

LIKE A BOAT ON A STORMY SEA, I tossed back and forth on the waves of my troubled thoughts. All the concerns of my life seemed to be crashing into my mind at once. I lay awake for more than an hour in the darkness, longing for rest that wouldn't come.

At 2:00 I decided it was a useless activity to rehearse all the problems of the present and the "might-be" problems of the future. I got out of bed, picked up my journal and the current devotional book I was reading, and went into the living room to spend some time with God. I knew it was time to put all these concerns into His hands.

The chapter I read from *Next Door Savior,* by Max Lucado, focused on what happened when Jesus got into the boat with the disciples. The fishing suddenly became good after a night of failure; and the storm became calm when He spoke just a word. Lucado posed the question: "Have you got Christ in your boat?"

I want You to come into my boat, I wrote in my prayer journal. *I want to give my boat to You—my life, my struggles, my problems. With You in the boat, everything will be OK.* Then I drew a small sailboat in the margin of my journal and labeled it "My Health Problem." *Come into my boat, Lord, and take over my pain. I can't handle it—but You can!* I drew another boat and labeled it "My Workload." The next boat I named "Family Relations," and another boat I labeled "My Writing Project." Another boat I called "Financial Needs" and yet another "Our Future." Before I finished I had a whole fleet of eight sailboats on three pages of my journal. After each one I wrote a prayer, asking Christ to come into that boat, that part of my life, and take over and solve the problem.

The last boat I labeled "Sleepless Night." I wrote, *Please, Lord, come into this boat of mine. As You slept in the storm on Galilee long ago, You can help me to sleep amid the storm of my thoughts. Calm my mind and help me to shut down my brain and sleep for the hours of the night that are left. With You in my boats, I know I will be able to sleep.*

I climbed under the covers and snuggled down into the soft pillow. Immediately I was asleep, calmed by my hour with the Lord, who can work miracles when He comes into our boats.

DOROTHY EATON WATTS

At the Master's Feet

Develop an attitude of gratitude and always give thanks to God our Father
for everything in the name of the Lord Jesus Christ. Eph. 5:20, Clear Word.

I WELL REMEMBER THE DAY we chose Leah from the animal shelter. She was sitting quietly at the end of a cement enclosure looking very sad and dejected. We learned that this beautiful golden Labrador had to be left behind when her owners made an interstate move.

She offered no resistance when we led her from the shelter to our car for the ride home. Leah seemed as though she had determined to accept her fate, whatever it would be, and it became very obvious that we had one very dispirited animal. For many weeks she didn't bark, wag her tail, or respond to us. However, continual love and care have a way of healing hurts, and eventually, with confidence restored, she gave all of her doggy trust to her new family. Leah proved to be a good-natured and obedient pet, fitting into my family of four children well. They loved her, and she enjoyed their company.

I was intrigued by Leah's behavior when given a bone. She would completely circle the yard once, drop the bone at my feet, then come and lick my hand before retrieving the bone. She continued this act all her life, even after going blind from diabetes.

Throughout her life she showed her loyalty by her gentleness with the children, her barks of protection, obedience at home and in the car—and how she loved to ride!

I was out when Leah had one of her diabetic attacks, and without the treatment I usually gave her, she died. She left us many happy memories, plus a few lessons to draw from too.

Jesus, my Savior, did not resist being led to Calvary to give me life eternal. He left His Father and His home in heaven to come to this world to make me a part of His family.

Life isn't always smooth, and the disappointments and pain can leave me sad and forlorn. In darkness or unhappiness Jesus never leaves nor fails me, but shows me joy and happiness through His constant love and care.

His promises are sure—but do I always remember to drop my "bones" of worry and care and kneel at my Master's feet to say thank You?

LYN WELK-SANDY

We Shall Be Like Him

Beloved, now we are children of God; and it has not yet been revealed what we shall be, but we know that when He is revealed, we shall be like Him, for we shall see Him as He is. 1 John 3:2, NKJV.

ONE DAY IN LATE SUMMER my husband brought in a beautiful caterpillar that he'd found in his pecan grove. It was a beautiful brilliant green with two rows of light-blue round knobs on both its sides, and two rows of orange knobs with black hairlike spikes on the knobs that went down its back between the rows of blue. I had a book on butterflies and how to raise a butterfly from the caterpillar stage, so I followed all the instructions. We kept it in a clear glass jar, and daily I cut fresh pecan leaves for it to eat.

When a friend came to visit one day I showed the caterpillar to her. She had relatives who knew a lot about such things, so she called them. They said it was a luna moth, and that it should build a cocoon in about a week or so. Sure enough, eight days later it began to build the cocoon, a process that took a couple of days. When completed, the caterpillar was housed inside (the pupa stage). As I write, we are anxiously waiting to see how and when it will emerge. Some moths or butterflies winter over in the pupa stage, so we may have a long wait.

We, too, are in a stage of transformation. In this life we are being transformed into His image, into His likeness. By beholding we become changed. We must take in our spiritual nourishment daily, which is more important than the physical food. For what is physical is temporary and will not last. I don't know what will emerge from the pupa in the glass jar, and it is written that it has not yet been revealed what we shall be. But we know that when He is revealed, we shall be like Him, for we shall see Him as He is. First Corinthians 15:51, 52 says, "Behold, I tell you a mystery: We shall not all sleep, but we shall all be changed—in a moment, in the twinkling of an eye, at the last trumpet. For the trumpet will sound, and the dead will be raised incorruptible, and we shall be changed" (NKJV).

DONNA COOK

Thought: Take the time to read all of 1 Corinthians 15:50-55. It contains a beautiful promise. If you know those who are worried about death and the future, share this text with them.

Unexpected Influence

Let us not become weary in doing good, for at the proper time we will reap a harvest if we do not give up. Gal. 6:9, NIV.

NANCY SERVED AS THE DIRECTOR of nursing at the nursing home I administered. Planning to move out of state, she submitted her resignation. As was my custom when a member of the leadership staff left, I wrote Nancy a letter of appreciation. I cited some of the enhancements she had initiated that had made for more efficient and effective nursing care. I thanked her for her contributions and wished her well.

Several years later I encountered Nancy again at a national nursing home convention. After leaving Michigan, she had decided to study to become a nursing home administrator. She wrote the required examination, passed it, and found a position. However, after a short term of service, she was fired, without any reason given for the dismissal.

In my mind I saw Nancy as a tough person who could deal with any situation in a confident manner. But not so; she told me that this turn of events had devastated her. She felt worthless and depressed. Contemplation of suicide plagued her mind.

Between jobs, with extra time on her hands, she decided to do some sorting and cleaning at home. While looking through a drawer, she found the letter I had written, and decided to read it again. The accomplishments mentioned there gave her renewed hope. Maybe she wasn't worthless after all!

This experience greatly humbled me. The results of my intention went far beyond my expectation. It brought home to me the importance of acts of kindness. They often take only a few minutes to perform and require very little effort, but may have far-reaching consequences.

Recorded in the Bible are many, many acts of kindness performed by Jesus when He was here on earth. He delighted in making sick people well, sad people glad, and demon-possessed people free, along with many other liberating miracles.

When we extend ourselves to bring joy into someone else's life, we are being Christlike. Isn't that our aim in life? Doesn't it delight our souls when we learn that we helped lift someone's burdens or made their day?

MARIAN M. HART

God With Skin On

I can do everything through him who gives me strength. Phil. 4:13, NIV).

IN OUR BIBLE STUDY GROUP we discussed how God wants us to reach out to those around us and allow Jesus to work through us. The phrase "God with skin on" was used. At the time it wasn't significant, but I believe God ordained that I was part of that discussion.

A few days later I received a phone call from a woman who lived in another town. We have a mutual friend; at the time, I had spoken on the phone with her, but we had never met. She wanted me to visit her daughter, whose husband is dying of cancer. She knew I had recently lost my own husband to the same disease, and thought I could help her daughter in some way.

It was a tall order. My own bereavement was so new and raw, but I said I would go, and begged God to give me wisdom. There is always a danger of talking about your own situation rather than listening to the one who is seeking help. I needed wisdom to avoid that.

We met, and I was taken to a local café for a cup of tea. My host was a wonderfully vibrant woman of great faith, and as we talked we realized we were friends already.

At the daughter's home my first thought was *She is too young to be going through this.* Her husband had had cancer for a number of years, but he had now reached the stage of "weeks to live." He was desperately thin, and yellow with jaundice. He had fought this illness all the way, and continues to do so. His wife is trying to hold down a full-time job (they live on her salary) and still attend to all his needs and the constant visits of people who often get in the way of mealtimes and other care.

I found we had much in common, except for our ages, and it was easy to answer her questions. *How did you feel about such and such? Is it OK to pray that God will cut short the suffering? Did you ever get angry about the situation? How did you cope with visitors?* And other questions. Despite our faith, we still have doubts and fears. I found it much less traumatic than I had anticipated. I had a wealth of information and insight I could pass on. God had known I could help her if I was willing to put my personal feelings aside. He helped me to do that.

If God gives you a tough assignment, pray about it, for you may be uniquely placed to do that particular piece of work. He will give you the strength and wisdom to do it.

VALERIE FIDELIA

Heaven's Secret Service

The angel of the Lord encamps around those who fear him, and he delivers them. Ps. 34:7, NIV.

MY HUSBAND AND I and three friends had traveled 280 miles (450 kilometers) that September day from our home to attend the homecoming weekend at the boarding high school we had attended. The day was marvelous! We enjoyed various musical groups—choirs, singing groups, duets, and solos—and visited with old friends. We decided to stay until the end of the last program, which was entitled "How the Angels of God Care for His People."

On our return home, just before reaching our town, my friends and I awoke to my husband shouting, "We are going to die!" I saw two headlights coming the wrong direction directly toward our car. Then the light mysteriously disappeared without any crash or accident.

Badly frightened, my husband admitted that for a few seconds he had fallen asleep at the wheel and had suddenly awakened with the bright headlights in his eyes. I know that heaven's secret service was beside us during the entire trip, and at the right moment they appeared in the form of light, waking him up to keep us from a fatal accident.

Heaven does have a secret service. Throughout history and in every place, angels have been close to faithful followers of Christ, keeping God's children from harm. The word "angel" appears in 34 of the 66 books of the Bible, more than 100 times in the Old Testament and more than 150 in the New Testament, where we find stories of angels speaking to Abraham, Lot, Gideon, Daniel, Zechariah, Mary, Paul, Peter, John, and many others. They have orchestrated great miracles of salvation, as in the case of the destruction of the Assyrian army, which was unseen by anyone. They are the same angels who, when Christ returns, will take our hands and lead us to our heavenly home.

We need to better understand the mission of the angels. "It would be well to consider that in all our work we have the cooperation and care of heavenly beings. Invisible armies of light and power attend the meek and lowly ones who believe and claim the promises of God" (*Christ's Object Lessons*, p. 176).

MARICÉLIA DE ALMEIDA SILVA

Thought: You might enjoy studying the functions of angels; you can begin with Hebrews 1.

Transforming Tastes

So whether you eat or drink or whatever you do, do it all for the glory of God. 1 Cor. 10:31, NIV.

I WAS BORN IN LAMAS, a relatively small town in the jungle region of northeast Peru. Lamas has a very agreeable climate and is called the three-story city because geographically it is situated over three levels. The city is inhabited by natives, who speak Quechua, and by mestizos.

The people are generally kind, happy, and simple. They have a characteristic intonation in their accent as they speak Spanish, which at times may seem funny and can cause those who hear it for the first time to laugh. They have many customs, beliefs, traditions, and tastes that make them different.

Until I was 13, I lived in the country region, surrounded by all kinds of animals and luxuriant vegetation. And, of course, I followed the popular customs of the people. When it came to eating, my family and I ate meat from every kind of animal imaginable.

When I read the Word of God in Leviticus 11 for the first time, I understood the message regarding my health and accepted it. But the change was not so easy. Over time God gradually changed my tastes. It was difficult for me in my work as a maid, as my duties included meal preparation for the family, who followed the local traditions.

The year after finishing my secondary studies, the Lord gave me the privilege of taking my superior level studies in Lima as a dormitory student at the Peruvian Union University. This was another world for me—everything was new, and there was much to learn. My eating habits took a 180-degree turn, because the school follows a vegetarian diet. Many foods the school cafeteria served I had never seen before, and at first I didn't like them at all. And one of these different foods was radish salad. I hated it!

Then I began to ask God to transform my tastes and to help me to develop a taste for all healthy foods. And God worked this miracle! Now I prefer a vegetarian diet.

The Lord wants us to be healthy. If necessary, He can change your tastes, as He did with mine. I have learned that a vegetarian diet is a healthy way to eat. Whatever God is leading you to do to improve your health, He will guide and help you.

MARGOLÍ SAAVEDRA PANDURO

The Bath Is Too Big

Fear not, little flock; for it is your Father's good pleasure to give you the kingdom. Luke 12:32.

THE AREA CHURCH LEADERSHIP had reassigned us again. We found a small but suitable two-bedroom house just a few miles from the famous Bluefields Beach in Westmoreland. I missed the lush green fields and vegetable gardens of South St. Elizabeth, but the proximity to the beach made up for everything else.

We loved to go for refreshing early-morning swims or late-evening dips, completing the day's activities with an inspiring sunset worship right there on the beach, and watching the most magnificent orange-red ball of sun slither deep into the sea. We'd wait until the last flicker of daylight faded before heading home.

Milton and I just loved the sea, but we couldn't say the same for 2-year-old Kadia. She was quite content to stay on the beach, playing in the sand. Her refusal to play in the water was always accompanied with the explanation "The bath is too big."

"Come and put your feet in the water; Daddy will hold you."

"The bath is too big." Although Kadia loved to take baths at home, the sea was too big for her. She could not understand how the bath was so big.

Kadia isn't that different from many adults. Often our days are spoiled with anxieties, caused by worrying over situations that either never happen or could never happen. Like Kadia, instead of wading into the soothing waters, we stand and look.

God wants us to enjoy today to its fullest. You might perceive today's to-do list as too challenging for you—the bath is too big. But guess what? Whatever your need, God has already provided for it. There is nothing that both of you cannot accomplish together. Trust Him, He has done it before.

GLORIA GREGORY

Thought: What is the bath that looks too big and intimidating to you right now? It might be a school examination or professional board you need to pass. Perhaps it's a work assignment or a medical or physical challenge. Are you willing to put your feet in the water and let your heavenly Father hold you?

All God's Children

They shall be mine. . . . when I make up my jewels. Mal. 3:17.

THEY WEREN'T JEWELS, those rough-hewn brick stashed neatly beside the house. Yet all 2,160 of those damaged, chipped bricks with splotches of white and black on the sunbaked red were beautiful to me. Used brick, they were called.

Each could tell a story. . . Perhaps they were once a part of a stately mansion, a brick fence in a garden, a scorched fireplace, or a castoff in a junk heap. Each had served a purpose, now no longer needed. Yet they would be prized again for my garden.

I had dreamed of a patio garden for several years, ever since I had sat down in a rocking patio chair in a home store. Of course, that chair came with three other chairs that rocked—and a table. Then I had to have an umbrella to go over the table, and a barbeque, and dishes with pictures of lighthouses on them.

Then began my dream of a patio garden. What kind should it be? Wood, stone, cement? Since my house is a 1950s house, I decided on old brick, with lots of flowers.

My husband and I dug and hauled brick, leveled corners and pounded bricks into the sand. Three weeks later, our muscles sore and our energy exhausted, our project was nearly complete. The old bricks lay together in a beautiful design, providing a haven on warm summer evenings and a respite for butterflies. It was a sunny breakfast nook on cool winter mornings. That was what my patio meant to me—a place to dream, to read, to write. A cheery, peaceful place to entertain friends. A place apart from the busyness of life, and a place to meet God.

As I surveyed the brick neatly laid down in the basket weave, the colors blending into a pattern, I remembered my first thoughts when I saw the collection of ugly, damaged bricks stacked against the house. "They're like all God's children—there's not a whole one among them." Each of us is damaged in some way or other. Yet in God's sight we are all treasured. We are His jewels, just as the damaged bricks were my treasures. Each has a beauty and a purpose. In our place of serving Him there is harmony and beauty, like the bricks in my garden.

EDNA MAYE GALLINGTON

Dreams

I will lift up mine eyes unto the hills, from whence cometh my help. My help cometh from the Lord, which made heaven and earth. Ps. 121:1, 2.

In a dream, in a vision of the night, when deep sleep falleth upon men, in slumberings upon the bed; then he openeth the ears of men, and sealeth their instruction. Job 33:15, 16.

I HAD BEEN ACCEPTED to two graduate programs at two different colleges. I had to make a decision quickly, because the respond date was nearing. Uncertain which one to choose, I asked the Lord to give me a sign.

A couple days later I had a dream that I was among tall buildings, and I felt liberated. When I awoke, I was impressed by the Lord to choose the graduate program at the city college. In retrospect, I'm delighted and grateful for my experience at that college. I formed wonderful friendships with colleagues and faculty.

The semester prior to graduation was a very stressful time for me, as I was working on my thesis. There was one particular portion of the thesis that I just couldn't complete. I felt so overwhelmed that I began to doubt if I could make it through. I asked the Lord to guide me.

Then my mother called to say that she'd had a dream. A man, whose hair and beard were white, helped me with my thesis. Later a colleague and I were conversing about the difficulties we had with our thesis papers. She shared that she had seen a professor who had helped her, and she encouraged me to speak to him. I knew this professor; he had interviewed me for the program. However, I hadn't had the opportunity to have him as one of my lecturers.

I went to see him and spoke about my struggle. He was very helpful and suggested some options that were applicable to my thesis. It was as if a lightbulb had gone off in my head—the man in my mother's dream was this professor, whose hair and beard were white! I was convinced that God had given the answer to my problem through my mother's dream.

Within the semester I was able to complete my thesis and graduate with honors. Glory be to God, who can help us in ways beyond our imaginations!

SHRANDRA EDMEADE

Thought: Have you thought about how God works through friends, as well as dreams, to answer prayers?

Grateful

But I will hope continually, and will yet praise thee more and more. Ps. 71:14.

ALTHOUGH I LIVE in an out-of-town retirement village and love it, retirement has had some challenges. But God knows our problems and helps us to cope and get our situation sorted out.

Often, when we think about retiring as we near our sixty-fifth year, there are questions that can bother us: What am I going to do now? What am I going to do to keep occupied? How am I going to cope financially?

It's been more than 10 years since I "officially" retired. I am grateful that the Lord guided me into missionary service for more than two years. I am grateful that I managed, with His help, to plan ahead. I am grateful for reasonably good health and can include some daily walking. I am grateful for being able to still be busy, grateful for no boring or dull moments. I am still willing to be involved where needed. Presently I work at our primary school library two mornings a week, and I do a lot of crocheting and some knitting for charity sales or for the needy.

I am grateful, too, for the quiet, peaceful, hilly area in which we live, away from city hustle and bustle. When I first came here, I was intrigued with the quantity and variety of beautiful butterflies that flew around, and I continue to enjoy them.

I am also grateful for the buddy system we have that keeps us in touch with one another so that we can help each other when needed in the garden, with transport, or for just a friendly visit. On my birthday my two buddies, both older than I, came over and sang "Happy Birthday," although they had given me cards and gifts earlier.

Since retirement I have been a volunteer executive secretary at an overseas Christian hospital, communication secretary, church ministry secretary, and church clerk in my church, and have spoken at worship and prayer meetings when asked.

Two of my daughters live very far away, but my third daughter is only a 40-minute drive from me. She and her family do come and visit when possible, so I am very grateful for their visits.

Where God guides, He certainly provides.

PHYLLIS DALGLEISH

Her Best Gift

*There is a time for everything, and a season for every activity under heaven:
. . . a time to embrace and a time to refrain. Eccl. 3:1-5, NIV.*

FILL THE CAMELBAK. Pack the training video. Bring up the
bike. Mount the bike rack. Load the bike. Pack the helmet.
Keys—got keys? Say "Hi" to Jeffrey. Jeffrey! The Allen key set.
Run inside; grab the Allen keys. Run next door; return the Allen
keys. Exchange quick pleasantries. Say goodbye. Run, run, run!
Get in the car! You are L-A-T-E!

"Wait!" cried Jeffrey's 4-year-old daughter, running after me, her
brown arms outstretched. "You forgot something."

I paused and looked back at Monique, puzzled. What could I have forgotten? I had borrowed some tools from her father and had just returned
them. There was nothing else. Nothing but the hectic schedule that loomed
ahead of me. Nothing but the appointments I was already late for. I certainly hadn't forgotten those.

"You forgot to get your hug," she said sweetly, flinging her arms wide
as she extended her invitation.

For a moment time stood still. I stared at Monique from across the
street. She and Jeffrey gazed back at me, waiting for my response. "She has
just offered you her best gift," a little voice inside me whispered. "Go back
across the street and get it."

"But I am running *sooo* far behind," I argued against my better judgment, and then the decision was made. Time snapped back into motion. I
took a step toward my car as I replied, "Aww, thanks, Monique! I feel
hugged." And with that I wrapped my own arms around my body, as if receiving the gift I had just robbed her of giving.

Hollow. Empty. Unfulfilled. *My sweet little friend, I do not feel hugged.*
Pressured. Pushed. Harried. Tense. *No, definitely not hugged.* But thank
you. Thank you for reminding me of the one thing I did forget. And thank
you for offering your best gift so freely. Next time I'll take the hug.

A. GRACE BROWN

Thought: How and when does the Lord try to hug you? What is your response? When Mary offered Jesus a "hug," how did He respond? Read
Mark 14:3-9.

The Train Toward Heaven

*Choose you this day whom ye will serve . . . : but as for me and my house,
we will serve the Lord." Joshua 24:15.*

A LITTLE GIRL STILL LIVES in my soul today. A little girl only
10 years old, who realized maybe for the first time that she had to
choose whom she would serve.

The street to the railway station was full of hurrying people.
Some ran, having a precise goal; some just followed the crowd;
and others lingered on the road, looking but without understanding. I
didn't know too well, either, but I decided to find out. I had more reasons
to do so as I discovered loved ones, friends, and acquaintances among the
hurrying ones.

Soon I arrived at the railway station. Most of the people stopped on the
platform. A few got into two or three train cars that halted there. But the
hurrying people headed to a totally special train. All was brilliant white.
How wonderful!

I boarded the train and found a seat. But as the train pulled out, I asked
myself, *Where are we going? Am I leaving home? I didn't pack anything!* The
travelers around me were quiet, distinguished, calm, and beautiful. But I
was leaving my world behind. I didn't stop too long to think—I hurried to
the door, and because the train was moving slowly, I got off. I looked
around. All seemed deserted and dark. In the eyes of those around me I
could see envy, hatred, resentment! Then I understood. This was not my
world! This was not where I wanted to live!

But the train was slowly departing. I started running, crying out for it
to wait for me. I started to lose hope. But suddenly, out of the last door of
the train, Somebody leaned over and reached His hand out to me. He was
the most beautiful man I had ever seen, and I knew immediately that He
was the only one who could help me correct the greatest mistake that I
could ever make—the decision to get off the train. I stretched out my
hands, and between heaven and earth a bridge formed. Especially for me!

I woke up. It was only a dream. But this dream had a lasting effect on
me. Every time I have to make a decision, I say to myself, "I am not getting
off the train!" In my soul a little girl still lives. A little girl who chose, maybe
for the first time so consciously, whom she would serve.

Stay on board!

ANDREEA STRÂMBU-DIMA

God Is Aware of Necessities

Casting all your care upon him; for he careth for you. 1 Peter 5:7.

I HAD READ today's verse many times, but I never completely understood what it meant until the day God gave me 10 cents.

It was a Sunday, and my singing group was going to make a presentation in a nearby church, but I had no idea how to get there. I had gotten directions and the advice that I should arrive before dark—the area was dangerous, and being alone at night in that location would not be wise.

I was only 16, and I was completely bewildered and lost. And very frightened. I stopped to ask for information and discovered that I would have to catch two buses to reach the church. Before getting on the last bus, I discovered I had 10 cents less than the bus fare. I was literally paralyzed. Without the exact amount I knew that I wouldn't be allowed to ride the bus. It was beginning to get dark, and I didn't know what to do.

As I sat down on the sidewalk and began to cry, the verse I had read that morning came to mind: "Casting all your care upon him; for he careth for you." I began talking with God, asking Him to guide me, to protect me, and to give me the courage to get on the bus with the money I had—but I didn't feel encouraged. I looked up in an attempt to get God to look at me and take care of my need. Out loud, I said, "Lord, You can do anything! I need only 10 cents!"

I had just finished speaking when I saw a bus closing its door as it passed by. Then I heard the sound of a coin falling onto the pavement. It rolled in my direction, and stopped right beside me. Quickly I picked it up. A dime! God had just answered my prayer—exactly! My eyes could hardly believe what they saw. God's promise had been clearly fulfilled in my life at that exact moment!

Friend, do you need 10 cents today? God wants to give you much more than that. He promises, "And all things, whatsoever ye shall ask in prayer, believing, ye shall receive" (Matt. 21:22). Why not give Him all of your cares?

ELIZABETE ROCHA BOGER

Thought: When you have a need, do you tell God your need or do you tell Him how to answer your need?

Serenity Rules

I have suffered much, O Lord; restore my life again, just as you promised. Lord, accept my grateful thanks and teach me your laws. Ps. 119:107, 108, NLT.

SHE STALKED INTO MY OFFICE ONE DAY, 98 pounds of elegant fury. I had heard about her from distressed professors who were saddened at her unused potential. I had seen her raging at an unsuspecting classmate on the sidewalk. I had heard her ranting in the university library about fines on her account. Now it was my turn to meet her face to face.

"And you're not going to throw me out of this place just because I had a few words with campus safety!" (I knew that her "few words" had turned the summer air blue.) "I had to speed. My daughter was sick. Everyone else was speeding. But did they stop them? No! They've been picking on me ever since I set foot in this wretched place, but I am not leaving. I will graduate."

A line from a passage I had just read sprang to mind: "By maintaining a connection with God, we shall be enabled to diffuse to others . . . the light, the peace, the serenity, that rule in our hearts" (*Thoughts From the Mount of Blessing*, p. 85). Silently I prayed for that serenity.

"We both know that you know what the university expects of you. We both know that you know how to behave." I spoke gently as I moved to the computer. "Now we are going to make a contract, listing at least seven principles that you can promise to abide by until you graduate in June."

So began a 10-month relationship. Rita shouted. I swallowed. She raged. I soothed. She blossomed. We both grew.

"I think I know how you did it." Her English professor gave me a glowing report on her progress in the early spring. "Rita told me yesterday that you act just like Jesus." Humbled, I realized that it was my prayer connection that had made the difference. In both Rita and me.

God had shown me how to defuse her ire, snarl by snarl. He had given me the serenity to welcome her into my office. He had pointed me to that powerful passage on serenity. When an ecstatic Rita graduated that June, I felt that I was the one who received the diploma.

Thank You, Master Teacher. Little becomes much when we place it in Your hands.

GLENDA-MAE GREENE

A Matter of Perspective

Always giving thanks for all things in the name of our Lord Jesus Christ.
Eph. 5:20, NASB.

 HAVE YOU EVER GONE THROUGH a time during which you thought you couldn't handle another problem—only to be hit by another one? At times like these you can relate to Job. That was the kind of week I had when we got home from vacation.

I had problems with both my computers. A friend came to work on them, and basically everything had to be wiped out and reprogrammed. I lost all the work I had saved in Word. I was so discouraged, because I had just spent hours the previous Monday preparing a youth program.

On Wednesday morning I went to work, and just as I backed into the stall in the underground parking garage I noticed smoke coming from under the hood. I got out of the van and saw green liquid pouring out. I called my mechanic and arranged to have the van towed. I gave the driver my automobile association membership number and thanked him for his assistance. He indicated that I owed $10.50 for the tow, as the membership covers only the first three miles (five kilometers). I had only a $5 bill in my wallet, so had to count all my change to pay the bill.

We put ceramic tiles on our bathroom floor, and then I noticed a watermark on the kitchen ceiling below. The plumber who came to look at it asked a few questions and determined that we needed to put in another wax ring immediately to seal the toilet. He went to his truck and brought in a $6 seal and put it on in a jiffy—and I was shocked when he handed me a bill for $110.75.

The washing machine broke, so we called a repairman, who came that same day. He indicated that the sensor had stuck on the mini cycle and suggested that I use the medium setting next time. He added that this problem was a rare one. *Not for me; not this week!* I was on a roll with problems. He reminded me that when people have the week I was having, it is to remind us of how blessed we are.

On the news that night I saw the families who had lost everything in a fire and the teenager who was killed by a drunk driver, and realized that I really didn't have problems. I am blessed. No matter what your circumstances, in all things give thanks, because it could be worse. It's all a matter of perspective.

SHARON LONG (BROWN)

A Different Sign

And the bow shall be in the cloud; and I will look upon it, that I may remember the everlasting covenant between God and every living creature of all flesh that is upon the earth. Gen. 9:16.

SIGNS ARE IMPORTANT. You see them wherever you travel in this world—in cities, towns, and countries—each serving a purpose. "For Sale" signs, protest signs, traffic signs—the list could go on and on.

I drove the same route to and from school each day, being aware of the speed limit sign: 40 miles per hour. One day had been a particularly trying one, working with 27 first graders. I was taking my usual route home when I heard a police siren. In the rearview mirror I saw that an officer was signaling for me to pull over and stop. *This can't be for speeding*, I thought.

The officer informed me politely that I had exceeded the speed limit, that at noon that day the speed limit sign had been changed from 40 miles per hour to 30.

I learned that it is important to be watchful at all times. Jesus told His disciples to "watch ye and pray, lest ye enter into temptation" (Mark 14:38).

There is another sign I saw while driving down East-West Highway on my way home, thinking about what I had accomplished that day and listening to one of my favorite songs, "You Raise Me Up," on the radio. Suddenly I found myself stalled in traffic. I wondered what the problem was. Minutes passed, and I became a little weary. Suddenly my thoughts were directed to look up, to the left. There, high above in the sky, was a beautiful rainbow. I remembered one of my favorite songs that the children and I enjoyed singing in the kindergarten department at church. Remembering that we would wave our rainbow banners as we sang "Who made the beautiful rainbow? I Know, I know." I found myself singing more of the song. "God made the beautiful rainbow, that's why I love it so." As I began singing, the traffic began to move. As I drove, I looked for the rainbow, and with every turn there it was, so bright, so clear, showing that God is always near.

Thank You, Lord, for the beautiful rainbow and its promise. Help me to continue reading Your Word and following Your signs so that I will never be caught in Satan's snares and with his fake signs.

ANNIE B. BEST

Rest Your Weight on Me

Instead, I am content and at peace. As a child lies quietly in its mother's arms, so my heart is quiet within me. Ps. 131:2, TEV.

WE USED TO HAVE A BEAUTIFUL BORDER COLLIE DOG named Zack. One winter day we noticed that he was not his usual self, and that his leg was swollen and hot. In fact, the cat was snuggling up to his leg to keep warm. So we took Zach to the vet to see what was wrong. We found out that he had cancer. We had the choice to put him down or have his leg taken off. It was a shock to think of having to part with him so suddenly, so we chose to have his leg taken off.

On the way home from the operation he lay in the back seat with his head on my lap. Zack always loved to look out the window; in fact, he usually jumped from one window to another. The anesthetic had almost worn off, and he decided he wanted to see where we were going, so he strained to lift himself up a bit to see. As we were bumping along, he tried to steady himself with the leg that he didn't know was not there anymore. He seemed a bit confused, so I patted him and told him, "It's all right, Zackie; lie back down." He eventually relaxed and seemed relieved to lie down and rest his whole weight on me. It was as if he were saying, "Life's a bit confusing and wearisome at the moment. You know what's best. Even though I would have liked to see where we are going, I'll do what you say."

God says that He wants me to trust Him like that. He wants me to give Him my worries, my future, my wounds, and to rest all my weight on Him. I have the cancer of sin, and it makes me think I don't need Him. I strain to see ahead, and I think I need to navigate through the problems of life. But God says, "I am here; I know the future. I made you; I care about you. Rest your weight on Me; trust Me!"

My dog knew something was wrong, but didn't know exactly what was happening to him. Nevertheless, he trusted my reassuring words that everything would be all right. Unlike my words, our God who controls the universe can, and has, promised us that everything will be all right if we put our trust in Him.

Lord, I want to be content in Your care today!

CASSANDRA BARON

The Best Policy

So in everything, do to others what you would have them do to you, for this sums up the Law and the Prophets. Matt. 7:12, NIV.

 IT WASN'T MY FAULT that the young checker left off that T-shirt from the list of charges and that I didn't realize it until I got home and looked at the receipt. The total had seemed less than it should have been, but it was her mistake! She had bagged all my stuff and totaled up the charges; I had paid and left. So why should I be concerned? Hadn't I had been so glad to find that color I had been looking for so long?

Then bedtime came, and I was ready to say my prayers for the night, to thank God for His care all day, and to ask Him to watch over me, take care of my family members, all the mission work around the world, and all the media outreach, etc. But as I started to pray, I couldn't! All I could see in my mind's eye was that receipt and that T-shirt. Then I remembered the words of Jesus in our verse for today. If I were on the other end of this transaction I wouldn't want to be cheated out of my dues. Maybe the young checker was new and inexperienced. Would she lose her job over it? I began to feel very guilty for my previous opinion, and my decision, and the thought that it wasn't my concern.

I went to my desk and got the receipt. I found the price tag that was on the T-shirt, with the bar code and price on it. I laid it together by my purse. In the morning I would go back to that store and explain the situation. Maybe they would not really dismiss that young girl who made that mistake checking out my purchases.

Immediately I felt 100 percent better, and I could pray and hope! The next morning I stopped by that store the first thing. I explained it all at the customer service counter. The woman looked astonished and very pleased as she commended me for being so honest. She said very few people would do that. I told her about not being able to pray, and that the Holy Spirit had talked to me about it. She understood.

At home I looked up a quotation by Ellen White in *My Life Today:* "In all the details of life the strictest principles of honesty are to be maintained" (p. 330).

Thank You, Lord, for Your Holy Spirit in my life—to keep me honest!

BESSIE SIEMENS LOBSIEN

Extreme Makeover— Heaven Edition

In My Father's house are many mansions; if it were not so, I would have told you. I go to prepare a place for you. And if I go and prepare a place for you, I will come again and receive you to Myself; that where I am, there you may be also. John 14:2, 3, NKJV.

THE RECENT HOT, NEW TYPE OF TELEVISION SHOW has been the reality show. I often chuckle as I think, *How real can life be as a slew of cameras are rolling, as the people do whatever it is they are doing—knowing full well that millions of people are looking at them all the while?*

I'm not usually a big fan of these shows, as you might be able to tell, but one evening while flipping through the channels a show caught my attention and captured my imagination. It was called *Extreme Makeover: The Home Edition.*

The premise was simple enough. Someone would write in about a family, other than their own, who they felt needed or deserved a new home. All the members of the selected family would be sent off for a seven-day vacation, during which time their house would be changed by a host of craftspeople and imaginative interior designers. In some cases the design team simply bulldozes the old homestead and starts literally from scratch, the "clean slate" approach.

The difference between the before and after photos was nothing short of amazing! In seven days they totally transformed the old house—or built a new home. Simply astonishing! And the level of detail that the design team goes to in trying to capture the spirit of the family and that of each individual's space was just fun to watch. I must admit that by the end of the show I was not only hooked but jealous as well. I looked around my house and suddenly wanted an extreme makeover. What the Lord had blessed me with was nice, but what my eyes had seen was nicer. Yes, I wanted a new home.

Then it dawned on me that I had already been promised an extreme makeover. Long before the show's creation and popularity, Jesus had promised a makeover so extreme that He said, "No eye has seen, no ear has heard, no mind has conceived what God has prepared for those who love him" (1 Cor. 2:9, NIV). He has promised a home that will be beyond my wildest dreams, more that I could ever ask for or imagine. Now, that's a makeover!

Jesus, I can hardly wait. Come soon.

MAXINE WILLIAMS ALLEN

Directions, Please

After this, David asked the Lord, "Should I move back to Judah?" And the Lord replied, "Yes." Then David asked, "Which town should I go to?" And the Lord replied, "Hebron." 2 Sam. 2:1, NLT.

AS A CHILD I REMEMBER LISTENING to the many intrigue-filled stories of David. Our little eyes bulged with astonishment when we learned that little David killed the giant Goliath. We loved the stories of the shepherd boy who was anointed king, of David and Jonathan as best friends despite King Saul's hatred for David, and of David running for his life from King Saul. As I grew older I was introduced to the "other side" of David—those dark times he stumbled and fell into sin. The record of lust, adultery, and murder is not easy to read, but the stories remind us that even great people who try to follow God are susceptible to temptation and sin.

Reacquainting myself with the story of David as recorded in the books of 1 and 2 Samuel brought one important theme into focus—David continually asked God for direction in his life each step of the way. In today's verse King David asks God where he should move and settle with his family after Saul's death. This is amazing, because he knew that he was anointed to be Israel's next king. His dream was about to be realized.

As I reflected on this theme I thought about the times that I have forged ahead of God without consulting Him regarding the affairs of my life. Feeling self-assured and confident, I have tried to solve my own problems. My fingerprints are all over the plan. I must admit that at times I have made a bigger mess than if I had invited God to give me directions and waited for His answer. Just having to wait for a few days or months caused me to become impatient and start the problem-solving process, but David had to wait for years to realize the promise of becoming the king of Israel.

Lord, when I am tempted to jump ahead of You, help me to wait. Even though I feel the anointing, help me to realize that You control the timing. I need Your guidance today and always. I need to understand that the difficult circumstances in life and the times of waiting often refine, teach, and prepare us for the future responsibilities You have for us.

ANDREA A. BUSSUE

More Than Luck

For He shall give His angels charge over you, to keep you in all your ways.
Ps. 91:11, NKJV.

STORIES OF ANGEL INTERVENTION in the lives of fellow travelers through this world always attract my attention. When our sons, David and Rodney, were quite young, I prepared for a trip to town. Having put Rodney in his stroller, we were ready to walk to the bus stop. As I was about to open the front door, David said, "Mommy, pray." We had already had our morning worship and asked God for His protection and blessing that day, but we closed our eyes and asked Jesus to take care of us while we went to town. Then we headed out for our trip.

We walked around town doing the planned errands, then stood waiting on a corner for an opportunity to cross the road. A small truck carrying a load of timber came around the corner in front of us. Just as it passed us, perhaps a little too fast, a length of timber fell from the load and landed right in front of the stroller. Apart from a fright, it caused us no harm. Had we stopped any closer to the road, we would have had a different story to tell that night. I pushed the stroller over the timber and crossed the road. As we passed a woman walking in the opposite direction, she said, "That was lucky!" I knew it was more than luck. Our angels had been at work in answer to our prayer. The piece of timber was of a size to cause serious injury, perhaps even death, to a small child, yet I believe it was guided by angel hands to a place that it did no harm.

We didn't need to see an angel that day to know that God had sent one to protect us.

These days, angel and cherub pins are worn as some kind of insurance policy against bad luck. Angel motifs appear as a decorative theme in craft projects. Recently I even saw a "kangaroo angel" pin. Do we pass off God's loving care for us as merely good luck, as did the woman I passed on the crossing?

How privileged we are to know from Scripture that there is Someone more powerful than any good luck charm; He sends His angels to protect those who trust in Him. These wonderful beings stand in the presence of the God of the universe, yet they have an interest in our lives. In heaven we will learn of the times these guardians did indeed keep us "in all our ways."

ANNE CRAM

On My Back

God did not send his Son . . . to condemn the world, but to save the world.
John 3:17, NIV.

I AM AN "HONORARY" JAMAICAN—guilt by association, no less! I've heard there is nothing like Jamaica's beaches—pure aqua waters, white silky sand, and velvet blue skies. I can attest that these superlatives are true, for I experienced Doctor's Cave Beach in Montego Bay when my girlfriend invited me to join her and her family for a reunion. I loved it so much that my friends renamed the beach "Lady Ev's Beach."

Sometimes the Lord has to put you on your back just so you can look up and see His salvation. It was at this pivotal point, while floating on my back in the beautiful waters of Jamaica, that my body, mind, and spirit acquiesced into a serene slumber of silence. And then I heard His quiet, still, irrefutable voice: "Yes, but you forgot something! When I first told you no, you followed the dictates of your heart instead. However, I did not condemn you; I loved you." There it was, sweetly placed before me. So once again the Lord put me on my back so that I could ask His forgiveness, and so that He could save His stiff-necked daughter.

You see, I had been having some problems. The Lord has three answers for prayer: yes, no, and wait! I preferred a yes or no answer, but the Lord placed me in the wait mode for almost a year. Evidently there was a lesson for me to learn! Throughout the process of waiting, the Lord placed strategic phase gates to instill His messages in me. He sent the niece to call and expound on anger and forgiveness just when I was at the height of my bitterness. He sent the prayer partner to encourage me to be a friend to my offender, although I felt like walking away. He sent problems on my job that mimicked what I was experiencing in my personal life just so I could learn to "love my enemies, and bless those who despitefully use me" (Matt 5:44, my version). It was not an easy lesson, but along the way I must have passed the test, because I reached the ultimate destination of compassion and forgiveness. However, that day, on my back, I learned the final phase of my lessons.

When we trust in the Lord with all our heart and believe that He knows what is best, we are assured that we are pleasing Him. But even in moments of failure, His grace and mercy always embrace us.

Lord, thank You for unfathomable mercy, depth of compassion, and unbelievable love.

EVELYN GERTRUDE GREENWADE

Looking Through Appreciative Eyes

[Love] keeps no record of wrongs . . . [Love] always hopes. 1 Cor. 13:4-7, NIV.

I WAS WORKING TOWARD MY MASTER'S DEGREE in family therapy. The course was long, involved, and exciting, but also emotionally draining at times. As part of the course we had to video our sessions with clients and watch them so that we could observe ourselves very closely, noticing things such as our style, our questions, and the responses of our clients. Watching the videos was very painful. I was good at noticing things that I thought were my mistakes, and I would soon feel discouraged, wondering if I could ever be good enough to be a family therapist.

I finally plucked up the courage to talk to my supervisor. "Karen," he said, "you are doing just fine for this stage in the course. You have the potential, if you keep on working and learning, to be a good family therapist."

"But when I look at my videos I see myself as clumsy and awkward!"

"I have never noticed that," he said. "I'm just looking at the things you do well, and I see that you are doing more things well every time you work. That's how I evaluate you. Next time you look at your learning videos, look at them through my eyes, eyes that are looking appreciatively at your work. When you watch other students' work, you always notice the things they're doing well, so just try doing that with your own work."

It was hard. I was so accustomed to looking at my work through critical eyes. But slowly I began to learn to look at my work differently, and to notice that sometimes even my "mistakes" opened new possibilities for talking with my clients.

Later I wrote a self-assessment about my progress. I wrote about my self-doubts and my struggle to be more confident. My report was returned with a comment from my supervisor: "Karen, I've noticed your increasing confidence. I'm looking forward to seeing what you will become."

Those few gentle words kept me going through many challenging moments. They also helped me to better understand how God sees us. It's not that He is blind to our faults; but He is more interested in looking at what we are doing well. More than anything, He is looking forward to what we will become. When God looks at you through appreciative eyes, what does He see, and what are His hopes for what you will become with Him?

KAREN HOLFORD

The Lord Goes Before Me

And the Lord went before them by day in a pillar of a cloud, to lead them the way; and by night in a pillar of fire, to give them light; to go by day and night. Ex. 13:21.

THE LIGHT OF GOD HAS GUIDED (either literally or in a figurative manner) thousands of people throughout history. When He provides physical light it must be marvelous; however, the spiritual light that He gives is something fantastic.

One morning I woke up thinking of a difficult problem I needed to solve. I had been praying about it for some time. Before opening the devotional book, I prayed as usual that God would be with me. When I opened the book, my eyes caught the title "Light That Guides." I smiled with joy as I understood that it was exactly this light from God that I needed. Then I read the verse and remembered the children of Israel as they walked through the desert. Are we not walking in a desert called "life on earth"? Our feet grow weary, and we become discouraged.

We are all companions in pain, suffering, and uncertainty on this earth. However, God goes before us. He knows the future, and each day He reveals Himself to us in some manner. He is the cloud by day, consoling us and enjoying Himself with us, bringing the shade of rest and peace. In the periods of greatest pain and uncertainty He is the pillar of fire, warming our hearts with hope and faith, and illuminating our way when we are blinded with pain. The presence of God—cloud or pillar of fire—was constant for the Israelites "to give them light; to go by day and night."

The light of God in our life has a purpose; we are to walk in the spiritual life, day and night, whether we are in conflict or in times of peace. We should continue our walk because it is dangerous to stop in the spiritual life.

As in the physical world, light overcomes the darkness. The Bible states, "The light shines in the darkness, but the darkness has not understood it" (John 1:5, NIV). The light that illuminates our way overcomes the darkness. We can be certain of this. Paul says, "For you were once darkness, but now you are light in the Lord. Live as children of light" (Eph. 5:8, NIV). More than being illuminated by Him, we become light in Him. May we walk in the light of God today, allowing Him to illuminate our way.

IANI DIAS LAUER-LEITE

Hands

I, the Lord, have called You in righteousness, and will hold your hand; I will keep You. Isa. 42:6, NKJV.

SHE WAS A VERY CONFIDENT, SELF-SUFFICIENT LITTLE GIRL— on the outside, that is. But she was a very lonely child, the only child of very young parents who divorced before she really knew her father. She and her mother went to live with her father's parents. Her young mother worked nights in a drugstore downtown, returning home very late at night.

The little girl's grandparents ran a large boarding house with paying boarders. They didn't feel comfortable with putting the little girl to bed alone on the third floor in her mother's room, so they pulled two large, overstuffed velvet chairs together each night to make a bed for her. Though the little girl was happy, she still was very insecure. So each night Grandma pulled the chair-bed very close to her bed and reached out to hold her hand until she fell asleep. As that soft, warm grandmother's hand encircled hers, all feelings of fear, loneliness, and insecurity would leave.

She was a young woman, confident and self-sufficient—on the outside, that is. But she was very lonely. Then a young man came into her life. They married and started a life together, and once again her hand would reach out to another for security in the night. As his strong, workworn hand encircled hers, all the feelings of fear, loneliness, or insecurity would leave, and a wonderful peace would come over her.

Then the time came when she was again alone. She was no longer confident, no longer self-sufficient. She reached out a trembling hand, but no one was there to grasp it. Emptiness filled her very soul. She clasped her hands tightly together, but there was no comfort.

In the still of a sleepless night she once again stretched out her arm and cried softly to God. Suddenly a feeling of warmth came over her outstretched hand, as if a strong hand was there, encircling hers. Was she dreaming that she was once again a small girl and Grandma's hand was there to comfort? Was the strong, young man taking her hand in love and security? No, this hand encircled hers with an unusual strength. A strange sense of peace spread throughout her body. And she knew she needed never fear loneliness or insecurity ever again, for there was a nail-scarred hand encircling hers.

BARBARA SMITH MORRIS

Receive

Ask, and it shall be given you. Matt. 7:7.

IN SPITE OF MY BEING BORN INTO A CHRISTIAN HOME, at some point in my life praying became wearisome, and it was not long before my life was in jeopardy. "Lord," I asked, "why aren't my requests answered?" I did pray; I just expected the Lord to give me what I asked for. Sometimes I'd mumble a prayer, and afterward I'd sense that my words hadn't gone even beyond the ceiling.

One day while I paged through my hymnal, my eyes fell on the hymn "Blessed Hour of Prayer." For the first time in my life I read through the stanzas carefully and listened to the words. Guess what? I found why my requests weren't being answered. "If we come to Him in faith, His protection to share" pricked me. I went over the stanzas again and found Jesus as my Savior and a friend, my compassionate friend. It told me to "cast at His feet every care," trusting in Him, and the blessings we need "we'll surely receive." "In the fullness of His trust we shall lose every care."

Above all, I learned that I lacked faith. I then prayed harder than ever, following the promises in the hymn. Finally I asked Jesus to give me faith the size of a mustard seed, because I knew that when He planted this seed in my heart I could trust Him to make the seed grow in me, and surely He has! I can now see there have been times that I had to practice faith, and when I did, by His grace my prayers were answered and my requests heard.

When word arrived that Aunt Margaret had died after a long illness, I wanted to attend the funeral and give moral support to her children. I had just spent a large sum of money on a family matter, and had only a day's time to travel between Umtata and Port Elizabeth, a nine-hour journey. I started the journey by faith. The Lord was very wonderful to me. The next day I arrived at the doorstep of the house, and it cost only $10 (R70).

After the funeral service I booked a seat on a bus. Although it cost $18 (R130) and I had only $17 (R120) in my purse, unexpectedly my niece, Zoleka, gave me $6 (R40), and my sister, Esme, gave me $3 (R20). God supplied the need because I asked in faith.

When all around you seems dark and dreary, ask God in faith for the help you need.

ETHEL DORIS MSUSENI

Wake Up With the Sparrows

Look at the birds of the air; they do not sow or reap or store away in barns, and yet your heavenly Father feeds them. Are you not much more valuable than they? Matt. 6:26, NIV.

EVERY DAY, VERY EARLY IN THE MORNING, I wake up with the pleasant singing of small sparrows at my window, which faces the trees in my backyard. Just like a good clock that keeps the time precisely, they instinctively know exactly the right time to wake up each day.

Enthusiastically chirping at 5:00 a.m., they are my alarm clock. Slowly, they awake and begin their joyful song that seems to be an offering of their praise to God. After several minutes listening to their pleasant chirping, I know it's my turn to get up and offer my praise and thanksgiving to my God.

As I open the door in the morning I look upon such a beautiful scene! There the little birds are, right in front of me, enjoying the water and food that's been left there. Happily they peck at the food and fill themselves up. I know that every morning the little birds will be there for their early-morning breakfast.

Many people don't have, or perhaps have never had, the privilege of observing such a beautiful view in the early-morning hours. God's creatures teach us many valuable lessons. As I watch them I remember the words of Jesus in today's text: "Look at the birds of the air; they do not sow or reap or store away in barns, and yet your heavenly Father feeds them. Are you not much more valuable than they?"

Then I think about God's care for His creation, how He lovingly protects even these small, defenseless creatures. In the same way He is concerned for us, His children. He gave His own Son to save us. He is aware of our necessities, and He knows when we go to bed and when we arise. For this reason, we should not worry. If we do our part, He will fulfill His promise.

These words of Jesus fill me with comfort. Every time I read them I renew my hope and my gratitude to the Lord, and each day I dedicate my praise to Him. I know that the One who cares for the sparrows will also care for me!

Maria Sinharinha de Oliveira Nogueira

Thought: How does Philippians 4:6 relate to today's text? Is it helpful to you?

God's Surprises

But my God shall supply all your need according to his riches in glory by Christ Jesus. Phil. 4:19.

IT HAD BEEN A LONG DAY, and I really wanted to go home. At the end of the afternoon I hurried to finish attending to the last patient so that I could catch the bus that would take me on the hour-and-a-half bus ride from the clinic where I worked. The clinic was near the bus station, so I could hear when the bus arrived.

My work was still not finished when I heard the arriving bus. I asked the receptionist to call the station to see if it was my bus. They told her that it wasn't, so I didn't worry. I finished with the patient, organized my desk, gathered my belongings, said good night to the receptionist, and walked to the bus station.

As I turned the corner, I saw my bus leaving. I hurried to the station to confirm what I already knew. The next bus would leave after 10:00 p.m. I would have to stay there and wait, and I was so tired. I prayed, "Lord, I need a miracle; I need to go home."

Returning to the office, I decided to call the bus station again. I don't even know why—I knew there were no other buses, but I called anyway.

The attendant asked me to wait a minute. Then he informed me that he had spoken to the driver from another bus company, and a bus had just arrived that would pass through my city. The driver agreed to give me a lift since I couldn't purchase a ticket for this bus line. I ran to the station.

The heat outside was tremendous, but the bus was air-conditioned, and the seats were very comfortable. I thought to myself, *I have never traveled in such a nice bus.* I thanked God for answering my prayer. He had given me something much better, and I didn't even have to pay for the ticket.

The Lord surprised me, and I believe He was also delighted with my reaction. I really did not know how to thank Him for being so kind to me! What a marvelous God we serve!

REGINA MARY SILVEIRA NUNES

Thought: When something great like this happens, how should we thank God?

Bambari

I have come to the brink of utter ruin. Prov. 5:14, NIV.

WE WERE LIVING IN A HOUSE that in colonial times had once been one of the best in the whole town of Bambari, Central African Republic. We felt safe on the large balconies located on three sides of the house. My children usually stayed with me on this terrace. Our daughter, Nadia, who was about 16 months old, had the urge to explore the surroundings outside our little secure world. So I sometimes let her play in front of the house, where I could see her well from my observation point. Out in front was a beautiful frangipani tree with pink flowers that her older sister loved to climb. But Nadia was too small for climbing. After a while she left the safe surroundings of the house. "That's far enough!" I said, and asked Thomas, our servant, to fetch the child back.

Nadia had smelled the scent of the wide world and didn't want to be brought back home. She started to run toward a shack where cowhides were hung up to be dried. But there was a deep pool between her and the shack. Thomas saw her running directly toward the pool and sprinted after her. He reached her just in time to pick her up as she fell into the filthy water. He fished her out of the pool and carried her back home.

What a shock for all of us! I took her into my arms and bathed her to get her clean and comfortable. Nadia had swallowed some of the filthy water and got an instant fever, but it didn't last long, and the next day she was well again.

How happy I was that nothing serious had happened! I hadn't even known that the pool was there. How easily she could have drowned in it! How thankful I was that Thomas had reached her in time! I will always thank God for that. He didn't want anything to happen to our daughter.

Only in eternity will we find out how often God has saved us and our loved ones from danger. God saved my daughter's life. How happy I am that every one of us has a guardian angel who takes care of us. I am sure it was Nadia's guardian angel who whispered in my ear, "That's far enough!"

HANNELE OTTSCHOFSKI

Lessons of Love

A new commandment I give unto you, That ye love one another; as I have loved you, that ye also love one another. John 13:34.

 MY MOTHER WILL BE 70 in September 2008, and she has been living in the United States for the past few years. This means it's not so easy for me to surprise her for weekend visits. She also feels the distance from many of her friends back home in St. Lucia. I told her she was in the right place to have access to technology, so I would teach her by long distance to use the Internet instead of waiting for my busy sister to contact persons for her every time she wanted to be in touch. If she would learn, then she could be in touch with everyone on line. As an added bonus, I could chat with her every day!

My mother is a wonderful woman who had given up her nursing career 47 years ago. She had devoted her life to raising and nurturing her 11 children. Therefore, I considered nothing too difficult to do for or with her. I deemed this experience to be a labor of love. She was enthusiastic about becoming technologically proficient, so although we were thousands of miles apart, our Internet lessons began. I'm a teacher, so I thought this would be easy. After all, what could be so difficult in walking Mommy through? Wrong thought! First, all computers and Internet servers are not the same, and all computers do not have the same programs. Second, I hadn't used my sister's computer when I had visited them a few months earlier, so I was clueless about its setup. Obviously I was blindly leading her, which was sometimes quite frustrating to her. You see, she hadn't done even much in the line of typing in quite a while, and she was technologically challenged.

We eventually began to make progress. You can imagine our jubilation when she was able to get online, receive her own e-mail, and chat with her loved ones. I got to chat with her every day. Although we are not physically in the same place, we still feel close.

God wants us to be close to Him, too. He doesn't have e-mail by which we can contact Him, but His Word tells us that the Holy Spirit is with us always. He is just a prayer away. He patiently walks us through those difficult and trying times. If we follow His instructions carefully, we'll come through successfully every time without falling prey to the wiles of the devil. We—and God—can rejoice in our victory.

BRENDA D. OTTLEY

Situation Vacant

Then I said, I have laboured in vain, I have spent my strength for nought, and in vain: yet surely my judgment is with the Lord, and my work with my God. Isa. 49:4.

FROM TIME TO TIME all of us look at our lives—and our work, in particular—and feel tired, bored, frustrated. underpaid, overworked, and discouraged. So the logical conclusion is to look for a new job. We think, *I've labored for no purpose; I've spent my strength in vain and for nothing.*

Realizing how prominent this feeling is, I took the opportunity to look up a job for anyone in that position: Wanted: servant. Meek, quiet, and willing individual to do:

• hard work
• heavy lifting
• electrical repairs
• eye surgery
• probation duty
• doorkeeping (exit only)

In our ambitious world many of us aspire to a profession with an elevated status and an impressive title. So the road sweeper becomes the "road sanitation engineer"; the cook, cleaner, and laundry worker becomes the "hospitality executive"; and the shelf stacker becomes the "stock control and monitoring auditor." But who wants to be a servant? Yet this is a title to which believers would do well to aspire. Jesus, "my servant, . . . my chosen one in whom I delight; I will put my Spirit on him. . . . He will not shout or cry out, or raise his voice in the streets" (Isa. 42:1, 2, NIV). He is the one who lifts heavy burdens, brings light, anoints eyes with eyesalve, saves us from our sins, and shows us the way out.

When seeking employment, think "Let this mind be in you, which was also in Christ Jesus" (Phil. 2:5). He "made himself nothing, taking the very nature of a servant. . . . He humbled himself and became obedient to death—even death on a cross" (verses 7, 8, NIV).

There's a situation open. The work is hard and often thankless, but the reward is out of this world. Will you apply?

JUDITH PURKISS

Are You Guilty?

Well done, good and faithful servant; thou hast been faithful over a few things, I will make thee ruler over many things: enter thou into the joy of thy lord. Matt. 25:23.

I RECENTLY RECEIVED A NOTICE requiring that I report for jury duty. Because I had never participated in the jury system, this was all very new for me. As the judge began asking questions of other potential jurors, I felt certain that many of my affirmative responses would eliminate me, rendering my participation inappropriate for this case. After a brief period of deliberation with the attorneys, the judge returned and began numbering the jurors. "I meant to call Ms. Curry first. Ms. Curry, we would like for you to serve as the forelady for this case."

Quite frankly, I didn't know whether to feel honored or run for the door. But as it was too late for the latter, I marched with the other jurors to the jury box, and we began taking notes on the testimony of the case. Clearly the attorneys worked hard at presenting the evidence and arguments for their clients. In the end it was the evidence and its clear presentation that allowed us, the jury, to reach a unanimous decision.

As I was reflecting on this experience a couple of days later, I remembered a conversation with a fellow juror, Mike. Both Mike and I claimed to be Christians. Mike was very familiar with my church, and I was aware of the services at his. One afternoon following a long day of testimony, Mike turned to me and asked, "Curry, do you think that if we were ever brought before a court of law and accused of being Christians there would be enough evidence to convict us?"

I thought for a moment on this question and all that it implied. Certainly I want to reflect Christ and His mission, but am I doing it adequately? Are my efforts genuine? Am I truly guilty of being a Christian?

When Christ returns, I want it to be clear that I am His follower. When people meet me, there should be no guesswork. I determined after that conversation with Mike that if I were ever accused of being a Christian my actions would shout, "Guilty as charged!"

Father, help me to live each day pleasing You. I want it to be known that I am Your daughter and that You are my Father. Thank You. Amen.

YVONNE CURRY SMALLWOOD

I Am With Thee

I am with thee, and will keep thee in all places whither thou goest.
Gen. 28:15.

IT WAS ALMOST MIDNIGHT when, after my second shift, I walked out of the hospital to the apartment building next door. There was no elevator, and I lived on the sixth floor. Feeling exhausted, I began climbing the stairs ever so slowly. Suddenly I heard the voices of people coming down the stairs. Usually at this time of night the building was quiet. I looked up and saw four young men, all strangers, with a young boy who looked to be about 9 years old, who was a son of a family living in the building. Seeing this boy among these strangers raised a red flag in my head. I was scared, but acted very calm as I stepped aside to give them room to pass.

Suddenly one of them pushed me into a corner with a knife pointed to my neck, and another man pushed his knife against my ribs. The other two pointed their knives toward me. Everything was going so fast that my mind blurred with fear, but somehow I lifted a prayer to heaven, asking God for ideas about how to get out of the danger. I then remembered I had three friends waiting for me in an apartment on this floor. So when these men asked where I was going, I pointed to that apartment door. I could feel the pressure of the knives against my neck and my left side and was convinced that they were going to kill me. When they rang the doorbell, I heard my friends calling my name. How surprised they were to see me with strange men with knives pointed at me.

These men tied us up and stuffed our mouths with whatever they found. Inspiration came, and I discovered that by moving restlessly I could signal the men that I wanted to speak to them. They pulled the gag out of my mouth, and I told them that I was expected back in the hospital by the doctor in charge. To my surprise, it scared them, and they picked up whatever they had stolen from the apartment and left. We helped untie each other and, though still scared, thanked God for our lives. This experience affected all four of us women, and three of us still keep in contact decades later. I will always hang on to God's promise in Genesis 28:15.

Lord, thank You for protecting us in all places. Keep us faithful to You and make us Your useful witness everywhere we go.

EUNICE URBANY

What We Should Eat

Blessed are they which do hunger and thirst after righteousness: for they shall be filled. Matt. 5:6.

 WE ALL NEED TO EAT IN ORDER TO LIVE, but if we ate only for this reason it would become a chore. We eat because we enjoy food, not just to keep ourselves alive. God gave us pleasure in eating when He created foods of varied tastes and colors. Then He gave us the talent to prepare food to enhance our enjoyment further. And God has made our stomachs to feel hungry. If we were never hungry for food, I suppose we would neglect eating and wouldn't eat properly. Besides hunger, God has given us the appetite for food. Some people are small eaters; others are big eaters. It's important to establish a balance between the two in order to maintain health.

As a result of sin, our appetites include a craving for harmful food and drinks. Sometimes such harmful things become more important than proper food. It's true that we've also lost our taste for the spiritual food that feeds our soul. We are no longer hungry for it and begin to crave only the things of this world, even though we know that that is the way to death.

We can't get anyone to eat unless the person has an appetite. Neither can we force spiritual food—a person must have a desire. God has put in every heart the desire to worship. Most people don't know how to satisfy that longing, and in ignorance find false gods and false ways to worship.

When visiting foreign countries, we're introduced to different types of food. We try to sample them and learn to appreciate different tastes. We need to introduce the Word of God to those who don't know it, and encourage them to taste. Our own experience with God will help encourage others to try. Psalm 34:8 says, "O taste and see that the Lord is good: blessed is the man that trusteth in him." When we love our friends, we invite them to our homes for food. Likewise, love should make us happy to share God's Word with them.

As we taste spiritual food we will find it more important to us than anything else. Christ won the battle with Satan by using the Word of God. Job said, "I have esteemed the words of his mouth more than my necessary food" (Job 23:12). God will fill our hungry souls with goodness, satisfaction, and eternal life.

BIRDIE PODDAR

Close Call

He that dwelleth in the secret place of the most High shall abide under the shadow of the Almighty. I will say of the Lord, He is my refuge and my fortress: my God; in him will I trust. Ps. 91:1, 2.

MY 16-YEAR-OLD SONS, Ron and Roy, were feeling all grown up. They had permission to use their dad's work truck for a weekend of camping with their friends, Del and Dave, and they were going on their own. They carefully planned the weekend food, trying to think of everything. As they were leaving I called out, "Be careful—and no showing off!"

"Don't worry, Mom," was the reply.

I watched them pull out of the driveway, then went back to work. Before long the phone rang. They wanted to know if they should put gas in the truck before leaving town. An hour later the phone rang again. They were starting up the mountain and wanted to know if the cell phone still worked. While we were eating supper the phone rang again. It was Ron. "We have a small problem. Can Dad come with a tow truck?" A few questions confirmed that the problem wasn't small, and we had better go.

Inexperience and loose gravel had caused them to lose control, and the truck had rolled, bouncing on every side, before landing back on its wheels. The truck canopy, camping stuff, guitar, and all the carefully packed food were scattered across the road. Roy and Del had been taken by ambulance to be checked over and were later released with only bumps and bruises. The truck was a write-off, but we were thankful that the boys had been wearing their seat belts.

"You know that you had angels with you today," I told them. Yes, they knew.

While this experience was still fresh in our minds, I found this passage: "Times without number God has interposed to avert death, to keep men, women, and children in safety when Satan purposed a result wholly disastrous" (*My Life Today*, p. 291). This side of heaven we won't know if this was a lesson in consequences or Satan's plan to destroy.

Lord, help us ever to remember how quickly life can change; may we abide in You daily.

ELIZABETH VERSTEEGH ODIYAR

Thought: In life it's easy to lose control and take a roll, physically or spiritually. Communication with home, as in today's story, is important. How do you maintain that?

You Asked for It!

If a man digs a pit, he will fall into it. Prov. 26:27, NIV.

 IT WAS VACATION and family reunion time. Relatives from various places had assembled for a Jamaican get-together in Miami. Odors floating from the kitchen gave assurance of delicious dishes and tasty treats.

At dinnertime everyone unabashedly devoured all the choice Jamaican eatables. However, most people passed up the cassava bread (bammy), exclaiming, "It is too hard—overcooked or something." But that didn't stop me. I remembered the ones my mother used to fix. They were so good! I reached in and took a small piece of the bread and experienced a practical instance of the breakable coming into contact with the unyielding. All of a sudden my top and bottom molars crunched together on something hard, and the pressure touched a nerve.

All the enthusiasm of the salivary glands had failed to soften the bammy sufficiently to allow the molars to grind that bread successfully. Undeterred, I urged them on, crunching and testing until—ouch!—something cracked. My tongue located something gravel-like, one small bit, then several pieces, loose and ragged. Other small gritty bits made me realize these were all from one of my molars.

The pressure had touched not only a physical nerve but, even worse, a "guilt" nerve, and my groaning didn't help the situation. I was embarrassed. Accusing eyes, sympathetic but reproachful, were riveted on me, and verbal bullets were fired in my direction. "You asked for it!" "You knew that the bammy was too hard!" "You had to try it!"

The physical pain was nothing to compare with the uncertainty and mental anguish that I endured prior to my visit to the dentist. He recommended surgery to uproot the pieces of the tooth still embedded in my jaw. The pain eventually wore off.

I could have avoided the embarrassment, the pain and suffering, and the inconvenience. I clearly understood my siblings' warnings: "Some things are better left alone!"

Now I heed Solomon's advice: "The prudent see danger and take refuge, but the simple keep going and suffer for it" (Prov. 27:12, NIV).

QUILVIE G. MILLS

A Cry for Mercy

Praise be to the Lord, for he has heard my cry for mercy. . . . will give thanks to him in song. Ps. 28:6, 7 NIV.

I HAD TAKEN THE CHALLENGE: read my Bible through in 90 days. That meant 12 pages a day, which took me about an hour to read, depending on the material. As I read through the history of all the wars of the judges and kings, I was amazed that the quality of life for God's people was so dependent upon the lifestyle of their rulers. When they chose to do what was "right in the eyes of the Lord" (1 Kings 22:43), everyone fared well. Either they lived in peace with the other nations or, if they went to war after seeking the Lord's counsel, He gave them the victory. Following all His commands, they were blessed. Asking the Lord for help against their enemies and in times of need is mentioned often in the Bible. The Lord does answer the prayers of His people.

One week we studied in our Bible lesson the importance of making God the Lord of our praise. I committed to leading the praise singing for our church that weekend. The Thursday before, I caught an awful cold, but I was determined to have praise songs for the service. At practice the night before, I thought I would supply the songs and be there for moral support. Then only one other person came, so I had to sing! We were both altos, and I was singing soprano!

The morning of church was another story. My voice was very low. Praying I would still be able to sing, I began coughing as I waited our turn in the program. Exiting, I drank water in between coughing spasms, and prayed desperately to God for help. "I have read often how You helped when people called out to You. Now I'm crying out, because You alone can keep me from coughing and sneezing. You alone can restore my voice." As I prayed I relaxed and quieted down. Thanking God for answering my prayer, I returned to the pew just in time for us to sing.

The Lord did honor my request. The praise singing went smoothly, and I offered the morning prayer. Not once did I cough. Praise the Lord for His loving-kindness!

LOUISE DRIVER

Thought: Take time to read some of the Old Testament stories. Why did God say He gave His people victories?

Kitten Without an Owner

Cast your cares on the Lord and he will sustain you; he will never let the righteous fall. Ps. 55:22, NIV.

WE HAD MOVED from one city to another not long before. Everything was beautiful, and each day something new appeared for me to see and admire. Little by little I came to know the neighbors and their pets and see the care that they offered them.

Then I met a cat that didn't have an owner. For most of the day the cat walked from roof to roof, apparently without any destination. One morning I heard her meowing as though in pain. I observed from afar, because she didn't allow anyone to approach her. There were marks on her small body that indicated that she had been cruelly hurt. Certainly this was the reason for her lament. From my hiding place I began to throw a little food on the roof. When she crept closer to eat, I saw a very deep cut on her back, and I wondered what I could do for this cat. How could I help her if she wouldn't even let me get close to her?

Then I remembered the words of Ellen White in her book *Patriarchs and Prophets*. She affirms that the lower order of beings "cannot understand or acknowledge the sovereignty of God, yet they were made capable of loving and serving man" (p. 45).

This little cat had worked for the neighbors, chasing away mice that attempted to enter their homes. She deserved to be attended by someone, and I was there and could help her. Since she wouldn't allow me to go near her, I decided to do something that never fails: pray. I asked God to cure the wound that was causing such pain to the kitten and that was putting her life in danger.

Two days later I saw the cat again. When she came close to eat, I could see her injured side. It was better, and she no longer cried. Of course! I had asked the Creator to cure her. This incident took place more than a year ago. The cat comes every day to eat the food that I put on the roof, and I admire her each day, but she still never lets me get close.

Lord, thank You very much for caring for this cat who has no owner! Now I better understand that if You care for an abandoned animal, how much more You care for me!

CLARA HORNUS DE FERREYRO

Piano Lessons

Happy are those whom you discipline, O Lord. Ps. 94:12, NRSV.

YEARS AGO I GAVE PIANO LESSONS to young children. It was both a rewarding and frustrating experience.

Four years ago we moved our home into a fourth-floor apartment. We soon realized that a young pianist was hard at work on the piano in an adjacent apartment. His daily offerings jarred my nerves and sensibilities, as I was very familiar with the pieces he attempted to play. I used to cry out, "No! Wrong timing!" and other such utterances to my apartment walls. I would send unspoken messages to his piano teacher: *Why aren't you helping him correct his errors? Why does he make the same mistakes week after week?*

Sometimes I met the boy in the elevator, and even though we had a language barrier I always tried to encourage him. His father translated for me, and I would receive a shy smile in return. Over the years we adjusted ourselves to his practicing. Recently, however, I realized that it has become a delight to listen to him play. All his perseverance has resulted in a very good command of the piano. He plays beautifully!

On a recent visit to my homeland, my son asked if I would help my granddaughter with her piano exam pieces. They weren't "quite right," as he put it. No, they weren't! Much was very good, but certain passages were sure to get her a very mediocre grade, or even an F. I sat beside her at the piano, and we talked about it. She reluctantly agreed that instead of playing the entire piece all the time, it might be a good idea to work on those weak passages in particular. We discussed techniques and agreed on a plan. I'm happy to say that she applied herself to the needed areas, and she did very well in her exams and is now working on the next level.

Is your spiritual life a bit like my granddaughter's piano pieces—very good in parts, but with areas of grave concern? Mine certainly is! If I keep living my life the way I do, the "areas of concern" will not get the attention they need. I want the heavenly Teacher to advise and counsel me. I need to ask Him to sit beside me and help me work through the difficult passages in my life. I want all aspects of my life to be a sweet melody. I want to move up to the next level. How about you?

VALERIE FIDELIA

In a Special Way and the Right Time

Delight yourself in the Lord and he will give you the desires of your heart.
Ps. 37:4, NIV.

HAS GOD EVER FULFILLED YOUR NEEDS in a special way, and just at the right time? My answer is "Always!" We don't think often enough about the provisions God has given to us. He has allowed many of my dreams to come true, and answered each prayer, so I have dedicated myself to Him constantly.

As an adolescent I dreamed of studying in a Christian high school. When my family and I visited the boarding school nearest my home, I was 13. Unfortunately, our finances were not enough, so I began sending letters, requesting a scholarship. One day I received a letter from the school stating that I hadn't received a scholarship. They said, however, that I could participate in Think Big, a new program offered by the institution. Through a program of selling educational and religious literature, I could pay for my studies. When I was 16, I was on the first student book sales team. Although my sales didn't reach the amount necessary for the annual tuition, selling books opened doors that helped me accomplish many dreams.

By working in two departments at the high school, I received a half-scholarship and was able to graduate there. Singing in a marvelous choir, participating in taping two CDs, and making friends for eternity were wonderful opportunities. God blessed me more than I deserve.

After spending one year away from the campus, I returned as an off-campus transfer student to the same institution to enroll in a university course. Tuition debts began to increase each month, and continuing my studies at this institution looked difficult, almost impossible. My second year of college ended, but my heart was heavy. I couldn't continue working on my degree the following year, and again I returned to selling books. After working one semester, praying, and dedicating myself entirely to God, I earned funds and returned to my studies. I fulfilled my pacts with God, and He kept His promises to me.

Many times God has proved that He loves me and cares about my dreams. I cannot even begin to imagine the plans He has for me—they are perfect and make me happy as I remember that this wonderful God is leading my life. He will do the same for you, so dream big!

Jenniffer Paola Cunha Ferreira

Take Time to Praise

O magnify the Lord with me, and let us exalt his name together. Ps. 34:3.

WHAT DO YOU PRAISE GOD FOR? Take a moment to make a list of things that cause you to praise God . . . Well, how did it go? Was it a long list, a short list, or are you still thinking? What did you put on the list?

Most of us praise God for the big things, and that's good. But what about the little things—the things God does that we don't acknowledge because they are so small? Or the things we know nothing about? One day God taught me to praise Him for all things—big and small.

I was shopping with a friend at a very expensive department store. I never, ever go on my own to shop at that store—it's just too expensive. They were having a sale, but I knew I would find nothing that I could afford.

As we walked around this very exclusive store I began to see various items that I *could* buy. How wonderful! That day I purchased six blouses for an unbelievably low price. While waiting in line to pay, the woman in front of me turned around and began to give God the praise for her purchase. She didn't know me, but she was so excited that she had to share it. She had come to buy a skirt of a particular color and had asked God to help her. At the first rack of skirts she found the skirt. Now she was praising God for what He had done, not just to me but to anyone who would listen!

I must admit I was a little thrown by the fact that she was so willing to talk about God to complete strangers. After I paid for my purchase I hurried to the car to wait for my friend, and as I sat there I thought about this woman and the way she had behaved. I was embarrassed for her. Then God spoke to me and asked, "What about you? Didn't I do something wonderful for you today? Where is your praise?"

I immediately felt ashamed. God had done something unexpected for me, and I had kept it to myself. I gave Him no praise, and I was critical of the woman who did praise God. Now I praise God whenever I can for whatever He does—big or small.

So go back to that list; try again, and you'll be amazed at what God has done for you—so give Him the praise!

HEATHER-DAWN SMALL

God's Children

For God so loved the world, that he gave his only begotten Son, that whosoever believeth in him should not perish, but have everlasting life. John 3:16.

WE HAVE TWO SONS AND A DAUGHTER, and it's safe to say that I love them more than life itself. Over the years we've tried to teach them right from wrong. We've endeavored to give them a set of values—the meaning of honesty, integrity, and truth. We've tried to foster in them a love for God and respect for others. We've taught them that Jesus is always there for them in times of trouble. I've always tried to set a good example, and I'm usually proud of the young adults my children have become.

However, one day not so long ago one of them made some choices that disappointed me, and I confided my sense of failure as a parent to my friend Brenda. "I want my children with me in heaven," I lamented.

She smiled and replied, "Fauna, don't you realize that your children are not yours to drag into heaven with you? You can teach them and provide a good example for them, but you cannot save them. Only God can do that. Our children are not really our children. They're God's children, and He has only given us custodial care for a short while. He loves them so much more than we ever could and doesn't want to see any of them lost. So you can trust Him to look after them and love them, no matter what they do."

I had to admit she was right. I was thinking that if I tried hard enough, if I was a good enough mother, my children would follow my lead. That's what God wanted from me. But a failure on their part doesn't necessarily mean that I have failed. I can't save my children. That's not my job. That's God's job. And He's so good at it that all I need to do is trust Him.

After all, He sent His only Son into the world for each of us. And He loves us so much that if I had been the only sinner He still would have sent His Son to die just for me. So how can I think that He would love my children less than I do?

Lord, I look forward to Your coming more than ever. Be with my children and let them know that they are always loved—by You and by me. Don't let them be left behind when you come for all Your children. Amen.

FAUNA RANKIN DEAN

How Old Is Too Old?

I can do all things through Christ which strengtheneth me. Phil. 4:13.

MURIEL, REGAL AT 92 YEARS OF AGE and well poised if slightly stooped, lingered in the hostel library. The reading table had been cleared of magazines, and in their place stood three not-so-young computers.

The invitation to "have a go" was resisted as Muriel considered herself far too old to become involved in such modern technology. A friend clicked the mouse a few times, tapped a few keys, and up came a beautiful colored photo of her late husband, a daughter, and herself. It was an article on her centenarian husband, who had been a diabetic for more than 60 years and described how he managed his illness.

Immediately Muriel began a love affair with the computer and its seemingly magical powers. What joy she experienced when she started doing simple jigsaws and then became very skillful at completing very difficult ones.

She was thirsty for more computer knowledge, so she advanced to having her own private e-mail. Now she was able to keep in contact with her family, especially grandsons who were overseas. They shared their exciting adventures in the form of stories and photos. Surfing the Internet for information, recipes, side effects of her prescribed tablets, and much more gave Muriel great pleasure.

During the same year Muriel not only stepped out in faith to master the computer, but also began writing her reflections on life's memories and aging. Some articles were submitted and printed. That brought encouragement not only to her but also to the readers. At the end of the year she was granted a Hinson award for the best devotional of the year.

How old is too old? Is it the number of years, or state of mind? It's been said that old age is youth in a different dress. What shapes our lives depends 10 percent on what happens to us and 90 percent on how we react. If oil, bread, sand, and shavings are put into a fire, they all react differently. So it is with our lives—we all react differently to a given situation

When confronted with a seemingly difficult task, may I always say "I can do all things through Christ which strengtheneth me."

JOY DUSTOW

Substitutions

Remember the former things, those of long ago; I am God, and there is no other; I am God, and there is none like me. Isa. 46:9, NIV.

AS I LOOKED THROUGH THE RECIPE BOOK that came with my new oven, I saw a recipe for a ham-and-egg casserole that looked good, and decided to fix it for lunch. The recipe called for green onion, but I didn't have any, so I decided to substitute a Vidalia onion that I needed to use up. I didn't have white bread, either, but I figured the commercial wheat bread I had in the freezer would do, so I cubed it. Of course, I didn't have ham, either; a soy protein went in instea. The recipe suggested that I add dry mustard and a dash of hot sauce, but I didn't have dry mustard and thought I would just leave the hot sauce out—people could add hot sauce if they wanted it.

If you're an experienced cook, you can guess that the casserole turned out just fine. It struck me funny, though, that I had made so many substitutions. As I thought about it, I realized that it also had some valuable lessons in it. What if I tried those kinds of substitution tricks in other areas of my life? What if I tried using bleach instead of fabric softener in the washing machine? Or have you ever grabbed a tube to brush your teeth and discovered that it was not the toothpaste? (I've heard of people brushing their teeth with all sorts of disgusting pastes.) Or what if I used turpentine when mixing a fertilizer for my African violets? Or how about using some made-up figures or items on my income tax return?

While mixing my casserole, I thought about my spiritual life. People try to use all sorts of substitutes. They try all sorts of idols (oh, I know, they don't call them that, but that is what they are) instead of the Creator God. They try numerous drugs instead of letting the Holy Spirit work in their lives. Some think that if they just change their spouse for another, they'll have happiness. Others try to get enough money, have enough insurance, own enough property or stocks and bonds, to have peace of mind in these troubled times. These substitutions don't work, but that doesn't stop people from trying.

Isaiah 46 is worth reading from time to time. Israel was substituting all sorts of things in place of God. But He cannot be substituted. He alone can bring peace, joy, happiness, and, best of all, eternal life. Who would want a substitute for that!

ARDIS DICK STENBAKKEN

Blackout

Watch therefore, for ye know neither the day nor the hour wherein the Son of man cometh. Matt. 25:13.

"VINCE! DANA!" I could hear my mom's voice, but I didn't want to acknowledge her. In the grogginess of my mind I wondered what time it was. Surely it wasn't time to get up to take my daughter to the nursery. All was quiet. Since I hadn't answered, I assumed that my mom had gone. I went back to sleep.

"Dana! Dana!" I could hear my mom again. This time I answered. It must be serious. When I met my mom, she told me that at 3:00 that morning there had been a fire at the Bermuda Electric Light Company. As the *Royal Gazette* put it the next day: "With the majority of residents in their beds yesterday, scores of firefighters battled courageously in unimaginable heat to quell 60-foot flames that exploded into life just after 3:00 a.m.—sending menacing plumes of thick, black smoke spiraling across the night sky." Thus, we had an islandwide electric blackout.

For an island that already had a water shortage because of a lack of rain, this was a disaster. We had to dip water from the tanks under our houses. Since we had an electric oven, my family had to eat at my parents' house, as they had a gas stove. Some took the experience in stride; they saw no big challenge. For them this was a time for flashlights and "lights out" parties. Such was the case with my family. We went swimming. For others, hurricane-style panic buying was the order of the day at gas stations, hardware stores, and supermarkets across the island. There was no way anyone could have prepared ahead of time.

As I reflect back on that day that will stand out in Bermuda's history, I think of a future time that there will be a spiritual blackout. Will we be ready, as were the five wise virgins who had oil in their lamps? Or will we be foolish virgins and have no oil? Those who live their lives daily according to the Word of God and are in constant communion with God will have no fear. There will be no panic—instead we will be looking forward to that time. "Immediately after the tribulation of those days shall the sun be darkened, and the moon shall not give her light. . . . and they shall see the Son of man coming in the clouds of heaven with power and great glory" (Matt. 24:29, 30).

DANA M. BEAN

Fearfully
and Wonderfully Made

I praise you, for this body is incredibly and wonderfully made. Your whole creation is amazing. Ps.139:14, Clear Word.

FOR MORE THAN SEVEN YEARS I suffered from osteoarthritis of the knee joints. In January 2005 I had total knee replacement surgery in my right knee. That Thursday morning I prayed, "Dear Lord, please be with Dr. Kouba and his staff, and let the operation be successful." My daughters took me to the hospital, and after brief preparation I was whisked into surgery at 7:30.

When I awoke in the hospital room, my daughters shared the news that the surgery had gone well. With my son-in-law, William, they visited with me each day until I was taken to the rehabilitation center to relearn how to walk. With the Lord's blessings and visits from my church family, I healed quickly.

Six days later my daughter Nicolette took me home. I was walking with a walker. She stayed two weeks, helping me through the most difficult time. By the second week I was able to attend church, surrounded by family support. My four other daughters—Sonia, Yvette, Linda, and Claudia—each spent one week attending to my needs. My son, Mario, came on the weekend to repair the shower and do other things around the house.

I thank God for the way that my family took care of me and how He protected them as they traveled. His providence and my family's care greatly enhanced the healing process.

Two months after the surgery I completed therapy to regain range of motion and strength in the right knee. My range of motion is now 120 degrees, which is very good, but before surgery it was 127 degrees. Because the titanium and plastic used to replace the cartilage is not flexible enough, I can no longer kneel to pray.

When God created us, He gave us limbs that work wonderfully. He has endowed people with the ability to replace worn-out limbs, but they don't work as well as those from the Creator. I look forward to the day that our bodies will be without any trace of the ravages of sin and age.

"Our citizenship is in heaven. And we eagerly look forward to the coming of our Savior, the Lord Jesus Christ. At that time, He will subdue all things, and by His power He will change our weak and sinful bodies to be like His sinless and glorious body" (Phil. 3:20. 21, Clear Word).

WILMA C. JARDINE

The Blessing of Peace

May the Lord strengthen His people and bless them with peace. Ps. 29:11, Clear Word.

WHEN MY HUSBAND AND I left for a six-year mission appointment in Kenya, I told my mom that I would be returning for furlough after two years, and together we would attend the entire General Conference session (a worldwide church conference) in Toronto, Canada. I asked her to promise that she would stay well. We did make the trip and had a great time together.

Two years later she developed health problems and had to have surgery. A year after that she began to develop some mild discomfort that steadily became worse. Since we were returning home for a family wedding, I decided to also spend time with my mother. I could get more details on her health condition and assist my sister.

My mother didn't attend the wedding. This was unusual, because she never missed any family gatherings. However, her birthday came and, together with family and her church friends, we joyfully celebrated with her. She enjoyed the occasion very much.

One day before we were scheduled to fly back to Kenya, four of us accompanied my mother to the hospital, where she was to have various tests. Being a nurse, I stayed very close to assist her on and off examination tables, as well as help her undress for her procedures. She seemed quite weak, but tried not to show it. We talked and prayed during her waking moments, and sang and prayed some more. I left her in the care of two sisters, a brother, and under the watchful eye of my oldest son, a cardiologist.

After two days of travel I called to inform my family that we had arrived safely, only to hear that my mother had been admitted to the hospital. Within four days she peacefully fell asleep in Jesus. Even though I wasn't with her in those final moments, I was at peace, knowing that we had spent quality time together over the years.

It is very comforting to know that God has promised to strengthen each of us and to bless us with peace in time of need. "We do not want you to be uninformed, brothers and sisters, about those who have died, so that you may not grieve as others do who have no hope. For since we believe that Jesus died and rose again, even so, through Jesus, God will bring with him those who have died" (1 Thess. 4:13, 14, NRSV). That is comfort!

LYDIA D. ANDREWS

He Answered Before I Called

Before they call I will answer; while they are still speaking I will hear.
Isa. 65:24, NIV.

MY SON WAS SENTENCED to three years in Marion Correctional Institution in Ohio. The first year I drove from Detroit twice to see him. Then they moved Russell two times before moving him to Lima, Ohio, Correctional Institution. I went to see him twice and took my daughter with me. Later in the year, I received a note in the mail, written on an old envelope:

"Mom, please call the sheriff's department, a lawyer, and the warden of the correctional institution. I need help now; please help me, and hurry. They put me in a hole, and I didn't do anything—I don't have any points or tickets on my record. I don't know why. I've been in this hole two days so far. Please, please help me!"

I felt sick and was so upset. I stopped reading and began praying. *Lord, I can't go back down the highway. Please, Lord, You will have to take care of my son. You handle whatever the problem is.*

The letter was still in my hand as I tried to understand it. Before I could say amen, the phone rang. It was my son. He told me that there had been a mistake and that he had been taken out of the hole early that morning. "I am just reading the letter," I told to him. "It is still in my hand!"

My heart pounded, and I cried. It was all I could think about. The Lord knew and had taken care of everything before I had even read the letter. He knew my heart and what I would pray. Now I believe and trust in His Word more than ever before! This is my miracle, and if I never hear or see another, this one is enough for me. I am amazed and overwhelmed each time I think about it.

I always believed in the Lord and know there are miracles in all our lives, but now this is so real in my life. It's almost too much to bear! The love that was shown to me is sometimes overwhelming. I cry when I think about the miracle that happened that day. The blessings just keep on coming in my life. To God be the glory!

As it says in Psalms 18:6: "In my distress I called to the Lord; I cried to my God for help. From his temple he heard my voice; my cry came before him, into his ears" (NIV).

BERTHA SWANSON

The Lesson From the Gas Burner

If we confess our sins, he is faithful and just and will forgive us our sins and purify us from all unrighteousness. 1 John 1:9, NIV.

"NOT AGAIN! OH, NO! IT CAN'T BE!" I couldn't deny reality. The proof was there, right before my very eyes. A minute of distraction, and once again the milk was spilled, covering the entire stove top, filling the air with a burnt odor.

Cleaning the stove top and scrubbing the burners is one of the most unpleasant tasks for me, especially when food has spilled and has been burned onto it, leaving it black. But I couldn't leave this task undone. Slowly I wiped the stove top and then began the unpleasant task of cleaning the burners, leaving the one that was covered with burnt milk until last. I scrubbed and scrubbed with dish detergent, then a scouring pad, but there was a stain that would not budge. I thought about giving up and leaving it (after all, it was just a little stain, almost unnoticeable).

Almost immediately, however, a thought came to me: *And if this were your heart? Wouldn't you want Jesus to keep working to remove just one little stain of sin?* That thought paralyzed me! How many times have I failed, and displeased the Lord with my actions, my temperament, my words? How many times have I stained my heart? "No, Lord, I do not want You to give up on me," I prayed. "My Lord, continue working in my life. Do not allow even one stain of sin to keep me from shining for You. Please, Lord, do not give up on me!"

From that moment on, that stain on the burner became a challenge to me. I wasn't going to give up until I had completely removed it. What a great relief when it was totally gone!

Don't you think that God has a hard task to do in our lives? He needs to do a complete housecleaning so that we can reflect His character. As David wrote in Psalm 51: "Wash away all my iniquity and cleanse me from my sin. . . . Cleanse me with hyssop, and I will be clean; wash me, and I will be whiter than snow" (verses 2-7, NIV).

May we be more sensitive to the work of the Holy Spirit of God in each of our lives throughout this day and every day.

CRISTINA FLORÊNCIO

Thought: What makes it hard for God to clean us up? Is it Him, or are we holding on to the sin?

God Sent an Angel

See, I am sending an angel ahead of you to guard you along the way and to bring you to the place I have prepared. Ex. 23:20.

I WAS 18 YEARS OLD when I decided to study at Mountain View College in the Philippines. I had heard that this school accepted working students, so I decided to work and to study. I had never been to the school, but my friend had been attending, so I asked her how to get there. She gave me a map and assured me that she would help me find a job. So I boarded the midnight bus alone for the six-hour trip to MVC. I sat near the driver so that I could ask repeatedly if we were there yet. Other people were sleeping, and I wanted to sleep too, but was afraid that I might miss my stop. The driver assured me that it was still a long way to Valencia, so it was safe to sleep.

When I reached the college, I stowed my suitcase and went to look for my friend, who lived in a nearby village. When I found the house, the owner said that my friend was away in another city. I walked back to where I had left my bag, and sat down on a bench to cry. I cried so much, but I also secretly prayed earnestly to God, asking Him to help me, because I really wanted to study and I didn't know what to do.

Suddenly an old woman appeared and asked me what had happened. I told her everything. I told her how much I wanted to study at that college, but I didn't know how. She told me that she would help. She took me to the girls' dormitory and helped me apply for work. The supervisor wasn't there, so we went to another dormitory and spoke to the assistant dean. She told us that their dean was resting and couldn't see anyone, but the old woman was insistent. The dean came out, and I applied for work as an assistant to the dean, and was hired. I was so happy—I thanked her so much.

I asked her where she lived. She told me she lived somewhere in a forest, so I walked with her as far as the main road. When I turned back, the old woman had disappeared. I couldn't see her anywhere, so I headed back to the dorm, praying and thanking God.

Do you think the woman was an angel? I think so, because people assured me that no old woman lived in that area. I praise God for caring so much for me that He sent the help I needed.

JOCELYN HERUELA

My Favorite Gift

Thanks be to God for his indescribable gift. 2 Cor. 9:15, NIV.

I WAS SO EXCITED! I was going to be 6 years old and have my first birthday party! It was toward the end of the Great Depression in the United States, so times were hard. When I was 3 years old, my mother had become a single parent who worked hard in a sewing factory.

A new family had just moved to town and opened a five- and ten-cent store. We lived in a small town with few shops, but we could find almost anything we needed at Bergens' Five and Dime. At Christmastime they had the most beautiful dolls a 5-year-old had ever seen!

The Bergens' son, Albert, was close to my age. Mother must invite him to my party; I thought he would probably bring me a wonderful gift! Maybe a game, paper dolls, or a toy.

Mother and I sat down and made a list of children to invite. Of course, the list included all five of the first graders at the Christian school I attended. She suggested we invite two older girls, Kathy and Jenny. "Not Jenny!" I protested. "She is very poor and not very well liked. She wears old clothes, and she probably wouldn't bring me a gift." This outburst brought forth a kindly lecture from Mother, and Jenny was invited. The party was a success—everyone came, including Albert and Jenny.

It is now decades later. I can't even remember the gift Albert brought me, nor what I received from any of the others. My favorite gift was from Jenny. Her mom had made red and green Jell-O and cut it into little squares. I thought that was the neatest idea ever!

I think now how selfish I was back then. I hope it helped teach me to be more caring and kind to others. When I told Jenny how much I liked her gift, she just beamed with happiness. It seemed that after the party everyone was nicer to Jenny. We didn't mind that her clothes were old; we found she was funny and would keep us laughing.

I am still longing for the most wonderful gift of all—an invitation to go home with my heavenly Father. Talk about presents! There will be no green or red Jell-O! Instead, there will be gates of pearl and streets of gold—and even mansions! But a cottage will be fine with me—and I hope it's right next door to Jenny!

NELDA BIGELOW

Direct Connect

But let him ask in faith, nothing wavering. James 1:6.

DID YOU EVER WANT TO ASK SOMEONE A QUESTION but were afraid what the answer would be? And then you decided to step out in faith?

My sister was dying of cancer, and the cancer was spreading fast throughout her body. I was 800 miles away and hadn't visited with her in more than a year, so I knew that I had to go see her. My brother told me, "If you want to see your sister, you should come now." I had been undecided about when I would go, but my brother's statement made my decision very clear—I needed to go now.

I informed my employer and started packing my bags. I also had to make arrangements for my husband, who was going to remain at home. He has an eye disease that has left him legally blind, and he has difficulty dialing the telephone. I had to make sure things were convenient for him.

My husband and I have cell phones that are also walkie-talkies. The walkie-talkies allow us to communicate with each other locally with the push of a button whenever it's necessary. My cellular phone company offers a feature that enables one to talk to anyone in the United States who has the same type of phone as mine. With this feature I would be able to talk to my husband directly while I was visiting my sister; however, we didn't have that particular feature on our phones, and we couldn't afford to pay the extra. I decided to call the company in faith and explain my situation to them and see if they could help me. After talking with a representative, I found out that I was calling at a time that there was a special: I could get nationwide direct connect free for 30 days, with 60 extra free minutes. God had answered my prayer! I was able to go see my sister, use my push-to-talk nationwide coverage, and keep in close contact with my husband.

You know, we all have nationwide—universewide—direct-connect lines with our Savior, Jesus Christ. You don't have to hesitate or be afraid to use your prayer line to connect instantly from wherever you are. It doesn't cost you any extra. You don't have to dial a number or push a button. Just ask in faith.

ELAINE J. JOHNSON

Picked Up by an Angel

When Pharaoh shall speak unto you, saying, "Shew a miracle." Ex. 7:9.

"I'M LATE AGAIN!" Ally exclaimed, "Dr. G is going to be angry at me yet again! Why isn't morning a little bit longer?" She finished tucking her niece into the stroller and sped away, barely looking both ways as she crossed streets.

Every morning Ally had to get up early, bathe her 1-month-old niece, shower, dress them both, and drop off her niece at the babysitter's on her way to class. She was helping her sister, who had to be at work by 4:30 a.m. and couldn't take the baby with her. The job was straining. It seemed as if she was never fast enough, was always 15 or 20 minutes late to Dr. G's class.

"Ally, I can't allow you to come late to class anymore without taking points off your grade," Dr. G had warned her the day before. His words echoed through her head as she kissed her niece goodbye at the babysitter's house. Then she took off running. *Oh! How I wish the college were closer!* she thought as she ran. *Lord, I need a miracle—I need You!*

Ally saw a man in a white limousine on the opposite side of the road, waving at her and smiling. He motioned her to wait as he turned around. Convinced that the limousine was an answer to her prayer, she waited. Very soon the gentleman stopped right in front of her, asking if she needed a ride. "Thank you, sir! I'm going to the college on top of the hill. I really need the ride."

"You know, you shouldn't climb into strangers' cars these days," the gentleman warned.

"Well, I did it because I know you are my angel. You are the answer to my prayer," she replied, confidence dripping from every word. "I prayed for a miracle, and you are it." Soon they arrived, and Ally jumped out of the car and shouted, "Thank you!"

"You made it, Ally! You are here!" Dr. G greeted, surprised and happy at seeing her. "I told you that you could get here earlier if you just tried a little bit harder."

"No, Dr. G.! The Lord sent His angel to get me here on time," Ally replied, gasping for air. "Didn't you see that limousine?" Ally asked, pointing toward an empty parking lot.

"What limousine?" asked a puzzled Dr. G. "I just saw you run in. I saw no limousine."

GLADYS S. (GUERRERO) KELLEY

303

No More Fear

When I am afraid, I will trust in you. Ps. 56:3, NIV.

WE LIVE IN A WORLD OF FEAR. As I talk with people, the word I hear most is "fear" about something. Fear comes from within us and is then attached to people and problems outside of us. Our many fears can be reduced to a few categories: fear caused by hurtful memories, fear of rejection, fear of failure, fear of losing control, fear of sickness and death, and fear of the future. All of this fear in our lives can cause a paralysis so that we cannot do what God wants us to do.

Members of a psychology class once asked 500 people, "What are you afraid of?" Those 500 people listed more than 7,000 fears. In my life I have had to face my fears many times in order to move on, to face situations that were bigger than I could handle. When I became pregnant with my second child, I got sick. It was a very difficult time. Fear came into my life, draining my energy. After many exams I decided to go ahead with my pregnancy. The waiting time was a fearful time. I spent days and nights thinking about the baby. After nine months of dealing with my fears, God was there, taking care of me and my son. Andre was born on a beautiful Friday morning, healthy, fine-looking, and full of energy. Whether my fear was realistic or out of proportion, my greatest refuge was Jesus Christ.

Fear is a powerful emotion, affecting all of us regardless of our age or position in life. But despite our fears, there is a blessing. There are more than 75 "fear not"s in the Bible. God doesn't condemn us for being afraid. He tells us to turn to Him when those fearful times come. He is there for us in the middle of the fear-causing situation.

Perhaps you are afraid today. Examine your fears. Allow God to work with you through those that seem unmanageable right now. "Do not be afraid," Jesus is saying to you. God can be trusted. There is nothing unknown to Him. He is always in control. Store these words in the memory bank of your heart: "When I am afraid, I will trust in you." That's why He has given us this verse. What fears are you battling today? Write them down and give them over to God in prayer.

Thank You, Lord, for being my refuge in times of fear, and for Your comfort and strength. Give the assurance I need to move beyond my fear, knowing that I am safe when I trust in You.

RAQUEL QUEIROZ DA COSTA ARRAIS

Seashells

And he shewed me a pure river of water of life, clear as crystal, proceeding out of the throne of God and of the Lamb. Rev. 22:1.

A YEAR AGO 5-year-old Ashley Anne, her mother, and I had decided to take a trip to California to see all our relatives there. After visiting several places, we decided to cut across to the Pacific Ocean and stay one night in a hotel. We found one at beautiful Pismo Beach and watched the sun go down over the water with waves gently lapping the shoreline. Seagulls walked around enjoying the coolness of the air. We too enjoyed all that God has created for His people.

Ashley was up at 5:00 the next morning, wanting to collect shells. (Only grandchildren can get you to do that!) We found so many pretty shells, and Ashley found many sand dollars, too.

My now-6-year-old Ashley snuggled in bed with me early one morning. While we were reading books, which is one of our favorite things to do, she suddenly started to cry. I asked gently, "What is the matter?" She said she felt sad at losing both her great-grandmas during the past year. I reminded her that when we get to heaven we will be reunited with them.

"I want to go get more shells from the ocean so that when I go to heaven I can take them to my grandmas," she explained. (Her grandmas just loved collecting shells by the seashores.)

My first reaction was to inform her that we weren't taking anything with us to heaven—but I stopped myself. The Holy Spirit must have inspired me because I could just see in a mind's flash the crystal sea. I told Ashley, "Oh, honey, you won't have to take shells with you. The Lord has a most wonderful sea that you and the grandmas can go to collect the most beautiful shells and rocks!"

I told her how very wonderful it will be and that God has promised, "Eye hath not seen, nor ear heard, . . . the things which God hath prepared" (1 Cor. 2:9) for us.

I really felt so close to God at that moment, and grateful that He gave me just the insight I needed to rightly answer a little girl. As it says in Mark 10:15: "Verily I say unto you, Whosoever shall not receive the kingdom of God as a little child, he shall not enter therein."

ANNE ELAINE NELSON

Misplaced Books

Hypocrite! First remove the plank from your own eye, and then you will see clearly to remove the speck from your brother's eye. Matt. 7:5, NKJV.

FOUR BOOKS LIE IN A ROW, and mine is the fourth book. Every morning and evening it lies at the end of the row, and each time I pick it up to sign by my name to mark my attendance.

One day I came, as usual, and picked up the fourth book and opened it to sign. I looked for my name—it was missing. I wondered what had happened. I turned the pages to verify that I was looking at the right page. Yes, I was. The person standing next to me asked what was wrong.

I replied, "I'm a bit confused—I can't find my name."

I knew that my name is number 57 in the book, so I checked again and found that the last number was 34. My name was not the only one missing. I was a bit embarrassed. Others were already lining up behind me to sign. I calmed myself a bit and noticed that the last name in the book started with M, whereas my name starts with T. Slowly it began to dawn on me that the book I picked up from the row was actually the third book that someone had placed in the fourth place by mistake. Immediately I dropped the book I was holding and looked for the fourth book—the *real* fourth book— found it, opened it, and with great relief found my name and signed.

Though it was not a crime, simply a misplacement, it caused a lot of confusion and wasted time not only for me but for all those who waited in line, not knowing why I was looking blank. My first reaction was to condemn the person who had misplaced the book. He or she should have been more careful to put it back in the right place. "What a waste of time it caused!" I murmured. I realized much later that to find fault with others is the easiest way to cover up one's own mistakes. Instead of criticizing others, I should have looked for the right book. If I had done my part well, I could have saved others from wasting their time.

Little acts of negligence or ignorance can cause a great deal of inconvenience. Why aren't we more careful in our duties and activities? "He that is faithful in that which is least is faithful also in much: and he that is unjust in the least is unjust also in much" (Luke 16:10). God wants us that way.

MARGARET TITO

And Everything?

And we know that in all things God works for the good of those who love him, who have been called according to his purpose. Rom. 8:28, NIV.

AND ALL THINGS WORK FOR THE GOOD? Everything? It is really difficult in the midst of a crisis, or when we feel anguish, to consider that this can be possible. But this promise has strengthened me at the most difficult times I have faced, because I know that it is salvation for me.

My son was to return to Spain to finish his second year of volunteer service. My feelings were mixed—a mother's pride to learn that he had been asked to return because of his good work, and the desire to have him closer. Only three days until he would travel, and I could not conciliate my thoughts and feelings.

That night my son returned home from taking care of documentation, pleased that he had finished everything. As he was about to show us the papers that he'd put in his wallet—Where was the wallet? We searched and soon felt despair, because everything that he needed for his trip was in that wallet—visa, tickets, money, some personal items that had special meaning for him.

I forgot my feelings and became concerned with my son's feelings. What could we do with so little time? Where could he turn to solve the problem? We didn't know. We looked for direction, for somewhere to turn that would enable him to replace the lost airline ticket and to get the necessary visa again so that he would be able to enter the country. "Lord, help us to find the wallet," we prayed.

The night was long—no one could sleep. The following day my son felt worse, but then we remembered the promise that everything that happens to us is for the good. We decided that we should live what we believe. We prayed again, and when we finished the prayer, the telephone rang. The wallet had been found by a neighbor. She had begun to call all the telephone numbers that she found inside so that she could return the wallet.

God showed me once again that He directs my life, and that I should not concern myself with problems. I need only ask Him to be the captain of my life, and He will be in charge, giving me the peace that is necessary.

NANCY CANO DE ZIEGLER

There Is No Distance for God

You answer us with awesome deeds of righteousness, O God our Savior, the hope of all the ends of the earth and of the farthest seas. Ps. 65:5, NIV.

THERE ARE SOME THINGS that give me great pleasure and joy, and one of them begins very early in the morning when I prepare for my daily time with God. My first reading is always the women's devotional book. The messages that other women write bring me peace and comfort for difficult days. I especially like the experiences that women share regarding answers to prayer and help in times of affliction. I think of those women who are far away, in countries from east to west, but who reach our hearts through what they have written.

When the experiences of these women touch me, I want to know where the author is from. Quickly, I turn to the biographical sketches to learn where they live or work. I've developed the habit of writing this information at the top of the page. I think about these experiences; then I tell these stories whenever I have the opportunity to witness to someone about our great God.

One of my desires is to be able to correspond with some of these women, to exchange ideas, to become friends. I would like to be able to send them e-mail messages. Many times I pray about their problems, struggles, and difficulties so that God may be with them and their family members. Although we are distant because of the geography of this world, our thoughts are upon our God through the Written Word. Even at great distances we can support one another in prayer.

There is a hymn in my Portuguese hymnal entitled "Lindo País" (Beautiful Country). It is one of my favorites because it talks about a country that God is preparing for His children. Through faith I think of the day that we will all be one people, in one country, and with one God. Nothing will separate us then, nothing will keep us from being friends, because there is no distance for God.

Lord, help me to trust in You in such a faithful, patient manner that I can give all to You—then I will be able to wait.

NICÉIA TRIANDADE

We Catch Them— God Cleans Them

Fear not; from henceforth thou shalt catch men. Luke 5:10.

I'M THE TYPE OF PERSON who always sees people for what they are, not what they can eventually become, or what purpose God may have for them. As a matter of fact, I was downright proud of myself for my judgment, and could defend my point without blinking an eye.

People from my native county see obstacles as stepping-stones. People don't necessarily have all the proper training or education for a job, but, combined with talent, they are able to do all kinds of things. A few years after I gave my life to Jesus I noticed a certain young man who did minimum-wage jobs to make a living. I'd been acquainted with him before I gave my heart to the Lord, and I thought he looked as though he wouldn't be interested in Jesus, so I never witnessed to him. Then as I grew in faith, I got involved in witnessing to a very hard-to-reach community. I felt this was where God wanted me to be in gaining souls for Him, not realizing—or even thinking—that *everyone* we meet is a potential candidate for heaven.

My friend Julianna invited me to a nearby congregation to worship. As I walked in, I saw the young man I had ignored. Of course I was awestruck. I asked Julianna if he was a baptized member. To my surprise, he was. But this shouldn't have been a surprise. He looked so happy and well groomed, worshipping God. I really could see the change in him.

God call us to be colaborers with Him; no one should be prejudiced against anyone.

This experience changed my perspective. Sometimes we think that just because people dress or look a certain way, they aren't Christians, even if we see them in church. With the help of the Holy Spirit, I began to see that I needed to focus on myself, not on others. In the end, they are the ones who will stand before the judgment throne for themselves. I have to concentrate on my relationship with Jesus so that He can clean me up.

Jesus said that He will make us fishers of people. He didn't say anything about us cleaning the fish. That's His job, not ours. We should focus on catching as many as we can, and He will do the quality cleaning.

Only You alone, Lord, should be our focus. Help me keep my eyes on You.

DONNA DENNIS

Am I My Brother's/Sister's Keeper?

And the King shall answer and say unto them, Verily I say unto you, Inasmuch as ye have done it unto one of the least of these my brethren, ye have done it unto me. Matt. 25:40.

AN INTERESTING STORY CAUGHT MY ATTENTION. It was reported on the local news that a man in Winnipeg, Manitoba, Canada, had recently been found dead. That may not seem unusual, but it was the fact that he probably died in 2002 that was hard to believe. According to *The Electric New Paper*, Jim Sulkers had been dead from apparently natural causes for nearly two years before being found. His bills continued to be paid through automatic withdrawal accounts.

Sulkers, in his 50s, had multiple sclerosis. The Winnipeg *Sun* reported that Sulkers' niece, Nicole Kurtz, described Sulkers as "incredibly warm and loving." Jim had worked in the city engineering department until 1992, then retired early because of illness. Eventually he sold his car and motorized scooter, isolated himself in his apartment, and made less and less contact with people. He would not answer the phone or the door.

Some people were curious about why they didn't see Sulkers anymore. The mailman left mail, but took it back when the box was full. Shortly before Sulkers was found, the manager told the mailman that Sulkers no longer lived there. How prophetic his words were. Some thought he was on vacation. Finally police entered his condo and found Sulkers in a mummified state.

When I researched this story, two points stood out. First, this man was dying way before he died. He chose to close his life to others. For years prior to his death he slowly detached himself from family and friends. The *Sun* reported that Kurtz said, "When our mail started coming back, we thought it was the next step in his withdrawal."

Second, how can a person get lost among so many people? *Today's Paper National* reported that a relative, who described himself as a "distant, distant cousin," said dozens of relatives lived within driving distance of Sulkers.

We are not lost in Jesus. He knows exactly where we are. But as fellow Christians, do we know where our family is? Not just our biological family, but people we go to church with or work with. How many times are we impressed to check on someone and ignore it? For poor Jim Sulkers there was an unfortunate result. My hope is that his death can mean more than his life apparently did.

MARY M. J. WAGONER ANGELIN

He Means It

If you keep the Sabbath holy, not having your own fun and business on that day, . . . I will see to it that you . . . get your full share of the blessings. Isa. 58:13, 14, TLB.

I WAS ATTEMPTING to get caught up on my scrapbook, and the store from which I get my supplies had a promotion for a $500 gift certificate. I wanted it badly. My trips to the supply department became more frequent. Soon I had accumulated five entries. On the back of the slips it said the drawing was at 4:00 p.m., May 10. I wrote it on my calendar, sure I would be that lucky person.

One day I noticed that the date of the drawing was on a Sabbath. I was raised to refrain from secular and business activities on Sabbath, but I rationalized, *It is they who will be doing the drawing, not me.* It also stated that one had to be there to win. *I will sit on a chair—I will not actually be involved.*

The day of the drawing came, and I went to church. I came home, did some reading, and lost track of time. When I did look at my watch, it was 2:40! I rushed out the door with my coat half on. I hadn't looked at my slips for many months, and had forgotten to turn them in.

I rushed into the store. Only one person was there, and by the door was a large sign: "Congratulations to Liz on Winning!" I didn't care about the last name—it wasn't mine. I guess I looked bewildered, holding the slips in my hand, because a clerk said, rather casually, "Oh, yeah; that was last week."

Walking back to my car, ashamed to be in the parking lot, I looked at the slips, not believing my eyes. I had absentmindedly thought the drawing was today, May 17.

Throwing the now-crumpled-up slips into my car's garbage receptacle, I broke down in tears, feeling just terrible. Not that I had lost, but at the overwhelming thoughts that raced through my mind. I had placed winning ahead of my relationship with Jesus.

The Lord knew right from the start that He would confuse my mind and not allow this terrible violation of His day to happen. The Holy Spirit's voice said, "I mean it when I say to keep my Sabbaths holy." Overcome with shame, I hurried home to get on my knees and ask forgiveness.

VIDELLA MCCLELLAN

A Different Type of Punishment

All your children shall be taught by the Lord. Isa. 54:13, NKJV.

FROM THE TIME SHE WAS VERY YOUNG, my mother, a student of the Scriptures, was enchanted with the truth she found there, and she wanted to tell everyone. On Saturday afternoons she would go from house to house in our neighborhood, offering a Bible study to people.

Soon Mother had many homes to visit, filled-out lessons to pick up, and Bible questions to answer for her Bible students. I was only 6, and easily agitated and restless, so I was chosen to go with Mother on her visits while my older sister stayed home and took care of our younger sister. For a fidgety child like me it was very difficult to go with her, and her explanations, as short as they may have been, tired me out.

One day a very arrogant man, speaking with the utmost diplomacy, said he wanted to stop taking the Bible course. He said that because he was a lawyer, it was very difficult for him to discuss the subject with someone as uneducated as my mother, who had only a fourth-grade education. He said, "Ma'am, did you know that in science there is a great deal of discussion about which came first, the egg or the chicken?"

My mother quietly listened with attention. Already impatient with the conversation, I blurted out, "What is the difference? Both the egg and the chicken need a Creator, right?"

The man looked interested and added, "That's true; it seems so simple that even a small child can answer this." And with that, he decided to continue with the studies.

However, these studies, without my being conscious of it, became very important in my life. When I was 9 years old and had a little brother at home, I wanted to stay and play with the children, but this was not how my mother thought. Bored with the studies that lasted for more than an hour in the home of a physically disabled woman, I decided to hold school for the children in the neighborhood. Now I was excited! I could tell stories and sing with them! So each week I spent my free time looking for pictures for the stories.

What did this mean in my life? I still love to work with children. How wonderful that Mother's "punishment" for her restless, agitated daughter was so wise that it could produce wonder fruit and touch the lives of so many children!

SÔNIA MARIA RIGOLI SANTOS

Sticks and Stones

Let the words of my mouth, and the meditation of my heart, be acceptable in thy sight, O lord, my strength, and my redeemer. Ps. 19:14.

A POPULAR CLICHÉ THAT I LEARNED from my grandmother during my childhood was "Sticks and stones may break my bones, but words will never harm me." Mama could get me to believe almost anything, so I truly thought that words could not do any physical harm to anyone. When children called me names or said ugly things, I didn't feel any physical pain, so the saying seemed true. Although I was taught that name-calling was wrong, I would call others names as well, and I never witnessed anyone crying as a result, so I thought, *How bad could it really be?* Wrong, wrong, wrong!

It was after I became an adult that I realized that Grandmother's goal was to prevent me from becoming involved in fights with other children. I have learned as an adult that words can hurt, destroy, and even kill. Name-calling, lying, using profanity, degrading, and exhibiting vindictive and obnoxious behavior toward others does hurt! This often happens in the home, at school, on the job, and in the street. Sometimes it isn't *what* is being said but the manner in which it is said. One's tone of voice can make a difference in delivering a message.

Who is calling the names can also make a difference. If we hear something from a parent, coworker, instructor, or a so-called friend, words hurt! What makes matters worse is that it takes time and spiritual nourishment for these wounds to heal—if they ever do. Sometimes a person has to take medication because continuous hurting can cause physical ailments leading to hypertension, stroke, and possibly death.

Something that makes words even more harmful is that words cannot be recalled, like a defective product, although one can sincerely ask for forgiveness. If my words are pleasing to God, they should be pleasing to my fellow human beings also.

Lord, my heart is focused on You. Please let my words and actions be acceptable to You and to those with whom I communicate today and every day.

CORA A. WALKER

Thought: James 3:3-6 has a lot to say about the tongue and words. Read it in several versions. Other texts about words that are worth studying: Romans 3:13; Job 5:2; Hosea 7:16.

Little Miracles

Happy is he who has the God of Jacob for his help, whose hope is in the Lord his God. Ps. 146:5, NKJV.

 I WAS SITTING IN HIS CHURCH because my daughter, Marina, had been asked to sing, and I was there to support her. After her solo, the young minister's thoughts captured my attention. He reminded us that many times God performs miracles, but we fail to notice and appreciate them because they are not big events.

Several days a week I like to walk for exercise. Most of the time I walk alone but feel safe because I'm in my own neighborhood. However, I had become concerned that if I should get sick or perhaps fall, nobody would know how to contact my relatives. So I prepared a small 2" x 3" emergency card that I could attach to my clothing.

A few days after I had heard the sermon on little miracles, I clipped on my little white card and started down my neighborhood street. After I returned home, I reached for my identification card and discovered that it had slipped out of its plastic card cover. I was immediately alarmed, because so much of my personal information was on it. My daughter was visiting me at the time, so I told her of my dilemma. "Let's retrace your steps," she suggested, rushing out the front door. We hurried to my car, and I drove slowly down the street while she looked out the passenger-side window. We had just passed a parked motor home where several people were visiting together when she said, "Stop! I think I see it." Jumping out of the car, Marina reached down and picked up something. "Here it is!" she called out to me.

Both of us had been praying silently to our heavenly Father, the one in whom we had placed our hope, and now we thanked Him out loud for performing one of His little miracles. In time the dust and rain would have destroyed my card, and God could have prevented anyone else from finding it or using it to my disadvantage, but instead He chose to calm my nerves by allowing my daughter to see it lying on the ground at the back of the motor home. The young preacher was right—God does perform small miracles every day. We need only to look for them. May you find your miracle today!

MILDRED C. WILLIAMS

Perfect Peace

Great peace have they which love thy law: and nothing shall offend them.
Ps. 119:165.

AS WITH ANY YOUNG CHRISTIAN WOMAN, through experiential knowledge I came to realize that having genuine peace, calmness, and composure even during challenging times comes not by chance but through a close relationship with Christ. The peace referred to in today's text can exist in spite of one's circumstances, since the decision to have peace is a choice.

We can choose peace even during persecution. We can choose peace in pain. We can choose peace through perplexity. We can choose peace in broken relationships. We can choose peace in spite of broken dreams. We can choose peace in divorce, in childlessness, in abuse. We can choose peace in unemployment and in the loss of a loved one. In other words, we can choose peace.

The concept of banking can be used to illustrate the Christian's experience with Christ, the giver, and us, the recipients. As the receiver, one stands a better chance if he/she has deposits of spiritual peace in the bank. This usually boosts confidence, and then the incidence for failing is greatly diminished, if not nonexistent.

In the spiritual realm those who make an effort to know God personally will find themselves with eternal deposits that are weightier than any earthly deposit. Our loving Father executes grace and mercy—but also justice. We cannot assume that we can simply withdraw from our spiritual account in an emergency, when we actually have a "malnourished" account. Replenishing this account is a daily task through much prayer, meaningful reading of the Word, Christ-centered meditation, and living a life above reproach. In our postmodern era, one's spiritual climate is tested not by what is said but rather by what one does—it really is the life we lead. The success we anticipate will come only with human will and divine power. We spend time with Jesus, and He deposits peace in our life.

Our Savior waits for us to withdraw copious amounts of peace from His account. Again, the greatest advantage of this type of peace is that it is universal and free; and its greatest disadvantage is our unwillingness to withdraw it.

Lord, I accept Your peace today.

ALTHEA Y. BOXX

The Second Coming

Thine eyes shall see the king in his beauty: they shall behold the land that is very far off. Isa. 33:17.

 I AM WALKING ON THE BEACH. I've been watching the news around the clock, as a hurricane is battering the state of Florida. We track the storm as it crosses into the state, and watch the pictures of devastation on TV. We have concern for our friends and the people living there.

Now we too are affected by this stormy weather. Our ocean waves roar loudly, lapping the sand and sliding back into the sea. Again and again the beach is battered by the waves. It becomes a great day for surfers.

I walk on in the waves, enjoying some of their ferocity as they slip and slide back and forth over my feet and the sand. I enjoy the coolness of the waves on this early fall day.

As I turn back, I look to the sky. I find that the dark clouds have increased. They have encircled the still brightly shining sun. The sun is widely encircled by its rays of light and white clouds. As I gaze at it, it is like a great beacon light in the midst of the tumultuous dark clouds.

It reminds me of the many pictures of the second coming of Jesus that I've seen again and again. I picture the many artists' renditions of the exceedingly bright cloud that every eye will see in the heavens as Jesus appears to all on earth. The dark clouds around the bright light appear as the darkness of the devastation of the earth. I watch this beautiful scene for some minutes, thinking on that great event that many of us are waiting for.

I realize this day is not the reality of His coming. I notice the people on the beach with me—some couples hand in hand, family groups, little children building sand castles, and the surfers. Have they heard the message of His impending return? Jesus waits so that you and I may in some way help to tell people in our own neighborhoods, or in lands beyond, of His soon coming. I must hasten on about my Master's work; I must help prepare people to be ready to behold Him with joy when He does appear. And I must be ready myself to meet Him in those glorious clouds that every eye will see.

DESSA WEISZ HARDIN

Thought: How does one keep the reality of the Second Coming alive every day?

The Cleansing

Purge me with hyssop, and I shall be clean: wash me, and I shall be whiter than snow. Ps. 51:7. Create in me a clean heart, O God; and renew a right spirit within me. Ps. 51:10.

MY HUSBAND AND I were doing a long-overdue cleaning of our fish aquarium. He carefully removed the fish to safety; then we took apart all of the components. When they were thoroughly scrubbed and sparkling clean, we put in fresh water and replaced the clean components. I put together the pump and filter and plugged it in. I actually heard the pump working, but I didn't see any water moving. We waited awhile, because we needed to be sure all was well before returning the fish. The pump was indeed working, but not as it was designed to, which meant there was a blockage somewhere. After removing that portion of the pump that I thought contained the blockage, I went to the sink and started purging it, and watched the large amounts of scum and algae come out in big clumps. When we put the pump back together, it started pumping the water through the filter as it was designed to do.

Our heart pumps are a most important part of us, similar to the pump in the aquarium. The arteries and veins to and from the heart may become blocked, and even though the heart is trying to pump, it can't get blood past the blockage. Because of the blockage, the heart can't receive a full measure of fresh oxygenated blood. In that case, surgical intervention is required to save the person's life.

The Holy Spirit works within us in the same way. Any resentment, envy, malice, greed, covetousness, jealousy, lust, or hatred that we have acts as a blockage. As the Holy Spirit attempts to commune with us, we can't receive the message because of heart blockage. We need a fresh infilling of the Holy Spirit to refresh and invigorate us every day.

As David asked the Lord to "purge" him, so I ask the Lord to purge me. Every time I attempt my own purging there are missed areas, and I make a bigger problem. My desire is for the Lord to use me in His service, drawing me nearer yet nearer to Him.

Lord, I want Your cleansing to order my steps so that I do Your blessed will in every phase of my life. I don't want any blockage in my spiritual system. Create in me a completely clean heart system. Thank You. Amen.

BETTY G. PERRY

Helen of Troy

I know whom I have believed. 2 Tim. 1:12, NIV.

"HELEN OF TROY WAS A REAL PERSON, RIGHT?" The question came tumbling out even before she had finished taking off her coat and flinging it over the back of the lounge. Before I could craft an answer, Melissa flopped down beside me and continued reporting on her field trip to the museum. When she finally wound down, I suggested that she fetch volume H of the encyclopedia. She was back in a flash, and we looked up Helen of Troy. The entry began: ". . . in Greek mythology, the most beautiful woman in Greece, daughter of the god Zeus . . ."

Melissa's face collapsed in disappointment. "No!" she cried. "It can't be! I saw a picture of her and the Trojan horse at the museum!" And that sparked an ongoing discussion of myths, legends, fables, allegories, and parables, and how they were often part of an aural tradition.

"People were more likely to remember a story," I explained, "when things weren't written down. Storytellers often recalled it and passed it down to the next generation."

"But it *was* written down—in a poem by Holer or Hoter or—Homer!" Melissa said triumphantly. "Maybe Homer just wrote down the story the way it had been told to him."

"And a grand story it is," I said. "Remember, it's one thing to enjoy a story and learn something from it, and quite another to decide whether it happened exactly as portrayed, or whether it simply described some natural phenomenon that the people couldn't explain any other way, or encompassed an idea that was prevalent at that time."

"Are there other stories that are myths, like Helen of Troy?" she wanted to know. By way of response we headed for the library to check out the book *Legends, Lies & Cherished Myths of World History*. "And the parables in the Bible?" Melissa skipped along beside me.

"Some were undoubtedly actual experiences, while others, like the parable of the rich man and Lazarus [Luke 16:19-31], are in the category of allegories."

"So we can learn from all of them, but it's important to know the difference," she said flatly. I waited. "Between something that's just a story and something that actually happened." *Yes, Melissa,* I thought to myself. *It can be critically important!*

ARLENE TAYLOR

God Said, "Wait Awhile"

Delight thyself also in the Lord; and he shall give thee the desires of thine heart. . . . Rest in the Lord, and wait patiently for him. Ps. 37:4-7.

WHEN I WAS SMALL, I was taught that God answers prayers. When He did answer my requests with a yes, I was happy. But I wasn't so sure about Him when it seemed that He had forgotten about my prayers, and that they might not be answered at all. As I grew older, I learned that sometimes God says no, and sometimes His answer is "Wait a while."

I've always loved cats, and I thought it would be nice to have a yellow and orange-striped tabby, just like little Puff, in the Dick and Jane series reading books. I could picture myself playing with my kitten, and having the kitty curled up at night, sleeping next to me on my bed.

But I was afraid to actually put this desire into a direct prayer request to God, because after our dog, Jack, was run over, my parents didn't want to have any more pets. So I didn't see how God could answer that prayer for me. Yet the longing stayed in my heart.

Thankfully, my husband, Carl, is OK with having cats as pets. During the course of our marriage, we've had quite a few. When we'd been married about nine years, we were given an orange-striped tabby kitten by an elderly couple who didn't know much about the care and feeding of cats. (They were upset when it refused to eat carrots!) The kitten didn't bond well with them, and it ran away a few days after it was given to us. I guess it thought that people weren't that great, and it would rather be someone's barn cat.

Ten years ago we became the owners of Catie (pronounced Katie). Catie looks just like the little Puff of Dick and Jane fame. She is just as pretty, playful, and affectionate as the storybook kitten. She also is a talented masseuse. When I come home from my part-time work, from running errands most of the day, or I'm get ready for bed, she'll come to the sofa or bed and knead the tired muscles in my arms, neck, and shoulders. She even naps on our bed.

Although I'm middle-aged, I enjoy and appreciate her just as much as, if not more than, I might have had I had her when I was younger. God gave me that desire of my heart. Catie was well worth waiting for! My prayer for you is that He will grant your heart's desire for some good thing.

BONNIE MOYERS

His Right Hand

I will say of the Lord, He is my refuge and my fortress. Ps. 91:2.

NINE WOMEN FROM OUR SMALL CHURCH had made arrangements to attend a retreat, and we were eagerly and excitedly making preparations for the trip. Our plans included visiting the hospital to see one of our members, a dear, energetic Christian woman who'd had knee surgery two days before. Two of the women, Shu-Shu and Daphanie, agreed to ride with me.

Everything went very well until we were a few blocks from our destination. As we approached a heavily traveled intersection, the traffic light changed to red. My foot automatically shifted to the brake pedal. I pressed. There was no response. I pressed harder. Still no resistance. I kept pressing more firmly.

"No brakes! No brakes!" I shouted. My first impulse was to keep going straight across the intersection, but at the instant the light changed, I observed a dark blue vehicle approaching the light at high speed from the opposite direction, heading directly into the lane I was about to enter. I didn't know what to expect.

Rising tension, suddenly heightened by the reality of imminent disaster, seized control. My hands tightened on the steering wheel and jerked the car to the right. The next thing I knew, the car had made a perfect 45-degree turn and had settled, comfortably, across the curb, having barely missed oncoming traffic, a gigantic cement block, and a heavily wired utility pole. In less than five minutes the police and the fire truck were on the scene. My friend Shu-Shu called the auto club. Problem solved, we resumed our trip to the hospital.

My hand on the wheel? Left to me, the car would have collided with that dark blue car that was competing for the same space and rushing toward me. I was speechless but calm; perhaps too stunned, too shocked, to be nervous or feel afraid. Later, when we had recovered, one of the women confessed to imagining several lifeless bodies and several wrecked automobiles.

I know now that my friends were praying earnestly, and our guardian angels were with us. And to this day we continue to lift grateful hearts to God for the miraculous deliverance wrought by His right hand! "Your right hand, O Lord, was majestic in power" (Ex. 15:6, NIV).

QUILVIE G. MILLS

Angie

For he will command his angels concerning you to guard you in all your ways. Ps. 91:11, NIV.

A FEW YEARS AGO I CAME HOME after eating out for lunch. I pulled up to my mailbox, retrieved my day's mail, and parked my car. Since the pullover sweater I wore had no pockets, I laid my keys on the car's dashboard. A big mistake!

Taking my walker from the back seat, I put the plastic food container from Shoney's in one of the pockets of the apron across the walker's front. A cup of cold drink fit into a smaller pocket. The mail fit in with the food, and I draped my purse strap over the right handhold of the walker. I locked the car door and turned to go to the house.

Too late, I saw my keys inside the car! Now what? I didn't have extra keys in my purse—another mistake. I immediately sent up a prayer: "God, please send someone to help me."

There seemed to be no activity in the houses near mine. I decided to stay beside my car so I could flag down any car or person that came my way. I leaned against the car and used my walker as support for about 15 minutes. I thanked God for strength to stand and for sending help.

Then I heard voices two doors down. The woman and her two youngest boys walked to her car. "Tracie!" I hollered.

"Do you need a ride?" She called back.

"No! I locked my keys in my car."

Tracie put her boys in their car seats, got in, backed around the circle to where I stood. "Did you try all the doors?" she asked

"No, but when I lock the driver's door, all the doors lock."

Tracie tried the rear passenger door. It opened! Then she unlocked the driver's door, and handed me the keys.

Angie (my angel) knew what I was about to do, and kept the door from locking! How can I be sure? The following Wednesday when my helper, Kathy, came, she tried all the keys. After unlocking the car, she relocked it, and tried all the doors. All four were locked.

"Before they call I will answer" (Isa. 65:24, NIV).

Thank You, Lord, for Angie—and for answered prayers.

PATSY MURDOCH MEEKER

Miracle in the Rain

He sends from heaven and saves me, rebuking those who hotly pursue me.
Ps. 57:3, NIV.

 WE LEFT VERY EARLY for the retreat that was to be held far from our home. We were happy, because an event like this always brings joy. Besides participating in the program, we would see dear friends again. However, we couldn't imagine what that day would hold.

Everything went well until it started to rain. The wet highway became dangerous, because there was an oil residue on the pavement that made it very slippery. This required much caution and attention to maintain control of the car.

Then it happened. On a curve, my husband was not able to control the steering, and the car skidded and crossed into the other lane of traffic, where two large trucks were speeding in our direction. I placed my hand on my husband's arm and waited for the impact, when suddenly we felt something strange take place. Before hitting the guardrail that protected the other lane, we were suddenly pulled back, and the car stopped on the shoulder of the highway in the lane in which we had been driving initially.

We felt the sensation that an angel had extended a hand and pulled our car out of the way, saving us from certain death. Speechless, we got out of the car to verify that we were safe. The car that had been behind us had witnessed the scene and stopped to see how we were. The driver, a faithful Catholic, exclaimed, "You can hold a Mass, because this was a miracle. You were saved!"

We knew this. God had sent His angels to save us from a certain accident. It was unquestionably a miracle!

Since nothing happened to us or the car, we continued our trip. Arriving at the retreat, we could joyfully witness with gratitude about God's kindness and how He saved us.

As we told of our blessings, we also thought about the love of our heavenly Father, who sent His angels to protect us. It was just as He has promised in the verse for today: "He sends from heaven and saves me, rebuking those who hotly pursue me."

Only eternity will reveal how many times God's children were protected from death by the ministry of angels!

NELCI DE ROCCO LIMA

How Can God Resist the Prayer of a Child?

The Lord is nigh unto all them that call upon him, to all that call upon him in truth. He will fulfil the desire of them that fear him; he also will hear their cry, and will save them. Ps. 145:18, 19.

IT WAS THE 1930S. Neighbors were gathering at the shack to help with the cooking, cleaning, and the care of the seven children. Their mother was very ill, almost to the point of losing consciousness. For weeks she had been suffering from high fevers and other symptoms that had her near death. To make the situation worse, they were living in a very remote area where access to doctors and hospitals was almost impossible. There wasn't much hope; they dreaded the worst.

Fearing that her mother's death was imminent, Mercedes, the oldest at 12, woke up all her brothers and sisters and made them follow her to the back of the farm. Their knowledge of God was very limited, but she had heard the priest at church talking about Jesus healing very sick people. She hoped God could do something to heal her mother.

In the middle of the pasture she gathered all the children and told them to be quiet—she would ask God to heal their mother. Most of them didn't understand what she was about to do, but they knew it was something serious. She began her prayer with something like this: "God, our mother is very ill. Please heal her, and if You do so, take the best two cows we have on the farm." The children then returned home very quietly.

Later that day their mother, who had been unconscious for several days, woke up and asked for a glass of pineapple juice. Everybody thought it was her last wish. They gave her the juice, and she slept for almost two days. After that she began to recover, little by little. Two weeks later lightning struck and killed the two best cows on the farm.

My grandmother lived into her late 70s. Years later, thanks to the tenacity of missionaries, my family all became Christians. Mercedes, now 75 years old, has been a faithful member of the church for more than 60 years. Today 90 percent of my family of more than 150 are active members of the church. The gospel has been a blessing in our lives.

HANNELORE GOMEZ

Thought: Why do you think God allowed lightning to strike the cows? To build faith? To confirm that it was God who answered Mercedes' prayer? Look again at today's text.

Of Dogwoods and Firs

For with thee is the fountain of life: in thy light shall we see light. Ps. 36:9.

WHILE TRAVELING WITH MY HUSBAND on a recent trip, I noticed it: a road lined with lovely green fir trees on either side. On the left, seeming to appear out of nowhere, was a beautiful white dogwood tree in full bloom, right in the middle of the greenery of hundreds of firs. Even though it was the only one of its kind among the green firs, it seemed to stand tall and unashamed, snow-white branches turned upward, almost proud to be there.

I began to think about Christians and what their impact and influence is on the world. Do we stand out like sore thumbs, annoyances because of our peculiarities? Or are we a welcome refreshing sight to those looking on, who may be in need of something different, a change? Do we turn people off because of our "strange" ways, or do we seek to help others understand what we believe, and why? Do we flaunt our differences when witnessing, or do we seek to find common ground where we can agree before gently yet confidently sharing our Bible-based distinctions and convictions?

As born-again Christians, we are indeed to stand out, but as refreshing stimulants, as pick-me-ups for a world gone bad. Like the dogwood tree in the middle of the firs, we are to be who we are—children of God, shoulders square, standing straight and tall, unashamed and unapologetic, proud to represent our Father to a world looking on, even as He represents and pleads our case before His Father, the God of the universe. As we represent God we are to be mindful that He has not called us to be weird, pathetic, or different for the sake of difference. He has called us to share His love with a dying world—to stand out so that others can see there is something pleasantly different about us. This difference should compel them to ask what causes us to glow in a dark world. They should see the Light that we reflect. The universe is looking on. What does it see in us?

Lord, help us to be a positive influence on those who watch us. Help us to be reflections of Your love and character, points of light showing a better way in a sin-darkened world.

GLORIA J. STELLA FELDER

Thought: Today's text mentions/implies water and light are both beneficial. Might this also indicate how we are to be seen?

Little Is Much

For thus says the Lord God of Israel: "The bin of flour shall not be used up, nor shall the jar of oil run dry, until the day the Lord sends rain on the earth." 1 Kings 17:14.

AS A CHILD, one of my favorite stories was Elijah and the widow of Zarephath. I was amazed at the miracle that God worked in the life of the widow and her son. She had so little, but when she gave it to the servant of God, God made it much. I always thought that was just a Bible story until I began to work in women's ministries and travel to different countries. Again and again I have seen God use the little that His daughters have and change it into "much."

While traveling in eastern Africa, I had the opportunity to visit some women's ministries projects. Each of these projects was begun by women with very little (in some cases, nothing at all). Yet this didn't stop them from reaching out to help others.

I think of the widow's project in Kisumu, Kenya. This group of HIV/AIDS widows and their children came together to see how they could support their families. They started a project of making charcoal, and then taking it to market to sell. As a result, they not only have been able to feed their families, but also have helped to support some of their children in college, and to help others go to school. They started with nothing but a desire and a prayer, and God turned that "little" into "much" so that they could help themselves and others.

Then there's the young women's project in Rwanda, a country that is still struggling to recover from the horrendous genocide of 1994. The lack of funds didn't stop these women, for they had a vision and trusted God. So they started a training center for young women who were orphans as a result of the genocide (and there are many, many such orphans). The women teach these young women a skill so that they can help support their families.

When I think of the Zarephath widow and the women I meet around the world, I see that they have two things in common, even though their stories are centuries apart: the desire to change their circumstances, and a trust that God could do that for them.

So what about you? What impossible situation are you facing? Don't worry; take another look at the widow's story found in 1 Kings 17 and be encouraged! He is the same God today as He was yesterday.

HEATHER-DAWN SMALL

Where You Going?

Trusting oneself is foolish, but those who walk in wisdom are safe.
Prov. 28:26, NLT.

 IT WAS TIME FOR MY CHECKUP, and even though I'd been going to this doctor only a short time, I had driven to his office often enough that I should have had no problems. But somehow I missed the turnoff, so I decided to take the next right turn. I thought that should take me to the corner of his building, which is a converted house in a residential area in which each block looks very similar to other blocks in the neighborhood.

As I came to the house and looked it over, I thought that something didn't look right. . . Perhaps it was the second door on the front that I didn't remember, or the swing set in the yard that confused me. But the parking lot appeared about the same, so in spite of my mounting doubts, I parked my car and walked up the sidewalk to the front entrance. As I slowly opened the door, I was immediately met by a woman who blocked my entry. We stared at each other for just a moment. Then I heard three words that stopped me short: "Where you going?" she asked.

My first impression was she was in the office doing some cleaning, but as I looked around I saw a living room where the waiting room was supposed to be, and a dining room in place of the nurses' station. I realized I was in the wrong building—and even on the wrong street!

"I'm so sorry," I apologized. "I was looking for my doctor's office, but this is your home, isn't it?"

Still eyeing me suspiciously and holding her place at the door, she said, "Yes, it is." With another hasty apology I made a hurried run for my car and drove away. I promised myself that next time I would be more diligent in knowing exactly where I was going.

No one was hurt that day, but the misunderstanding and embarrassment could have been avoided if I had just taken the time to recheck my options at the very first hint of doubt. Proverbs 14:12 says, "There is a way which seemeth right." But if it only *seems* right, that may not be good enough. I trusted in my own mind, and, as I found out, I was a fool.

Lord, please help me always to walk in wisdom.

CLAREEN COLCLESSER

Thought: What is the difference between making an honest mistake and being a fool?

Tomato Basket Upset

The angel of the Lord encamps all around those who fear Him, and delivers them. Ps. 34:7, NKJV.

A PICTURE IN A FAMILY ALBUM of a sweet little girl brought back a vibrant memory that was some 25 years old. The recollection was so vivid that it sent chills up my spine. I used to enjoy going to the Jamaican market in the early morning when the produce was fresh. The brilliant colors of the ripe tomatoes, oranges, mangoes, and pineapples made me imagine their mouthwatering taste.

One morning my little daughter and I walked down the aisles, selecting the choicest items for our table. The traffic was congested that day; buses and trucks seemed bent on almost colliding with each other. Suddenly a large truck came into view, bearing down directly on my precious child. Without thinking of my own safety, I pulled her to me. Then, having nowhere else to go, I sank into the safety of a nearby basket of tomatoes. I felt the moist squish of the vegetables beneath me, but I knew my child was safe, and I praised God! Though the market woman's precious red tomatoes were destroyed, we both were unharmed.

Embarrassed and relieved at the same time, I took out my wallet to pay the merchant for her damaged vegetables. "Oh, no, ma'am," she objected. "I couldn't take your money. Just last week a little boy broke his foot when a truck did the same thing and crashed into him." But knowing that her weekly income depended on bringing home money for her products, I insisted.

Thinking about that incident still sends chills up my spine. I now realize it mirrors my heavenly Father's relationship with me. He watches me enjoy the goodness on this earth and is ready to snatch me from danger if I should wander too far afield. In one of my favorite books Ellen G. White makes a powerful yet comforting statement about God's protection: "Not one that in penitence and faith has claimed His protection will Christ permit to pass under the enemy's power. The Savior is by the side of His tempted and tried ones" (*The Desire of Ages*, p. 490).

Thank You, loving Savior, for the reminder that You watch over me constantly. In penitence I claim Your protection. Thank You for staying by my side.

VERONICA CAMPOS

Buyer's Remorse

Delight yourself in the Lord and he will give you the desire of your heart.
Ps. 37:4, NIV.

Keep company with God, get in on the best. Ps. 37:4, Message.

I COULDN'T BELIEVE IT—IT WAS MINE! The excitement caused me to tingle from head to toe. The whole experience took on a surreal feeling. *I must be dreaming,* I thought as the deal finalized. My head whirled, and the voices around seemed muffled and distant as my own mind shouted and rejoiced so loudly that I marveled that no one else could hear the commotion in my brain. I anticipated the sheer joy of ownership that awaited me.

The euphoria, though, lasted only until I awoke the next morning. What had I done? Was I crazy? I tried to think of ways to get out that wouldn't land me in court. Had I really prayed about it? Had I wanted to hear the answer yes so much that I ignored everything else? Was I being a good steward? The questions poured down just as hard as the torrential rain outside, each drop filled with a new question. "Lord, what do I do now?" There was silence from above.

Just then the phone rang. It was a good friend, with whom I had shared my plans, calling to find out what had happened. I poured out my feelings and concerns. Now she too was quiet on the other end of the phone line for what seemed an eternity. Then I heard it—it started as a snicker, building to a giggle before erupting into uncontrollable peals of outright laughter—deep, honest-to-goodness, contagious laughter.

"What's so funny?" I asked. "Here I am sharing my heart's concerns with you, and all you can do is laugh at me!" She struggled hard to control herself, and then explained with profound simplicity, "The Lord has truly blessed you—just say thank You and enjoy it."

She was right. None of us are deserving of even God's smallest blessing. How ungrateful I was being with my questions and doubts. He Himself had admonished us to ask, and it would be given; seek, and we would find; knock, and that door, which seemed to be locked and totally inaccessible, would be miraculously opened, as long as we submit it to being done according to His will (Matt. 7:7).

Lord, I say simply, thank You. Thank You for the good days, as well as those that are more challenging. Thank You, Lord—thank You. Amen.

MAXINE WILLIAMS ALLEN

To See His Face

For now we see indistinctly in a mirror, but then face to face. Now we know partly, but then we shall understand as completely as we are understood. 1 Cor. 13:12, MLB.

MY FRIEND SUE AND I often meet at the cafeteria at work and chat over lunch. I know she enjoys the opportunity to talk together—I see how her face lights up when she sees me—but our communication has some limitations. There are times that I find her speech difficult to follow, or that she has trouble understanding me. We both speak the same language, but the problem is that Sue cannot hear my voice—or her own—at all. She's been deaf since birth and relies on lip reading. As well as following my lip movements, Sue watches my gestures and facial expressions closely and is alert to any indication that I may not have caught her meaning. She's quick to pick up a paper napkin and a pen to write down a difficult word. Even so, misunderstandings do occur now and again, such as the time she said that she'd like to go to Fiji, and I thought she was saying that she'd like to go fishing!

Subtitles on television programs and movies make things easier for Sue, but she can't use a regular telephone. The advent of mobile phones by which one can send and receive text messages has been a real boon for her, although she finds that a long and detailed text message conversation can be a time-consuming and frustrating task.

The communication challenges that Sue and I experience remind me of some aspects of the Christian life. It's wonderful to be able to talk to God in prayer, but there are times that I'm not quite sure that He has understood my question, because the answer just doesn't seem to match. If I could see His face when we talk, it would be easier to know if my message is really getting through. And if only I could actually hear Him speak to me in reply! "I need you to be specific here, Lord," I sometimes say. "Do You want me to choose this course, or that course—or something else entirely?" How can I be completely certain of which way He is directing me? How can I tell whether His apparent silence means "No" or "Wait awhile"? His "text messages" in the Bible do help, of course, but to hear His voice, to see His face, and to touch His hand—that's what I'm waiting for!

JENNIFER BALDWIN

Thought: My heart says to You, "Your face, Lord, do I seek" (Ps. 27:8, ESV).

Blessings Via a Neighbor

Before they call I will answer, while they are yet speaking I will hear.
Isa. 65:24, RSV.

I RECEIVED AN INVITATION one Thursday evening from a dear sister at church, inviting me to her seventieth birthday celebration, to be held the following Monday. Since Monday was a holiday and the stores would be closed, Friday was the only day I could buy a gift.

I didn't have much money. In fact, the money I had was supposed to be used to buy a gift for a newborn baby and a pair of winter gloves for myself, as I was planning to attend a congress during winter. I thought, *Now I'll have to go without the gloves in order to buy my friend a gift.*

I chose something for the baby, but then curiosity still led me to the glove section. Looking through the various pairs, only one pair was my size—and they were so beautiful! I asked the sales assistant if she could put them aside for me, as I had to buy a gift for someone and was afraid I wouldn't have enough money for both articles. But she said they might get lost or stolen, so I paid for both the baby's gift and the gloves, and left.

Why I bothered to go into the gift shop next door, I don't know. I had spent the money I had, but I thought that at least I could check out what gifts they had. So I browsed through the aisles and checked prices. As I was checking, I looked up and saw my neighbor, whom I hadn't seen for a long time. She asked how I was, and then asked me what I was looking for. I told her I was looking for a gift for a special friend. "Choose what you like," my neighbor said, "and I'll pay for it." She didn't even know my predicament!

"I'll pay you back," I stammered.

"No," she said. "Please don't. Because you are so good and kind to everyone, I want to pay for this for you." I couldn't believe what I had heard!

Our text for today played again and again in my mind as I walked home, praising the Lord.

Heavenly Father, You are so great and wonderful! Thank You for loving me. I am so unworthy of Your wonderful love! Thank You that You solve my problems when I least expect it—or even before I ask. I love You more every day.

PRISCILLA E. ADONIS

Amazing Love

For God so loved the world, that he gave his only begotten Son, that whosoever believeth in him should not perish, but have everlasting life. John 3:16.

GOD IS SO AMAZING! The way He loves us is out of this world! He shows us this love in so many ways. Have you ever noticed that those times that you're too busy to spend time with Him are the times He sends love notes your way? How many can you think of right now?

His expressions of love touch each of us in different ways. As you awake, the birds sing their morning songs. He paints the sky with a magnificent rainbow after a rain shower. The beginning and ending of each day is marked by the beauty of the rising and setting sun. He shows each of His children how He loves them individually, often in amazing ways, and always at the right time, even when we don't realize that we need that hug from our Father.

These are some of His ways of spending time with us, but how He must long for us to "be still, and know that [He is] God" (Ps. 46:10). This world is full of so much sorrow; it's easy to rush through each day and see only sadness. Why not slow down? Admire the wonders of nature. Read the love notes of beauty He sends our way. He's just letting us know that there is still hope and love. If you look for sorrow, you'll find it. Whatever you are looking for, you'll find it.

So take a look at the many loving ways our Father shows us His love. All He wants in return is time with us. Stop focusing on how much you do for Jesus and start spending time just getting to know Him. When Jesus walked on this earth, He spent most of His time visiting, talking, healing, feeding, and communing with people. He could not get enough of our company.

Well, my friend, it's still that way today. He waits patiently for time, His time, to spend with us. He sends us these special gifts in hope that we will value "His time." He wants an intimate relationship with you, dear friend. Don't keep Him waiting. Stop! Take a deep breath. Allow yourself to feel the presence of our Lord surrounding you. He longs to make you one with Him. Let Jesus have some time today. Every day.

We love You, dear Jesus. Teach us this day how we should spend our days in Your presence, listening to Your every word. Amen.

Tammy Barnes Taylor

331

You Need to Spank Them

Behold, happy is the man whom God correcteth: therefore despise not thou the chastening of the Almighty. Job 5:17.

 MY TWO GRANDSONS, fittingly named James, 3, and John, 18 months, have sibling rivalry. (Ironic, isn't it?) Both vie for the affections of their mother. They push, kick, hit, and move each other out of the way to see who gets the "higher position" in their mother's arms.

One day as I was talking to my daughter on the telephone, I heard her reprimand James for hurting his little brother. As we continued to talk, she told me that they continue to fight with each other. At times James even will revert back to the stages of infancy to get attention. I exclaimed, "You need to spank them!" There was silence. Since I didn't get an immediate response, I emphatically repeated my statement a second time.

Just then I heard her phone receiver drop, and a little voice called out tearfully, "Mommy, Grandma . . . said . . . you . . . need . . . to . . . spank . . . us!" Unknown to me, my daughter had put the phone down to go discipline James, and little John had picked it up and listened to my conversation. And he didn't like the idea of being spanked!

How about discipline in terms of God's relationship to us, His earthly children? There are times that He corrects us for wrong actions or for the way we treat our brothers and sisters (whether blood or spiritual siblings). God says in His Word, "As many as I love, I rebuke and chasten" (Rev. 3:19). What a blessing to know that chastisement, though not pleasant or desired, is done by a loving God who cares enough to correct the defects in our character and prevent us from taking wrong courses of action.

James and John, by God's grace, will one day grow out of their sibling rivalry. We too, as God's children, one day will grow out of sin and into a saving relationship with Jesus Christ. So despise not chastening when it comes, because our heavenly Father is demonstrating His love and His desire that we become more and more like His Son, Jesus Christ. As we are faithful and obedient, the work of sanctification will culminate in our seeing Christ one day, face to face.

Father in heaven, help us, Your earthly children, to endure times of chastening. We know that it is done with a loving heart, and that the end results are for our best good. Amen.

CHERYL D. COCHRAN

I Will Be With You

When you pass through the waters, I will be with you; and through rivers,
they shall not overflow you. Isa. 43:2, NKJV.

AFTER WAITING SEVERAL HOURS for a vehicle that failed to
arrive, we decided to walk. We were eager to reach a high school
located in the highlands of Guadalcanal in the Solomon Islands.
We quickly filled our backpacks with the essentials we would
need overnight.

Accompanied by two young men from a local village, we set off just as
the sun was setting. Darkness comes quickly in the tropics, and we were
soon finding our way by flashlight. Rain had recently fallen, making the dirt
road a maze of corrugations, puddles, and mud. Our guides easily negotiated these obstacles while we did our best to stay upright.

After passing through a village, we quickly managed our first river crossing through knee-deep water. Hours passed, and we crossed again through
the now-rising river. When we arrived at our third crossing, the waters were
rising fast because of rain in the mountains upstream. I took a firm grip on
the arm of one of our guides, and by the light of our flashlights, we stepped
into waist-deep water. The water rushed around us, making progress slow.
Looking into the darkness to the opposite bank, I prayed that we would make
it. The water had reached my armpits when my guide decided it was too dangerous—we would have to go back. As we turned, the force of the water suddenly swept my feet from under me, and I was stretched out on top of the
water like a rag doll, buffeted by the current. With a flashlight in one hand
and holding a large bag with the other hand, my guide could only stand firm
against the flow and hope that I could keep my one-handed grip on his arm.
Unpleasant thoughts of what might happen if I lost my hold crossed my
mind as I struggled against the force of the water. Ever so slowly my guide
dragged me toward the riverbank while I desperately tried to get my feet
down on the river bed. At last, close to the bank, we found quieter water, and
I was able to stumble out, shaken but unharmed.

In church a few weeks later the speaker read a verse in Isaiah. As I
scanned the page of my Bible, today's text caught my attention. I nudged
my husband and pointed out the verse to him. Of course, I had read this
verse before, even underlined it in my Bible. Now, though, I read it with
new meaning, in the light of experience.

ANNE CRAM

Answered Prayers

And he went a little farther, and fell on his face, and prayed saying, O my Father, if it be possible, let this cup pass from me: nevertheless not as I will, but as thou wilt. Matt. 26:39.

I BELIEVE GOD ALWAYS HEARS and answers our prayers. Often it's a yes answer, and many times it's "No," "Wait a while," or even "Not just yet." I must accept His answer, and I pray, "Help me to accept Your will graciously," and I plead that I may be able to cope "according to Your will."

When Jesus was in Gethsemane, He pleaded with His Father God. Matthew 26:42-44 says, "He went away again the second time and prayed, saying, O my Father, if this cup may not pass away from me, except I drink it, thy will be done." Jesus then went to the disciples and "found them asleep again. . . . And he left them, and went away again, and prayed the third time, saying the same words."

We face difficult times too, and we need God's help. I've pleaded with God to help me and to guide and lead me. I pray, "Lord, keep me calm." Several times I've been very unsure about what to do, and He has helped me to accomplish my task calmly. Attitude is important, and it's helpful not to be upset.

When the answer is no, asking God to keep me calm has soothed me many times, and I have coped with the no answer, which is an answer to prayer in itself.

Sometimes unexpected incidents happen. Perhaps someone has promised to visit, and you're expecting something that you've asked them to bring and they weren't able to do it. That is most disappointing. Then it's necessary to hand it over to God and not be unhappy or frustrated.

I still do knitting and crocheting for the retirement center at which I used to stay. Sometimes the knitting machine seems to do something crazy, and I want to finish the article I'm making. *Now what do I do?* I say to myself. Then I hand the problem over to the Lord, and He sorts it out. and I say to myself, *Our incredible God even knows how to knit.*

Thank You, Lord, for Your help and care. God is only a prayer away.

PHYLLIS DALGLEISH

Can You Keep a Secret?

A talebearer revealeth secrets: but he that is of a faithful spirit concealeth the matter. Prov. 11:13.

"ISN'T IT SAD THAT AILSA'S NEPHEW IS IN PRISON?" Sandra asked as we filled in our time cards.

"How do you know?" I countered.

"Ailsa told me so herself when we worked together yesterday. She said not to spread it around, but you're her best friend, so I knew you'd know."

The conversation continued along other lines, but my thoughts were racing. Ailsa and I were close friends, and she had told me in strict confidence about her nephew. "I don't want anyone else to know," she had ended. "I know that I can trust you." Yes, she could trust me—I hadn't mentioned it to anyone. But she couldn't trust herself.

Long ago I learned not to tell anyone anything that I didn't want the world to know. I once told someone a private matter. As soon as I'd done it, I knew I had made a mistake and begged the person not to pass it on. She promised, but then she told her sister, whom she knew she could trust. The sister told her best friend, and her best friend told her mother. That misplaced trust cost me dearly and made me change my mind about telling private matters to friends.

Now I work on the assumption that if I can't keep the information to myself, how can I expect anyone else to keep it secret? How many hurt feelings, strained friendships, even broken marriages, have resulted from people not keeping secrets entrusted to them?

We all know what it is like to have problems, sorrows, wounded ego, fancied or real slights, worries, or wonderful joys that we long to tell someone about, but they are too private. I've found the solution—I share my pleasure and pain, and all my secrets, with my Best Friend. He knows all about them anyway. I can't explain how He can be interested in all that concerns me, but He is. He is equally as interested in whatever concerns you—and the billions of other people who inhabit the earth. He loves us all. If we take Him as our confidant, we can't go wrong. He will never, ever tell our secrets to anyone else. Trust Him.

GOLDIE DOWN

A New Name

I will also give him a white stone with a new name written on it, known only to him who receives it. Rev. 2:17, NIV.

 THE FRONT PAGE OF THE WEDNESDAY NEWSPAPER was truly horrifying. There, in a large photo, was a severely injured dog—still alive! When the animal was found wandering the streets of the city, someone quickly called the animal shelter so that he could receive immediate care. The necessary but delicate surgery was preformed. Through this act of generosity the veterinarians were able to save his life without any side effects. Although the injury had been to his head, his coordination was perfect, proof that there had been no brain damage. Fortunately, the newspaper also carried a smaller picture of the totally recovered animal.

After the successful surgery one of the veterinarians explained that the recovery would have to take place from the inside out, so the little dog would have to stay at the animal shelter for several more days, but he would soon be ready for adoption. The newspaper published a telephone number for anyone who was interested in adopting this animal, and the following day the telephone didn't stop ringing. People from everywhere in the state called, wanting to adopt the dog. The employees at the shelter named him Astro, such was his fame.

Astro was finally adopted by a resident in the capital city. She took him home, fixed a comfortable house for him, and gave him food and a great deal of love and attention. And she gave him a new name, Nick, so all the things that he had suffered would be forgotten. "Now he has a new name and a new life!" she stated in the interview.

And that's what's going to happen with us. Our heavenly Father wants to give us a new name and a new life. He wants to heal our hearts, remove the wounds, the doubts, and the nightmares from us. He wants to take us to live in the heavenly "capital city," the New Jerusalem. There everything really will be new: a new name and a new life! A life in which we will no longer remember the pain or suffering we have experienced in this world.

What a privilege is ours to be adopted by the King of kings, to live with Him forever in that home that He has prepared for us.

ANA MARIA B. HONORATO

A New Beginning

But this one thing I do, forgetting those things which are behind, and reaching forth unto those things which are before. Phil. 3:13.

FOR YEARS I'D BEEN SAVING THE ARTICLES I'd been writing, the sermons I'd given, the studies, special letters, and even the beginnings of a book I had hoped to publish someday—and more—all on my computer. Then one day, with a simple right click in the wrong place, all this precious material was erased. Gone. I called in a computer expert, who tried for almost two hours to retrieve my information and finally announced that it was a lost cause. I couldn't believe it! In just a moment documented years of my life had been erased and could not be found.

That same week my mail was stolen, and for my protection I had to open a new checking account, request new credit cards, and almost start all over again.

I will confess that I felt a bit lost, and even a bit dazed, at the reality that so much of what seemed to identify me was either gone or changed. I believe the Lord allows things to happen to us for very specific reasons, so by His grace I decided to turn this negative into a positive. Rather than thinking that I've lost so much, I decided to view it as an opportunity to begin again—a new page in my life, so to speak. So much of what I had written was about the past—where I've been and what I had done, who I've met. Perhaps now was the time to think of new things, look toward the future.

Nothing in life is dependable, except Jesus. He is the only reality, the one thing that is sure and solid and can never be erased or taken out of our lives by mere circumstances. To reject Him from our lives requires a very intentional act, not a simple wrong keystroke. My identity must be wrapped in Him, and not in anything else. His faithfulness to us is great, His forgiveness is complete, and His mercies are new and fresh every morning (Lam. 3:22, 23).

Every day the past is gone, erased, never to be retrieved again, and we can be grateful that with Jesus, life—rich and meaningful life—does indeed go on.

I may have had to change credit cards and checking accounts, but I can be certain that God never changes (Num. 23:19; James 1:17), and that, too, is for my protection.

CYNTHIA MEJIA

Lottie's Legacy

So now you've become an example to all believers. 1 Thess.1:7, Clear Word.

 SOME OF THE MOST PROFOUND LESSONS in Christian living I've learned from the humblest of people. Whenever I need to review my list of wise things to remember, I often think of my friend Lottie.

Lottie was a sweet woman, a widow, and mother of six grown children. Her youngest, a girl with Down's syndrome, lived with Lottie. Their home was across the street from our church, and they were always among the first to arrive for worship service.

One day Lottie's telephone rang. A little girl asked to speak with Mr. Wall. Lottie said, "I'm sorry, but there's no Mr. Wall here." Then the child asked to talk with Mrs. Wall. Lottie explained that no one by that name lived there. The girl then wanted to know if there were any Walls there. Lottie assured her that there weren't.

The child queried, predictably, "If there are no walls there, what holds your house up?"

Without missing a beat Lottie answered, "Why, honey, Jesus holds my house up. Do you know Jesus?" I never knew what the little prankster said or thought, but the wisdom I gleaned from Lottie still helps me in my walk with the Lord.

Lottie focused on Jesus, not on self. Her concern was for the salvation of others, and she never missed an opportunity to witness. She was so filled with the Holy Spirit of God that it spilled out in her actions and her conversation. Her obvious love of the Father and her close relationship to Jesus made her oblivious to the careless and unkind words of others. Lottie had little of this world's goods. However, her lifestyle was her show-and-tell for living the Christian life, her gift to those who knew her. I doubt if she realized it.

Today Christian values are severely challenged. Things are taking place that we could never have imagined only a few years ago. We may not like the changes or what's happening. However, when trials come, because of the promises of God we can hold steady and calm in a shaky world. If someone should ever ask, "How do you manage to hold up when things go wrong and you're under a lot of pressure?" I hope we can answer, "Friend, Jesus holds me up. Do you know Jesus?"

MARCIA MOLLENKOPF

A Fragrance or a Reek?

So then, just as you received Christ Jesus as Lord, continue to live in him, rooted and built up in him, strengthened in the faith as you were taught, and overflowing with thankfulness. Col. 2:6, 7, NIV.

A SMALL TUBE OF LOTION is one item you will always find in my purse. It just feels refreshing to rub on some lotion every now and then.

I was in a crowded mall one day, stressed and tired. I'd been on my feet for almost a half day, so when I noticed an empty chair in the corner I went and sat down to rest for a while. You know how it feels to be able to sit after long hours of just walking and standing. And it's even better it you can couple it with a rub of cold, sweet-smelling lotion. That's exactly what I did. I opened my purse, took out my tube of lotion, and started rubbing my hands with it. Then I noticed people turning to look back, trying to see where the sweet fragrance was coming from.

Another time I was in a meeting, and the item under discussion was a heated one. I was quiet, trying to figure out my stand. As usual, I quietly opened my purse, took out my tube of mango-mandarin hand cream, squeezed a little in my palm, and began rubbing it through my fingers. Then, in the midst of the discussion, someone commented, "What a fragrance!" I smiled when they spotted me.

One time we were driving from Loma Linda, California, to San Francisco, enjoying the scenery and beautiful music on the way. Then, all of a sudden, everyone in one voice exclaimed, "What's *that?*" The air simply stunk!

As we drove on, I wondered, *Does my life bring a sweet, inviting fragrance, or does it reek to those around me? Do people smell the sweet fragrance of Christ's life in me, or are my human tendencies so strong that people try to avoid me?*

"But thanks be to God, who always leads us in triumphal procession in Christ and through us spreads everywhere the fragrance of the knowledge of him. . . . To the one we are the smell of death; to the other, the fragrance of life. And who is equal to such a task?" (2 Cor. 2:14-16, NIV).

Lord, I want to have only Your fragrance this and every day.

JEMIMA D. ORILLOSA

A Vote of Thanks

Give thanks in all circumstances, for this is God's will for you in Christ Jesus.
1 Thess. 5:18, NIV.

OUR CHOIR HAD PRESENTED a wonderful Thanksgiving concert that year. At the end of the program it was my turn to thank them for the long hours of practice they had put in and the hard work they had so obviously done. That, I knew, was an easy job. The choir had been so good.

Moving to the podium, I began talking about the six-letter word "thanks," so fast becoming endangered. The word can literally bring emotional and psychological healing and spiritual uplifting when expressed to God for His love to us.

Folding my notes, I walked back to my seat. "You did such a marvelous job," a church member congratulated me as we left the church. It was clear that we were all grateful to God for the many gifts He has given to us.

My little talk reminded me of how God had spared me from what could have been a terrible accident on May 20, 1994. I was very tired that evening as I made my one-hour ride home. I literally drove and slept with my eyes wide open. About a mile before my exit I saw that there was a car about a half mile ahead of me. Suddenly I woke up to find my car only a yard from the back of the other car. I had no clue when, or how, I got so close.

Shaking, I thanked the Lord for sparing my life. Pulling over to the side of the road, I rested awhile, thanked God again, and asked Him to take the other driver and me home safely. At that point I realized that I could not continue working so far away from home. It was much too tiring. I asked God to make a way out for me.

He provided me with a job minutes away from my home! I transferred to the new job four days later without having to give notice. Ellen White once said, "We are the constant recipients of God's mercies, and yet how little gratitude we express, how little we praise Him for what He has done for us" (*Steps to Christ*, p. 103). I now thank Him for His mercy every day.

Lord, I thank You for Your love and merciful kindness. Help us all to do our part to keep thanks alive by precept and example. Help us to be grateful for every trial You allow in our lives—it's the trials that make us pure gold.

CAROLLE H. WALKER-HAY

God Supplies
My Need in Advance

But my God shall supply all your need according to his riches in glory by
Christ Jesus. Phil. 4:19.

I NOT ONLY COUNT MY BLESSINGS; I tell of them and I journal about them. In this way I will always remember what the Lord
has done. In December 1998 I needed 20,000 Jamaican dollars
(approximately US $560). As far as I could recall, this was my
first major financial crisis, because God usually supplies my needs
in advance. In fact, I would say, "I am God's spoiled child, because whatever I need, He supplies." God has been very faithful to me, so I do more
thank-You-Lord prayers than Lord-I-need prayers.

But what's happening this time, Lord; have You forgotten me? Did I upset
You? You always supply my needs even before I ask. I need this money
urgently. I have checked out all my financial resources, but nothing is happen-
ing. What is going on, Lord? After praying for about a week, I sat at my office desk one morning when the Lord spoke to my heart. "Jackie, when was
the last time you read your salary statement? Why don't you take it from
your handbag now and look it over?"

As I looked at the statement the Lord spoke to me again. This time He
said, "What about that item on the car loan that you've been repaying? Don't
you think it's time to stop?" I immediately got the message, crystal clear.

Picking up the telephone, I called the business office and inquired how
much longer until my car loan was repaid. The person at the other end
quickly accessed my account, and with a big laugh she said, "Girl, you have
money."

"I have money? What are you talking about?" I asked.

"Well," she said, "you have overpaid your loan. We owe you approximately J40,000 (US $1,111). Come on up to the office and request your
money."

I was stunned, unable to move. But I learned my lesson well. Jesus
wanted us to talk. I was to stop taking Him for granted. He was still supply-
ing my needs in advance; He has not changed—no one can upset Jesus. And
so after one week of fellowship with Him, He opened my eyes to money He
had provided in advance. *Great is Thy faithfulness, Lord, unto me!*

JACKIE HOPE HOSHING-CLARKE

Failing to Heed the Signals

For yet a little while, and he that shall come will come, and will not tarry. Heb. 10:37.

FOR MORE THAN A MONTH I'd been planning a trip to a new outlet mall in Virginia. In fact, I had even talked with my mom about taking a day off to travel the 50 miles with me. "Come on, Mom," I begged. "I'll be on maternity leave by then—with a whole week before the baby is due." After some hesitation she finally consented.

But on the day of our trip there was a problem, and I'd made up my mind not to talk about it. Prior to our departure I'd begun showing signs of early labor—some minor cramping, but no real discomfort. *We'll be back long before it's time for the baby to come,* I reasoned. *Walking the mall will do me good.* As this was my second child, and I had been in labor for more than 18 hours with the first baby, the last thing on my mind was the possibility of a quick delivery.

"Are you all right?" Mom observed my obvious discomfort after four hours of shopping.

"Uh—well, I'm in labor!" I confessed.

"You mean you were showing signs, and you didn't heed the warnings?" she scolded.

I hung my head, quickened my steps, and headed straight for the car for the long commute home and, ultimately, to the hospital. Fortunately, all went well, but the lesson still sticks with me. We start each day by observing the warning signs of Jesus' coming. Newspapers and the television and radio morning news all but scream that He is coming. There are wars, constant natural disasters, murders, rapes, and deaths from unnatural causes—all warning us that Jesus is coming soon.

But often, my friend, our actions suggest we'd rather ignore what's happening around us and go about the business of satisfying the urgency of our desires. But His word is sure, and He who has promised to come will come. I tried desperately to ignore the warning signs of my daughter's impending birth just to satisfy my own wishes. Fortunately, no damage was done. But I don't want to miss His signs. I want to be ready, and I know you do too!

Dear Jesus, You have sent us many signs of Your coming. Help us to heed the warnings and be ready. Amen.

YVONNE CURRY SMALLWOOD

Patterns

According to all that I shew thee, after the pattern of the tabernacle, and the pattern of all the instruments thereof, even so shall ye make it. Ex. 25:9.

I WAS ONLY 10 when I joined a 4-H club in the little Vermont town in which I was born and raised. Soon after joining 4-H, I was introduced to the magic world of sewing. Since my stepmother had passed away, I was supposed to eat at the restaurant for each meal, but I found that for only 15 cents I could buy a clothing pattern. Another 25 cents would buy pretty fabric. At that time, 21 meals a week cost only $5; I could buy a pattern, some cloth, and get a soda and chocolate bar for my meal. My mother had passed away when I was 4, and then my stepmother when I was 10, and my father worked very long hours to pay our debts. I was alone much of the time; no one was there to tell me that my meal plan wasn't very nutritious.

The first pattern I bought was for a pair of pajamas. I had no trouble following the pattern and cutting out the material, and sewing the top part was fairly easy. But putting the pants together was another story. With many prayers for help, I sewed them together and took out the stitches and sewed them together again about five times before they actually looked like pants. I was a very stubborn and persevering young woman, even at the age of 10, and I determined to sew those pants correctly.

I soon learned a great deal about sewing, and pants, and following patterns. As I grew older I found a different set of patterns—I found the Bible and many patterns within it. I found Jesus, who is our pattern for living life more abundantly, for loving others, for character building, and for avoiding wrong paths.

I particularly enjoy reading about the pattern that God gave Moses in the wilderness for the earthly sanctuary. The Bible tells us it is patterned after the one in heaven. The earthly sanctuary has a rich history that can be very helpful for Christians who wish to learn more about God and the plan of salvation. My prayer for you, dear reader, is that you will explore God's plan—His pattern—for you through His Word.

LORAINE F. SWEETLAND

Thought: To learn more about this sanctuary, study Exodus 25-40 and Hebrews 8-10.

Deceptive Appearances

Good understanding giveth favour. Prov. 13:15.

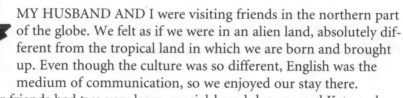 MY HUSBAND AND I were visiting friends in the northern part of the globe. We felt as if we were in an alien land, absolutely different from the tropical land in which we are born and brought up. Even though the culture was so different, English was the medium of communication, so we enjoyed our stay there.

Our friends had two very large, special-breed dogs named Keta and Kota. The very sight of their thick, shaggy coats and wolflike faces gave us a fright. They were kept at the entrance of the house, so we had to pass them whenever we went out and came in. Their masters had a good rapport with them, but we weren't so comfortable with them around. To appear at ease, my husband would call them by their names when he came near them. They would immediately respond, and, closely watching their expressions, my husband would skirt around them. One day our friend said, "Pastor, when Kota and Keta respond, just put out your hand and pet them a little. They like it, and this is what they expect. They are confused when they are called by name but not petted." I knew that my husband would rather ignore them than touch or pet those huge dogs.

By the end of the holidays, though, we had become good friends with Kota and Keta, who turned out to be the best watchdogs we had ever known. Our fears vanished, and a strong bond was created. We could pet them boldly. Their size and appearance didn't change from what we saw at the beginning, but it didn't matter to us now, as the relationship had become sweeter and closer. Given the expected patting and petting, they were ready to obey any commands given.

A four-footed animal taught and trained to respond tenderly toward a two-footed animal who offers love and attention is a thing to be admired. They made us happy during our entire visit.

Don't be swayed by appearance. I learned on that trip that sometimes appearances can be deceptive. Have you also discovered that this is true? It is only when we have a good understanding that we make the correct judgments—about animals or people.

MARGARET TITO

Rest

Come unto me, all ye that labour and are heavy laden, and I will give you rest. Matt. 11:28.

PEANUT BUTTER, contact lens solution, and bread—a few of the essentials my husband and I gathered when we shopped in Costco one evening. Then I told him I would be in the book section as he was off to hunt for batteries. I browsed the best sellers in numerous stacks: *The Purpose Driven Life;* books on Reagan and on Hillary and Bill Clinton. Suddenly someone thrust a small piece of paper in my hand. She said, "I would like to give you this," and then she was gone. I looked down at the paper in my hand. It was a tract entitled "Have You Found Rest?" I decided to keep it, and I stuck it in my purse, intending to read it later because I was impressed with her commitment to share.

I forgot about the tract the next day. Then, sometime later and for some unknown reason, I decided to mend my purse strap, which had been broken and frayed for several weeks. As I cleaned out the purse I came across the small tract. Still intrigued by the brief encounter in the book section, I curled up in the corner of the couch to check out the tract's content.

Stamped across the back of the pamphlet was the name of a local church, but the pamphlet had but one message: to invite one to "come to Jesus and let Him give you rest." It offered no doctrines, no cleanup job of one's life, nothing the reader needed to do—just come as you are. I was touched. Sometimes we make coming to God so complicated. We polish and manipulate our little sayings about who and what God is, hoping to deliver some clever religious message, all the while forgetting the simple gospel that God commissions us to share. "Take my yoke upon you, and learn of me; for I am meek and lowly in heart: and ye shall find rest unto your souls. For my yoke is easy, and my burden is light" (Matt. 11:29, 30). His gift is peace, rest, and relief from your work, your struggling, your efforts. Receive this peace by knowing Jesus.

Dear Jesus, show us our Father. Thank You for the invitation to "come" and find rest and peace by simply knowing You. Help us to share this simple gospel with all we meet.

JUDY GOOD SILVER

Happy Birthday

I will declare the decree: the Lord hath said unto me, Thou art my Son; this day have I begotten thee. Ps. 2:7.

 WHO CAN FORGET THE EXCITEMENT OF A BIRTH—the first pains; the breaking of the water; the mad dash to the hospital through traffic (and sometimes through a storm), with or without the legendary suitcase; the intense contradictions. Lights, faces, voices, orders. And then the final pain of the child's arrival. Birth is painful, but what a joy to have the infant, to hear that first lusty cry, to be a part of it all as mother, father, aunt, grandparent, or even as a friend.

Now comes the excitement as the news spreads, picked up by cell phones, e-mail, and word of mouth: "The baby is born!" "It's a girl!" or "It's a boy!" or, maybe, "It's twins!" Soon gifts and festive balloons tell the story in blue or pink.

Is this how the Lord feels about us coming into His family by baptism? "This day have I begotten thee." Does He announce our new birth with celestial festoons, or does He dispatch angels to the other worlds, angelic messengers sharing the best news in the world? My child is born again!

However, like children, how soon we forget the day of our birth! Without the prospect of gifts at a birthday, how many of us would remember that day anyway, especially as we grow older? How often the relationship begun with such joy is disregarded—children and parents not speaking to each other. Sometimes this happens to our relationship with Jesus, who has given us a new life. Are we still on speaking terms with Him in prayer? Are we listening to Him, reading His Word? Are we meeting Him at His house of worship? How soon we return to "business as usual," as if there had never been a birth, as if we came here all by ourselves.

What does your baptism mean to your Lord? What does it mean to you? Though you may forget it, He, like a good parent, never will. He recalls every pain, every triumph. Your birth still means everything to Him. Today may be the day for you to remember, to go back to the place where you began your life with Him. He has declared, "Thou art my [child]: this day have I begotten thee." Let this be the day that you too remember, and renew.

Annette Walwyn Michael

346

An Example

The path of the righteous is like the first gleam of dawn, shining ever brighter till the full light of day. Prov. 4:18, NIV.

THE PLACE WAS ALMOST LIKE PARADISE. On one side, flowerbeds filled with the most beautiful and varied flowers, and on the other, a wonderful orchard. Many trees surrounded the property, and often they served as houses and hiding places for our childhood games. The beautiful wooden veranda, built by our father, allowed us to contemplate one of the most beautiful views in that region. We could see the large river that flowed nearby, and we remembered the times we had camped on the riverbank in the summers. On that veranda each afternoon we heard Bible stories, told to us by our father. Abraham, Isaac, Jacob, and Joseph were true heroes to us.

One hot afternoon, as we returned from school, I took off my shoes as I walked along behind my mother. Suddenly I stepped on something cold and screamed for my mother. We quickly realized that I had been bitten by an extremely poisonous snake.

Not even three minutes had gone by, and I could no longer see anything. I was given first aid by a farmer who took me to his house, about two thirds of a mile away. My leg was drawing toward my body, and I was very thirsty. Everyone was in a panic. Our father was working, and there was no way to communicate with him. My little sister suggested, "Let's pray so that God will send Daddy home now. He is going to ask God, and God will perform a miracle."

Not more than 10 minutes passed after our prayer when my father arrived. He knelt by my side and told God that he was not prepared to lose me, that he wanted God to save my life. He picked me up in his arms and immediately took me to the hospital. The doctor there said that I needn't have come to the hospital, because if I was going to die, it would have happened within the first two hours after the snake had bit me.

My father's example and the certainty that he had in his prayer being answered remain in my memory to this day. Our God is like this, incredible, marvelous, and answering His children's prayers. May this God inspire you today to serve Him and love Him forever.

EVA MARIA ROSSI MELLO

Thought: Eva knows her life was saved and that God has a purpose for her. Do you know yours?

Sister, Sister

Say, I pray thee, thou art my sister: that it may be well with me for thy sake; and my soul shall live because of thee. Gen. 12:13.

 HAVE YOU EVER ASKED GOD FOR SOMETHING and were impatient to accept His gift, or unaware that God had already answered? I often asked God for a sister close to my age, someone to play with, to talk to, and to share special moments. For many years I felt that my prayers were unanswered, or that God had abandoned me. This feeling of loneliness began at an early age.

I am the youngest of seven children in my family. My parents, who have now gone to sleep in the Lord, divorced when I was very young. My father remarried and started another family with "other children." Being the youngest child in a single-parent home with a working mother and active brothers and sisters made me feel isolated and alone. Consequently, I entertained myself by playing games and reading to my imaginary friends. I became very bitter and resentful because my dad devoted more of his time to the "other family" than he did to me. When you're young, you form your opinions based on the opinions and feelings you've heard from others who are closest to you. Fortunately, my spiritual growth allowed me to overcome many of my negative emotions.

While attending funerals for immediate family members over the past few years, I had an opportunity to talk with my "other sisters." I realized that I was feeling an intimacy that I hadn't experienced earlier in life. I had lost two sisters—and gained four, who were there all along, but I didn't appreciate them because of my emotions. I thought about all those wasted years of resentment, frustration, and loneliness. I began to accept the blessings I had been missing.

After I became an adult and learned more about the Lord, the animosity and dislike for the "other children" vanished. My life is more complete, and my love for my family has grown tremendously. My mother taught me about our Father in heaven and His unconditional, everlasting love. I also learned about my Father's riches; whatever I needed, all I had to do was ask in His name and believe. Sometimes we have to just let go and let God.

I thank You, Father, for allowing me the opportunity to be a witness to the "other children," whom I am blessed to call my sisters and to share in the new birth of sisterhood!

ELAINE J. JOHNSON

I Will to Wait

But they that wait upon the Lord shall renew their strength; they shall mount up with wings as eagles; they shall run, and not be weary; and they shall walk, and not faint. Isa. 40:31.

I'VE ALWAYS BEEN A GOD-FEARING INDIVIDUAL, and I was certain that God was leading me, yet my relationships with the opposite sex, no matter how hard I tried, just failed miserably. I got really tired and disappointed, so I decided to have a little chat with God. Dear God, if it be Your will that I remain single and serve You better, then Your will be done. If this isn't Your plan for my life, then please provide for me. So ended my prayer one evening before retiring for the night.

The following week, on a Friday evening after having my evening devotion, I tarried a little longer on my knees because of the fatigue that I felt from my hectic workload at the office. Then some unknown power was propelling me off my knees to the computer.

"I am too tired for this tonight," I argued.

I hesitated awhile, but eventually lost the battle and took a seat at the computer desk. I logged onto one of my favorite Christian chat rooms and listened attentively to the topics being discussed. It wasn't long before I began to ask questions to someone—someone whom I never anticipated would be my husband today. I've learned that prayers are not always answered in the manner that we anticipate. This kind man, who endeavored to answer my questions as well as possible through God's Word, asked me whether I would like to be his prayer partner. I agreed, and we've been prayer partners ever since.

Many large bodies of water separated us, but we finally decided to meet. The answer to my prayer on that lonely night followed me all the way to the Caribbean. He visited my family and me twice. We knew also that he was running away from the cold weather back home. (Wouldn't you?)

I am constantly reminded of today's text. Not only did I ask, but I learned to wait, also. Today we are happily married.

Lord, continue to let Your will be done in our lives. I know that You hear and answer prayers. The important principle is for us to listen, and then follow as You lead.

MATHELDA JEFFREY

349

Nellie Clara

And in all the land were no women found so fair as the daughters of Job: and their father gave them inheritance among their brethren. Job 42:15.

NELLIE CLARA WAS BORN DECEMBER 7, 1907. She was a surprise baby—there were five older sisters and one brother—but Nellie was welcomed into a loving, hardworking family.

Life was not always easy. Early in life Nellie's mother had attended evangelistic meetings and given her heart to the Lord. Nellie also dedicated her heart to the Lord. The decision caused difficulties between her mother and father. Soon Nellie and her mother found themselves living in a small shack behind her father's house. Mother was faithful through the years, not only caring for her husband but also to the vow she made to follow Jesus. She worked hard, taking in laundry to make ends meet. Nellie walked five miles to school in town. She would pick up coal along the tracks on the way home to help heat their "little house." Through it all Mother showed how to have a loving, positive Christian heart by her example. Most of all, Nellie learned from her mother to love the Lord and let Him lead in her life.

Nellie did grow up loving the Lord and letting Him lead. She studied to be a nurse with her best friend, Morene. She met Ludwell, the man who would become her lifelong companion. In later years she would chuckle, telling everyone how the Lord had "closed a school" so she could meet the man she would marry.

Both Nellie and Ludwell worked many years in the field of medicine. She was supportive of his decision to become a medical doctor. When he graduated, they opened a practice in New Mexico. Nellie "retired" after 18 years as a nurse. Retirement was a short three years, because they adopted a son, John, and then a daughter, Mary. Nellie now found herself "working" again.

Through it all Nellie let the Lord lead. There were joys and sorrows, laughter and tears, and a beloved granddaughter named Emily. One of her greatest joys was finding this entry in her father's Bible: "Nellie Clara, born Sabbath, December 7, 1907." It was her confirmation that her father had given his heart to the Lord.

After a journey of 85 years Nellie went to sleep in Jesus and now awaits His call. Nellie Clara is my mother. I am eternally grateful for her and Grandmamma Ellen's example of letting the Lord lead.

MARY E. DUNKIN

A God-sent School Fee

But my God shall supply all your need according to his riches in glory by Christ Jesus. Phil. 4:19.

IT WAS THE FIRST WEEK OF DECEMBER. Outside was frosty, and my heart was just as chilly. My savings had been depleted, and we were living from week to week on my small paycheck. I had separated from my abusive husband, and now my two boys and I were experiencing hardship. I just didn't have the funds for my son's school fee for the month of December.

My younger son attended Duluth Junior Academy and Christian school while my older son was in public high school. I explained the financial situation to my younger son, to prepare him for a school transfer. He didn't deal very well with the news, because he didn't like public school. I suggested that we pray about it, but I wasn't hopeful, and began worrying as human weakness set in.

I told the principal and my son's classroom teacher about the situation. I also informed the school treasurer. The teachers and I discussed alternative ways to get financial help. I checked out the sources we had discussed, but was turned down by everyone. It was a pretty dim outcome.

My son's fifth-grade teacher asked that we continue to pray. One day my older son noticed that I was still worried and said, "Mommy, why do you worry when you can pray? Isn't that what Christianity is about?" This strengthened and encouraged me to pray more and have greater faith in God.

Just before the Christmas holiday my phone rang. It was the treasurer at the school, who said, "Your prayers have been answered! Your son's school fee has been paid for the rest of the year." I was in a state of shock as I praised and thanked God for helping. I asked who had been so kind. She told me that a man from another church found himself with some extra money and decided to donate it to a needy child getting a Christian education.

The donor paid the fees in full for the rest of the school year. My sons and I experienced the power of God through prayer. I sent a thank-you card for the anonymous donor, and I pray that he will thrive in God's goodness to bless many more of God's children in need.

MARVET FURZE

Prayer Emergency Room

God is our refuge and strength, a very present help in trouble. Ps. 46:1, NKJV.

WHEN WE FACE TURBULENCE IN THE AIR, we wish for solid ground. When we come upon a storm at sea, it is our desire to reach dry land. But when the solid ground is shaken, we crave heaven, because there is no place in this world that is safe. The only secure place is in Jesus' arms. Many times God has calmed the storms in my life, but at other times He has let the storm roar around me and has calmed my heart, which was filled with fear.

The day had been pleasant. We were all at home in a cozy place in the middle of nature. Toward the end of the afternoon, I decided to take a walk. When I arrived home, I learned that my son, Wilson, had suffered an accident with a glass door. The cuts on his hands and arms were so serious and deep that he had been taken immediately to the emergency room.

I made the most difficult decision of my life and decided to stay home that night in my "prayer emergency room" instead of rushing to the hospital. It was the longest and most anguishing night that I have ever spent, pleading with God for Wilson's life. "He is just a little boy, and I want so much to attend his baptism!" So many things went through my mind, so many uncertainties. The entire night was spent in prayer.

My friend Jesus dried my tears and comforted my wounded heart. The following morning, as soon as day broke, I went to see my son in the hospital. The nurses were changing the bandages. He had undergone emergency surgery, but the doctor couldn't guarantee that he would regain movement in his hand. However, I believed that God had performed a miracle during that night of prayer.

Fourteen days later 54 stitches were removed from his wounds, and Wilson had returned to school and was already writing! Three months later I discovered the proof that God had totally healed him when I found him playing and throwing weights in our yard.

Great joy touched my heart when, 40 days after the accident, Wilson and his best friend were baptized in our little church on our farm.

Our God is a God of the impossible. I believe in the miraculous power of prayer. *Thank You, Lord, for hearing our prayers!*

JANA TEIXEIRA ARSEGO

The Lioness Award

Your goodness is so great! You have stored up great blessings for those who honor you. You have done so much for those who come to you for protection, blessing them before the watching world. Ps. 31:19, NLT.

IT CAME IN THE MAIL ONE DECEMBER MORNING, a card on which a sleek lioness, stretching on a vista of green, had been painted. Curious, I opened it and read: "Dear Dr. Greene, I am presently flying at 35,000 feet above China, en route to Hong Kong. What better time to write a word of encouragement to one of my favorite administrators of all time? This card is an award that is given only to people who have shown me a strength that I know comes from Jesus Christ, the lion of the tribe of Judah."

I smiled as the kudos flowed on the hand-printed pages. "With this award comes no plaque, no gift certificate, no money. All you receive is the awareness that you have been the source of light to an individual in deep darkness."

There is a word that we counselors often use: metaperception. Roughly translated, it means our perception of others' perception of us. In other words, what we think others think of us. Ironically, I hadn't really thought about how others saw me, but this card got me thinking. What were others seeing?

The lioness award seemed to trigger numerous unrelated awards, or maybe my own heightened awareness of the tributes. First was the Honorary Alumna of the Year from a college at which I had served. Then came the Outstanding Dissertation Award for a work I had enjoyed developing. But one of my most valued awards came by e-mail from a former student who now lives in Vietnam. She was writing, she said, on behalf of the young women I had mentored.

Her words framed my lifework—past and present—in simple poetry: "Thank you for showing us that we can be articulate, well-dressed women who make an impact without being bulldozers." The apostle Paul's pungent prose, however, summed up the matter: "The only thing that counts is faith expressing itself through love" (Gal. 5:6, NIV).

I can't wait to get to heaven so that the Lion of the tribe of Judah can give me His award, because He helped me display the only important thing. How about you?

GLENDA-MAE GREENE

VIP Seats

But my God shall supply all your need according to his riches in glory by Christ Jesus. Phil. 4:19.

 ONE PLEASANT DECEMBER 11 EVENING my friend Carolyn and I went to the U.S. Army Band Christmas concert in Washington, D.C. Since the concert was beginning at 8:00 p.m., we left early to get close parking and good seats.

We got there an hour ahead of time and drove around for 45 minutes to find street parking—but to no avail. By now it was nearly 8:00, and I was so anxious I even prayed to find parking. In desperation we drove around once more. When we passed in front of the concert hall once more, we slowed down and carefully looked to see if any car was leaving. Just then a car pulled out, and we were thrilled to get a spot right in front of the hall.

We were already late for the program. At the door we saw some people being turned away. I was confident that we would get inside, since we already had tickets. But when we arrived at the door, the usher refused to let us in, saying that the hall was completely full and that we couldn't go in even if we had tickets.

We were so disappointed to hear this after driving so far, spending so much time to park, and having tickets. I didn't give up easily. I tried to explain to the usher that parking took a lot of time, and we had come from afar. At first he only sympathized with me, and Carolyn was ready to leave. Then the usher said to wait, and he would see what he could do for us. I was so happy to hear those words!

In a few minutes he returned with a woman in military uniform, and she apologetically affirmed that there were no seats left other than a couple of seats in the VIP area, and we could sit there, if we liked. I could hardly believe my ears! I was so happy and excited that I thanked and hugged her and the usher for being so kind to us.

We were seated in the VIP area, just above the stage, where we had the best view. I thanked God for not only giving us the best seats but also a convenient parking space. Certainly "my God shall supply all your need according to his riches in glory by Christ Jesus."

STELLA THOMAS

Praying for God's Will

Your will be done. Matt. 6:10, NIV.

TWO WEEKS BEFORE CHRISTMAS 2001 we finally moved into our home after waiting 14 months. When we moved from Cheltenham to London, we figured that buying a house would be easy. We resigned ourselves to purchasing a small house with no garage, no garden, and no study for me, and no separate bedrooms for each of our daughters, as London is an expensive area to purchase property.

However, nothing worked out the way we planned. We ended up renting a small flat with nothing of our own, apart from our computers, one filing cabinet, one bookcase, and one suitcase of clothes each. Everything else went to storage.

No matter what we did, we were unable to buy a house. We signed contracts on three houses, started contract procedures with two others, and looked at so many houses that real estate agents readily recognized us each time we visited them. Why wasn't God helping us? He knew we needed a home. My husband and I found it difficult to minister fully in our church, and our children longed for a place to really call home. We were confused. Why wasn't God answering our prayers?

During that whole time we had prayed that "God's will be done," though secretly I had hoped that God would find us a house in a particular area. When we lost the last house in October, I had had enough. I told God I was now willing for Him to choose our home, wherever He wanted it to be.

God answered that prayer immediately. And guess what? We are living in the very place I never wanted to live. We are living in the very estate that I never wanted to live in, yet I am happy! The house is far better than anything that we had looked at previously. It also has all those things that we planned to do without—a garden, a garage, a study large enough for my husband and me to share, individual bedrooms for our girls, and a living room large enough to have church members over for lunch.

Don't be afraid to ask God for His will to be done in your life. You may save yourself a lot of pain if you do. You may also discover that God knows exactly what you need to be happy!

MARY BARRETT

The Element of Suspense

But if we hope for what we do not see, we eagerly wait for it with
perseverance. Rom. 8:25, NKJV.

EVERY WEEKDAY I TROT OUT TO THE MAILBOX charged
with an element of suspense, thinking, *What will be in the mailbox*
today? Will I get a letter? Or will there be just some bills and un-
wanted advertisements? The same kind of suspense brings me to
check the e-mail on my computer. Perhaps it's a feeling experienced by other women. There is so much comfort in belonging to someone—family, friend, or acquaintance. And the hope of communication with
them is eternal.

I had received many lovely cards and letters at Christmastime, but
Christmas Day came and went without a greeting from my son and his
wife, who live in another state. I was downcast, but I knew they were very
busy, so I told myself to wait patiently; they always send something. I even
watched for the delivery truck that had come last year with a box containing gifts. But the day ended—nothing.

Two days after Christmas a beautiful card came from them, and inside
was a gift certificate to be spent at a well-known store. It was a sizable
amount, and I was excited and eager to use it! But first I thanked them, lovingly, promising to tell them what I had purchased with their generous gift.
And I later did just that. The waiting and suspense was worth it! I had not
been forgotten.

I thought about the letter from my Savior. I can read it again and again,
finding more truths each time, much like an unlimited gift certificate. I read
daily in His Word, so eager to know Him better; I am constantly blessed. And
the suspense of His soon coming thrills my heart. It truly is the blessed hope,
"looking for and hastening the coming of the day of God. . . . We, according
to His promise, look for new heavens and a new earth in which righteousness
dwells" (2 Peter 3:12, 13, NKJV).

If I look for that day as eagerly as I look for the daily mail, I'm sure my
suspense will be rewarded more than I can imagine. I want to hear Him call
my name and say, "Well done."

It will be worth the wait.

BESSIE SIEMENS LOBSIEN

Please God
Rather Than People

And behold, a voice out of the heavens said, "This is My beloved Son, in whom I am well-pleased." Matt. 3:17, NASB.

THERE ARE INDIVIDUALS who are called "people pleasers." They seem unselfish—always doing for others. But sometimes they do it for the wrong reasons. When I was a child, I remember telling my grandparents to buy Christmas presents for my siblings, and if there was any money left over they could get something for me. I didn't fuss over material things, and put the needs of others before myself.

Have you ever had things happen to you that made you wonder if you are good enough? I had my first child on my sixteenth birthday, fathered by a man 10 years my senior. When I was baptized, it was to please my mother and grandparents, as I knew that would make them happy, and I thought that was my purpose in life. When I was 28, my grandmother was concerned that I was still single. She took it upon herself to provide a plane ticket for a prospect she had chosen, and sent him to Canada. We were married three months later, still virtual strangers, but Christians nonetheless.

To make peace and please my husband, I agreed to buy a house that was beyond our means. That major commitment didn't bring the peace I was longing for. We had three children, and I stayed in that situation because I didn't want the children to grow up without their father as I had. My attempt to please was futile, and the marriage eventually ended 10 years later.

Throughout my journey I have come to realize that I put my faith and trust in the wrong people and things. What I needed to do was to please God, not people. As I reflect on my past mistakes I can see how God was there for me in spite of me.

He is there for you, too. No matter what you may have done or denied yourself of in order to please others, God can help you to do His will. God said about Jesus, "This is My beloved Son, in whom I am well-pleased." He also says, "This is My beloved daughter, in whom I am well-pleased." God has revealed Himself to me in many wonderful ways—all I want to do is to please Him. What is getting in the way of your pleasing God? Take a moment and pray to Him now, and He will help you do just that.

SHARON LONG (BROWN)

The Birthday Suit

Humble yourselves in the sight of the Lord, and he shall lift you up. James 4:10.

BIRTHDAYS ARE USUALLY SPECIAL TO US, all the more when we have passed the age that is considered youthful. That's how it is with me! Whenever a birthday comes around, I pay special attention to it. I take extra pains with my appearance to ensure that I look different. I guess "different" is what I achieved this year. My birthday was on a Wednesday, so I had to go to school. I thought I looked special and was very confident when I faced my classes that day.

A beautiful bouquet had been delivered earlier in the day, and by afternoon most of the students knew it was my birthday and were extending birthday wishes to me. I couldn't wait for the students from my favorite class to come in. When they did, they were tumbling over themselves with good wishes and telling me how pretty I looked. However, one boy looked really puzzled. "Is it really your birthday, Miss?" he asked without changing his expression.

"Yes, Jamie," I responded.

His next statement was a shocker. "But Miss, that isn't nice. The color isn't nice. It makes you look—" He hesitated without finishing the statement, but turned up his nose.

At this point I should have been crushed, but I was amused. The color was obviously different, not one I had ever worn before, so he probably didn't see it flattering me. Whatever the reason, my outfit that day didn't meet his approval. Even though the other students tried to convince him that I looked pretty, there was no changing his mind.

I was amused at his innocence in pointedly stating his dislike. His childlike innocence was obvious. It didn't allow him for one minute to consider that he could hurt my feelings, and he had meant no ill will in stating an opposing opinion, either. An adult would have quickly said how nice I looked, even if he or she honestly felt otherwise.

Christ said, "Except ye be converted, and become as little children, ye shall not enter into the kingdom of heaven. Whosoever therefore shall humble himself as this little child, the same is greatest in the kingdom of heaven" (Matt. 18:3, 4). We need to express the humility and innocence of a child and put away all guile and deviousness in our relationships with others and God. God wants genuine people to stand up for Him. Can He count on you and me today?

BRENDA D. OTTLEY

He Left All

Then Peter began to say unto him, Lo, we have left all, and followed thee.
Mark 10:28.

WAS PETER TELLING THE TRUTH? Was he reminding his Master about the disciples' sacrifice? Was he expecting a reward? Of course Peter was telling the truth—they had left their homes and businesses. What if Jesus were here on earth right now, and He came to me and asked me to follow Him? Would I leave all, as the disciples did? Our home, our property, our vehicles, our assets are all very important to us—but the disciples left all.

My mother used her land, her money, and all for the Lord. She told us, "You girls go wherever the Lord calls you. Don't put your mind on our land and properties." This we did. On her deathbed she said, "Do not set your eyes on my bank account—that is for evangelism." She also told us to take care of her friend, who was a poor widow. We have tried our best to follow her advice, and the Lord has taken care of us, too.

Jesus left heaven with all its glory and comfort. He stooped low, experiencing poverty, suffering, pain, and death for our sake so that we might have life and a home in heaven. We really do not need anything as long as we have Jesus.

With all the calamities around us, how do we feel when we have all that we need, and we know of people who have lost all? It is so pathetic to see those whose homes were destroyed by an earthquake, for instance. They have nothing but the clothes on their backs. They have to be supplied with provisions, medicine, and shelter. As we watch the news we see them suffering even more because of the rain, and then winter is about to set in. They are in sorrow over the loss of loved ones. Their future is uncertain. They need more than the temporal things—they need our help and love. They need Jesus.

In reply to Peter's statement, Jesus said to him and to those who have left all, "Verily I say unto you, There is no man that hath left house, or brethren, or sisters, or father, or mother, or wife, or children, or lands, for my sake, and the gospel's, but he shall receive an hundredfold now in this time, houses, and brethren, and sisters, and mothers, and children, and lands, with persecutions; and in the world to come eternal life" (Mark 10:29, 30).

What reward could be better than that?

BIRDIE PODDAR

Weather Changes in Life

I will never leave you or forsake you. Heb. 13:5, Clear Word.

ONCE AGAIN WE WERE ENJOYING A HOLIDAY BREAK at Port Vincent, a seaside town one never tires of revisiting. From our van site the view extends across the sea. As the tide comes in and goes out, the scene ever changes, revealing clean sand, gently washed when the tide returns. The seabirds are prolific, including flocks of pelicans, terns, seagulls, and cormorants. It's very peaceful, and I thank the Creator who has given such things to enjoy.

I vividly remember the evening that the sea breeze changed to gusts, then turned into a violent storm. All night the van rocked and the annex shook. I prayed for safety, but I'm sure that God could see my fearful heart. Thankfully, by morning the storm had abated, and I emerged to assess the damages. Trees were down, tents flattened, and vans askew; however, I had survived with minimal damage.

Relieved by the return of stillness, I reflected upon the changes from peace to storm that I had encountered in life over the years: the lost job, sickness, financial difficulties, death of loved ones, disappointments, and so forth. In and through it all, God sees the fearful heart tossed about by the storms of uncertainty and sadness. His eye notes the damage left behind by the hurts and pain of situations that come along.

Like the tides of the sea coming in and out, my circumstances have changed, altering my view on life. When the storms have hit hardest, there is one thing I've learned that has always seen me through: our God never changes. His love, mercy, and care are constant. His hand is continually over us, and He knows our need and is always faithful.

We are assured that after the nights of storm will come the day Jesus will return and take us to heaven, where we will have peace eternal. How wonderful!

As I write this I am gazing across the seascape. There is a gentle breeze carrying the sound of the birds once again. I am comforted, for I've come through life's storms this far, and I see afresh God's love and watchcare. How peaceful!

Thank You, Father, for You are only a prayer away and can help me find peace when the weather changes in my life.

LYN WELK-SANDY

The Theft

Bless them that curse you, and pray for them which despitefully use you.
Luke 6:28.

ONE SABBATH I NOTICED the Bible held by the soprano sitting next to me in choir. It was obviously much loved and much read: the cover was gone, the pages marked and tattered.

Impulsively I asked, "Would you like me to recover your Bible for you?" She handed it to me without question. A week later I returned it to her with a new hand-tooled leather cover, and her name, Dilcia, engraved on the cover.

Ten years later we both belonged to the Women's Intercessory Prayer Group. One particular Sabbath Dilcia brought her mother in her new Bronco. She asked for prayers for her finals starting the next day. After the prayers the group lingered to fellowship. Dilcia excused herself, saying she had to study. Moments later she and her mother burst back into the room. "My car has been stolen!" Dilcia cried.

We quickly reconvened the prayer circle. The women prayed for Dilcia, for relief from her shock and pain, and for the swift return of her car. Dilcia's prayer was for the thieves. She asked God to woo them to Him through this incident. After prayers Dilcia told us her schoolbooks were in the car, and now she couldn't study for her tests. That was bad enough, but it was evident that something else was distressing her more. She finally told me:" "My Bible—the one you covered—was with my schoolbooks!"

Within days police found Dilcia's stripped Bronco. Her schoolbooks were in the back seat, but her Bible was not. It was the only personal item the thieves took!

A week after the Bronco was returned to her, Dilcia told the congregation how the Bronco had been restored to perfect condition by the insurance company. God brought her studies to remembrance, and she passed her finals with good grades. And she also told the congregation that she was convinced that God had allowed her Bronco to be stolen so that her marked Bible could be taken by the thieves. She said, "God is using my Bible to woo the thieves to Him."

Dilcia knows how to put today's text to the test. It is my prayer that we may each live His Word.

DARLENEJOAN MCKIBBIN RHINE

How Is Our Faith Today?

For we walk by faith, not by sight. 2 Cor. 5:7.

 "DAVID IS COLLAPSING!" shouted the children. Hearing this, I dashed out and found several boys holding David by his arm, leading him to the dormitory to his bed. The doctor checked him over and gave him medicine to get rid of parasites (roundworms). But even after taking this medication, David would suddenly collapse or stagger, and mumble to himself. When the doctor checked him again, he concluded that David should be taken to a psychiatrist.

In the meantime I invited David home to talk concerning his problem. I looked into his eyes and asked, "David, why do you mumble something when you fall ill?"

Taken aback by this question, he paused and then said, "I hear someone talking inside me. I try to talk back to him."

I asked what language the voice spoke and asked what that someone talked about; David couldn't remember. "But he talks to me in my dialect and in a kind voice." David comes from one of those remote hill areas of Jharkhand in eastern India. The tribes of this area are animist who believe in spirits. So David knows what spirits are. But after learning from our Bible class, he also knows about the true God.

After my conversation with David, I looked at him and said, "This someone is no one but the evil spirit. It is only by asking God to help you that you can be cured. Do you believe?"

David did, so I also told him, "Whenever you hear someone talk to you, say this, 'In the name of Jesus Christ, go away. I am Jesus' child.'"

However, after a week or so David's condition turned from bad to worse. He became violent toward his classmates. I happened to be with David when suddenly he collapsed. I grabbed him by his arm and held him tight, and said in a loud voice, "In the name of Jesus Christ, get away, you devil!" With that rebuke, everything was over! David was all right but very weak. So I took him home with me. From that time onward David was never again troubled by the evil spirit. With a grin on his face, he said, "When I grow big, I will tell my people how God chased away the evil spirit from me, and to worship only the true God, the Creator."

"When the son of man cometh, shall he find faith on the earth?" (Luke 18:8).

ANNIE M. KUJUR

Lessons From Butterscotch

The wolf also shall dwell with the lamb, and the leopard shall lie down with the kid . . . ; and a little child shall lead them. Isa. 11:6.

SHE WAS BEAUTIFUL TO BEHOLD. She was dependable, caring, protective, and most of all she was forgiving. Butterscotch came into our lives when she was only 6 weeks old. Instantly she won the hearts of family, friends, and neighbors.

My family and I were out for a Sabbath afternoon walk when a vehicle went by bearing a sign offering free puppies. We had recently moved to Guelph and had had to give Sacha away to a farmer. The children were heartbroken. They were eager to have a replacement. My husband was not quite as eager, since he remembered the training process involved in the acquisition of a puppy. After sunset that evening a station wagon drove up our driveway with several beautiful puppies. We later learned that our 6-year-old, Karimah, had memorized the phone number on the car we had seen earlier on our walk and had called, requesting that the owner bring us a puppy. Her little scheme worked. The owner placed all the puppies on the floor in the foyer of our home. Leon and I were determined not to make a commitment based on emotion. As the owner scooped up the puppies to leave, one hid itself under the table. That did it! The decision was made. We decided to keep her since she had chosen us. Omar and Karimah named her Butterscotch.

Over the years the children kept their promise to love and care for her. My husband took care of her training, including obedience school. When the children went away to our church-run school, Butterscotch became my close companion. She was faithful in ensuring I did my daily walks, which benefited both of us. She was instinctively protective of the family, and strategically placed herself where she could guard us while we slept. She welcomed us home each day with such exuberance that it made coming home a sheer delight. Indeed, Butterscotch couldn't speak to us in human language, but she communicated volumes. She taught us lessons of love, caring, dependability, and forgiveness.

For us, Butterscotch represented a segment in the portrait of God's creative masterpiece. Isaiah 11:6-9 speaks of God's peaceable kingdom, where the young child, the wolf, the bear, and the cow shall live and play together and not hurt each other. I long to be there, don't you?

AVIS MAE RODNEY

Unanswered Prayer

So is my word that goes out from my mouth: It will not return to me empty, but will accomplish what I desire and achieve the purpose for which I sent it. Isa. 55:11, NIV.

IT WAS TIME to attend the Singing Christmas Tree program at the local church. I had decided not to go that year, but my adult daughter offered to go with me, so we went. At the intermission, when they started drawing the names out of a container to win a prize, I was sorry that I had even turned my name in. I began praying, "God, please don't let me win. I can afford to buy anything I want, so have them choose someone who needs it." Besides, of the three books you could choose from, one was a cookbook, and I'm not a cook. The second book was *The Purpose Driven Life,* which I'd already read. The third choice was *The One-Year Bible.* I had lots of Bibles and didn't need another one.

The weird feeling that I was going to be chosen persisted, so I begged God not to let them pick my name. But they did. My prayer seemed to have been unheard. We were to pick up our choice after the program, so I decided that I might as well stop at the counter and tell them that my name had been chosen. I decided on the Bible, and saw that it was laid out so that one could read some from the Old Testament, some of the New Testament, and some from Psalms and Proverbs each day of the year. I took it home, told my husband I had won it, and added it to the stack of books on the end table. My husband and I don't usually study together, but on January 2 I got the idea that maybe we could read this Bible together. He had already thought of that and had read the first day on his own.

When we got to Leviticus and Numbers and Deuteronomy, the books that bog many people down, we just kept plugging away. My husband just reads; we don't discuss it, but I keep claiming God's promise that His Word will not return to Him void but will accomplish what He has planned.

God is so wise. I wasn't going to attend the program, but when I got there I turned in my name for the drawing (which I usually don't do). I begged not to win the drawing, but God knew what He was up to. He knew that my heart's desire would be for my husband and me to read His Word together, and He worked it out through unanswered prayer.

LANA FLETCHER

364

My Passport Miracle

"For I know the plans I have for you," says the Lord. "They are plans for good and not for disaster, to give you a future and a hope." Jer. 29:11, NLT.

I WAS PREPARING to go to the United States to pursue further studies. My passport had expired, and I had applied for a new one and was given a date to pick it up. On the day appointed, I decided to take my lunch break to run into the passport office, pick up the passport, and return to work within the hour. When I arrived at the passport office, I was given the frustrating news that it wasn't ready and that I would have to return another day. I was very upset. It would cost me time off from work and more taxi fare.

Dejected, I walked out of the passport office. As I neared the street I saw a gentleman walking toward me. I recognized him from his visits to the hospital with his dad. We greeted each other and he asked, "Nurse, what are you doing on this side of town?" Without thinking about it, I complained that the passport office had told me that my passport would be ready but it wasn't, and I would have to come back. He said that he was sorry and that I should go with him.

I followed as he entered the passport office. He asked me to have a seat, and he went to an office. He soon returned, handed me my passport, and wished me good luck with my travel plans. When I opened my new passport, I saw that he had signed as the passport officer. I expressed my profound gratitude to him and walked out of the passport office in jubilant shock.

When I was growing up in Barbados, I frequently heard my dad say, "Cast your bread upon the water and you shall find it after many days." Mr. Boydkin's father was once an outpatient at the hospital where I worked, and often when he came for medical treatment I would get a wheelchair and assist him while Mr. Boydkin parked the car. I never dreamed that I would be rewarded for my kindness.

Sitting in the taxi, I thought how awesome my God is to turn what seemed an impossibility into reality. Although I had walked out of the passport office angry and had neglected to pray, He provided an instant answer before I called. It is wonderful to have a heavenly Father who is always looking out for us. Isn't it amazing how He works things out for our good? His plans give us hope and a future.

SHIRLEY C. IHEANACHO

Farmed Out

Like a shepherd's tent my house has been pulled down and taken from me.
Isa. 38:12, NIV.

I WAS 11 YEARS OLD when I first heard that I was going to be farmed out for the summer. "Farmed out" is the country expression for sending children away to live with other families. Traditionally, a family with too many mouths to feed would send a child to live with a relative or friend. The child was expected to earn her keep and not be a burden on her foster family.

So now it was my turn. My sister was very ill with kidney disease and had had several operations in an effort to avoid an actual transplant. I had already started babysitting and was used to being home alone, but my folks didn't want me to be alone all night, as they frequently stayed over at the hospital.

First, they sent me to my grandma's house. She was always a whirlwind of activity, and I spent my days there helping her with her huge yard and feeding stray cats. Then I was sent to my other grandma's, where I cooked and sewed. After that, I was sent to live with a neighbor family. They had four girls and a swimming pool, and my duties consisted of routine chores and keeping track of the youngest girl.

I wasn't truly unhappy in any of the three places I stayed, being very aware of one thing—none of them were home. Many nights I would cry from homesickness. I knew that my sister needed my parents more, but I felt as if I were being shoved aside so as not to get in their way. I felt cut off from everything comfortable and familiar.

Jesus was basically farmed out to be raised by His human family. Mary and Joseph may have been excellent parents, but Jesus was still cut off from the physical presence of His heavenly Father. He may have loved His home here, but how He must have longed for His true home in heaven! Earth must have seemed a poor place in comparison.

In a sense, we are all living as exiles, not just those of us who have had to live apart from our families. No matter how happy we are with our earthly possessions, no matter how much time we spend painting and wallpapering our houses, we won't really be at home until we are reunited with our Creator.

GINA LEE

Thought: Thank Jesus for coming to live with us as Immanuel—God with us.

Angels of Protection

The angel of the Lord encamps around those who fear him, and he delivers them. Ps. 34:7, NIV.

 AFTER SEVERAL YEARS WITHOUT A VACATION, we finally would be spending Christmas and New Year's at our friend's beautiful getaway more than 300 miles (500 kilometers) from home. Our plan included visiting relatives, and we were radiant with joy! The trip had been postponed four times, but finally, on December 24, we were ready to leave. We read Psalm 121 for our worship, we prayed again in our car, and we were off.

We arrived in Amparo in rain. Oily pavement caused the driver to lose control as we rounded the last curve. Violently hitting the embankment, the car rolled over three times and finally stopped upside down, the wheels spinning in the air. What a terrible situation!

After a loud noise and breaking windows, everything was silent. Only the beautiful voice from the CD could be heard still singing: "Thank you, I have given myself to the Lord, today I am transformed." During those moments of panic we called out to God for help. No one had the courage to look at the others, fearing a fatality.

I turned up the volume on the car sound system, and everyone agreed that we had experienced a miracle—a Christmas miracle. It was as if we had all been born again! We didn't have any cuts or broken bones, praise God! He heard our prayers. Bruises, bumps, headaches (as well as nightmares), but no serious injuries.

One of the individuals who offered first aid was impressed. "Are you Christians?" he asked. "So am I. You know that the angels of God protected you. We received information that the accident had been fatal. This is a miracle! Consider life as a Christmas present."

We were very saddened to learn that three other cars had lost control as well, but fortunately there were no fatalities. The Lord had spared everyone. The fright was tremendous for all the travelers, and required a great deal of work for tow trucks. It was goodbye vacation; however, we are immensely grateful to the Lord and His angels, to the people who offered first aid, and to those who helped us return to our home.

We were literally born again, sustained in His arms. Praise the Lord for another Christmas gift!

PALMIRA J. J. DE CAMARGO

Every Day Is Christmas

For God so loved the world that he gave his one and only Son, that whoever believes in him shall not perish but have eternal life. John 3:16, NIV.

 CHRISTMAS IS THE SEASON of lights, trees, beautiful sights, sounds, and smells. It is a time that the streets are transformed with colors and lights. People everywhere are looking for the best gift, running against time.

I remember my last Christmas in Brazil. It was such a wonderful time with all my family together. Everything was well planned—the dinner, the music, the tree, and the worship, with the participation of all. Everyone was excited about doing something to help. As always, my mom was attending to the last details for the best meal ever. The kids were asking for their gifts, bored with the waiting. That Christmas was very precious to me because I would be moving soon. I still remember the fun time we had together, with my father-in-law acting as Santa, bringing a gift for everyone. The scene in my mind is unforgettable; it was all something difficult to leave behind.

How important life is—important to me, important to my family. In this season it is so important to think about the best gift ever—Jesus Christ, who gave His own life in order to give life. Any number of things can happen tomorrow, but nothing can rob you of the assurance you have in Jesus—another gift.

Years ago I read a book about miracles by Emilie Barnes. She explains how important it is to receive Jesus as a gift every day. Every moment of your life is precious and important, to be received with gratitude and unwrapped with joy, and then shared like a box of chocolates.

There is an interesting thing about this gift. With the gift of life, the more you give away, the more you receive. Heaped up. Overflowing. With a big red bow on top.

"For God so loved the world that he gave his one and only Son, that whoever believes in him shall not perish but have eternal life." Which means that for every one of us who chooses to receive that gift, every day of our life is going to be Christmas! So, Happy Christmas!

Father God, my life has been full of wonderful blessings from You. Every day I am thankful for Jesus and for the opportunity to live Christmas as a daily experience.

RAQUEL QUEIROZ DA COSTA ARRAIS

Miracle on Christmas Morning

I will answer them before they even call to me. Isa. 65:24, NLT.

CHRISTMASTIME IS A BUSY TIME for all women. In 2004 Christmas fell on a Sabbath, and I worked extra-hard to make sure I finished all my work before sundown on Friday. My husband was also busy on Friday, preparing his sermon for Sabbath. He was at the computer for much of the day. Since the printer hadn't been working for several weeks, he couldn't print out his sermon notes, and he couldn't write them out because he gets writer's cramp easily. So each Friday I copied his notes from the computer by hand. That afternoon he made the same request, but didn't press me because of how busy I was.

The house was full by evening, as our three sons and their families had arrived for the weekend. As usual, I was up early on Sabbath morning and reading my Bible when my husband called me. I went downstairs to find that he needed me to copy his notes from the computer. I replied that I was in the middle of my personal devotions and that I would do it as soon as I was through. Then he said, "See this!" I looked at the paper in his hands and realized it was his sermon outline, printed out. Surprised, I exclaimed, "Oh, the printer is working!" He answered, "Yes, but only one page got printed." He had tried to print out the story accompanying his sermon, but the printer had failed again. It had printed one page and stopped, but he could tell the story without notes.

The printer never worked again until we took it to the dealer for repairs. God didn't fix the printer; He just provided the one page that needed to be printed. He performed a miracle, knowing that I was busy and that my husband couldn't write for very long.

That Sabbath afternoon we gathered after lunch in the living room for a family sing-along. In between songs, stories were read or told. At the close I told the family about the miracle that God had performed that morning for their dad. I added that the God we worship and serve is a real God, a God who loves us and knows our needs, a God who never fails His children. A God of Christmas miracles.

BIROL CHARLOTTE CHRISTO

Thought: The day after Christmas is a good time to take inventory of the many blessings—miracles—God has provided at this special season, and all year long.

The Cabin in the Woods

Be still, and know that I am God. Ps. 46:10.

WE DROVE PAST THE CABIN AT SAND LAKE, and it stirred up some long-forgotten memories. There have been many changes over the years. The cabin no longer sits alone in the woods by the shore of the lake. Now it's surrounded by cottages, stores, a gas station, a bar—all signs of progress. When Grandpa Gallant retired from General Motors in Bay City, Michigan, the cabin was the logical place to move to. For some time my grandparents had been preparing the cabin for permanent residence, adding on, installing a heating system and adequate plumbing, until it was a suitable place to retire, taking the place of their comfortable home in the city.

Originally the cabin had three rooms, a wood-burning stove in the living room, a kitchen of sorts, and one small bedroom. The toilet, a "one-holer," was at the back of the unattached garage, at the end of a well-worn path. But how we loved to go up to the cabin, where the children could swim in the lake and the menfolk could fish or hunt while Grandma and I could sit and chat over a cup of tea.

When the remodeling was finished, a huge living room had been added, with a dining area at one end adjoining the kitchen. The original kitchen became a full bath. A large bedroom took over the original living room, and a good-sized closet was added. The small bedroom opened off the new living room, in which a mammoth fieldstone fireplace took center stage opposite a row of windows overlooking Sand Lake—just right for Grandma's collection of African violets on the ample ledge. Underneath the house, space was excavated to provide a heating system, water heater, and room for a washer and dryer.

How we used to love to drive to the cabin for weekends of peaceful quiet. I still remember the wind rustling the leaves on the oak trees around the cabin, winter and summer. It was a peaceful place, set apart from the fast lanes of life. But there have been many changes since the old folks died and the cabin sold. It's no longer a place to enjoy the peace and quiet. Instead there is the noise of motorboats on the lake and the traffic on the road that now passes the cabin. There aren't many moments of peace in our fast-paced lives today, but a true Christian will take time to be with God. "Be still"; it will bring peace and quiet to the soul.

LAURIE DIXON-MCCLANAHAN

Words Thrown to the Wind

A gentle tongue is a tree of life, but perverseness in it breaks the spirit. Prov. 15:4, RSV.

I REALLY ENJOY OBSERVING NATURE. The golden sunset, the waves of the ocean, and stars in the heavens are things that leave me marveling, but the color, the diversity of forms, and the pleasant fragrance of flowers are what I most admire about nature.

As we observe the flowers, we notice those, such as the delicate orchids, that are more sophisticated and appear to be dressed for a fashionable party. These flowers exist in an immense variety, and the color combinations are fantastic.

Since childhood I have admired the dandelion, a small flower with delicate seeds. It has a lively yellow color and is small and simple. After a few days of blooming, it develops very light, featherlike seeds that easily spread on the wind. When I was a child, I always searched for these seeds to blow into the air so that I could watch them glide slowly on the wind.

Dandelion seeds are like our words. Just as the wind hits the seeds and carries them everywhere, so words are spread. Good or bad, offering comfort or criticism, encouragement or discouragement, hope or despair, words, once said, spread everywhere, leaving their influence upon the people who receive them.

Sometimes we don't realize that the things we say—and how we say them—will influence others. See what wise Solomon wrote in Proverbs 12:18: "Reckless words pierce like a sword, but the tongue of the wise brings healing" (NIV). He also wrote, "Words can bring death or life! Talk too much, and you will eat everything you say" (Prov. 18:21, CEV).

We, and those around us, are benefited or destroyed by our words. James compared the human tongue to a fire that can spread evil throughout our entire body (James 3:6).

Let's allow God to direct our words in such a way that they may be a positive influence on the people around us. May our words uplift, encourage, and comfort, leading people closer to Jesus.

Lord, help me today to be aware of each word that I speak so that I may show others Your wonderful love through what I say.

LUCIANA RIBEIRO DE MATTOS

It's All About Me

Do not think of yourself more highly than you ought, but rather think of yourself with sober judgment, in accordance with the measure of faith God has given you. Rom. 12:3, NIV.

A FRIEND TOLD ME ABOUT THE LATEST GET-TOGETHER with her birthday bunch. They had been going out for lunch on their birthdays for years, with the birthday girl as the honored guest and not having to pay. March was Della's birthday, and the group gathered in her honor.

After everyone had placed her order, the five women began to chatter as only women who have been getting together for years can do. Suddenly Della interrupted the chatter and announced, "It's all about me today!" Then she told how one of her grandchildren had said that line at a recent birthday party when attention had drifted from him. My friend said they all gave a polite laugh and the conversation continued, but she was shocked into silence at hearing an adult demand such attention. She thought this might have been cute when a child innocently broadcast his needs, but not so cute when an adult did.

At their next get-together Della once again used that it's-all-about-me line. My friend no longer thought it funny or appropriate. She questioned the selfishness of such a statement.

Selfishness. The dictionary defines it as "caring chiefly for oneself or one's own interests or comfort, especially to the point of disregarding the welfare or wishes of others." We can all become selfish at times in wanting, or even demanding, our own way. Selfishness can become an insidious form of idolatry, with "me" as the idol!

Today's verse admonishes us to not be high-minded beyond what we ought to be, but instead contemplate ourselves with sober (well-balanced or controlled) judgment. This is a strong warning against overestimating ourselves. We need to become acquainted with the weak as well as the strong points of our character so that we may constantly be on guard against crediting ourselves with more attention than we deserve. Life should be comprised of denial of our own selfish ways, and of opportunities to be of service to others.

Lord, my prayer is that You will help me think less of my own needs and the desire to control everything, and to think more of the needs of those in my path. Life doesn't revolve around me. Let my life today revolve around following Your example and serving others.

Nancy Van Pelt

He Cares for Us

No evil shall befall you, nor shall any plague come near your dwelling.
Ps. 91:10, NKJV.

IT HAD BEEN THE MOST BEAUTIFUL NIGHT in December. Flowers, lights, smiles, melodies, perfume, and much love all joined together harmoniously like a choir of voices to make my wedding one of the most memorable ever held in the church in my town.

The church was filled with guests, since my future husband and I were well known in our community. The minister and his wife, groomsmen, bridesmaids, ring bearer, and other children walked down the red-carpeted aisle, everyone to their proper places.

Elegantly dressed, the groom began to sing with his melodious voice, "My love, I want to tell you I love you, I love you more, much more . . ." while I walked down the aisle, dressed in my beautiful wedding gown. The ceremony was memorable and meaningful for both of us. Yes, it was, without a doubt, the happiest day of my life!

Five days later, as we were going by bus to a Christmas party held by the company for which I worked, the driver, going at a high speed, lost control of the bus on a slope, and the bus overturned. A terrible panic filled the vehicle, which was loaded with company employees and their families. The majority were young people who had left their homes to participate in the much-anticipated Christmas party.

Screams of horror, tears, and pain suddenly replaced the joy and happiness so typical of youth. After the terrible shock I discovered that I was lying on the roof of the bus, because I could clearly see the seats above me. Frightened, I looked for my husband, but I couldn't find him. A horrible feeling washed over me as I thought of the possibility that something more serious could have happened, and I began to pray. Fortunately, soon my husband spoke: "I am here, my love, close to you!"

Thank You, Lord! Thank You very much! I prayed in gratitude.

We were all taken to the nearest hospital. My husband had some stitches in his right elbow, and I had broken my pelvis. It took five long months for me to have a complete recovery, but I am certain that God took care of us at that time, saving our lives—for now and for eternity. Have you too thanked God lately for saving you?

RUTH MENEZES NUNES

Blessings to You

Because of your father's God, who helps you, because of the Almighty, who blesses you with blessings of the heavens above, blessings of the deep that lies below, blessings of the breast and womb. Gen. 49:25, NIV.

EVERY MORNING parents bless their waving children as they drop them off at school. Daily, in thousands of high-rise buildings, workers offer short prayers for their coworkers before leaving. Departing travelers acknowledge God as they board trains, planes, and ships. Even those who fight against God bless others as a part of their daily ritual. Laws are enacted that demand that graduates refrain from praying; and villages, towns, and cities remove crosses from hills but speak words of blessing in their concluding remarks. Fortune 500 companies provide detailed training for all their staff to bless those who call, and, amazingly, nobody objects.

In the Bible's very first book we find God blessing the seventh day of Creation. In chapter 9 God blesses Noah and his sons, and Noah asks God to bless Shem. Melchizedek blessed Abram. God blessed Sarah, and Rebekah's family blessed her as she left her homeland to be wed. Jacob begged for a blessing from the One with whom he wrestled, and he received it. At the end of Jacob's life he spoke a final benediction over his sons and grandsons. Some form of blessing occurs more than 60 times in Genesis.

Today we practice leftover rituals that remind us of those Bible blessings. Many parents take the time to have their children dedicated, or blessed, in special church services. Some religious schools begin the school year with a dedication service. Many weddings include special dedication prayers. These services all ask God's blessing and continued presence to be with those being blessed. How does all this happen?

All over the English-speaking world people say "goodbye." The benediction "goodbye" is an alteration of the phrase "God be with you." Over time the phrase was modified and shortened to "good" for God, and "bye" for "be with ye." The phrase has been further shortened to bye or bye-bye, but it still means "God be with you." Without ever realizing it, millions daily acknowledge God's presence with a farewell wave and a friendly "goodbye."

SHIRLEY KIMBROUGH GREAR

AUTHOR BIOGRAPHIES

Betty J. Adams, a retired teacher, is a mother, grandmother, and great-grandmother. She has written for *Guide* magazine and her church newsletter, and is active in community service. She enjoys writing, her grandchildren, scrapbooking, and traveling—especially on mission trips. **Feb. 5, Apr. 9, June 18.**

Priscilla E. Adonis and her husband, Peter, are retired but now "retreaded" in South Africa! Priscilla enjoys preparing sermons and Sabbath school programs, playing Scrabble, and updating her vocabulary. **Feb. 9, Apr. 12, Nov. 17.**

Maxine Williams Allen, a licensed real estate professional, currently resides in central Florida with her husband and two sons, Brandon and Jonathan. She enjoys writing, traveling, meeting people, and experiencing new cultures, and has a special interest in family ministries. She often quips, "Speak, Lord, for Your servant is finally listening." **Sep. 17, Nov. 15.**

Maria Odete D. de Almeida lives in Tocantins, Brazil. She has three children and four grandchildren. She has worked with children for 30 years and loves nature, and loves to read, do handicrafts, and care for her garden. **Aug. 11.**

Lydia D. Andrews is a certified registered nurse, certified midwife, mother of three adult children, wife, and grandmother of two boys. She and her husband spent six years in Kenya in mission service. She now resides in Huntsville, Alabama, where she works as a clinical instructor in two nursing programs. Her hobbies include reading, travel, music, and spending time with her grandsons. **Mar. 19, Oct. 15.**

Mary M. J. Wagoner Angelin lives in Ooltewah, Tennessee. Mary, a stay-at-home mom, and her husband, Randy, have two children, Barbara and Rachel. She works one day a week as a social worker. Her hobbies are therapeutic humor, exercising, hiking, writing, vegan cooking, and volunteering with the Make-A-Wish Foundation, Regeneration, and Kids in Discipleship. **July 10, Aug. 28, Oct. 28.**

Conisia Anthony is a business management consultant and trainer in South Africa. She is also a trainee pastor who is involved in the ministry of writing, praying, and preaching. Her passion is to encourage and empower other women to pray, write, and preach the gospel of Jesus Christ. She published her first book, *Prayer Power,* in 2005. **Jan. 3, Feb. 8, Aug. 8.**

Raquel Queiroz da Costa Arrais is the associate director for women's ministries at the General Conference of Seventh-day Adventists. Raquel is the wife of Pastor Jonas Arrais and the mother of two sons: Tiago, 22, and Andre, 19. Raquel loves reading, walking, playing the piano, and collecting pictures of women's faces. She enjoys spending time ministering to, and learning from, them. **Oct. 22, Dec. 25.**

Jana Teixeira Arsego is a nutritionist, family therapist, and professor in Brazil. She is married and has two children, Anelise and Wilson. She enjoys being with her family, talking to friends, taking walks, reading, and giving seminars. **Dec. 9.**

Jennifer Baldwin writes from Australia, where she works in clinical risk management at Sydney Adventist Hospital. She enjoys church involvement, travel, and writing, and has contributed to a number of church publications. **Nov. 16.**

Cassandra Baron lives in Brisbane, Australia. She has been women's ministries leader in her local church for three years. She is passionate about flower arranging and is a member of the Floral Art Society of Queensland. She also enjoys camping, reading, decorating, vegetarian cooking, and studying God's Word. **Sep. 15.**

Mary Barrett, writing from England, has been trained to work as an associate in pastoral ministry with her husband. She is also a writer and a speaker. She and her husband have two grown daughters. For relaxation she loves to spend time with family and friends. **July 12, Dec. 12.**

Marianne Toth Bayless experienced some changes in her life this past year. She retired after 17 years working as a secretary in a local high school. She became a great-grandmother, and she recently was married! South Florida living agrees with both her and her new husband. Creative scrapbooking is a new hobby for her. A Family Heritage Album is in progress. **May 9.**

Dana M. Bean, a second-grade teacher in Bermuda, is married with a daughter. In 1993-1994 she was a student missionary to Rwanda. Dana enjoys photography, writing, reading, telling children's stories, and swimming. This is the second time she has contributed to the devotional book series. **June 17, Oct. 13.**

Dawna Beausoleil and her husband, John, live in a cozy cottage in the northern woods of Ontario, Canada. A former teacher, she loves singing, reading, and cats. She's been published in numerous journals. **Feb. 7.**

Annie B. Best is a retired teacher in Washington, D.C., and a mother of two grown children. She enjoys being with her three grandchildren, reading, and listening to music. Working as leader in the children's departments of her church inspired her to compose a song that was published in *Let's Sing Sabbath Songs*. Her husband of 53 years passed away in 2001. **Mar. 20, Apr. 10, Sep. 14.**

Nelda Bigelow is a widow with two daughters, six grandchildren, and three spoiled cats. She became Sabbath school secretary at age 14, and has been a Sabbath school superintendent for more than 50 years, an office she still holds. She retired for nine months 10 years ago, but went back to work part-time because she enjoys being with people. She lists reading, cross-stitch, and writing letters among her hobbies. **Apr. 18, Oct. 19.**

Dinorah Blackman lives in Panama with her husband and daughter, Imani. At the time of this writing she was the academic coordinator at a Jewish elementary school. **July 7.**

Juli Blood has been happily married to Gary since 1994. They were missionaries in South Korea for a year. Juli now fills her days with raising her two active sons and enjoys reading and writing, when she can find the time. She has a cat named Sandy, who didn't enjoy South Korea as much as she and her husband did. **Mar. 14, June 9.**

Elizabete Rocha Boger lives in Canoas, Rio Grande do Sul, Brazil. She is married, and likes to accompany her minister-husband on his visits. They have one son, Herbert William. **Sep. 11.**

Althea Y. Boxx is a graduate nurse from Northern Caribbean University who lives in Jamaica. She was the recipient of the Inter-American Division women's ministries scholarship in 1996 and 1997. She enjoys reading, writing, traveling, and cooking. **Nov. 2.**

A. Grace Brown enjoys reading, writing, the outdoors, and sharing meaningful conversations with other people. She lives in Columbia, Maryland, and works as a copy editor and graphic designer. Grace attends church in Fulton, where she leads small group ministries. **Feb. 4, Sep. 9.**

Kristina Brown, previously an educator in a prekindergarten class, is currently pursuing her M.A. in developmental psychology at Columbia University. She attends Bethesda Adventist Church. She likes to read and write, and enjoys music and educational media. **Jan. 6.**

Margret Nyarangi Bundi enjoys teaching at a girls' school in Kenya. She loves instrumental music and desires to develop this talent, but lacks the instruments for practice. She enjoys sewing, crocheting, and writing. She hopes to pursue graduate work in guidance and counseling. **Jan. 15, May 6.**

Darlene Ytredal Burgeson is a retired sales manager. Her hobbies include sending notes and seasonal cards to shut-ins and people living alone. She also enjoys writing, gardening, and photography. **Jan. 5, Apr. 7, June 6.**

Andrea A. Bussue was born on the Caribbean island of Nevis. She holds a master's degree in education, and currently works as an administrator in Washington, D.C. In her local church she started the children's choir, and has been a Sabbath school superintendent for years. Andrea is host of the radio program, *Children Are Precious.* She enjoys reading, traveling, sewing, and meeting people. **Apr. 13, July 6, Sep. 18.**

Joy Butler, born in New Zealand, is the director of women's ministries for the South Pacific Division. She, with her husband, Bob, has worked as a secretary, teacher, chaplain, and missionary in the Pacific islands, Australia, and Zimbabwe. Her passion is to help women who are abused, such as Thailand's child prostitutes in the Keep Girls Safe project. **June 28.**

Palmira J. J. de Camargo lives in Paraná, Brazil. She is a teacher and makes greeting cards, boxes, and souvenirs. She enjoys reading, playing the piano, and contemplating nature. **Dec. 24.**

Veronica Campos is a wife, mother, and grandmother who lives in Jamaica, West Indies. She recently retired after more than 40 years of active service as an administrative assistant at West Indies Union, where she worked with six union presidents. She revels in gardening, writing poetry, traveling, and watching her five grandchildren grow up. **Nov. 14.**

Terri Casey has been married to Mike for more than 20 years and has been blessed with two children and two grandchildren. She works as a lab supervisor for a dermatology and laser practice, and is a safety officer and consultant for several medical practices in Canada. She teaches the youth Bible class, loves to walk, Rollerblade, quilt, read, camp, and, most of all, to write. **July 13.**

Birol Charlotte Christo lives with her husband, Gerald, in Hosur, India. Beginning her church employment career as a schoolteacher, she also worked as office secretary, statistician, and the first Shepherdess coordinator of the Southern Africa-India Ocean Division of Seventh-day Adventists. Her hobbies include gardening and creating craft items to raise funds to help needy children. Birol has five grown children and 12 grandchildren. **June 5, Aug. 15, Dec. 26.**

Cheryl D. Cochran is a registered nurse in a small community hospital in Athens, Alabama. She is actively involved in her local church with the prayer ministry and adult Sabbath school. She is a single mother of three adult children and two grandsons. She enjoys watching plants grow, singing, writing, preaching, teaching, and reading. God is her first love. **Mar. 13, Aug. 4, Nov. 19.**

Clareen Colclesser, a retired nurse and widow, has two children, seven grandchildren, and six great-grandchildren. She enjoys family, and quiet times with a good book. Clareen stays active in her church as Sabbath school superintendent and communication secretary. Hobbies include writing letters and short stories, and her collection of interior decorating magazines. **Jan. 4, June 19, Nov. 13.**

Donna Cook attends church in Decatur, Arkansas. She likes to crochet, quilt, garden, and help those in need. She is a hospice volunteer and loves to spend time with her husband and grandchildren. **Feb. 29, Aug. 31.**

Anne Cram from Australia is married with two married sons, one daughter, and four grandchildren. For the past 11 years she has been involved with mission trips (her addiction) to the Solomon Islands, Vanuatu, and Kiribati in the South Pacific. She enjoys knitting, crocheting, patchwork, her garden, reading, and being a grandmother. **Sep. 19, Nov. 20.**

Celia Mejia Cruz is a pastoral assistant, church secretary, elder, and women's ministries leader at the 600-member church in the Atlanta area where her husband is the pastor. She is the mother of five adult children and grandmother of seven. Celia enjoys entertaining, playing with her grandchildren and her dog, and collecting Siamese cat figurines. **July 14, Aug. 13.**

Phyllis Dalgleish is officially retired but is still very occupied. She lives in an apartment in one of South Africa's retirement villages, away from the city pollution and noise. Phyllis volunteers at a primary school library, and also enjoys being helpful to the residents in her community. **June 13, Sep. 8, Nov. 21.**

Tânia Celeide Teixeira Damasceno is a student in Brazil. She likes to visit different places and read in her spare time. **Jan. 17.**

Dalry Dean is an administrative secretary at Canadian University College in Lacombe, Alberta, Canada. Music is a large part of her life, and she enjoys playing the piano for her singing friends and making Christian music together to bless others at churches and in nursing homes. She also enjoys gardening, golfing, and spending time with friends and her three grown children. **June 7, Aug. 9.**

Fauna Rankin Dean is a writer-photographer who writes from northeastern Kansas, where she lives with her husband of 25 years. They have two grown sons and a teenage daughter. They live on a "golden retriever ranch" and enjoy the country life. **Feb. 28, Oct. 10.**

Donna Dennis is from the Cayman Islands in the British West Indies. These are her first published devotionals in the women's ministries devotional book series. **Feb. 6, Oct. 27.**

Silvia Dima is the women's ministries director of the Romanian churches, wife of a pastor, mother of one, and a grandmother. She thinks that God blessed her with more than she asked for, and she is happy to discover daily the miracles that God does in her life, for her family, and in the church where she is serving, through the programs of women's ministries. **June 10.**

Laurie Dixon-McClanahan, a former Bible instructor for the Michigan Conference of Seventh-day Adventists, is now retired. Old age prevents many activities, but she enjoys reading and living with family and her cat, Benjie. **Jan. 18, Mar. 28, Dec. 27.**

Leonie Donald and her husband moved back to New Zealand in 2003 to be near elderly parents. She enjoys reading, exercise, and gardening. Leonie takes an active part in church activities at the retirement village where her parents reside. **Feb. 2, June 20.**

Goldie Down and her husband, David, did evangelistic work in Australia and New Zealand for 20 years, and served as missionaries in India for another 20 years. Goldie was a prolific writer who had 23 books and numerous articles published. She was the mother of six children, whom she home-schooled. Goldie died in 2003. **Feb. 3, May 21, Nov. 22.**

Susan Drieberg, a registered nurse and driver's education teacher, has a master's degree in education and teaches health occupations at a vocational school. She has four daughters and three grandchildren. She and her husband, Denver, enjoy many outdoor activities. Her hobbies include oil painting, gardening. **Mar. 25, Aug. 7.**

Louise Driver and her pastor-husband, Don, recently retired to Boise, Idaho. They have three grown sons and four grandchildren. She enjoys being involved with praise music. Her hobbies are singing and music, reading, gardening, and traveling to historical places. **Oct. 5.**

Trudy Duncan is a mother of two, and a medical technologist by profession. She loves helping in the children's department of her church. Her hobbies include traveling, singing, and nature activities. **June 29.**

Mary E. Dunkin is still a "muttlets mom" to her three dogs. She has served in Pathfinders for more than 45 years, as well as in other areas of church leadership. She owns a small business, Your Concierge, and has earned her masters degree. Her greatest joys include her "babies," creating fun stuff (such as prickly pear truffles), making history fun, and traveling in her home state. **July 4, Dec. 7.**

Joy Dustow is a retired teacher who enjoys taking an active part in the social and spiritual activities of the retirement village in Australia where she resides with her husband. They read the devotional book each day and receive pleasure in knowing that from the sale of the book many have an opportunity to receive an education in a Christian environment. **Mar. 22, Oct. 11.**

Shrandra Edmeade, a first-time contributor, has a master's degree in education and is a counselor. She and her husband live in New York with their two children. An active member at her local church, Shrandra enjoys singing and reading. **Sep. 7.**

Gloria J. Stella Felder lives in Atlanta, Georgia. She and her retired pastor-husband share a family of four adult children and five grandchildren. Gloria enjoys music, writing, speaking, and spending time with family, especially her grandchildren. She has written articles for several magazines, and for six editions of the women's devotional, and is working on a second book. **Mar. 12, Aug. 6, Nov. 11.**

Jenniffer Paola Cunha Ferreira is in her third year of phonoaudiology at Paraná Adventist Academy, Parana, Brazil. She likes to sing and participate in school programs. **Oct. 8.**

Clara Hornus de Ferreyro writes for us from Argentina, South America. **Oct. 6.**

Valerie Fidelia has lived and worked on the Mediterranean island of Cyprus for the past 14 years as women's ministries director for the Middle East Union of Seventh-day Adventists. Widowed, with four grown children, she rejoices in her seven grandchildren. Local church activities include being worship leader, musician, and children's Bible class teacher. **Sep. 2, Oct. 7.**

Edith Fitch is a retired teacher who lives in Lacombe, Alberta, Canada. She volunteers in the archives at Canadian University College, and enjoys doing research for schools and churches, as well as individual histories. Her hobbies include writing, traveling, needlework, and cryptograms. **Apr. 5, June 4, Aug. 24.**

Lana Fletcher is a homemaker who lives in Chehalis, Washington, with her husband. She has one adult daughter. Her younger daughter was killed in a car accident in 1993. She is the church clerk, has attended Toastmasters for several years, and enjoys making Creative Memories albums, gardening, and writing. **Mar. 11, Apr. 14, Dec. 21.**

Cristina Florêncio lives in Pernambuco, Brazil. She is a minister's wife, and the mother of two children, Thiago and Alisson. A chemistry teacher, she enjoys reading, crochet, embroidery, and crossword puzzles. Currently she works with women's ministries. **Jan. 19, Oct. 17.**

Lidia Floricel comes from a family that has always been active in the church. She is a member of the Alexandria church in Romania. Her son is a pastor, and her daughter is married to a pastor. She has three grandchildren who, most surely, will have a word to say in the future progress of the church. **May 12.**

Marvet Furze is a Jamaican woman who loves Jesus. She is the mother of two teenage sons, and is a certified nursing assistant. She enjoys cooking and reading. **Dec. 8.**

Edna Maye Gallington is part of the communication team in the Southeastern California Conference of Seventh-day Adventists, and is a graduate of La Sierra University. She is a member of Toastmasters International and the Loma Linda Writing Guild. She enjoys freelance writing, music, gourmet cooking, entertaining, hiking, and racquetball. **Jan. 22, July 8, Sep. 6.**

Marlene Esteves Garcia, from Brazil, has a degree in education. She is married to Pastor José Garcia, and has two children: José Newton and Joselene. She enjoys listening to music, taking walks, and cooking. **Feb. 11, May 13.**

Evelyn Glass lives with her husband, Darrell, in northern Minnesota on the farm where Darrell was born. They are delighted to have their son and daughter-in-law and grandchildren living next door. They also have two grown daughters and one son-in-law. Evelyn writes for their weekly newspaper, and she is active in speaking, a local writers' group, and a quilting group. **Mar. 21, Aug. 5.**

Hannelore Gomez, from Panama, currently teaches Spanish in a high school in Virginia. She is working on her master's degree and Ph.D. in international studies. Her hobbies are reading and traveling. Knowing the gospel since she was born has been her greatest blessing. **Nov. 10.**

Elizete Borges Goulart lives in Sombrio, Rio Grande do Sul, Brazil. She is married, has a daughter, and is a businesswoman. She enjoys reading and admiring nature. **Mar. 27.**

Mary Jane Graves worked at many jobs before retiring with her husband, Ted, in North Carolina. As a part of women's ministries, she started—and maintains—the church library. She also enjoys gardening and sharing the results with friends and neighbors. **Aug. 14.**

Shirley Kimbrough Grear writes from New Jersey, where she lives with her husband, Carl. She is the mother of C.J. and Michelle, and has four grandchildren. She is active in women's ministries, writes, lectures, and provides workshops. **Jan. 16, Apr. 15, Dec. 31.**

Glenda-mae Greene, a chronicler of the everyday moments in her life, is a former university educator. She writes from her wheelchair in Palm Bay, Florida, rejoicing in the fact that she now has time to count the many blessings that God has showered so lavishly upon her. **Feb. 12, Sep. 12, Dec. 10.**

Leila Fay Greene writes from Florida, where she and her husband have retired. She is the mother of five adult children and the grandmother of six. She is the Bible school superintendent in her church. **Jan. 23.**

Evelyn Gertrude Greenwade, mother of two young adults, is the Pathfinder and Adventurer area coordinator for western New York. Her passions are youth ministries, reading, inspirational writing, travel, and being a keynote speaker for women's issues. She has been a member of the Akoma Women's Community Gospel Choir for nine years, and has worked for 25 years at Xerox Corporation. **Sep. 20.**

Gloria Gregory is a minister's wife and the mother to two beautiful adult young women. Gloria works as director of admissions at Northern Caribbean University in Jamaica. She believes that each person was born to fulfill a special mission for God and that we are precious in His sight. **Mar. 18, Apr. 17, Sep. 5.**

Dessa Weisz Hardin lives in Kennebunk, Maine, with her husband, Bart. She is a mother of three, and grandmother of two charming boys. Dessa enjoys the ocean, traveling, writing, art, music, reading, and working with children. An added dimension is grandparenting. **Jan. 24, June 22, Nov. 3.**

Marian M. Hart, a retired elementary teacher and nursing home administrator, works with her husband in property management. As a member of the Battle Creek Seventh-day Adventist Tabernacle for 28 years, she has served as a volunteer in many different capacities. She is the proud grandmother of six and is a first-time contributor to the devotional book. **Mar. 6, June 14, Sep. 1.**

Denise Dick Herr teaches English at Canadian University College in Alberta, Canada. She enjoys books, words, and the exciting possibilities of a blank sheet of paper. **Jan. 25.**

Jocelyn Heruela is a first-time contributor who writes from Mountain View College in the Philippines. **Oct. 18.**

Karen Holford works with her husband in family and children's ministries in southern England. She has authored more than seven books, and she is especially interested in creative approaches to prayer and worship. The Holfords have three teenage children. She is a family therapist, and enjoys quilting and walking in the English countryside. **Feb. 15, May 3, Sep. 21.**

Ana Maria B. Honorato is a high school student in Brazil. She enjoys reading newspapers and biology and physics books. Her hobbies are listening to music, painting, and playing the transversal flute. **Nov. 23.**

Jackie Hope HoShing-Clarke, an educator since 1979, has been a principal, assistant principal, and teacher. She now serves Northern Caribbean University (NCU), Jamaica, as director for the precollege department. She is married to Pastor Bylton Clarke, and they have two children, Deidre and Deneil. She enjoys writing, teaching, flower gardening, and housekeeping. **June 23, Aug. 17, Nov. 28.**

Norma Howell is a certified nurse assistant on a cardiac floor, and the personal ministries director of her church in Palm Bay, Florida. She enjoys spending her spare time playing tennis, going horseback riding, listening to music, and writing poetry. This is her first submission. **Feb. 16.**

Gloria Hutchinson is a registered nurse with an Associate in Science degree in computer network administration. She is the single mother of an adopted son, who is also her nephew. She works for an elder-care facility as an assessment nurse coordinator. At church she has served as Sabbath school superintendent. Her hobbies include sewing, reading, and working on the computer. **Mar. 29.**

Shirley C. Iheanacho enjoyed 24 years as an employee of Oakwood College in Alabama, including 21 years as an administrative assistant to various presidents, and is currently an administrative assistant to the provost. She is the mother of three adult daughters, Ngozi, Chioma, and Akunna. She has two grandsons, Nikolas and Timothy, and is grateful for her supportive husband of 37 years. **Feb. 18, July 3, Dec. 22.**

Wilma C. Jardine, originally from Panama, is a retired federal employee who lives in North Carolina. She has six children, seven grandchildren, and two great-grandchildren. At her church she is a soloist, chorister, and choir member. She is a jail ministry volunteer, and gives Bible studies at a local nursing home. She enjoys playing the piano, reading, and traveling. **Aug. 12, Oct. 14.**

Mathelda Jeffrey, is originally from the beautiful Caribbean island of St. Lucia, affectionately known as Helen of the West. Mathy lives with her husband, an assistant professor at Canadian University College. She loves cats, children, home decorating, and flowers. **Dec. 6.**

Lois E. Johannes is retired from overseas service in southern and eastern Asia, and lives near her daughter in Portland, Oregon. She enjoys knitting, community service work, patio gardening, and her four grandchildren and two great-grandchildren. **July 9.**

Elaine J. Johnson resides in the southern part of the United States with her husband-best friend of 39 years, Peter. She is active in her local church and likes to tinker with all types of electronics, especially her computer. **Aug. 18, Oct. 20, Dec. 5.**

Gladys S. (Guerrero) Kelley, from the Dominican Republic, came to the United States when she was 17 years old. She has a bachelor's degree in English education, and is working on a masters in second language acquisition. She teaches Spanish as a second language, loves to write, swim, read, play volleyball, and do extreme sports, such as bungee jumping and skydiving. **Oct. 21.**

Iris L. Kitching (formerly Stovall), now an administrative assistant at the Adventist world headquarters, previously worked 10 years in women's ministries. She enjoys doing personality assessments. She recently married Will, her high school sweetheart (41 years later), and together they enjoy their combined five sons, and four daughters-in-laws, one daughter, and eight grandchildren. **July 26.**

Becki Knobloch lives in Mountain Grove, Missouri, where her husband pastors more than three churches. One daughter, Natasha, is at Ozark Academy, and a second daughter is finishing the eighth grade through home school. She is still looking for work in her field of health education. Homemaking, gardening, writing, music, and women's ministries are her interests. **Apr. 8, July 15.**

Annie M. Kujur served the Adventist Church organization for 43 years as an elementary teacher. Now retired, she is a director of the registered Prabhudas Orphanage, Kurgi, Village in Jharkhand, India. She is author of five elementary school textbooks and several nonfiction books. She teaches piano to students from all walks of life. **Mar. 30, May 4, Dec. 19.**

Mabel Kwei, originally from West Africa, now lives in New Jersey. She is a former university/college lecturer, a mother of three, and a pastor"s wife. She loves to write, read, paint, and garden. **Mar. 23, July 2.**

Nathalie Ladner-Bischoff, a retired nurse, enjoys homemaking, gardening, volunteering at Gospel Outreach and the local hospital gift shop, reading, writing, knitting, and crocheting. She's published several magazine stories and two books, *An Angel's Touch,* and *Touched by a Miracle.* **Apr. 4.**

Ros Landless, from South Africa, works at the General Conference of Seventh-day Adventists in Treasury, programming the Web site and database for the interdivision missionaries. She and her husband, Peter, a doctor, have two grown daughters who have chosen careers in music therapy and occupational therapy. Ros collects stamps and thimbles and enjoys crochet and cross-stitch. **Apr. 11.**

Jeanine Xavier Názer Latif is married and has three teenage children: Samia, Ahmad, and Samir. Jeanine lives in Brazil and enjoys reading and writing, traveling, being with her family, and handicrafts. **Feb. 13.**

Iani Dias Lauer-Leite is working on her doctoral thesis about children's economic behavior. She likes reading about many things, but especially about prayer. She's involved with a prayer ministry where she lives in Brazil. **May 10, July 16, Sep. 22.**

Gina Lee has published more than 800 stories, articles, and poems. She enjoys working at the public library and caring for her family of cats. **Mar. 31, May 14, Dec. 23.**

Ruth Lennox, who has retired three times and is now being "retreaded," writes from Canada. In 1995 she retired from active medical practice, in 2003 from women's ministries for the British Columbia Conference of Seventh-day Adventists, and in 2004 from women's ministries for the Adventist Church in Canada. Ruth and her husband have three married children and four delightful granddaughters. **Feb. 26, Mar. 16.**

Cordell Liebrandt serves as the women's ministries director for the Southern Africa Union. She is a paralegal and is passionate about intercessory prayer and women's ministries. She also enjoys being involved in other positions in church. Cordell loves reading, spending time with people, and walking in nature. Her favorite saying is "You can make a difference." **May 7.**

Nelci de Rocco Lima is a minister's wife and has two children, Theillyson and Thaillys Caroline. She enjoys reading, writing, crocheting, knitting, swimming, playing the piano, and preaching where she lives in Brazil. **May 8, Aug. 3, Nov. 9.**

Olga I. Corbin de Lindo, a retired teacher and contracting officer for the United States Air Force, writes from Panama. Since the recent death of her husband, she has found writing to be therapeutic. Other hobbies include reading, gardening, playing the piano, and visiting her daughter and three grandchildren in Florida. She serves her church in women's ministries and as a pianist. **Apr. 27, May 15.**

Bessie Siemens Lobsien is a retired librarian who enjoys spending time with her grandchildren and two great-granddaughters. She likes doing simple mission projects, such as sewing for the community center and collecting used eyeglasses to send to the needy in Mexico, where she worked as a missionary librarian. **Mar. 24, Sep. 16, Dec. 13.**

Sharon Long (Brown) is from Trinidad, West Indies. She is a social worker who lives in Edmonton, Alberta, Canada, with her husband, Miguel. She has three adult children, one teenager, and two granddaughters. Three of her children live at home. Sharon is active in her church and sings in two choirs. She enjoys writing, entertaining, cooking, baking, and sewing. **Feb. 19, Sep. 13, Dec. 14.**

Terrie E. (Ruff) Long is director of field and associate professor in the Social Work and Family Studies Department at Southern Adventist University in Tennessee. She enjoys public speaking, bargain shopping, and reading. She describes herself as a "people person," whose life motto is "I'm too blessed to be stressed or depressed, and too anointed to be disappointed!" **Mar. 9, Aug. 27.**

Denise Múckenberge Lopes is a minister's wife and piano teacher in South America. She has two sons, Denisson and Willington. She enjoys working with decorations and literature. **Jan. 8, May 26.**

Denise Malcolm is a computer educator who attends church in Palm Bay, Florida. She has one daughter and a granddaughter. She enjoys reading in her spare time. This is her first submission. **June 3.**

Tamara Marquez de Smith writes from Bay Shore, New York, where she lives with her husband, Steven, and their two daughters, Lillian and Cassandra. Tamara is currently the youth leader, a deaconess, and the music coordinator in her church. **June 15.**

Maressa Steiner Marroni, from Brazil, is a medical student at River Plate Adventist University, Argentina. She enjoys reading, writing, and singing. **Jan. 26.**

Peggy Mason, living in Wales with her husband and one of her two adult sons, is a teacher of English and a writer. Her hobbies include dried flower growing and arranging, cooking, sewing, gardening, and reading. She is a pianist/composer, and enjoys working for her church and community. **Mar. 3.**

Luciana Ribeiro de Mattos is a minister's wife and a teacher who has two children, Thamires and Lucas. She lives in Ijui, Rio Grande do Sul, Brazil. She enjoys handicrafts, reading, and playing the piano. **Apr. 19, May 17, Dec. 28.**

Vidella McClellan is a caregiver for seniors in British Columbia, Canada. A mother of three and grandmother of seven, her hobbies are gardening, crossword puzzles, Scrabble, and writing. She also loves cats, reading, and gospel music. She belongs to the Toastmasters Club and does public speaking. She is active in her church, and helps with the yearly women's retreat. **Jan. 27, Apr. 28, Oct. 29.**

Patsy Murdoch Meeker has lived in Virginia for a number of years, but misses her home state of California. She has contributed to many of the devotional books. **Nov. 8.**

Cynthia Mejia is from Columbia, Maryland, and has served in mission service as director of the language school program in Bangkok, Thailand, and in Naña, Peru, at the Peruvian Union University Language Institute. She is currently at Weimar Institute in California, where she works with the NEWSTART program. **Nov. 24.**

Eva Maria Rossi Mello is a minister's wife in Brazil. She and her husband have three children: Joezer, Eduardo, and Jair. **Dec. 4.**

Antônia Rodrigues N. Mesquita is married and has two children, Jessica and Gabriel. She likes to read, walk, and admire the beauties of nature near her home in Brazil. **Mar. 8.**

Annette Walwyn Michael, from St. Kitts and Nevis in the West Indies, is an English teacher and a published writer of Caribbean literature. Reginald, her husband of 35 years, their three children, and three grandchildren bring her constant joy and inspiration. She is active in the children's and women's ministries at her local church. **June 24, Aug. 20, Dec. 3.**

Quilvie G. Mills is a retired community college professor. She lives with her pastor-husband, Herman, in Port St. Lucie, Florida. In church she serves as musician, women's ministries leader, Bible class teacher, and member of the floral committee. She enjoys young people, traveling, reading, music, gardening, word games, and teaching piano to children. **July 17, Oct. 4, Nov. 7.**

Marcia Mollenkopf, a retired teacher, lives in Klamath Falls, Oregon. She is active in her local church and has served in both adult and children's departments. She enjoys reading, music, sign language, and bird-watching. **Nov. 25.**

Esperanza Aquino Mopera is the mother of four adults, grandmother of five. She enjoys being a traveling nurse and gardening. **May 20, July 18.**

Elisabeta Moraru lives and attends church in Perieni, Romania. She has been involved in women's ministries, teaching a youth Bible class, evangelism, and as a deaconess. She says she has been sorely tried, but God has comforted her and given her power to go on. She longs for the day that our Lord Jesus will come, and she will meet dear ones once again. **Jan. 14.**

Walkiria Vespa S. S. Moreira is a pastor's wife and an educator. Her hobby is traveling. She has three children, and currently lives in Colatina, Espirito Santo, Brazil. **July 19.**

Barbara Smith Morris is executive director of a nonprofit retirement center, and presents a devotional over the speaker system daily. She served for seven years as a Tennessee delegate, representing housing and service needs of low-income seniors. Barbara is a presenter of seminars on elder life issues, mother of four grown children, and grandmother of six. **Sep. 23.**

Bonnie Moyers lives with her husband and three cats in Staunton, Virginia. She has two adult children and one granddaughter. Bonnie is a musician for a Methodist and a Presbyterian church on Sundays. She writes freelance, and her writings have been published in many magazines and books. She's a volunteer musician for her local church on Sabbaths. **Jan. 12, June 25, Nov. 6.**

Ethel Doris Msuseni is a single parent, professional nurse and teacher, and pensioner member of her local church in South Africa. Her hobbies include baking, sewing, gardening, and listening to gospel music. **July 20, Sep. 24.**

Patricia Calahan Muñiz, originally from Canada, is a special education teacher who works with special needs preschoolers in northern California. She is the proud parent of three growing children, and in her spare moments she loves to spend time with each one of them. **July 1.**

Clarice Turner Murphy lives in the mountains of western North Carolina and is the mother of a grown son. She is a social worker by profession, and the CEO of a hospice. **Apr. 26.**

Lillian Musgrave and her extended family make their home in northern California and love the closeness this provides. A new home will be finished soon, but there are no guarantees of retirement. She enjoys family activities and church responsibilities; music; writing poetry, stories, and songs; and belonging to the Sierra Christian Writers, who plan to publish a book soon. **Mar. 17.**

Julie Nagle is wife of one, mother of three, and is a professional working for the Australian Public Service. She is an indigenous Australian and is involved in many ministries, including those for women and the general public. Her motto is "in His service," and she is an ordained elder for Christ. She enjoys public speaking and continual learning. **Jan. 28.**

Anne Elaine Nelson, a retired teacher, tutors and does testing for schools. She has written the book *Puzzled Parents*. Widowed in 2001, she lives in Michigan. Her four children have blessed her with 11 grandchildren. Anne stays active as women's ministries leader and a Sabbath school superintendent. She loves sewing, photography, and creating memories with her grandchildren. **May 18, Aug. 21, Oct. 23.**

Doina Nicolae is an economist in Alexandria, Romania. She and her husband have two sons. She says she found God later than her husband, but this has changed her life. She is enthusiastic about telling others about God's love. **June 16.**

Maria Sinharinha de Oliveira Nogueira, from Brazil, is married and has two daughters and four grandchildren. She enjoys writing poetry, crossword puzzles, reading, and doing exercises. **Apr. 3, Sep. 25.**

Regina Mary Silveira Nunes resides in Blumenau, Santa Catarina, Brazil. She is a pastor's wife and a dentist. She has two daughters, Cristiana and Carolina, and enjoys cooking, giving counsel, and helping her husband in his pastoral work. **May 22, Sep. 26.**

Ruth Menezes Nunes is an English language professor at the university level in Brazil. She has published a book, *Henoch Andou com Deus* (Enoch Walked With God). Her favorite pastimes are writing, reading, playing the piano, caring for her plants, and handicrafts. **Dec. 30.**

Elizabeth Versteegh Odiyar, Kelowna, British Columbia, Canada, has managed the family chimney sweep business since 1985. She has twin sons and a daughter. Beth enjoys mission and road trips, being creative, sewing, cooking vegan, home decorating, organizing, and hopes to be a writer. She loves leading Pathfinders and vacation Bible school, and being church bulletin secretary. **Oct. 3.**

Viviane Fragoso de Oliveira has a degree in literature, has completed music courses, and has done graduate work in education. She lives in Brazil, and is the daughter and granddaughter of pastors. She enjoys reading, writing, cooking, and handicrafts. **Apr. 1, Aug. 22.**

Jemima D. Orillosa works with the Secretariat Department of the General Conference of Seventh-day Adventists. She is active in her local church in Maryland, where she lives with her husband and their two young adult daughters. She finds joy in organizing and joining mission trips. **May 23, Aug. 23, Nov. 26.**

Brenda D. Ottley was born in Guyana, South America. She is married to Ernest, a Trinidadian, and lives in St. Lucia, where she works as a secondary school teacher and e-tutor in the University of the West Indies distance education program. She and her husband are involved in radio ministry at PrayzFM. **Mar. 1, Sep. 28, Dec. 15.**

Hannele Ottschofski lives in southern Germany and is an elder in her local church. She has four daughters and one grandson. A pastor's wife, she is active in women's ministries and helps in the organization of seminars and congresses. **Jan. 29, May 19, Sep. 27.**

Margoli Saavedra Panduro was born in Peru, and now lives in Bolivia. She is a Bible instructor and nutritionist. She holds several positions in her church and is very involved in its activities. **Apr. 21, Sep. 4.**

Ofelia A. Pangan and her husband just finished two years of volunteer service at Mission College, Thailand, where she taught English as a second language. They're now enjoying being close to their three professional married children and nine grandchildren. She will enjoy gardening again, walking every day, reading more books, and playing Scrabble regularly. **Apr. 2, June 1, July 21.**

Revel Papaioannou, from Greece, is the wife of a retired-but-still-working pastor, mother of four, and grandmother of 10. She is a Sabbath school superintendent and teacher who enjoys visiting, gardening, mountain climbing (whenever possible), and reading. **Jan. 31.**

Betty G. Perry lives in Fayetteville, North Carolina, with her semiretired pastor-husband. An anaesthetist for 34 years, she also is now semiretired. They have two adult children and five grandchildren. Hobbies include playing the piano and organ, arts and crafts, trying out new recipes, and, most recently, quilting. **July 22, Aug. 25, Nov. 4.**

LaVella Pinkney retired after working in the retail nutrition business for more than 20 years. She and her husband, Dan, live in their motor home and travel in the winter, following the sun. They have a grown daughter and son and two grandchildren. She enjoys talking to the neighbors, reading, her small garden, going to garage sales, and writing and e-mailing on her computer. **Jan. 13.**

Birdie Poddar lives in northeastern India. She and her husband enjoy retirement but keep busy. They have two adult children, a daughter and a son, and four grandsons. Birdie enjoys writing and does handcrafts to console the sad ones and encourage those who need her prayers. **July 23, Oct. 2, Dec. 16.**

Janaína V.C.B. Portes lives in Engenheiro, Coelho, São Paulo, Brazil, where her husband studies theology. She is a math teacher who likes to read, cook, work with children, and camp, and has a great appreciation for nature. **Feb. 21.**

Judith Purkiss is a secondary school teacher originally from Birmingham, in the West Midlands, England. She now lives and works in London, where she is the Sabbath school leader in her local congregation. She enjoys reading, singing, cooking, and running. **Feb. 22, Sep. 29.**

Joana Vieira de Aquiar Ramos lives in the south of Brazil, where she is a retired literature teacher. She enjoys writing, public speaking, and gardening. **Mar. 15.**

Barbara J. Horst Reinholtz, semiretired, works as registrar for the North American Division Evangelism Institute extension school. Mother of three married children and grandmother of two, she has held several church offices. A published author, she enjoys people, music, crocheting, and other crafts. Best of all, she enjoys being wife and best friend to her husband, Laun. **June 12.**

Darlenejoan McKibbin Rhine was born in Nebraska, raised in California, and schooled in Tennessee. She is a widow with one grown son. She holds a bachelor's degree in journalism, and worked in the plant at the Los Angeles *Times* for 21 years. Now retired, she is an author who lives on an island in Puget Sound, Washington, and attends the North Cascade Adventist Church. **Mar. 7, June 26, Dec. 18.**

Maria Moreira de Almeida Ribeiro is a librarian in Brazil. She is married, and likes to walk, read, paint, and observe what is happening around her. **Mar. 4, July 24.**

Avis Mae Rodney is a justice of the peace for the province of Ontario, Canada, where she resides with her husband, Leon. Avis is the mother of two adult children and has five grandchildren. Her hobbies include early-morning walks, reading, and spending time with family and friends. **June 27, Aug. 26, Dec. 20.**

Sayuri Ruiz lives in Angwin, California, where she is a college student. She loves working with youth, children, and women's ministries. She is the president of the Spanish youth federation of the Northern California Conference of Seventh-day Adventists, and leads a sign language choir. Ruiz wrote the book *Tulip, Jesus is Watching You,* and she enjoys reading, writing, preaching, and signing. **May 25, July 25.**

Maria Sales worked as a missionary in Angola and is currently working as a secretary in the Seventh-day Adventist Church headquarters in Portugal. She is a widow who has two children and four grandchildren. She enjoys writing poetry, reading, traveling, and walking in nature. **Feb. 10, Apr. 6, July 5.**

Deborah Sanders shares from her personal journal, "Dimensions of Love," which has become a writing-prayer ministry. She lives in Canada with Ron, her husband of 36 years. They've been blessed with two children, Andrea and Sonny. Sonny is mentally challenged with psychomotor retardation and autism. She says, "Thank you for caring." **Feb. 17.**

Sônia Maria Rigoli Santos is a minister's wife and has her master's degree in theology. They live in Brazil, and have two children, Carlos Eduardo and Carla Beatriz. Her hobby is writing. **Feb. 23, May 16, Oct. 30.**

Dorothy D. Saunders writes from Pennsylvania. She is a first-time contributor to the women's ministries devotional book. **Jan. 11.**

Marie H. Seard is a repeat contributor to the devotional book project. She enjoys family, friends, writing, reading, traveling, and shopping. She lives in Washington, D.C., with her husband, and they have celebrated 48 years of marriage. **Apr. 16.**

Donna Lee Sharp is thankful that there were no injuries to her hands and arms (see "Tested but Alive"). She is again playing the piano for her church. She's active in community organizations and work for seniors. Gardening, reading, and recovery are her present pastimes. **Jan. 20.**

Rose Neff Sikora and her husband live in the beautiful mountains of western North Carolina. A retired nurse, she has written short stories and articles for devotional books, magazines, and their local newspaper, The *Times News.* Her interests include camping, helping others, and spending time with her three grandchildren. **Feb. 24.**

Elaine Aparecida da Silva lives in Ribeira, São Paulo, Brazil. She is a pastor's wife, and a teacher, and is studying education. She enjoys traveling, reading, and studying the piano. **Feb. 25.**

Maricélia de Almeida Silva enjoys listening to children, traveling, and working with children in Brazil. **Apr. 22, Sep. 3.**

Judy Good Silver has been married to her best friend, Phil, for 31 years. They live in Stanley, Virginia, in her great-great-grandfather's place in the mountains of Shenandoah Valley. Her children, Jill and Joel, and grandchildren, Jonah and Mary, are her most treasured gifts. She has written a book, *Forget-me-nots.* She enjoys gardening, reading, cross-stitching, and e-mail. **Jan. 9, June 2, Dec. 2.**

Sandra Simanton is a full-time mom in Sioux Falls, South Dakota, where she lives with her husband and three children. She enjoys sewing, stamping, and scrapbooking. **Apr. 29.**

Taramani Noreen Singh is a librarian at Roorkee Adventist College in India. She has two young sons. **July 31.**

Heather-Dawn Small is the director for women's ministries at the General Conference of Seventh-day Adventists. Heather-Dawn and her pastor-husband, Joseph Small, are the parents of an adult daughter and teenage son. She loves air travel, reading, embroidery, scrapbooking, stamp collecting, and ministry to women. **Feb. 14, May 11, Oct. 9, Nov. 12.**

Yvonne Curry Smallwood is a wife, mother, and grandmother. She writes from Upper Marlboro, Maryland. Trained as a scientist, she works in science administration. Her stories have appeared in several publications. **Sep. 30, Nov. 29.**

Katherine A. Smutka, a first-time contributor, is a 21-year-old junior at the University of Colorado in Colorado Springs. She is majoring in psychology, minoring in nutrition. She is an only child, and her parents own a ranch in Colorado. She enjoys reading, writing, singing, and being with those she loves. Many of her writings are inspired by nature. **Aug. 10.**

Kathleen Sowards is married to a wonderful man who has helped her grow into the woman she is. She is the mother of two adult sons and a daughter. She is an editorial assistant and has been a leader in children's Sabbath schools and at camp meetings, and a Vacation Bible School leader. She has also conducted a stop-smoking clinic and presented devotionals for women's meetings. **May 24.**

Ardis Dick Stenbakken is enjoying retirement and wondering how she had time to be director of women's ministries worldwide. She fits editing this book around spending time with her granddaughters and family, speaking, gardening, and enjoying the Colorado Rockies. She is looking for time for some quilting and painting, and to read a lot of books. **Jan. 21, Feb. 20, Oct. 12.**

Andreea Strâmbu-Dima is a first-time contributor who writes from Romania. She is 24 years old, graduated from the Academy for Economical Studies, and has a master's degree in marketing. She is the daughter of a pastor, and she and her pastor-husband have one child. She likes to work with children and women's ministries. She loves poetry, trips, and music. **Sep. 10.**

Rubye Sue and her husband, Bill, have the best of two worlds—the beautiful mountains of Tennessee in the summer, and the warmth of Florida in the winter. Although she has now celebrated her eighty-third birthday, she still enjoys secretarial work. She and her husband are grateful for all their children, grandchildren, and great-grandchildren. **Mar. 26, May 28.**

Carolyn Rathbun Sutton lives in Tennessee with her husband, where they are involved in their local church, prison ministry, and their own Building for Christ Ministries, a supporting ministry that raises funds for mission evangelism, church building, and orphan assistance. **Apr. 24, June 21.**

Bertha Swanson is a first-time contributor writing from Michigan. She is a local church women's ministries leader. **Oct. 16.**

Loraine F. Sweetland is retired in Tennessee. She is involved with church and community volunteer work, and enjoys writing, machine knitting, her three little dogs, computer surfing, gardening, and reading. **Mar. 5, Apr. 23, Nov. 30.**

Debbie Steyn Symes left Durban, South Africa, in 1981 for the Gold Coast, Queensland, Australia. She has been married to David for 21 years, and they have three lovely children—a son and two daughters. She is passionate about intercessory prayer and women's ministries. She has enjoyed numerous positions in her church, and enjoys the beach, reading, and spending time with family. **Apr. 30.**

Frieda Tanner, born in Colorado, will be 90 in August 2008. She and her husband live in Eugene, Oregon, and are members of the Springfield Adventist Church. They have two children and two grandchildren. Frieda, a retired R.N., and her husband make spiritual visual aids for children around the world. **Aug. 2.**

Arlene Taylor is risk manager for three Adventist Health hospitals in California. An internationally known speaker, she is the founder-president of her own non-profit corporation and the author of brain-function resources. In 2002 Taylor was one of 100 recipients of the American Biographical Institute's American Medal of honor for Brain-Function Education. **May 5, July 27, Nov. 5.**

Patrice Hill Taylor is a speech-language pathologist who is involved with the human relations committee at her school, where the children worked hard on a fund-raiser to assist Hurricane Katrina victims. She is not a published author, but loves to read devotional selections. Singing is a real interest of hers, and she is a member of her church choir in the church in which she grew up. **July 28.**

Tammy Barnes Taylor has been married for 20 years and has four great children; the eldest is 17, the youngest 3. She owns her own business, Little Cherubs Childcare. "The Lord runs it" with her every day, she says. She enjoys working on the women's ministries counsel, scrapbooking, and writing. She is women's leader in her local church, as well as a Sabbath school teacher. **Jan. 7, June 11, Nov. 18.**

Stella Thomas works in the Office of Adventist Mission/Presidential of the General Conference of Seventh-day Adventists. Her passion is to tell the world of Jesus and His soon return. **Dec. 11.**

Emily Thomsen is a massage therapist and wellness professional. She loves being self-employed and working from home. She enjoys cooking, home decorating, music, reading, writing, and photography. But backpacking is her passion—in the summer of 2003 she hiked more than half of the Appalachian Trail. **Apr. 20, June 30, Aug. 1.**

Margaret Tito, who works in the Southern Asia Division in India, enjoyed being an educator with children of various ages for almost 28 years. She and A.J., her pastor-husband, who is publishing director of the Southern Asia Division, have three grown children. **May 2, Oct. 24, Dec. 1.**

Nicéia Triandade lives in Niteroi, Brazil, in the state of Rio de Janeiro. She is married, the mother of three adult children, and has five grandchildren—her great passion. She enjoys entertaining friends, sewing, cooking, and writing poems. Her greatest joy is to travel with her family. She appreciates nature, and likes to meditate by looking at the sea. **Oct. 26.**

Gloria Lindsey Trotman is the women's and children's ministries director of the Inter-American Division. The Trotmans have four children and four grandchildren. Gloria enjoys reading, writing, music, people-watching, and having fun with her grandchildren. Her motto is "making a difference." **Mar. 10.**

Nancy Ann Neuharth Troyer and her husband, Don, have retired to California. They have one daughter, Stephanie. Nancy spent 24 years traveling the globe with her United States Army chaplain-husband. Nancy is noted for unique calligraphy pictures. **Jan. 10.**

Eunice Urbany is a mother of three and grandmother of five. She is now settled in Lakeland, Florida. She is a prayer warrior, running the women's prayer partners meeting every Tuesday evening. She is a Sabbath school superintendent and church elder who loves to read, write, and garden. **Oct. 1.**

Rebecca L. Usoroh lives with her husband, Isaac, in south Florida. They have two young sons, and are recent graduates of Andrews University in Berrien Springs, Michigan. **Aug. 19.**

Nancy Van Pelt, a certified family life educator, best-selling author, and internationally known speaker, has for 20 years been teaching families how to really love each other. She has authored more than 20 books, and her hobbies include getting organized, entertaining, having fun, and quilting. Nancy and her husband live in California and are the parents of three adult children. **May 29, July 11, Dec. 29.**

Cereatha J. Vaughn writes from Detroit, Michigan. This is her second contribution to the women's ministries devotional book series. **May 31.**

Donna Meyer Voth and her husband, Al, are in the retirement transition years. She enjoys traveling, camping, watercolor painting, quilting, and involvement with her church. **Jan. 30.**

Cora A. Walker is a retired nurse, editor, and freelance writer who lives in Fort Washington, Maryland. She is an active member of the little country church she attends in Charles County, Maryland. She enjoys reading, writing, swimming, classical music, singing, and traveling. She has one son, Andre V. Walker. **Jan. 1, Apr. 25, Oct. 31.**

Carolle H. Walker-Hay is a nutritionist who works at the Health Department in Melbourne, Florida. She and her husband have two adult children. Her hobbies include fashion design and the culinary arts. Harking back to her Jamaican childhood, she still harvests sorrel, sugarcane, sweet potatoes, and pineapples from her garden. **Nov. 27.**

Anna May Radke Waters is a retired administrative secretary. She and her husband of 50 years are retired in College Place, Washington, in the summer, and in Desert Hot Springs, California, in the winter. She enjoys being an internet volunteer for Bibleinfo.com and the Discover Bible course. She and her husband enjoy their four children and eight grandchildren. **Jan. 2, May 27.**

Dorothy Eaton Watts is an administrator for her church headquarters in India. Dorothy is a freelance writer, editor, and speaker. She has been a missionary in India for 25 years, founded an orphanage, taught elementary school, and written more than 20 books. Her hobbies include gardening, hiking, and birding (with more than 1,400 in her world total). **May 30, Aug. 29.**

Lyn Welk-Sandy works with bereaved children and aids young offenders attending court. She plays the pipe organ for a church in Adelaide, South Australia. She enjoys choir work and Christian fellowship, caravanning and photography in the outdoors with her husband, Keith. Lyn is the mother of four adult children and has nine grandchildren. **Feb. 1, Aug. 30, Dec. 17.**

Vera Wiebe has been in ministry with her husband for 33 years. They live in Canada. She has two sons and three grandchildren who bring a lot of joy to her life. Her hobbies include organizing music for her church and for camp meeting, and sewing and knitting for the grandchildren. **Mar. 2, July 29.**

Mildred C. Williams is a retired physical therapist living in southern California. She enjoys studying and teaching the Bible, writing, gardening, public speaking, sewing, and spending time with her grown children and granddaughter. **May 1, Aug. 16, Nov. 1.**

MeLissa Wilson is a pharmacy technician who lives in Alabama. She attends church at Oakwood College in Alabama and has published a book, *Conquering Regret.* Hobbies include ice skating, volleyball, Rollerblading, and tennis. **Feb. 27.**

Charlene M. Wright, a widow, is a member of the Dupont Park SDA Church in Washington, D.C., returning to the church after 30 years. She is a special education elementary school administrator and has a passion for children with disabilities. She is the women's ministries coleader, and enjoys Bible studies, reading, and spreading the gospel. **July 30.**

Nancy Cano de Ziegler is a music teacher and works with her husband in the Austral Union in Argentina. They have dedicated their lives to serve youth. They want to be a united family to see Jesus come. **June 8, Oct. 25.**

prayer requests

_____

_____

_____

_____

_____

_____

_____

_____

_____

Take me, O Lord, as wholly Thine.
I lay all my plans at Thy feet. Use me in Thy service.
Abide with me, and let all my work be wrote in Thee.
—Ellen G. White, *Steps to Christ*, p. 70.

prayer requests

_____

_____

_____

_____

_____

_____

_____

_____

Take me, O Lord, as wholly Thine.
I lay all my plans at Thy feet. Use me in Thy service.
Abide with me, and let all my work be wrote in Thee.
—Ellen G. White, *Steps to Christ*, p. 70.

prayer requests

_____

_____

_____

_____

_____

_____

_____

_____

_____

_____

Take me, O Lord, as wholly Thine.
I lay all my plans at Thy feet. Use me in Thy service.
Abide with me, and let all my work be wrote in Thee.
—Ellen G. White, *Steps to Christ,* p. 70.

prayer requests

_____

_____

_____

_____

_____

_____

_____

_____

_____

Take me, O Lord, as wholly Thine.
I lay all my plans at Thy feet. Use me in Thy service.
Abide with me, and let all my work be wrote in Thee.

—Ellen G. White, *Steps to Christ*, p. 70.

prayer requests

_____

_____

_____

_____

_____

_____

_____

_____

_____

Take me, O Lord, as wholly Thine.
I lay all my plans at Thy feet. Use me in Thy service.
Abide with me, and let all my work be wrote in Thee.
—Ellen G. White, *Steps to Christ*, p. 70.

prayer requests

_____

_____

_____

_____

_____

_____

_____

_____

_____

Take me, O Lord, as wholly Thine.
I lay all my plans at Thy feet. Use me in Thy service.
Abide with me, and let all my work be wrote in Thee.

—Ellen G. White, _Steps to Christ_, p. 70.